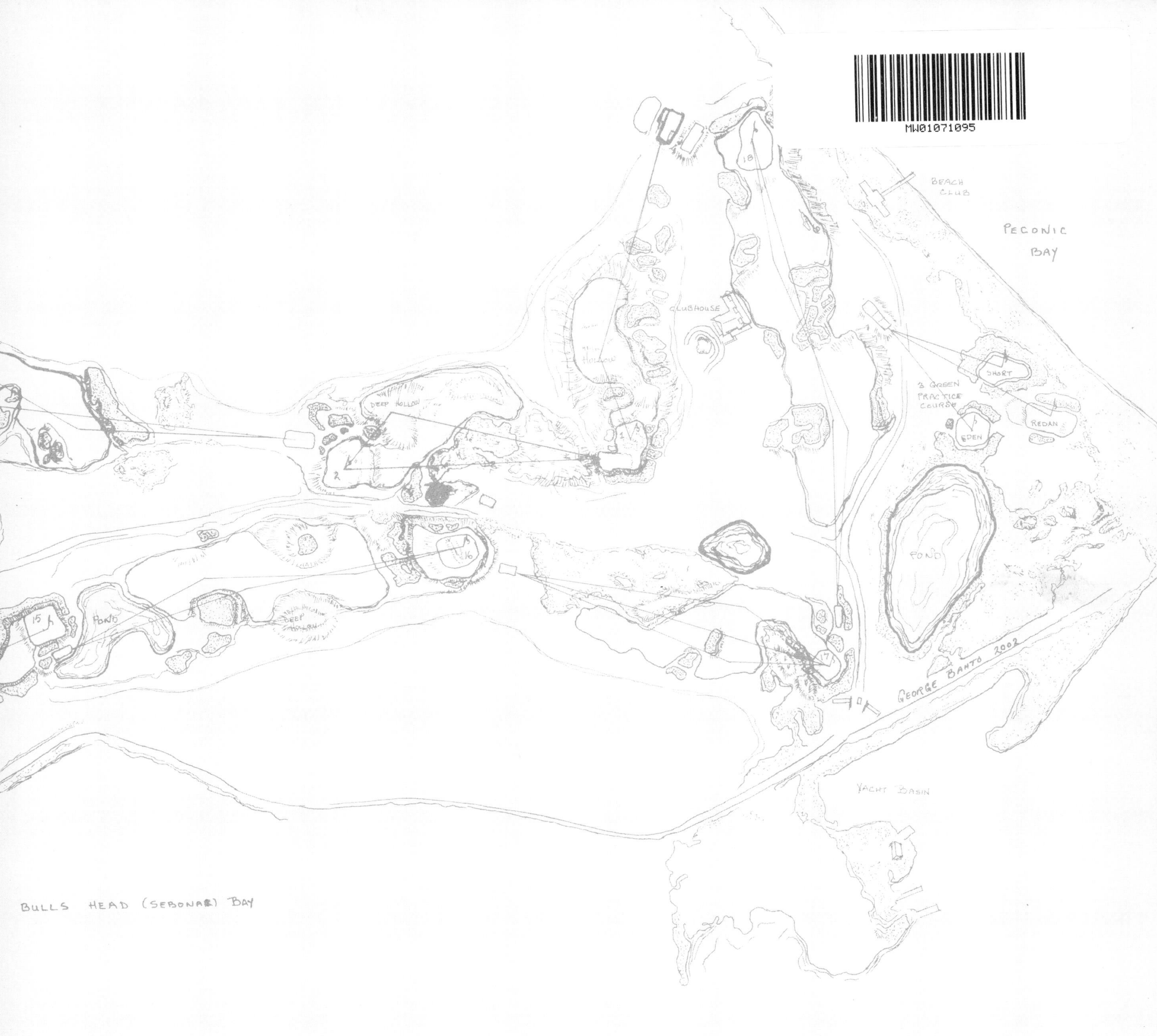
MW01071095
BEACH CLUB
PECONIC BAY
CLUBHOUSE
HOLLOW
DEEP HOLLOW
3 GREEN PRACTICE COURSE
SHORT
REDAN
EDEN
POND
POND
DEEP
GEORGE BAHTO 2002
YACHT BASIN
BULLS HEAD (SEBONAC) BAY

THE EVANGELIST OF GOLF

THE STORY *of* CHARLES BLAIR MACDONALD

by GEORGE BAHTO

Clock Tower Press LLC
320 North Main Street
P.O. Box 310
Chelsea, MI 48118
www.clocktowerpress.com

Printed and bound in Canada.

10 9 8 7 6 5 4 3 2 1

Library of Congress Cataloging-in-Publication Data
Bahto, George.
The evangelist of golf : the story of Charles Blair Macdonald / by George Bahto.
p. cm.
Includes index.
ISBN 1-886947-20-1
1. Macdonald, Charles Blair, 1855. 2. Golf course architects—United States—Biography. 3. Raynor, Seth J., 1874-1926. 4. Golf courses—United States—Design and construction—History. I. Title.
GV964.M3 B35 2002
712'.5'092—dc21 2002005260

TABLE *of* CONTENTS

FOREWORD *by Tom Doak*.....5

INTRODUCTION *by Ben Crenshaw*.....7

CHAPTER ONE: *The Early Years*.....9

CHAPTER TWO: *Chicago Golf Club*.....15

CHAPTER THREE: *Macdonald and the First National Championship*.....21

CHAPTER FOUR: *The Ideal Golf Links*.....29

CHAPTER FIVE: *Glossary of Holes and Green Complexes*.....39

CHAPTER SIX: *National Golf Links of America*.....61

CHAPTER SEVEN: *Seth the Surveyor*.....137

CHAPTER EIGHT: *Piping Rock Club*.....147

CHAPTER NINE: *Sleepy Hollow Country Club*.....155

CHAPTER TEN: *St. Louis Country Club*.....159

CHAPTER ELEVEN: *The Greenbrier Resort*.....163

CHAPTER TWELVE: *The Lido Club*.....169

CHAPTER THIRTEEN: *Shinnecock Hills Golf Club*.....185

CHAPTER FOURTEEN: *Ocean Links*.....191

CHAPTER FIFTEEN: *Links Club*.....197

CHAPTER SIXTEEN: *Practice Courses*.....203

CHAPTER SEVENTEEN: *Women's National Golf & Tennis Club*.....207

CHAPTER EIGHTEEN: *Gibson Island Club*.....211

CHAPTER NINETEEN: *Creek Club*.....215

CHAPTER TWENTY: *Deepdale Golf & Country Club*......221

CHAPTER TWENTY-ONE: *Mid Ocean Club*.....225

CHAPTER TWENTY-TWO: *Yale University Golf Course*.....231

TIME LINE *of* EVENTS.....247

COMPOSITE LISTING *of* COURSES *of* CHARLES B. MACDONALD, SETH J. RAYNOR, *and* CHARLES H. BANKS.....259

OBITUARY *by H.J. Whigham*.....263

ACKNOWLEDGMENTS.....269

EDITOR'S NOTE.....271

INDEX......273

In the overall scheme, man is only here on earth for a wisp of time. Most of us go through life working, raising a family, honoring our country, and responding in good turn to our fellow man. In a short time we are gone and although we did much good, besides the family we leave behind, we leave little that endures the test of time.

I admire the man who, through virtue of God-given or acquired talents, is able to leave his personal "mark" for others to admire and enjoy; a Shakespeare or Poe who left behind for us their written word; a Rembrandt or Rodin who left us their magnificent works of art; a Beethoven or Mozart who left their music for us to enjoy.

This book is dedicated to the golf course architects of the Golden Age who left us great classic courses to play over and enjoy. They cast their "footprint" on the face of the Earth—a golf course.

—George Bahto

FOREWORD

Some men prefer older women; I prefer older golf courses. Aside from the obvious benefits of maturity in the landscape, classic courses generally have more personality than modern creations, the kind of subtleties and quirks that one can grow to love.

While I'm a fan of many different architects, and have consulted in restoring the work of several, I feel most at home on the courses of Charles Blair Macdonald and his more prolific associates, Seth Raynor and Charles Banks. Like Macdonald, who was a student at St. Andrews University, I grew to love the "old game" in my year overseas on a scholarship to study golf architecture, based largely on Macdonald's precedent, and I returned to America with many questions about how modern golf architecture had evolved.

While in St. Andrews, C. B. Macdonald had been a first-hand witness to another, more profound evolution—from featherie balls to gutta-percha to the Haskell ball. In the transition, some previously-admired golf holes were "found out" as their challenge for the better players diminished. But as Macdonald noted, others held their challenge for all comers, because they required thought as well as stout hitting to conquer. Macdonald developed a boundless respect for the great golf holes he found at St. Andrews, North Berwick, Sandwich, and Prestwick, which had stood the test of time; and he made no bones about imitating their best features in his own work. He defended his style in *Scotland's Gift—Golf*: "I believe in reverencing anything in the life of man which has the testimony of the ages as being unexcelled, whether it be literature, paintings, poetry, tombs—even a golf hole... Another great landscape architect, Prince Puckler [said] 'Time is not able to bring forth new truths but only an unfolding of timeless truths.'"

As a result, playing a course by Raynor or Macdonald is like visiting an old best friend—the familiarity returns almost instantly, even if you have never seen it before! There is sure to be a par 3 in imitation of the Redan at North Berwick, a long shot to an angled, tilted green set above deep bunkers. Another of the short holes may have the vestige of a horseshoe-shaped depression (or even a ridge) in the center of the green. A third will be vaguely reminiscent of the famous 11th at St. Andrews, with deep bunkers at the wings of the green and an open central approach. And the fourth will often be a very long shot (220) yards to a lengthy plateau with a deep swale just in front of the flagstick, tagged on the scorecard with the odd name of "Biarritz."

When modern golf architects repeat their own work (and they do, all too often), I find it distasteful, wondering why they can't think up a fresh idea for a hole. But when I play another of Raynor's versions of the Redan, I confess a fondness for it. Am I a hypocrite? Perhaps, but I believe there is a difference. Macdonald and Raynor were paying homage to a classic form, and at the same time, trying to devise improvements to it based on the local situation. Their fourth at National Golf Links is better than the 15th at North Berwick, because the slightly downhill shot and lower intervening ridge afford a better view of the strategy of the hole, leading your eye to the target, while it cradles the layup shot just as well as the original. I have learned much about the Redan, and about golf design in general, by comparing Raynor's different versions and analyzing their strengths and weaknesses.

In modern design, we have the earthmoving power to produce exact copies of famous holes if we so desire. But the power to copy has become a curse, as few designers take the time to consider improvements to their original design. And where copies have been built, few have succeeded in getting the last six inches right, the nuances of approach and green that make the original a world-class hole.

Macdonald was the kind of golfer who understood those nuances, and after several years of boredom with the dismally dull golf courses of turn-of-the-century America, he set out to build a course that would honor and even surpass the best

British links. He personally chose the land, adjacent to the fledgling Shinnecock Hills Golf Club on Long Island, and enlisted the help of the local surveyor, Seth Raynor, to find the right places on the site to imitate the Redan, the Alps at Prestwick, and other ideas he had culled from courses overseas. The product of their work is the National Golf Links of America—fortunately for us, among the best-preserved courses in America, and still today, along with perhaps Dr. Alister MacKenzie's Cypress Point, the closest realization of Macdonald's ideal of building a course with the strategic interest, playability, and charm of the Old Course at St. Andrews.

Spurred on by the success of both Chicago Golf Club and the National, Macdonald went on to design a handful of other classic layouts, including St. Louis Country Club, the Yale University course, Mid Ocean in Bermuda, and the lost Lido Golf Club on the south shore of Long Island, once spoken of in the same breath as the National and Pine Valley. On most of these projects, Macdonald was not only the designer of the course but a critical force in founding the club and getting his elite social and business contacts involved. Yet he never accepted a fee for his work, preferring to keep it on the level of a hobby and a "good deed" for American golf. For this, he was deservedly christened by Herbert Warren Wind as the "father of American golf course architecture," and we all owe him a tremendous debt.

After the National, though, Macdonald saw that the demand for his services far exceeded the time he was willing to spend at his hobby. In addition, he was so enamored with his masterpiece that he found it difficult to maintain his interest in less ambitious projects for other clients. So he referred most of the enquiries to his protégé, Raynor, who was a working man and had the engineering background and the organized mind to plan courses across the country—from Westhampton near his home in New York to Waialae in Hawaii.

Raynor didn't have the artistic flair, the magnetic personality, or the overdeveloped ego of his mentor, and as a result, until recently, his work was sadly neglected. A dozen years ago, Pete Dye told me that Camargo and Fishers Island—both Raynor designs—were the best overlooked courses in America. Today, thankfully, they have both found their rightful place among lists of the elite. But wherever I have gone to search out another of Raynor's courses—from Yeamans Hall in the marshes of Charleston, to Lookout Mountain on top of a Georgia mountain—I have found solid and inspiring designs on sometimes magnificent properties. With Macdonald's social connections behind him, Raynor had first dibs on some of the most beautiful property in America between 1916 and 1926, when he suddenly died. He was then in the planning of a golf course at Cypress Point. Alister MacKenzie was chosen to replace him and he made the most of the opportunity.

I am unfortunately less familiar with the designs of former schoolmaster Charles Banks, who fell in with Raynor and Macdonald while they were working on the design of a course at the Hotchkiss School in Connecticut, not far from where I grew up. Banks was inspired enough by their work to quit his day job and join the firm, assisting with the Yale golf course and Mid Ocean, and building some truly dramatic holes on his own early efforts like Forsgate and Whippoorwill. But Raynor died and Macdonald became disinterested, and three years later the Depression put an abrupt halt to opportunities in the golf design business, leaving Banks understandably somewhat bitter about the whole thing.

I've been lucky to have had the chance to write a bit about golf architecture, but to call me an historian on golf architecture is certainly inaccurate, and the responsibility worries me. I seldom can find the time to do the research good history requires. Fortunately, George Bahto has made the time, and that makes his book worth reading. From now on I'll be content to read what he has discovered, and hope that my own work will be good enough to deserve the occasional reward of a game on a Macdonald, Raynor, or Banks course.

—Tom Doak

INTRODUCTION

Charles Blair Macdonald and his seminal achievement, the National Golf Links of America, in one fell swoop inaugurated the evolution of golf course architecture in America. From the crude obstacle courses that characterized the pre-1900 era, Macdonald introduced holes of strategic complexity that are as much a test of mind as body.

To his detractors, Macdonald was an opinionated autocrat, a stubborn and bullheaded dictator who felt appointed by providence to defend his romanticized vision of golf from contamination in America. To his many friends and admirers though, he was merely a traditionalist, a man who wished to bring the game he learned as a young student at St. Andrews University back to share with able sportsmen in this country.

And why not? His grandfather, a member of the Royal and Ancient, arranged a locker for him in the golf shop of Old Tom Morris. The Grand Old Man of the game introduced Macdonald to his son Young Tom, the wunderkind of his era who, before his tragic death, retired the championship belt with three straight victories in the British Open.

Those were the years that molded the impressionable young Macdonald, who could be found daily on the links, endlessly practicing his newfound passion with such verve that he soon could hold his own in the challenge matches that were the city's main form of recreation. Macdonald observed that the links were an extension of the very being of St. Andrews, with churchmen, parishioners, scholars, tradesmen, ladies and students, everyone playing on equal footing with honor, and strictly by the rules adopted in 1754 by the Royal and Ancient (the original Rules of Golf were constituted by the Honorable Company of Edinburgh Golfers in 1744). Golf at St. Andrews was more than just simple recreation, it was a game to be honored, that molded character. Macdonald was determined to plant the seeds of golf in America, and who among us could blame him?

Upon returning home to Chicago in 1875, according to his passionate memoirs, *Scotland's Gift—Golf,* circumstances were dire and opportunities to play nonexistent. He was to refer to this bleak period, lasting some 17 years, as "The Dark Ages." With the rare opportunity to play his beloved game only while traveling abroad on business, Macdonald found new life in 1892 by organizing the Chicago Golf Club, the first formal 18-hole course in America.

As golf gradually began to take root, particularly in affluent places, it became necessary to form an organization, an American authoritative body as it were, to govern the game. The first order of business was to define what constituted an "amateur" and to determine which clubs had courses of sufficient quality to participate in this new organization. Representatives from five clubs—Shinnecock Hills, The Country Club at Brookline, St. Andrews (Yonkers, N.Y.), Newport C.C., and Chicago G.C. (represented by Macdonald)—officially formed what was later to become the United States Golf Association. After much controversy and several false starts, to the surprise of no one, Macdonald won the first Amateur Championship at Newport in 1895.

A vocal and influential protectorate of the game's roots, Macdonald insisted that the traditions, customs, and most importantly, the rules, should strictly adhere to the Scottish model. He felt certain that any "Americanization" of golf would put the game in jeopardy as a passing fad.

Golf architecture, in Macdonald's mind, was where he could engender real and lasting change in an area he could truly sink his teeth into. To contribute something of permanence back to golf appealed to his educational, artistic, and emotional senses.

After moving from Chicago to New York in 1900, Macdonald became obsessed with building a golf course that would compare favorably with the finest links of Great Britain. In 1902 he returned to the British Isles with the expressed desire to compile sketches, notes, diagrams, and surveys of the holes that he and his many overseas friends felt to be timeless classics.

Patiently and methodically, Macdonald moved from course to course, devoting most of four summers to gathering detailed information. Satisfied that he had surveyed every possible hole of value overseas, he returned to look for a suitable piece of ground on which to build his course. Oddly enough, he found what he wanted right next door to Shinnecock Hills, about which Horace Hutchinson referred to at the time as "ladylike." (It might have been ladylike around the turn of the century, but it most certainly isn't today!)

When the National Golf Links of America had its unofficial opening in 1910, the landscape of golf in our nation was forever transformed, setting the benchmark for a new standard of excellence. All of golf paused to marvel at Macdonald's magnificent creation, the first attempt in this country to construct golf holes on classic lines, embodying the very best features of the famous holes of the British Isles. What a Herculean effort!

Among the legendary holes depicted were the Alps at Prestwick, the Redan at North Berwick, the Sahara bunker at Royal St. George's, and both the Road and Eden holes at St. Andrews. Some closely resembled the originals, while in other cases the underlying thought or principle was worked into the canvas of the landscape. There are many who feel the best holes at the National are entirely Macdonald's, original notes in a rhapsody of wonderful depictions that are as much links-like as any course in America.

The National Golf Links also marked the beginning of an important and meaningful collaboration, when Macdonald hired a Southampton engineer and surveyor named Seth J. Raynor. The two quickly gained such mutual respect that they immediately began a business relationship that must have been entirely sympathetic. Under the tutelage of Macdonald, the passion of constructing golf courses bit Raynor hard, and he went on to construct some marvelous courses in the image of Macdonald's National.

Some of Seth Raynor's best are Camargo, Shoreacres, Yeamans Hall, Fishers Island, and a masterful reconstruction of Macdonald's own Chicago Golf Club. Like his mentor, all his courses had a number of "classic" holes interwoven beautifully into the tapestry of the final product. While some may suggest that this is a redundant formula, the two gentlemen had an uncanny knack for adapting the particular hole in question to fit seamlessly both into the terrain, and most importantly, to be playable and functional for all classes of golfers.

Their scheme worked, and more importantly, works beautifully today. Playability, elasticity, and memorable features are just a few of the attributes that Macdonald and Raynor consistently repeated. Wherever Bill Coore and I are afforded the opportunity to build a golf course, their genius and legacy occupies our thoughts, guiding us to give golfers inspiration and hope, not endless despair.

—Ben Crenshaw

CHAPTER ONE

THE EARLY YEARS

It was early in August of 1872 when I was first introduced to golf. I was 16 years old then. My father desired that I should go to my grandfather in St. Andrews, Scotland, and there complete my education at the university, the United Colleges of St. Salvador and St. Leonard's. I left Chicago in July, placed in the care of a family friend, Mr. Kirkwood. We crossed the Atlantic on the Scotia, *a side-wheel steamer of the Cunard Line, the last of its character that ever crossed the Atlantic.*

Mr. Kirkwood hailed from Musselburgh, a town five miles to the east of Edinburgh. I was permitted to go with Mr. Kirkwood to Musselburgh and spend the night at his aged mother's home. Here it was that I heard of golf. I was much interested in seeing the red coats of the players and watching the leisurely way in which they lounged in the Musselburgh common–"common" to me, but "links" to them, as soon as I learned. It seemed to me a form of tiddledy-winks, stupid and silly, for never in my life had I known a sport that was not strenuous or violent.

We left Edinburgh the next afternoon at three from Waverly Station reaching St. Andrews about six.

—Charles Blair Macdonald from *Scotland's Gift—Golf*

During the train ride a family friend who accompanied them on the trip "tried to explain at some length the fascination of the game. I couldn't see it. My day had yet to come."

The town of St. Andrews, tucked into a remote corner of Scotland's eastern shore, charmed the young, impressionable Macdonald from the moment he arrived. He left the wounded city of Chicago and its population of 300,000, just seven years removed from the end of the Civil War. Chicago, slowly recovering from the aftereffects of the bloody conflict, suffered another tragedy when, just nine months before young Charlie left for St. Andrews, the city nearly burned to the ground. The "Great Chicago Fire," caused when a cow belonging to one Mrs. Patrick O'Leary, kicked over a lantern in a barn, destroyed many nearby structures before strong winds spread the fire still further. Within 24 hours the raging inferno destroyed three and a half square miles, wiping out the entire Chicago business district, destroying 17,000 buildings, killing 300, and leaving over 90,000 people homeless. Fully one-third of this great city was destroyed. With business and industry at a halt, the morale of the devastated population hit rock bottom.

The contrast between the chaos Macdonald left in Chicago, and the quiet and charming town of St. Andrews was pronounced. Impressed with the tranquility of this Scottish burgh and its "leisurely, delightful liftestyle," he quickly fell in step, describing the people of St. Andrews as being "absorbed in the past, while the people of the United States seemed absorbed in the future." Young Charles had yet to discover the historical treasures of this "cornerstone" of golf, a game he would come to love with a passion.

The tranquil atmosphere surrounding the town of St. Andrews had a calming effect upon the young man who had left behind a home in chaos. Macdonald would soon find himself immersed in the early history of the town, and its seminal place as golf's birthplace.

William Macdonald, his paternal grandfather, was a member of the Royal and Ancient Golf Club. The day following his arrival, he took young Charlie to meet with the "the genial and much-loved Tom Morris [Old Tom was 51 at the time] and bought me three or four clubs." Too young to be permitted in the Royal and Ancient, Macdonald was assigned a locker in the golf shop of Old Tom Morris. A round of golf was arranged with another youngster, and with grandfather along to offer

Macdonald's clubs at St. Andrews consisted of seven woods and four irons. He carried a driver, a grass club, the middle spoon, a short spoon (a "baffy"), a wood niblick, a mid-iron, a lofter, an iron niblick, and a wooden putter. During the '20s, with the hickory age all but gone, and the 14 club rule not yet in force, Macdonald felt the "modern" habit of carrying a myriad of clubs for every conceivable situation a violation of the spirit of the rules. Disgusted at what he perceived as a cheapening of the game, he played with only *six* clubs: a "bulger" (with the loft of a 2-wood), a driving iron, a light iron, a mashie, a niblick, and a putter—only one was a wooden club.

Below: St. Andrews Clubhouse. (Mike Daniels)

advice, together they set off to play. This beginning, in the cradle of the game, marked a starting point not only for Charlie Macdonald, but in many ways for golf in America. On that breezy afternoon in 1872, the Old Course planted the seed that he would carry back across the Atlantic and help germinate into the game we know today.

With nearly 20 hours of daylight, and school not yet begun, the smitten Macdonald spent his days enthusiastically pursuing his newfound passion. Often stopping only to eat and sleep, around the course he went, the exception being Sunday, when the Old Course was (and still is) closed in observance of the Sabbath. "My only interesting Sunday diversion, at first, was to explore the ruins of the castle, the ruins of the cathedral, and the transcept of Blackfriars Chapel, or to climb St. Rugulas' Tower—then to read of them in the evening as directed by my grandfather."

As time went on and the desire to improve took hold, Macdonald and his fellow students would often sneak out on Sunday afternoon to the Old Course, retrieving clubs they had hidden in the gorse bushes. There they would practice in hidden areas of the course, out of sight of the deeply religious townsfolk.

Golf was a simple game in those days at St. Andrews. "The earlier rules of play always suggested a code of honor. One rule alone governed the game after driving off: the player must play the ball as it lay and not interfere with his opponent's ball." The ball was not to be touched with anything but a club until it was holed out; the only exceptions were a lost ball or a ball in water. Macdonald took this basic precept of the game to heart. An unwavering defender of golf's code of ethics, he firmly believed the 13 original rules, as laid down by the ancients, were more than sufficient to cover any circumstance.

Touching a ball in play without penalty "was anathema to me, a kind of sacrilegious profanity." Macdonald was unshakable in this feeling of reverence for the sheer honesty of the game. A look at today's confusing, and often contradictory Rules of Golf would only reinforce his convictions.

Charlie quickly became proficient at the game and by the second year he was invited to play in matches with Old Tom, his son Young Tom, and celebrated players like David Strath and brothers Willie and Jamie Dunn. Matches were arranged in many creative formats at St. Andrews, mostly because Young Tom and Davie Strath were considerably better than most of the others. Strath would often play the better ball of three, or there would be three vs. two, or four vs. two. Macdonald was very proud of these many matches, and in his reminiscences *Scotland's Gift—Golf*, he looked back fondly back at the more important ones.

The charm of the Old Course, and its rolling windswept expanse, was the measuring rod by which Macdonald evaluated golf courses. He described it as "the most entrancing course in the world besides being the finest test of golfing ability."

It was a magical time and place for young Charles Macdonald. Molded by the true spirit of the game and its traditions, he would later go on to spread its gospel on this side of the Atlantic.

His studies completed, young Charlie Macdonald said a sad goodbye to Scotland in September of 1874. By now he was an accomplished golfer and a hardened match player, able to hold his own against most any caliber of opponent. During those two crucial years, Macdonald took the

Above: At age 16, a young Charlie Macdonald spent 25 months at St. Andrews University. It was here his love of the game flourished and before he left he was playing with and against the best golfers in the British Isles, including the legendary Young Tom Morris pictured above with his father. Both men won four Open Championships; Young Tom won four straight before he reached the age of 21. (George Bahto Collection)

Above: Allan Robertson, 1815-1359, St. Andrews, Scotland.

Allan Robertson died at the young age of 44. He left a legacy of accomplishment that would be difficult for anyone to equal. He was recognized as the greatest ball-maker of his day, the greatest golfer of his day, and holds the distinction of being recognized as the first professional golfer. Robertson was the first person ever to break 80 at the Old Course (1858); a feat no one ever felt could be accomplished.

In 1842 he modified the Old Course at St. Andrews by widening the existing fairways and creating St. Andrews' huge double greens. He added the great 17th 'Road' hole to the St. Andrews layout and is also recognized as the first golf course designer. (*Golf Illustrated*)

Opposite: Famous portrait of Old Tom Morris. (*Golf Illustrated*)

opportunity to play and study other great courses of the British Isles and portions of Europe. This experience polished off his education, and served as the foundation upon which he would later build his ideal course, the National Golf Links of America.

Macdonald's Dark Ages: 1875-1892

Returning to Chicago in the fall of 1874, eighteen-year-old Charles Macdonald found the city still in total devastation. The fire of 1871 was followed by "The Panic of 1873," a depression of unprecedented magnitude. Men fortunate to find work toiled 12 to 16 hours a day. The thought of participating in a leisure activity was inconceivable. Wrote Macdonald, "Certainly, bankers would call in a loan—if one was fortunate to get so rare an accommodation—of anyone who attended to anything outside of business."

Visited by a Scottish classmate, Macdonald recalled a fruitless attempt at playing golf in America. It was August of 1875, a year removed from both golf and St. Andrews. Taking some of Macdonald's old clubs, the pair ventured out to an abandoned Civil War campsite and "cut in a few holes utilizing some old tin cans left behind by the troops years before." After a bit of play and some reminiscing, the pair was accosted by " hoodlums from the vicinity who tormented us to death. Evidently they thought us demented." Discouraged and embarrassed by the ignorance of his countrymen, Macdonald reluctantly put away his clubs until he could go abroad and play "real golf."

For the next 17 long years, "real golf" was confined to the occasional business trip to Europe, as his clubs—and desire—languished in a dusty closet. Golf in America was totally out of the question because there was neither the time to play nor a golf course to play on. It was a dispiriting situation for a man who learned the game under the wing of Old Tom Morris, only to be deprived for half of his lifetime. By 1892, C.B. Macdonald was 35 years old. Yet the distance and years removed from St. Andrews did nothing to dampen golf's flame in his heart.

The beginnings of golf in America, crude as they were, first germinated on a 34-acre plot in Yonkers, N.Y. This rudimentary course was soon followed by a 70-acre cow pasture near

Chicago, a lawn in Lake Forest, and a seven-hole course in Boston "over undulating lawns with hazards consisting of avenues, clumps of trees, bushes, beds of rhododendrons and azaleas." Slowly but surely, the game set down roots, spreading its pollen wherever it would grow.

And grow it did. Wherever sportsmen gathered for leisure, this curious game with its strange looking sticks began to flower.

This tiny spark was all he needed, for Macdonald saw these simple beginnings as a signal from providence. Knowing that a decent course did not exist in this country, Charles Blair Macdonald believed he was divinely chosen to promulgate the game of golf in America. It would be an endeavor that would consume him for the rest of his life.

Charles Macdonald, the eldest son of Godfrey Macdonald and wife, Mary Blackwell Macdonald, was born in a house on Lundy Lane in Niagara Falls, Canada on November 14th, 1855 and although he was born in Canada, Mr. and Mrs. Macdonald were American citizens. Not long after, the family moved to Chicago, Illinois.

The family was wealthy, so life in Chicago as a youngster was well above the level of most, even though the city was in the throws of depression after the Civil War and the disaster of the Great Chicago Fire.

Wealth and stature came readily in the Godfrey Macdonald family, whose ancestry traced back to wealthy ancestor Sir William Johnson, an Irishman who at one time owned most of the Mohawk Valley. Sir William (1715 - 1774) was an American colonial fur trader, land speculator, soldier and, later, an Indian agent who exerted considerable influence on the Iroquois. He was a major general in the French and Indian War when British/Indian forces defeated the French at the battle of Lake George. As a result Johnson was made a baronet and soon thereafter appointed superintendent for northern Indian affairs. Johnson gradually acquired more than 500,000 acres of land in the Mohawk and upper Susquehanna valleys. He ruled the area from "Johnstown," his personal capital, with the iron hand of a feudal lord. How much of Sir William's wealth was passed down to the Macdonald family over the next hundred years is not known.

The birth date (year) of C. B. Macdonald has often been misidentified. Many publications and club histories have it as 1856. More confusion was added after his death when Bernard Darwin's written eulogy announced his life span from 1857 to 1939. Even his gravestone is inscribed with the birth year of 1857. In truth, Charles Blair Macdonald was born in November of 1855. In his book, Scotland's Gift—Golf, *the opening sentence of the text reads:*

"It was early in August in 1872 when I was first introduced to golf. I was then sixteen."

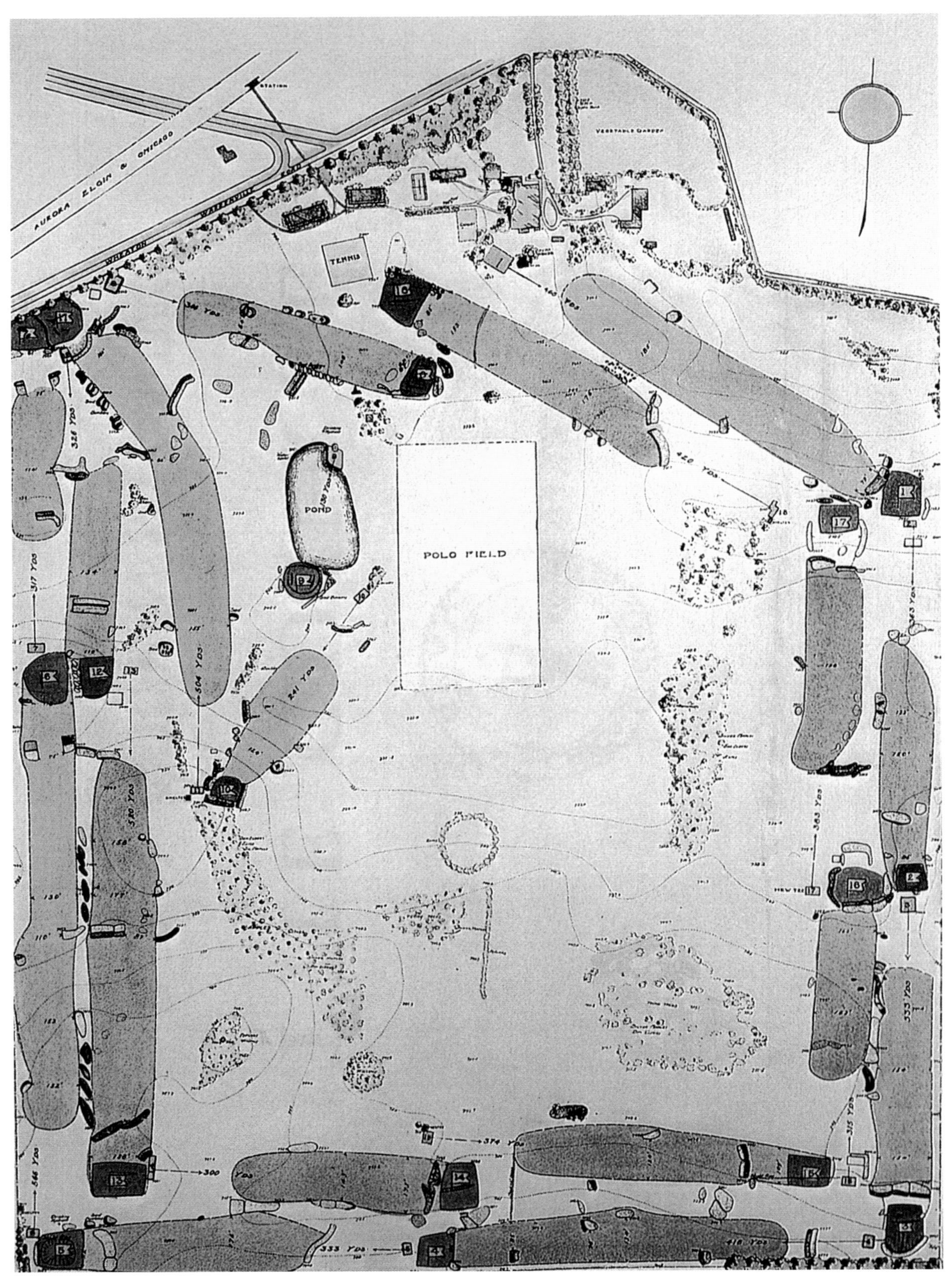

AURORA ELGIN & CHICAGO
STATION
WHEATON
TENNIS
VEGETABLE GARDEN
POND
POLO FIELD
420 YDS
504 YDS
241 YDS
300
374
333 YDS
418 YDS
NEW TEE 17

CHAPTER TWO

CHICAGO GOLF CLUB

A club whizzed through the air—a sharp click—and Charles Blair Macdonald drove the little sphere of gutta-percha far over the water of Lake Michigan in St. Andrews fashion. I looked at Macdonald in amazement, and then followed his eyes in the direction of the lake. He may have seen the ball, but I would have to take his word for it. That drive, however, started the golf craze in the West.

—From an article written by
Horace Chatfield-Taylor of Chicago in 1900

In early spring of 1892, C. B. Macdonald went to Lake Forest, Illinois, at the behest of his friend Horace Chatfield-Taylor to build a "golf course" on the lawn of the home of his father-in-law, Senator Charles B. Farwell. This spacious summer estate, resting on a high bluff overlooking Lake Michigan, was known in society circles as "Fairlawn."

The few courses existing in America in 1892 were just crude designs laid out randomly over existing land, with huge, ugly cross-bunkers gouged out of the earth. These artless roadblocks were normally stone-filled, muddy, or sandy ditches dug out of the ground, with the dirt simply thrown up to form a high rampart. The first set of bunkers, usually 150 yards from the teeing grounds, were designed specifically to entrap a topped or weak shot. Similar bulwarks placed further down the fairway added more penal horrors before finally finishing off the exhausted golfer just short of the green with a deep obstruction that effectively stymied the traditional running approach. These rudimentary courses, commonly laid out by beginners, were sadly devoid of strategic or aesthetic value. Indeed, playing over these contrived and unnatural landscapes, early golfers in America frequently found golf both wearisome and irritating.

The opportunity to build a golf course came partly because of the upcoming World's Columbian Exposition of 1893. This World's Fair marked the 400th anniversary of Columbus's discovery of America. Only the second World's Fair ever held in the United States, the event breathed new life into the city of Chicago. The Exposition, which unveiled such wonders as the Pullman car and the Ferris wheel, encompassed over 650 acres and glistened like white marble in the Chicago sunlight.

Sir Henry Wood, England's Commissioner General to the Exposition, counted among his visiting entourage a number of young college men who had played golf at their English

Opposite: The original golf course designed by Charles Blair Macdonald. (Chicago Golf Club)

schools and were brought to the exposition to help introduce this new game to America. The boys "were clamoring for some outdoor sport"—namely, golf. They talked incessantly about the game and, according to Macdonald, "created a willing audience."

One of those young men was Henry J. Whigham, whose father had been a schoolmate of Macdonald at St. Andrews University. Macdonald had written to Whigham's father David, urging that he send his son Henry to the Columbian Exposition. Henry, who hailed from Oxford, would later marry Macdonald's daughter Frances.

Though he found a sympathetic audience in these young men from England, this was hardly the case in America. In truth, C.B. had bored nearly the entire city of Chicago with his ceaseless pontificating about golf. Annoyed and weary of his endless speeches over the previous 17 years, even his closest friends began to steer clear of him. Chatfield-Taylor, a frequent victim of Macdonald's rambling, heard of the young men's desires and spoke to Macdonald about building a few holes for them on his property.

Horace Chatfield-Taylor recalled that first day's golfing experience:

"Macdonald teed another ball and handed his driver to me. I attempted to imitate his actions, and after a series of contortions which would have done honor to the rubber-man in Barnum's sideshow, tore up a foot of turf without any way disturbing the equanimity of the little white object I had striven so viciously to hit. Macdonald laughed, and I said, 'damn'... and I have been saying it ever since."

According to Horace, Macdonald looked about Senator Farwell`s property and "with supreme contempt, he eyed the trees and flower beds and said the grounds would never do." Eventually Macdonald recanted, deciding the venture worthwhile. "If only to give the game a start—and after a few glances about the place, he started out to pace off the holes."

Macdonald quickly drove stakes into the ground to mark where the holes would be, demonstrated the "trick" (the art) of hitting a golf ball once again, and left for town, leaving behind a few clubs and balls from his college days. This introductory course consisted of seven short holes, the first being 80 yards long, with four holes less than 75 yards, and none over 250.

Portions of the course wandered among the trees and flower beds, while other parts were routed into an adjoining park by the shore where sliced balls "went over the bluff and fell some 200 feet to the beach below." St. Andrews it wasn't, but it was a course. And the only one in the West.

Although the "hole-cups" were as yet not in place, the first game was scheduled the following Saturday. Urban Broughton, an Englishman living in Chicago, Horace Chatfield-Taylor, and Macdonald teed it up for a "go at the game.

"In a blinding storm," continued Chatfield-Taylor, "we waded around the nine holes [really seven], losing most of Macdonald's balls, and playing with the singular modification that holing out meant hitting the stake with the fewest strokes."

In short order, six sets of clubs with strange sounding names like "baffy" and "niblick" were ordered from the Royal Liverpool Golf Club in Hoylake, England. It seemed golf in earnest was to be inaugurated in the Chicago area. But during the summer of 1892 few Americans joined in to play, and according to Chatfield-Taylor, Americans "who passed the little links, stared in amazement, or, as was more often the case, laughed derisively at our antics." The following year, Commissioner Wood's presence in the Chicago area added some credibility and stature to the efforts of the golfers, and the club's membership began to improve.

Charlie Macdonald was far from happy with the course on Farwell's estate and was in search of more suitable land "where it could be possible to take a full swing without over-driving a hole." According to Macdonald, minor

Above: Horace Chatfield-Taylor requested that Charles B. Macdonald build a course on the estate of his father-in-law Senator Charles B. Farwell, a seven hole rudimentary design—it was a beginning. (*Golf Illustrated*)

"strong-arm and brow-beating" was required to recruit additional club members. In due time, however, donations of 10 dollars each was contributed by 20 or 30 of his friends to cover the cost of constructing a nine-hole course on the stock farm of A. Haddow Smith, an Englishman in nearby Belmont, Illinois. Scotsmen James B. Forgan and Herbert and Lawrence Tweedie were recruited to help lay out the course. Charlie was elated; his efforts were finally coming to fruition—or so he thought.

There wasn't a clubhouse, so a neighbor's barn was used as a place to store their clubs, and for shelter in the event of rain. Equipment was in short supply, so six more sets of clubs were ordered from the Royal Liverpool Golf Club. Soon all was set for the introduction of the game to the contributing members, who were asked to accompany Macdonald to neighboring Belmont. An elaborate luncheon was ordered for the event but, as fate would have it, the weather was not cooperative. Heavy rains would ruin the day, as only two players, Edward Worthington and Harry Wilmerding, showed up.

Undaunted, Macdonald handed out clubs, arranged some small wagers (making bets with novices already), and damn the weather, the match would go on! After five holes of play over the new course, the skies opened and torrential rains ensued. The three players took refuge in the nearby barn to pass the time hoping for the rains to subside. Charlie had brought a deck of cards, and they passed the time waiting for a break in the weather. Despite the delay, they were firmly hooked, for in Macdonald's own words, "I am happy to say that between each hand they ran to the door to see if the rain was over, each being confident he would win the next hole. The result of all this was that golf won over two of the most enthusiastic men I have ever known, and throughout their lives they never ceased to be devoted to the game."

In the spring of 1893 the course was increased to 18 holes and by July 18, 1893, the charter of the Chicago Golf Club was granted. The applicants were Charles B. Macdonald, J. Carlos Sterling, James B. Forgan, W. R. Farquhar, George A. H. Scott, and Urban H. Broughton. The driving force in the development of the Chicago Golf Club, and a member of the prestigious Board of Trade, 38-year-old Macdonald was hitting his stride. With a bright future ahead in both golf and business, he married Frances Porter, with whom he would eventually father two daughters, Janet and Frances.

Above: Charles Blair Macdonald in 1898 at age 42. (George Bahto Collection)

By 1894 the popularity of the game increased, and the Chicago Golf Club's membership increased to outgrow the modest course in Belmont. At Macdonald's urging, the club voted to purchase another tract on which they would build an improved golf course, one that would equal the best inland courses in the British Isles.

They purchased a marvelous piece of 200 acres of rolling meadowland—the "Patrick Farm"—a mile from the town of Wheaton, 25 miles from Chicago along the Northern rail line. Memberships in the Chicago Golf Club were sold for $200, with each a participant in the purchase of the new property. The lush, rolling meadow of the Patrick farm, with nary a tree, was perfect for the "first-rate parkland" course that Macdonald wanted to build. It was the start of a dream for Macdonald, but a nightmare for Mr. Patrick, an affable farmer and former property owner. Unable to cope with his newfound wealth from the $28,000 selling price, an enormous sum in those days, he eventually went insane and died in an asylum.

The abandoned course at Belmont was bought by a group headed by H. J. Tweedie, and the Belmont Golf Club was formed in 1899. About that same time, the small course on Senator Farwell's estate gave birth to the Lake Forest Club, using the nine holes at the McCormick farm until they purchased additional property to build a new nine. Lake Forest later added a second nine that was laid out by Macdonald's future son-in-law, Henry J. Whigham. The club eventually evolved into the Onwentsia Club.

Concurrent with the growth of the Chicago golf craze, the game was slowly taking root along the East coast. Started by wealthy men who had "discovered" the game while vacationing in Europe, the four other clubs that were to eventually form the nucleus of the United States Golf Association were building courses of their own.

The (new) St. Andrew's Golf Club, organized by Scottish exile John Reid, began in November of 1888 on an empty lot before moving to a nearby apple orchard in Yonkers. Then known as the "Apple Tree Gang," the first formally organized club in America quickly outgrew the orchard and moved to their present Mount Hope location in 1897. Reid, sometimes referred to as the "Father of American Golf," did nearly as much as Macdonald in helping to popularize the game here in his adopted country.

The Country Club, in Brookline, Massachusetts, later the site of Francis Ouimet's historic 1913 U.S. Open victory over English stars Harry Vardon and Ted Ray, was in the process of constructing a nine-holer on the property of local sportsman Laurence Curtis.

At about the same time, William K. Vanderbilt Sr., freshly returned from a visit to a course in Biarritz, France, had persuaded their professional, Willie Dunn Jr., to come to Long Island and improve their existing course in the sand hills of Southampton. The original 12-hole course, hand built by local Indians on a nearby reservation, was soon expanded to 18. The course would need a clubhouse, so the club commissioned Stanford White, the leading architect of his day, to design and construct the hilltop clubhouse that still stands guard today over the Shinnecock Hills golf course.

In fashionable Newport, Rhode Island, Theodore Havemeyer had also developed a passion for the game while vacationing in Europe. Upon his return to this country, the then 50-plus-year-old Havemeyer "sensibly deemed golf a game more appropriate than polo for a man of [his] age." He convinced a few newly-converted friends to introduce the game of golf to their summer habitats in Newport, and the first course, a short nine-holer, was laid out across 40 acres near scenic Breton's Point. However, with the introduction of the livelier Haskell ball around the turn of the century, the course was found to be too short, so Havemeyer persuaded 75 friends to invest in a 140-acre parcel then known as Rocky Farm. With that, the Newport Country Club was launched.

Back in Chicago, Macdonald, Henry Whigham, and James Forgan had laid out their new course at Wheaton, which despite one peculiar element was drawing universal praise. Routed in a clockwise manner along the perimeter of the property, sliced balls would break toward the center of the course, away from the surrounding cornfields. This was done at Macdonald's insistence, he being a chronic slicer. Hooked balls had to be hacked out of the adjacent farmland because there was no out-of-bounds on the course. Eventually, under pressure from the few unfortunate members afflicted with a hook, a local rule was adopted allowing shots in the cornfields to be replayed from the tee with a one stroke penalty. Macdonald was said to have never hit a shot out-of-bounds —a strange coincidence indeed.

Despite this design quirk, by any measure Chicago Golf Club was an outstanding course for its time. The "old" Chicago (later redesigned) course's par was 73. The great amateur champion Walter J. Travis, while in his prime, claimed his course record 69 to be "the only perfect round I ever played." A few years later, leading amateur Chick Evans, with better equipment, scored a 67. He also called it a near perfect round of golf. The virtues of Chicago G.C. quickly

Left: The clubhouse at Chicago Golf Club. (Chicago Golf Club)

spread to Europe, and drew the attention of no less than Horace Hutchinson and Bernard Darwin. The pair, who had a feature section in *Country Life* magazine, perhaps the most prestigious publication of its day, enlisted the writing skills of Chick Evans to pen this description of the Chicago Golf Club prior to the 1912 National Amateur:

> *The membership is composed of leading citizens of Chicago, and the club was one of the five clubs to organize the United States Golf Association. In the spring of 1895 the course was laid out under the supervision of Messrs. C.B. Macdonald, H.J. Whigham, J.B. Forgan and others well versed in the science of golf-course-building. How well they planned, the present condition of the course shows. They had a thorough British knowledge of the game, and they tried to import it whole, not even forgetting a flock of sheep to keep the course cropped. It is interesting to note that Mr. Macdonald has since laid out that unique course on Long Island, consisting of eighteen clever reproductions of historic British holes.*
>
> *The course at Chicago Golf Club is now generally recognized as furnishing one of the best tests in the United States. It has been much improved since the last United States Golf Association amateur tournament [1909, won by Robert A. Gardner], and still other changes are contemplated. At present it is in tip-top condition owing to the recent rains, which have done away with any fear of cracked or baked ground—a somewhat common condition during dry summers on other courses in Chicago. As on all American links, the fair green and rough at Chicago Golf form a sharp, straight line, but broken here and there by well-placed mounds and bunkers projecting into the course. Mr. Hilton's remark about the National Golf Links might well be applied here: Thank goodness, I don't have to play down between two straight lines. I am awaiting his opinion of this course with much curiosity. My own enthusiasm of it is so great, even after a tour of British and Eastern American courses, that I am anxious to hear an expert foreign verdict.*
>
> *Among the peculiarities of the Chicago Golf course are its system of traps and the excellence of its putting greens. We must remember that Nature has provided ideal greens for Britain, but America has been compelled to make her own. The much-desired gentle slope is here usually artificial, and each green at Chicago Golf has an individual roll and topography of its own. To me these smooth and velvety greens resemble "Old Country greens" and are flawless. The absence of clover makes them unusually true. Then directly in front of the greens the ground is what it ought to be. One does not have to pitch through bunches of grass when the greens get fast. On the holes where there are bunkers to catch a topped iron approach, there is plenty of fair green between the bunker and the putting green, which is imperative with the present fast ball. This ground is usually gently rolling, and I consider it even better than that on British seaside courses, where there are unexpected sharp humps and hollows just short of the green. One of the favorite methods of trapping at Chicago Golf is to run a number of mounds of irregular shape into the rough to catch a poor tee shot; they are used around the greens also, and every green is well guarded.*
>
> *To sum up, the excellent condition of the course has resulted logically from the first well-planned scheme down through the skilled management of the various presidents and directors, who were upheld, encouraged and advised by a most harmonious membership. In this manner the course has been adjusted without friction to every new condition of the game. The man who wins at Wheaton in September must be an accurate drive, for woe-betide him who gets off the course! The recent improvements were intended to emphasize the necessity of well-placed shots. The criticism has been made that there are no long carries; that is not exactly true. There is a long but narrow way for the elect, and the long, straight driver is doubly fortunate. The winner [of the 1912 Amateur] must also be a good mashie player, for that shot is necessary on many holes, provided the tee shots are well played. In fact, he should play every shot properly, for each mistake is heavily penalized. Therein lies the value of this course. As much as possible, mere luck had been eliminated, and, barring accidents, the best man must win. Finally, too much credit cannot be given to the professionals, the Foulises, father and son, for their faithful and practical assistance in the arrangement and upkeep of the course.*

Macdonald's original design was not dramatically altered for over 20 years with the exception of a few suggestions offered by famed British architect Harry Colt. With new and better courses popping up all the time, the architect of Sunningdale, at the club's request, tweaked the design to help keep the quality of the course competitive with some of the more modern layouts. Ultimately though, Chicago Golf

Club's design became antiquated and the club voted in 1922 to retain Macdonald's legendary protégé, Seth Raynor, to assist Macdonald in completely remodeling the layout .

Despite the fine reviews of 1895, Macdonald was still dissatisfied with the state of course architecture, and as far back as 1897 yearned to build what he felt would be a truly first-class links course in America. That year, he wrote an article that was to prove prophetic. In it, he observed that:

The ideal first-class golf links has yet to be selected and the course laid out in America. No course can be called first-class with less than eighteen holes. A sandy soil sufficiently rich to make turf is best. Long Island is a natural links. A first-class course can only be made in time. It must develop. The proper distance between the holes, the shrewd placing of bunkers and other hazards, the perfecting of putting greens, all must be evolved by a process of growth and it requires study and patience.

Not realizing it at the time, in three scant years he would move to New York where his dream of this ideal links would continue to grow. In a sense, Macdonald would find his inspiration with another article, this one also published in *Country Life*.

Above: Rare glimpse at the painting of C.B. Macdonald (circa 1895) that hangs in the grill room at the Chicago Golf Club (courtesy of the Club).

CHAPTER THREE

MACDONALD *and the* FIRST NATIONAL CHAMPIONSHIP

In 1894 it was proposed by Theodore Havemeyer and the membership of the Newport club that a national golf championship be held. It was felt a tournament of this stature would continue to promulgate the game, which was already in the throws of strong growth. St. Andrew's in Yonkers, The Country Club at Brookline, Newport in Rhode Island, and Shinnecock Hills on Long Island were quickly gaining converts. Havemeyer, Newport's founder, was very proud of their new nine-hole course at Rocky Farm, and proposed that the inaugural championship be held there. That this was agreed to by the other clubs, clear rivals for the attention the event would bring, is attributable in no small measure to Havemeyer's position as a nationally recognized public figure.

C. B. Macdonald was ecstatic. Considered the best golfer in the country, the opportunity to display his golfing prowess before his peers and winning America's first championship appealed to his enormous ego. He already fancied himself the first great American-born golfer, and what better way to usher in a new era of championship play than by taking his rightful place upon the throne!

With his background at St. Andrews, learning his golf under Old Tom and playing matches throughout the British Isles, there was no question, at least in his mind, that he would easily win the contest. After all, his skills and competitive experience were unmatched in this country.

The First Tournament: *Newport Country Club, Rhode Island*

In order to showcase their layout, the tournament committee at Newport set their course up as tough as possible, narrowing the fairways, allowing off-fairway areas to go unmowed, and placing the flagsticks in most difficult positions. There was some grousing from the competitors that the course had been made artificially difficult, but the powers at Newport felt this type of setup would produce a "true champion."In over 100 years, little has changed.

It was agreed that the event would be contested for 36 holes of medal play over two days. The tournament, played in September of 1894, began with a field of 20, but by the conclusion of the first round, 12 of the 20 had dropped out, leaving a field of only eight. Not surprisingly, Macdonald led after the first day, shooting a sparkling 89, followed by W.G. Lawrence of Newport, who was alone in second with a 93.What began as a smooth and dignified beginning to championship golf in America was soon to become an embarrassing debacle.

Disaster struck Charlie on the second day, when inexplicably, having lost all semblance of his game, he staggered in with an even 100 strokes.During the round his ball came

Map of the
Newport Country Club Golf Links
circa 1895

Hole 1.	210+	Hole 4.	188+	Hole 7.	301+
Hole 2.	351+	Hole 5.	340+	Hole 8.	330+
Hole 3.	172+	Hole 6.	484+	Hole 9.	327+

Total 2707+ yards

The first official championships of the United States were held here on the first week in October 1895.

The Championship was won by
Charles Blair Macdonald

POLO FIELDS
STONE WALL
BUNKER
904'
992'
OPEN BUNKER
OPEN BUNKER
STABLE
982'
EARTH BUNKER
1454'
OLD QUARRY
CLUB HOUSE
632'
SAND POT BUNKERS
SAND POT BUNKER
1054'
564'
517'
1021'
SAND POT BUNKERS

The length if the holes was measured in feet - not in yards

GEORGE BANTO 1996

to rest against a stone wall and he moved it away, deeming it an obstacle. The Newport tournament officials penalized him two strokes, ruling the wall was actually a hazard. This was to cost him the championship as W.G. Lawrence, who shot a 95 for a total of 188, defeated Macdonald by a single stroke.

All hell broke loose. Macdonald, in a childish fit of pique, berated the Newport Club's tournament committee for the manner in which the tournament was conducted. His complaints were many, but the main issue was his contention that a stone wall did not constitute a hazard. Not only was the penalty unjustified, but he also chastised them for using a stroke-play format, insisting that it should have been match play—anyone knew that! He issued a sweeping condemnation of the entire tournament, labeling it a fiasco. This seemed contradictory to many because Macdonald himself had sanctioned the event by participating in it. Obviously, had he won, there would have been no fuss made. The Newport Club was unsure of the correctness of their ruling against him, and accompanied by the tenacity with which Charlie attacked them, backed off and agreed to discount the tournament. Incredibly, Macdonald won the argument and the championship was to be replayed!

Convinced by Macdonald, or perhaps for the sake of pacifying him, the tournament committee agreed to hold a match-play event at a new venue, this time at John Reid's St. Andrew's Club the following month. Macdonald, who felt not the slightest twinge of embarrassment, was ecstatic at having a second chance.

Opposite top: Newport Country Club, Rocky Farm Golf Course William F. Davis designed a unique nine-hole course replete with hazards that included artificial grassy mounds, a quarry, deep sand "pot" bunkers, earth bunkers, and "stone wall" bunkers. There was even an orchard on the property that served as both a border and a natural hazard. For its day, this was truly a fine golf course. (George Bahto Graphics)

Opposite bottom: "The First Amateur Golf Championship." Currier & Ives print, 1931 (George Bahto Collection)

The Second Tournament:
St. Andrew's Golf Club—Grey Oaks Course, Yonkers, New York

Now with a new format and a new venue, the tournament was scheduled for October 11th through the 13th, 1894. The field was a bit stronger this time, with competitors from eight clubs entered. The nine-hole course was short, only 2,364 yards, and every hole but two had to be played across a road at some point. There was one long hole of over 500 yards; the next longest was a mere 338 yards.

During the first day's play, Macdonald won his opening match handily by 8 and 6. He also won his second match, this time by a 4 and 3 margin. Nothing could stop this steamroller! In his usual manner, C. B. was ready to celebrate. Attending a premature victory party that night at the old Waldorf given in his honor by famous architect Stanford White, Charlie made merry with his friends until close to dawn. Why worry—a man of his talents could win handily against this caliber of competition. With less than an hour of sleep, Macdonald took some strychnine (pep) pills on the advice of White, and was ready to go (sort of). Charlie had a breakfast engagement with his semifinal opponent Willie Lawrence—the "nonchampion" of a month before—and then managed to get his revenge by besting Lawrence 2 and 1 in the morning match.

His last opponent of the tournament would be Lawrence Stoddart of the host St. Andrew's Club who had defeated his opponent in the other semifinal match 5 and 4. Unlike many of the competitors who were unaccustomed to tournament pressure, Stoddart would prove to be a more formidable opponent. A transplanted Englishman, he was a member at the Royal Liverpool Golf Club in Hoylake. Charlie felt terrible—ill, tired, and hungover. He confided to Stanford White of his deteriorating condition and "Doctor" White prescribed a bottle of champagne and a large steak, hoping it would ease the terrible hangover. It was a very poor suggestion.

Off they went in a steady rain, and although Macdonald was fading fast, the match was even after five holes. Stoddart took the next three in a row, before Macdonald managed to halt the bleeding by finally winning the ninth. He was two down as they began again on the first hole for their second trip around. After halving the 10th and 11th, Stoddart hit a poor shot at the 12th...and Macdonald was only one down with six to go. The comeback was short-lived as he lost the 13th when his sliced tee shot found a ditch. A win at the next, followed by two halved holes, left Macdonald only one down on the 17th tee. Stoddart's badly missed tee shot, which bounded off an apple tree and ended up in the rubble of an old stone wall, led to a 1-stroke penalty for extrication. Macdonald played to the green and won the hole to even the match; no one seemed to notice that the last time a stone wall was involved, Macdonald had insisted there should be no penalty.

With the match even going to the 215-yard 18th hole, Macdonald had the honor. Brimming with confidence and with Stoddart on the run, Macdonald strutted onto the tee. Determined to finish like a champion, he reared back and took a mighty slash at the ball. It was not to be, for his old bugaboo slice reared its ugly head and a shocked Charles Blair Macdonald watched his tee ball sail far to the right into a field, coming to rest behind a muddy corn hillock. Stoddart, having seen enough strutting, sensed the kill and stroked a beautiful tee shot close to the green. In the meantime, Charlie left his second shot still in the field before hitting his third still deeper into the rain-soaked ground. Stoddart was on in three, Charlie's fourth finally found the fairway and was on the green in five. Lawrence Stoddart holed his putt to win the match and the championship. The final standings also showed that Archibald Rogers had won the Bronze by default when his opponent William Lawrence failed to show up. A crestfallen Charles B. Macdonald won the silver medal, and Larry Stoddart was awarded a gold and diamond medal as the first Amateur Champion of the United States.

Wrong again.

To the dismay of everyone, Macdonald was off again on a tirade, ranting and raving, discrediting Stoddart just as he had William Lawrence. He bellowed, illogically, that since Stoddart had not previously won anything, how could he possibly be National Champion? Who was the St. Andrew's Club to speak for the golfing community? One club could not speak for all of golf—only an association of clubs could bestow such an honor. On and on he went. Not even the tournament committee had the courage to put an end to this embarrassing diatribe.

Now two championships were in a shambles from the bullish and domineering personality of this displaced Chicagoan, and something had to be done.

Enough was enough, and it was evident that a strong governing body must be formed to keep order and prevent future occurrences of this nature. Fearing that a war between Midwesterner Macdonald and his supporters against the gloating East would be the beginning of continuing controversies, Henry Tallmadge, one of the original members of St. Andrew's, Laurence Curtis of The Country Club, and Theodore Havemeyer of Newport quickly joined forces in an effort to restore order and reestablish credibility to the sport.

Tallmadge wrote to the five clubs deemed most prominent in the country and invited them to each send two delegates to a dinner he was planning in New York for the purpose of establishing a governing body for their sport.

On December 22, 1894, less than eight weeks after Macdonald scuttled the first two events, an historic meeting was convened in New York at the Calumet Club. In attendance that evening were representatives John Reid and Henry Tallmadge of the St. Andrew's Club of Yonkers; Samuel Parrish from Shinnecock Hills (General T. H. Barber the second delegate was unable to attend); Laurence Curtis and Samuel Sears from The Country Club of Brookline; Havemeyer and Winthrop Rutherford from Newport; and Arthur Ryerson and Charles Macdonald from the Chicago Golf Club. This group, the core clubs at the forefront of the game in America, officially enjoined themselves and gave birth to the Amateur Golf Association of the United States.

Controversy arose immediately when several other prominent clubs, upset at being excluded in the original charter, threatened to break off on their own and form a rival organization. Theodore Havemeyer was "a man of great tact and unusual charm three hundred and sixty five days a year, and where other men might have failed, he was able to placate the members of Meadow Brook, Tuxedo, Essex Country Club and the other clubs who had felt slighted and persuaded them to join the association."

Electing Theodore Havemeyer as president of the new organization was probably the best decision they made. One of his first acts was to donate a handsome thousand-dollar trophy for the Amateur Championship. In addition, when-

Right: A painting of Macdonald being presented the Havemeyer Trophy by its donor, sugar magnate Theodore Havemeyer, after winning the first United States National Championship at Newport, Rhode Island in 1895. (National Golf Links of America)

Below: In 1898, an international match between Canada and the United States was played at the Toronto Golf Club. The U.S. team won easily, 27-7. C.B. Macdonald (seated in the center row second from left) won two points in his singles match with George S. Lyon. The competition may have been the first of its kind and may have served as a prelude to the Walker Cup matches. (Mike Tureski family)

ever there was a bill that organization funds could not cover, Havemeyer paid it. Hard-working Henry Tallmadge was also perfectly suited for his position as secretary. He was diligent, thorough in his duties, and—perhaps even more importantly—he seemed to have the gift of knowing how to handle the rambunctious Macdonald, who from time to time mistook the national organization for the Chicago Golf Club.

Quoting its historic first document:

Each club pledges itself to contribute, not to exceed fifty dollars, to a fund which shall provide for the expenses of formation of this association, and for suitable trophies for the amateur and open championships.

The purpose of this Association shall be to promote the interests of the game of golf, to promulgate a code of rules for the game, and to hold annual meetings at which competitions shall be conducted for the amateur and open championships of the United States of America.

The new organization would sponsor not only the country's Amateur Championship, but an Open Championship as well. This led to the name being temporarily changed to the American Golf Association, before finally settling on the United States Golf Association when the constitution was finally adopted. It was decided that the first sanctioned tournament of the new organization would be the United States Amateur Championship, held (again) at Newport Country Club. It would be the third and last time the "first" tournament was held.

The championship, held on October 1st through the 3rd in 1895, would be an invitational of 32 players, with no qualifying round; the players would compete in 18 holes of match play, with the finals being a 36-hole match. Newport was the perfect host for the festivities; Havemeyer arranged parties and personally paid the expenses for the entrants. Newport society turned out for the event. The ladies wore their gayest silks and the men wore their red jackets; tournament officials scurried about proudly, wearing their new red-white-and-blue badges. Despite the convivial atmosphere, the Easterners were a glum group—none of them had scored better than Macdonald in the practice rounds. It was reported in the New York *Herald* that "the man from the west" was playing better than ever and was regarded as the "probable winner." According to published reports, aside from Macdonald, "in the main [the other players] were gentlemen golfers—more gentlemen than golfers!"

There were also a few new characters included. One of them was a golfing minister, the Reverend William Rainsford. Another was Richard Peters, "who used a billiard cue on the

Above: Charles Blair Macdonald playing golf in his middle years. (National Golf Links)

Some Tournament Play *of* Charles Blair Macdonald

United States Amateur Activity

1895: Playing out of the course he founded, Chicago Golf Club, Macdonald won the United State's first National (amateur) Championship at Newport's Rocky Farm Course. He defeated Charles Sands of St. Andrew's, Yonkers, 12 and 11.

1896: Lost his 1st round match of the 2nd National Amateur Championship, played at the Shinnecock golf course in July. Macdonald barely qualified for the event with 88–90 / 178. Although he was suffering from ptomaine poisoning he competed but lost his opening match to J. G. Thorpe of the Cambridge Golfing Society, 3 and 2. Henry J. Whigham won the championship.

1897: In the semifinals, Macdonald lost to Rossiter Betts of Shinnecock Hills on the first extra hole after tying in 36 holes, 1 down. The championship was played at Charlie's home course, Chicago Golf Club. Henry Whigham won his second straight Amateur Championship by trouncing Betts, 8 and 6.

1898: Macdonald lost in the semifinals once again, defeated by Walter B. Smith. The championship was played at Morris County Country Club in New Jersey. Findlay Douglas (a close friend) defeated Walter Smith, 5 and 3.

1899: A frustrated Macdonald, still living in Chicago, lost for the third consecutive year in the semifinals. This time, at the Onwentsia Club, he was soundly beaten by the eventual winner, H. M. Harriman (who would become another of Macdonald's close friends), 6 and 4. Harriman won the championship by defeating Findlay Douglas.

1900: Macdonald did not compete in the event. Now a resident of New York (his office was in New York City) he lived in Garden City and officially played out of the Garden City Golf Club, a marvelous course built by Walter Travis in 1902.

1901: Macdonald qualified with a 174 for the championship, which was held at the Atlantic City Country Club in September. He won his first round match, 1 up, but lost to Walter Travis 7 and 6. They both used remodeled Haskell balls for the match.

1902: Macdonald was abroad during the time the Amateur was played.

1903: Macdonald was abroad again during the time the Amateur was played.

1904: Macdonald, now age 48, failed to qualify for match play. The tournament was held at Baltusrol Golf Club.

1905: Macdonald qualified for the Amateur, which was held at his old course, Chicago Golf Club, with a 170 but lost to Chandler Egan, 2 up, in the first round. Chandler Egan went on to win the championship.

1906: Macdonald did not compete.

1907: Failed to qualify—played out of Garden City.

1908: Macdonald did not enter.

1909: Failed to qualify—played out of Garden City.

1910: Macdonald, now age 54, failed to qualify—National not yet complete—still playing out of Garden City.

1911: Macdonald failed to qualify—played out of his own club, the National Golf Links.

1912: Macdonald, in his final appearance in the U.S. Amateur, failed to qualify—played out of his own club, the National Golf Links.

British Amateur

1906: Macdonald, 50 years old, appeared in his only British Amateur at Royal Liverpool Golf Club, Hoylake, where he was a member for many years. He lost in the second round. (*Golf Illustrated*)

greens, not because he wanted to clown around but because he was convinced he could putt better that way."

In truth, although Macdonald was a fine player, the weak field was mainly comprised of comparatively poor golfers with little experience. As expected, Macdonald easily defeated his first-round opponent Lawrence Curtis of The Country Club of Brookline, 7 and 6. His second opponent, Gerald Bement from Essex Country Club, was also easily defeated 8 and 6. C. B. was off and running, blasting accurate drives, staying clear of bunkers and sinking long putts. He appeared unbeatable.

A controversy arose during his next round, however, played against Winthrop Rutherford of Meadow Brook. Both Macdonald and Rutherford were using professional golfers to caddie and coach them throughout the round. This was technically within the rules, but drew criticism from other contestants who had a different understanding of what constituted "amateur" golf. Although Macdonald was only 1-up after the first nine, Rutherford failed to win a hole over the next six and was defeated, 5 and 4.

The semifinals saw Macdonald trounce Dr. C. Claxton of the Philadelphia Country Club. Claxton only won one hole in the entire match and lost to Macdonald, 8 and 7. The 36-hole final match was played on the 3rd of October. Macdonald's opponent was Charles Sands of St. Andrew's, who won his semifinal match over F. J. Amory from The Country Club. Incredibly, although he was a good athlete and an excellent tennis player, Sands was a rank beginner at golf, having played for about three months.

Both players had professional coach-caddies. Sands, in fact, had two: Sam Tucker and the great Willie Dunn. Charlie had his old friend Jim Foulis, the club professional from the Chicago Golf Club, to assist him.

By the 6th hole, Sands was down by four, winning only the 3rd hole. They traded wins on the 7th and 8th and Sands won the 9th when C. B. putted poorly. At the end of the first nine, Macdonald was 3-up. The back nine was fairly uneventful with Sand's first win coming on the 16th. At the end of the morning 18, Macdonald was 5-up and playing well.

The rest of the match was anticlimactic. Winning the first seven holes, Macdonald gained the victory with a 12 and 11 margin. To the surprise of few and to the disappointment of many, the incongruous Charles Macdonald emerged as the champion. He had finally done it: he had won the first U.S. Amateur Championship. He completed his round in an attempt to break the course record but failed.

C. B. was awarded the beautiful United States Golf Association Havemeyer Trophy—to be displayed at his home course, Chicago Golf Club, until the following year's event. With that, a grand tradition began as this great tournament was to become a springboard for many of golf's greatest players. One was Robert Tyre Jones Jr., who, unfortunately, was in possession of the original trophy when it was sadly lost in a clubhouse fire at Atlanta Athletic Club in Georgia (now East Lake Country Club) in 1925. The replica, made the same year, is the one still used today.

Almost as an afterthought, an Open Championship for professionals was held the next day. It was won by 21-year-old Englishman Horace Rawlins when he defeated the famous Scottish clubmaker and course architect Willie Dunn. Their stroke-play scores 171 to 173 were for four trips around Newport's nine holes.

Was Charles Blair Macdonald a poor loser? Absolutely. Ironically, his fatuous outbursts led directly to the stability of golf during a crucial period. Many of his actions did not endear him to the press, but his controversial reputation did not bother Macdonald in the least. He had made his mark, and though his objectivity and sense of fairness were a bit suspicious when it came to his personal aspirations, he was still the staunchest supporter of the ideals and integrity of the game. As he got older, and perhaps more circumspect about his past actions, he wrote a paragraph that clarifies his feelings on the often capricious inequalities of the game:

> *In golf the cardinal rules are arbitrary and not founded on eternal justice. Equity has nothing to do with the game itself. If founded on eternal justice the game would be deadly to watch or play. The essence of the game is inequity, as it is in humanity. The conditions which are meted out to the players, such as the inequity of the ground, cannot be governed by a green committee with the flying divots of the players or their footprints in the bunkers. Take your medicine where you find it and don't cry.*

The sentiment, no doubt, was aimed at everyone but himself.

CHAPTER FOUR

THE IDEAL GOLF LINKS

After playing golf at championship form for many years, Macdonald's game had slipped as he reached his mid-forties and he was no longer capable of competing at golf's higher levels. It was a bitter pill for such an enormous ego, and though the new, livelier Haskell ball had made its presence felt, his game did not improve proportionately. Driving contests during the era of the gutta-percha ball (gutty) would normally see winners slogging the ball a crisp carry of 170 yards in the air. With the advent of the new Haskell, 20 to 30 yards could be added to the tee ball, with proportionate increases to iron play. A two-shot hole was effectively shortened by 30 to 50 yards, many once difficult-to-reach par 4s became a drive and a mid-iron. The long par 5s, most barely over 500 yards, became fairly easy. Sadly, many of golf's best holes of the gutty era lost their design strategy virtually overnight. Holes such as North Berwick's Redan, though still formidable, were suddenly reachable on the fly. (Previously, many players had to lay up short of the left-hand bunker.)

The Haskell changed the game forever because entire golf courses became obsolete and in need of redesign. Even with the Haskell, Macdonald's drives lacked the punch and distance they once had, and with the rising level of competition, he was no longer a factor in tournament play. He was, increasingly, viewed as an ex-champion—an honorary contestant rarely challenging the leaders.

It was the realization that "one could not be the game's master" but rather "its servant" that convinced him to move on to other ventures while only playing the occasional tournament. Confining most of his golf to casual matches with friends was not easy for Macdonald to accept. Yet he was finally ready to acknowledge his time had passed. While his thoughts were still focused on playing golf, his position as an elder statesman of the game slowly changed his priorities. He continued to compete, confining himself to the more important tournaments, but began to realize the importance of serving the game rather than playing only to satisfy his ego. Though most of his friends and acquaintances in golf were rich and powerful people, he began to feel the game's popularity would be self-limiting if enjoyed only by the wealthy. His golfing roots had been established in Scotland, where everyone from bank president to common laborer played side by side on equal footing.

The first stumbling block in his desire to propagate the game was the fact that the vast majority of golf courses in America were bland in their design, lacking excitement and esthetics. Holes with alternate routes of play were unknown in early American golf, so everyone was forced to choose between laying up or driving over cross hazards. As it turned out, the spark that provided the original inspiration to construct America's first great course was an article in Britain's

WHY NOT BUILD A GOLF COURSE EMULATING THE SAME GREAT HOLES BROUGHT OUT IN THE DISCUSSIONS? WHY NOT DUPLICATE THESE HOLES? IF 18 OF THE WORLD'S GREATEST HOLES WERE INCORPORATED INTO ONE GOLF COURSE, WOULD IT NOT BE THE FINEST GOLF COURSE IN THE ENTIRE WORLD?—THIS WOULD CERTAINLY BE THE "IDEAL GOLF LINKS."

Golf Illustrated written by Hoylake's legendary amateur Horace Hutchinson. The 1901 article posed the following questions to the great golfers of the British Isles:

> *January 25, 1901*
> *Which Are the Most Difficult Holes in the World?*
> *by Horace Hutchinson*
> *Notice:*
> *For the purposes of this enquiry the questions to which we would request the answers of golfers of standing, both Amateur and Professional, are:*
> 1. *Which do you consider the best and most difficult one-shot hole?*
> 2. *Which do you consider the best and most difficult two-shot hole?*
> 3. *Which do you consider the best and most difficult three-shot hole?*
>
> *Golfers may make their answers as long or as short as they please and they will greatly oblige by sending them as soon as possible to us for publication. ED*

A two-time British Amateur Champion, Mr. Hutchinson's article went on to point out the necessity of distinguishing between objective and subjective difficulties in making their evaluations. He also suggested that participants not be influenced by "great shots played" or "favor a hole because that particular hole suited their game or flight of ball." In his usual colorful manner, he continued:

> *...perhaps, the influence of terror, of funk, that a man will feel at a hole where he has come to grief often, until he makes a "scunner" at it, as the Scotch say. It has a sort of a nightmare influence on him, quite out of proportion to the difficulties that it really presents. The player may be quite aware of this, but that does not make an atom of a difference; it is a question of nerves, and nerves are beyond the reach of argument and reason. Another way of expressing it is the more common one, in the golfer's mouth, that it is "the devil." The golfer, in practice, if not consciously, shows a very classical belief in the "genius loci," the god or demon that haunts this or that particular place—generally a bunker, although there are Elysian Fields. But you have to cross a bad place to reach them. One man will talk of a hole being difficult because its length makes it a hole that demands many good shots. Others talk of a hole only in regard of its "catchiness," of the bunkers around the green.*

Golf Illustrated agreed to publish the views of participants, both amateur and professional, as to holes they considered to be the best and most difficult, with Horace Hutchinson "promising to deal with the whole matter" when the results were published.

Such was the power of *Golf Illustrated* that over the ensuing weeks nearly 30 responses were received from the great champions of the day. The respondents included:

Harry Vardon: British Open Champion–1896, 1898, 1899; U. S. Open Champion–1900
J. H. Taylor: British Open Champion–1894, 1895, 1900
James Braid: British Open Champion–1901
Willie Park Jr.: British Open Champion–1887, 1889
H. H. Hilton: British Open Champion–1892, 1897; British Amateur Champion, 1900
Alexander Herd: (Future British Open Champion–1902)
John L. Low: British Amateur Champion–1897, 1898

Horace Hutchinson: British Amateur Champion–1886, 1887
Leslie Balfour Melville: British Amateur Champion–1895
Herbert Fowler: Later noted architect and partner of Tom Simpson

Responses were directed at a hole's difficulty, its fairness, and its good design. References were made to difficulty of greens and whether they were fair or just difficult. In soliciting responses, an essential by-product of the query in *Golf Illustrated* was not only to enumerate great holes in the U.K., but also to help clarify why they were revered.

Not surprisingly, the par-3 11th at St. Andrews ("High-Hole-In") was voted the most difficult par-3 hole. It was often referred to as the Eden hole in part because its green was bordered in back by the Eden River. Players, terrified of the Hill and Strath bunkers guarding the front, often overshot the green, landing on the beach. The chip back was nearly impossible owing to the radical back-to-front tilt of the green. The choice was simple: dare the hazards, or lay up.

North Berwick's infamous Redan hole, a French word describing an "impenetrable fortress," garnered nearly as much attention as the 11th at St. Andrews. Fiercely defended by an enormous sand pit at the left front, and peppered with pot bunkers to the right rear, the green is set at a 45-degree angle and tilted away from the line of play. Its greatness lies in the complex arrangement of hazards and greenside contours, demanding a complete reevaluation of strategy with every shift of wind strength or direction. (Although the Redan hole is probably now the most copied hole in golf, the stature of St. Andrews relegated its wonders to second place.) Other notables included in discussions were the Maiden hole at Sandwich and the notorious blind shot over the Himalayas at Prestwick.

In the category of best par 4, the Alps (#17) at Prestwick was the nearly unanimous choice by the giants of the game. Blind holes were still in vogue at the time and the notoriety bestowed upon the Alps was legion. The Sahara (#4 at Royal St. George's) with its enormous carry bunker off the tee was admired by many, as was the intimidating greenside bunkering at the 9th at Brancaster. (Sadly, like many great par 4s of the time, the challenge presented by their most notable features has become drastically tempered with the new equipment and lively ball.)

Known as the Alps, the par-4 17th at Prestwick was the preeminent blind shot in the British Isles. There were other similar holes (any time there was a high mound to play over, it was given the same moniker), but Prestwick's Alps was the epitome of this genre. Measured yardage from the tee box was 380 at that time, and even a solid swat from the tee would leave the golfer a substantial spoon shot over a towering sand hill to the green, hidden in an intimate hollow.

In his summation of the Best Hole discussion, it was Hoylake's Harold H. Hilton who so aptly described the Alps:

> *I know that many consider that the seventeenth hole at Prestwick has a great weakness in the fact that the edge of the bunker is too near the green, and it is almost impossible, when playing anything approaching a full shot, to remain anywhere near the hole. In addition the hole is blind, and the far edge of the bunker is also blind, so that there is a certain amount of uncertainty as to the distance to be carried. But it does not do to be too hypercritical, as there is no hole in all the world of golf in which it is not possible to find at least some little room for improvement, and although it might have been better in the case of this particular hole had the position of the bunker been reversed [behind the green rather than before it], and had the green been a wee bit more spacious, still, nature has decreed that it is not so, and we cannot quarrel with Nature, at least as Nature is represented at the famous "Alps at Prestwick."*

In selecting the best three-shot hole, there was much competition, although the 14th and 17th at St. Andrews commanded most of the attention. It was felt by most respondents that those holes were the best representations of the two distinct types of par 5. The first, known as "Long," demands players to plot points depending upon wind strength and direction to avoid hazards like Hell Bunker. The 17th (Road hole) was cited best as a risk/reward hole. Despite advances in equipment at the time, owing to its calamitous hazards the Road hole was still considered a three-shotter for all but the longest hitting professionals.

Hilton continues:

> *Certainly no hole in existence, except, perhaps, "Point Garry In" at North Berwick, has been the innocent cause of so many opprobrious epithets and language of a lurid hue as the "Road"*

hole at St. Andrews. It is difficult, no one can deny that, but the difficulties do not commend themselves to all, as they are such as necessitate a timorous style of play, which is not exhilarating to watch, or interesting to the player himself, at least that is an opinion I formed when I witnessed the very flower of Golfdom negotiate this in the Championship last year. It certainly can be said that it is open for the player to take a direct course for the hole and play a bold game. James Braid did it with more than a fair share of success, so did other players, but the majority were completely out of the hunt, and Braid cannot be judged by ordinary standards, his exceptional power forbids it, and the majority, including even the strong, accurate driver like Vardon, preferred the "old woman's game," round the corner so to speak.

In all, the discussion was a huge success and proved to be extremely interesting reading for the subscribers of *Golf Illustrated*. It appears that the comparison and grading of golf holes and courses was as popular then as now. These early articles, and the discussions they fostered, may well have been the original efforts to establish what we refer to today as golf architecture.

These discussions certainly caught the attention of Charlie Macdonald. Why shouldn't America have golf equal to that in the British Isles? In his mind, the content of the article was the definitive listing of those holes reverenced by the world's greatest players. If America was to have golf that compared to that in Britain, its courses must be based on the same timeless genius as those across the Atlantic. If this was truly a collection of the best holes from many courses, then would not a composite of all of them be a blueprint for the "greatest course in the world"?

The seed planted at St. Andrews was finally ready to germinate. Macdonald remembered:

I was intensely interested, and from this discussion I was urged to carry out the idea of building a classical golf course in America, one which would eventually compare favorably with the championship links abroad and serve as an incentive to the elevation of the game in America.

Why not build a golf course emulating the same great holes brought out in the discussions? Why not duplicate these holes? If 18 of the world's greatest holes were incorporated into one golf course, would it not be the finest golf course in the entire world? This would certainly be the ideal golf links.

He sailed for Europe in 1902 on a crusade to gather information and discuss the idea with his friends abroad. Most solicitations were encouraging, but there were also dissenters; many of them angered by the thought of Macdonald duplicating their golf holes. The very idea was sacrilege to them, and of all places to do this, in America! Undaunted, he concluded the concept was sound and returned to the United States more determined than ever. It would be a long road, requiring several years of planning and research. It was still early, but his "ideal golf course" was beginning to take shape.

Contrary to modern architecture, where the line of play is clearly delineated by the designer, many of the classic courses left decisions on the ideal line of play entirely up to the individual. Macdonald sought to make his course more than a simple objective test of skill, but strove to compose challenges that gave the game its essential subjective interest. This was the cornerstone of Macdonald's National School of Golf Design.

In 1904, Macdonald was off again to make a more detailed study of the holes he admired in Europe. Upon his return, he began a preliminary search for land on which to build his dream course. It was to take years. He scoured the East coast of the United States from Maine to Cape May, New Jersey, before deciding the best approximation of traditional links land was on New York's Long Island. While the search continued, his close friend Devereux Emmet spent a winter in the British Isles carefully measuring holes he felt noteworthy for Macdonald. A brother-in-law to Stanford White, Emmet was later to become a prolific course designer in his own right.

Less that two years later Macdonald returned to Europe to make a much more detailed study of these holes, making drawings, blueprints, and topographic surveys. He began to recognize that an exact duplication of the holes would be extremely difficult. There was no single site where the different topographies of these holes could all be located. For example, an Alps with its mountain or a Redan, required a natural site that would be extremely difficult to find. It also became apparent that a huge amount of soil would have to be moved to accomplish his objectives. The idea of shaping and contouring large quantities of earth was revolutionary. Prior to Macdonald, for better or worse, the existing terrain dictated the playing characteristics of a hole. Hell Bunker on St. Andrew's 14th hole was a natural evolution, developed over centuries on the links land of Scotland. If a Hell Bunker was to be built on his new course it would have to be dug out of the ground.

Most importantly, it became clear to Macdonald that his original concept of topographic duplication was not as relevant to the quality of the course as the individual strategic elements. This principle of variations on the strategies and shot values of these classic holes is the basic foundation of their classic courses.

Contrary to modern architecture, where the line of play is clearly delineated by the designer, many of the classic courses left decisions on the ideal line of play entirely up to the individual. Macdonald sought to make his course more than a simple objective test of skill, but strove to compose challenges that gave the game its essential subjective interest.

For Macdonald, there was much work to be done. He was aware there were a number of shortcomings of even these great holes. There were holes where the strategy from the tee was excellent, yet the second shot was uninteresting. On some holes, the green contours were perfect, but the route to them was bland. Simply copying the greatest holes by rote was not going to achieve the desired result, and he abandoned this idea early on. He recognized that the answer lay in applying scientific methods to identify both their strong and weak points. Macdonald reasoned that by reducing each great hole down to its unique elements, he could discard their weaknesses. A course with no weak point! Now this would indeed be an ideal golf course.

Feeling the strong conviction that every hole on an ideal course should present good and interesting golf shots, he was determined that there be no filler holes. The course should not be overly long, and should be built so that even the less skilled player could enjoy it as much as the scratch player. Never neglecting these players, leaving them an alternative route would be the heart of his designs. He desired that everyone—regardless of skill level—be able to enjoy himself.

1906 brought on four more months in Europe completing the research. He would return to the United States with detailed surveys of the most important holes and 20 or 30 sketches of his own reflecting a bunker or hazard here, a landing area there, as well as various stratagem that he could combine for some original hole designs.

> *These drawings were not necessarily copies of a particular hole from tee to putting green, but in most instances were the outstanding features which I thought made the hole interesting and which might be adapted to a hole of a different length. Two or three of such features might be put in a hole which would make it more or less composite in its nature.*

His plans were taking on more definition now and the excitement was building.

By now, news of Macdonald's plans had spread throughout the British Isles like wildfire, and given the size of his ego, we can be sure he made no attempt to suppress the news. Many Brits were furious, bristling not only at his overall plan, but most notably his contention that the many of their great holes were weak in some areas. What could possibly be wrong with the Road hole, the Eden, or the Redan? Open

Championships had been played over some of these courses for decades, and who the devil was this Macdonald fellow, an American yet, to critique the greatest holes of the British Isles?

An example of how his bold plan was playing across the pond was found in the June 23, 1905 issue of *Golf Illustrated*:

> *"Millionaires' clubs" are by no means novelties in America, but a millionaires' golf club, exclusively, is somewhat of a rarity, although one or two wealthy men, such as John D. Rockefeller, possess golf links of their own, where they can "do" the links free from the gaze of the curious crowd, in company of their friends. However, Charles B. Macdonald, a founder of the United States Golf Association and sometime champion of the country, has made known an idea to a small coterie of millionaire golfers of New York and Chicago that may possibly result in the formation of the most unique golf club in the world...Mr. Macdonald has not a very high opinion of American golf courses, and his scheme is to lay out the holes on English and Scottish models...From present signs, as regards to the course, it seems that Mr. Macdonald is anxious to counterfeit as near as possible some of the St. Andrews and Prestwick holes. How he will bring this about is difficult to imagine, unless a combined attack is made some dark night on the British shores, and the holes and putting greens are carried away bodily. Despite these few trifling and apparent difficulties, the links, it is said, will ultimately reproduce some of the world's most famous holes as nearly as topographical conditions will permit.*

Never one to back down from a controversy, Macdonald fired this volley back across the Atlantic:

> *Now why should not one try to absorb the sanctified tradition of each particular hole by copying its best features in another climate where in time tradition might sanctify its existence. The flowers of transplanted plants in time shed a perfume comparable to that of their indigenous home.*

Macdonald was a man used to success, and the building of his ideal course had become an obsession, a consuming desire he vowed to see through. To move forward there must initially be organization and funding. He prepared a prospectus to be offered to interested parties. The first two paragraphs outlined his proposal:

> *Any golfer conversant with golf courses abroad and the best we have in America, which are generally conceded to be Garden City, Myopia, and the Chicago Golf Club, knows in America as yet we have no first-class golf course comparable with the classic golf courses in Great Britain and Ireland.*
>
> *There is no reason why this should be so, and it is the objective of this association to build such a course, making it as near national as possible, and further, with the object of promoting the best interest of the game of golf in the United States.*

In Charlie's view, the ingredients for an ideal golf course could be numerically quantified and existed within certain parameters. Of special import was an article that C. B. wrote for the February 1, 1907 issue of *Golf Illustrated* in which he chronicled the key holes that he and his protégés would use as the basic blueprint for all of their courses:

The Ideal Golf Course

An American Expert's Theories on the Laying Out of a Championship Course

> *In discussing and comparing the merits of various courses, one is struck immediately with the futility of argument unless some basis of excellence is agreed upon which to anchor. In view of this, I have tried to enumerate all the essential features of a perfect golf course in accordance with the enlightened criticism of today, and to give to each of these essential characteristics a value, the sum total which would be 100, or perfection. Following is the result:*

Essential Characteristics		***Merit***
1. Course		*45%*
(a) Nature of the soil	*23%*	
(b) Perfection in undulation and hillocks	*22%*	
2. Putting Greens		*18%*
(a) Quality of turf	*10%*	
(b) Nature of undulation	*5%*	
(c) Variety	*3%*	

I BELIEVE THE COURSE WOULD BE IMPROVED BY OPENING THE FAIR GREEN TO ONE SIDE OR THE OTHER, GIVING SHORT OR TIMID PLAYERS AN OPPORTUNITY TO PLAY AROUND THE HAZARD IF SO DESIRED, BUT, OF COURSE, PROPERLY PENALIZED BY LOSS OF DISTANCE FOR SO PLAYING.

3. *Bunkers and other hazards*		13%
(a) Nature, size, and variety	4%	
(b) Proper placing	9%	
4. *Length of hole*		13%
(a) Best length of holes	8%	
(b) Variety and arrangement of length	5%	
5. *Quality of turf of fair green*	6%	6%
6. *Width of fair green of the course, 45 to 60 yards*	3%	3%
7. *Nature of teeing ground and proximity to putting greens*	2%	2%
		100%

1. Studying the above qualities, in detail, there can be but one opinion as to the nature of the soil the course should be built upon, as well as the contour of the surface of the green, running as this should in more or less gentle undulations as at St. Andrews, breaking in hillocks in a few places, more or less bold in certain parts as at Sandwich and North Berwick. The three courses above mentioned fulfill the ideal in this respect. There can be no real first-class golf course without such material to work upon. Securing such a course is really more than half the battle, though I have credited this phase of the question with only 33 points, the other 17 points blending themselves with the other features. Having such material at hand to work upon, the completion of an ideal course becomes a matter of experience, gardening and mathematics. The courses of Great Britain abound in classic and notable holes, and one has only to study them and adopt their best and boldest features. Yet in most of their best holes there is always room for improvement.

2. Regarding quality, nothing conduces more to the charm of the game than perfect putting greens. Some should be large, but the majority should be of moderate size, some flat, some hillocky, one or two at an angle; but the great majority should have natural undulations, some more and others less undulation. It is absolutely essential that the turf should be very fine so the ball will run perfectly true.

3. When one comes to the quality of bunkers and other hazards we pass into the realm of much dispute and argument. Primarily bunkers should be sand bunkers purely, not composed of gravel, stones or dirt. Whether this or that bunker is well placed has caused more intensely heated arguments outside of the realms of religion, than has ever been my lot to listen to. However one may be rest assured when a controversy between the "cracks" is hotly contested throughout years as to whether this or that hazard is fair or properly placed, that it is the kind of hazard you want and it has real merit. When there is unanimous opinion that such and such a hazard is perfect, one usually finds it commonplace. Fortunately, I know of no classic hole that doesn't have its decriers.

The eleventh hole at St. Andrews, which four out of five golfers (a greater consensus of opinion than I have found regarding any other hole) concede to be if not the best, second to no short hole in existence, is berated vigorously by some able exponents of the game. At the last championship meeting at Hoylake, Mr. H. H. Hilton told me it would be a good hole if a cross bunker was put in and Strath closed. Heaven forbid!

To my mind, an ideal course should have at least six bold bunkers like the Alps at Prestwick, the ninth at Brancaster, Sahara or Maiden (I only approve of the Maiden as a bunker, not a hole) at Sandwich, and the sixteenth at Littlestone. Such bold bunkers should be at the end of a two-shot hole or very long carries from the tee.

Further, I believe the course would be improved by opening the fair green to one side or the other, giving short or timid players an opportunity to play around the hazard if so desired, but, of course, properly penalized by loss of distance for so playing.

Other than those bold bunkers, I should have no other hazards stretching directly across a hole.

Let the hazard be in the centre or to the side or graduated in distance from the hole across the course. A very great number should be pot bunkers particularly to the side; bunkers in which one can take a full shot with a wooden club are a travesty—some such bunkers as they have at Sunningdale.

A burn is a most excellent hazard and is utilized with the greatest advantage at Prestwick and Leven.

As to side hazards other than bunkers, no doubt bent rushes and whins are the best. Long grass entails too much searching for balls. However, in the case of long grass from the fair green proper to the full growth of the grass the cutting should be graduated, being shorter nearer the line to the hole.

4. Treating length of hole, we must again, as in placing of hazards, revert to the experience history has taught us in the past to guide our judgment. Speaking roughly, the generally accepted best total length of a golf course is put at 6,000 yards. I have before me cards giving the distances of twenty of the first courses in the United Kingdom. The average distances of holes sum up as follows:

200 yards and under	*2*
300 yards and under	*2*
400 yards and under	*8*
499 yards and under	*4*
500 yards and over	*2*

I don't believe one can go far wrong if he takes the above as an approximate guide.

True, nearly all these courses were laid out before the advent of the rubber-cored ball, adding as it does twenty yards to wood and iron. Now, while the rubber-cored ball has marred many excellent holes, it has made just as many indifferent holes excellent. The majority of green committees have failed to realize this and have expended their energy in devising means to lengthen every hole. It would be much better if they would shorten some, lengthen some and leave the others alone.

The large majority of old golfers—notably Mr. Low, Mr. Horace Hutchinson and the Messrs. Whigham (men all brought up in different schools)—declare that bad as too short a course may be, too long a course is infinitely worse. What a golfer most desires is variety in one, two, and three shot holes, calling for accuracy in placing the ball, not alone in the approach but from the tee. Let the first shot be placed in relation to the second in accordance with the run of the ground and the wind. Holes so designed that a player can, if he so wishes, take risks commensurate to the gravity of the situation—playing, as it were, "to the score."

Let the two-shot holes over 380 yards call for long driving, less accurate than others where less length calls for greater accuracy. The more accurate the drive in placing the ball the better the approach.

Without generalizing further on the question of the best holes, following are eighteen holes which occur to me as being about right. Of course the reader must assume that the run of the ground and the hazards are correct:

1.	*370 yards*	*Similar to the bottle hole at Sunningdale, placing deep graduated bunkers in place of ditch and bunker the green properly.*
2.	*340 yards*	*Composite first shot of the 14th or "Perfection" at North Berwick, with a green and bunker guard like 15th at Muirfield.*
3.	*320 yards*	*Similar 3rd St. Andrews*
4.	*187 yards*	*Resembling Redan North Berwick*
5.	*510 yards*	*Suggested by 16th Littlestone, a dogleg hole. Direct length, 410 yards. Latter route could be made excessively dangerous by calling for long and accurate play.* Author note: This is the model hole for the fourth hole at Lido, the "Channel"
6.	*400 yards*	*Similar 4th Sandwich*
7.	*130 yards*	*Similar 5th Brancaster with tee raised so player can see where pin enters the hole.*
8.	*420 yards*	*Similar to 9th Leven*
9.	*350 yards*	*Similar 9th Brancaster*
10.	*240 yards*	*Similar 3rd, or "Sahara," Sandwich, making carry full 175 yards direct, then a fair run*

LET THE HAZARD BE IN THE CENTRE OR TO THE SIDE OR GRADUATED IN DISTANCE FROM THE HOLE ACROSS THE COURSE. A VERY GREAT NUMBER SHOULD BE POT BUNKERS PARTICULARLY TO THE SIDE; BUNKERS IN WHICH ONE CAN TAKE A FULL SHOT WITH A WOODEN CLUB ARE A TRAVESTY.

		to green with alternative to play around.
11.	*450 yards*	*Similar 17th St. Andrews, making very bad hazard where the dike calls for out-of-bounds, and while keeping the green same in size as at present would alter face of plateau approaching.*
12.	*160 yards*	*Resembling the 11th St. Andrews*
13.	*400 yards*	*Similar 3rd Prestwick*
14.	*490 yards*	*Like 14th St. Andrews, making green larger and run-up less fluky*
15.	*210 yards*	*Suggested by 12th Biarritz [orig. 3rd—"Chasm"] making sharp hogback in middle of course. Stop 30 yards from hole bunkered to right of green and good low ground to the left of plateau green.*
16.	*300 yards*	*Suggested by 7th at Leven, which is only 240 yards, with burn running at a bias, and green guarded by sharp hillocks.*
17.	*380 yards*	*Resembling 17th, or "Alps," Prestwick.*
18.	*360 yards*	*Resembling 8th St. Andrews, New, which is now too long for the bunkering.*
		A grand total of (a projected) 6,017 yards.

These distances are measured from the middle of the teeing space to the middle of putting green. With proper teeing space and putting greens each hole could be lengthened at will from 20 to 30 yards.

I have notes on many holes equally as good as a number of the above, but this list will convey to the mind of the reader a fair idea of what I have gleaned during the last few months as constituting a perfect length of hole consistent with variety.

5. For quality of turf throughout fair green there is no excuse for its not being good enough, so I have allowed only eight marks for it.

6. The tendency to widen courses is much to be lamented. Forty-five to sixty yards is plenty wide enough. This is wider than St. Andrews used to be thirty years ago, when the course was better than it is now. I note Mr. Deally, Mr. Lucas and Mr. Charles Hutchings in laying out the new course (the last word in golf) at Sandwich have kept a width of rather under than over fifty yards.

7. I would like to give proper width three marks, as well as two marks for good tees in close proximity to the putting green. This walking fifty to one hundred and fifty yards to the tee mars the course and delays the game. Between hole and teeing ground people sometimes forget and commence playing some other game.

The aggregate of all the above marks makes 100, which from my point of view is an ideal golf course—something yet to be attained!

Before closing I wish to enumerate a few defects, which unavoidably exist on some really good courses:

More than three blind holes are a defect and they should be at the end of a fine long shot only. Hills are a detriment. Mountain climbing is a sport unto itself and has no place on a golf course. Trees in the course are a serious detriment. Out-of-bounds should be avoided if possible. Cops are an abomination. Glaring artificiality of any kind detracts from the fascination of the game.

When questioned about his concept of adapting the strategies of the best holes from Europe as the basis of his architectural philosophies, Charles Blair Macdonald often referred to the following quote from *The Art of Landscape Architecture* (1797) by Humphrey Repton:

> *If it should appear that, instead of displaying new doctrines or furnishing novel ideas, this volume serves rather by a new method to elucidate old established principles, and to confirm long received opinions, I can only plead in my excuse that true taste, in every art, consists more in adapting tried expedients to peculiar circumstances than in that inordinate thirst after novelty, the characteristic of uncultivated minds, which from the facility of inventing wild theories, without experience, are apt to suppose that taste is displayed by novelty, genius by innovation, and that every change must necessarily tend to improvement.*

CHAPTER FIVE

GLOSSARY *of* HOLES *and* GREEN COMPLEXES

The cornerstone of Macdonald and Raynor's work is the use of recurring themes in their designs. Though no renditions of a given hole were ever identical, they consistently returned to tried-and-true strategies by emulating the salient features of the world's best holes. Because this philosophy of honoring the past was common to all of their courses, this reference guide to some common configurations used in their work may be useful when reading this book. Readers should bear in mind that many renditions have been altered from their original architecture, so some elements may be missing at a given hole. The particular holes listed as "best examples" are considered to be the purest unaltered articulations of their work.

The 17th at National Golf Links. (National Golf Links)

Leven

Origin: Old 7th hole of old Leven Links (NLE), Leven, Fife, Scotland. | **Length:** Short par 4, usually 330-360 yards. | **Bunkering:** Fairway bunker or waste area challenges golfer to make heroic carry for an open approach to the green. Less courageous line from the tee leaves golfer with a semiblind approach over a high bunker or sand hill to the short side of the green. | **Green:** Usually moderately undulating surface with least accessible cup placement behind sand hill. | **Best example(s):** 17th National Golf Links of America. Many second tier examples. | **Comments:** 17th at National rated one of top 100 holes in America—one of the great short par-4 strategies in golf.

The 4th Hole at National Golf Links. (George Bahto Collection)

Redan

Origin: 15th hole at North Berwick Golf Club (East course) East Lothian, Scotland. Architect: Ben Sayers. | **Length:** 190-215 yards. **Bunkering:** Deep sandpit guards direct frontal attack. Deep bunkering also beyond short side of green. Normally a "framing bunker" is positioned well short of the putting surface. | **Approach:** High shoulder along outside edge of the green is designed to deflect balls toward the center of the green. | **Green:** Putting surface oriented at 45-degree angle to tee, most renditions are boldly tilted to the rear. Every flagstick change or wind change dramatically alters the strategy of hole. Classic Redan green tilted from front-right to back-left. Many later versions (reverse-Redan) built as mirror image. | **Best example(s):** 4th at the National Golf Links; 3rd Piping Rock. Reverse Redan: 8th at Creek Club. | **Comments:** Considered the finest par-3 design in the world. National's 4th rated one of top 100 golf holes in America.

The 9th at Yale University. (George Bahto Collection)

Biarritz

Origin: 3rd hole (the Chasm) (NLE), Biarritz Golf Club, Biarritz, France. Architect: Willie Dunn Jr. 1888. | **Length:** 220-245 yards. **Bunkering:** Narrow strip bunkers guard the sides and rear of green. A framing bunker short of green often used to represent the original cliff-to-cliff carry over Bay of Biscay. | **Green:** Enormous green with deep swale either in front of or incorporated into putting surface when fully planted. | **Approach:** Original architecture featured only one tee. All shorter tees were added later by clubs. | **Best example(s):** First version built at Piping Rock. Most literal version had been 9th at Yale or 7th at Fishers Island until it was ascertained by Dr. Alister MacKenzie that the 16th at Cypress Point was originally suggested by Seth Raynor as part of his original routing there. | **Comments:** Macdonald never built a version at the National. Until recently only Yale and Chicago had the "landing area" short of the green planted as putting surface (20,000 sq ft). Presently there are over 30 such dramatic versions.

The 3rd at National Golf Links. (George Bahto Collection)

Alps

Origin: 17th hole at Prestwick Golf Club, Ayrshire, Scotland. Architect: Old Tom Morris. | **Length:** 400-435 yards. | **Bunkering:** Deep cross-bunker in front of green on far side of high hill. | **Green:** Depressed or raised punchbowl green with distinctive ridge or spine running through putting surface. | **Approach:** In purest form, a blind approach shot over a high hill. More moderate versions provide a partial glimpse of the target. Most common version positions the green over or at a rise in the fairway with Alps-type bunkering, mostly notably the frontal cross-bunker. | **Best example(s):** 3rd hole at the National Golf Links; 4th hole at Fishers Island; 5th at St. Louis. Many other fine examples remain. | **Comments:** Dismissed by some as a relic of the past, but a fun and unpredictable hole to play. Hill is often represented by a rising fairway to a semiblind green. A consensus of golfers who know the National well call the Alps one of their favorite holes.

The 13th at National Golf Links (Karl Olson)

Eden

Origin: 11th hole at St. Andrews (High-Hole-In), St. Andrews Old Course, Fife, Scotland. | **Length:** 160-170 yards. | **Bunkering:** Greenside: "Hill" bunker left, "Strath" bunker (technically a pot bunker) right. "Eden" bunker behind green represents beach of the Eden River (Scotland). "Cockleshell" (or "Shelly" bunker) short and right of the green frames the green complex. | **Green:** Original Eden severely tilted back to front; later versions feature much larger greens with moderate slope and undulations. In truest form, balls can be putted off the green into the Strath bunker. | **Approach:** True representations offer few easy cup placements. Most versions are a gentle interpretation of St. Andrews original. | **Best example(s):** National 13th; Chicago 13th; St. Louis 3rd; Lido 3rd. Many other fine examples remain. | **Comments:** Along with Redan, the Eden is considered one of the finest examples of par-3 strategies.

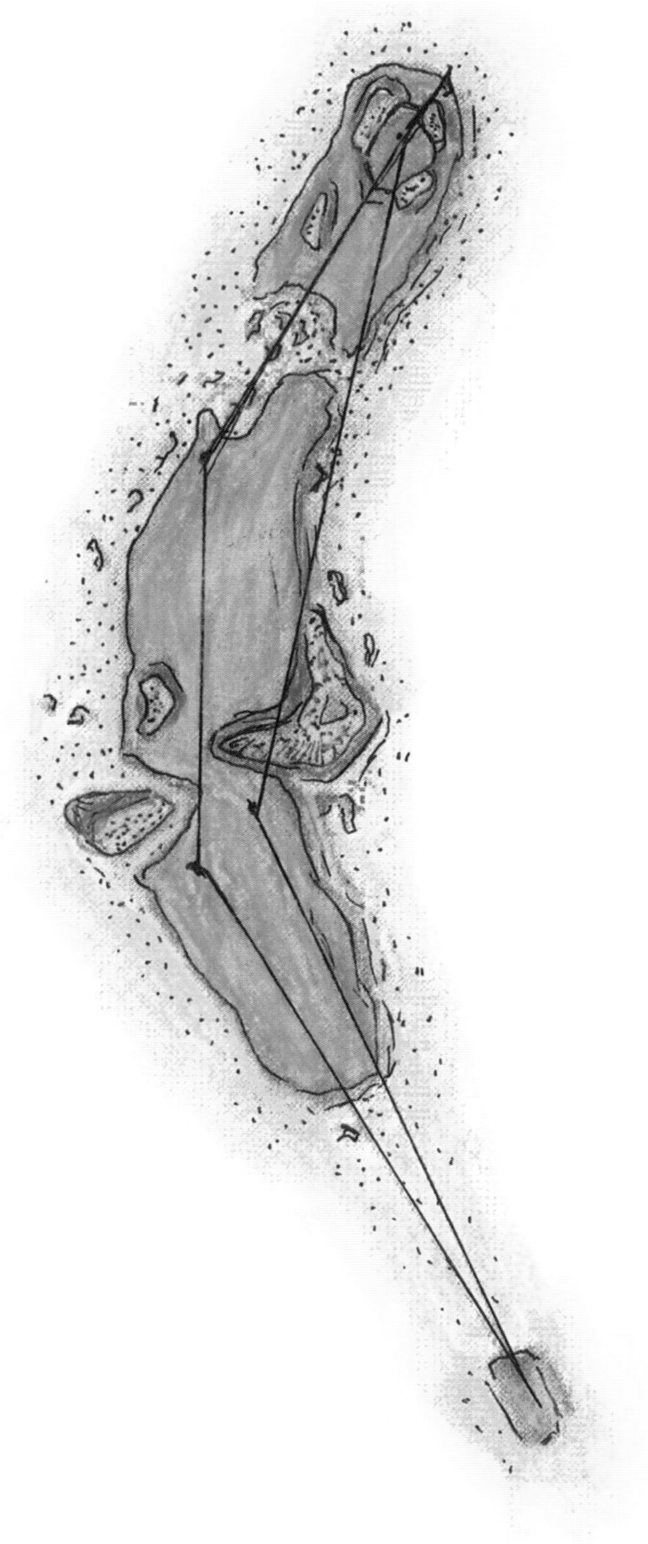

Raynor's Prize Dogleg

Origin: 6th at Lido, a reachable par 5 (493 yards). A Seth Raynor rendition combines two entries in the *Country Life* magazine design contest. | **Length:** 435-445 yards. After Lido, hole was designed as an unusually long par 4. In Raynor's own words, "a par four but a bogey six." | **Bunkering:** Severe fairway bunkering, especially at inside of dogleg. Play to opposite side lengthens hole considerably. | **Green:** Elevated green angled to the line of play; often "fishhooked" in the same direction as the dogleg. In later versions, green sites were often not bunkered. | **Approach:** Huge waste area 60 to 100 yards short of the green left golfer with a layup or go-for-it decision. Later versions more forgiving as the waste area was replaced with echelon bunkering. Even with modern equipment this hole is difficult to reach in regulation figures. | **Best example(s):** Sadly, it appears no unaltered difficult versions remain. Memberships unable to appreciate strategic excellence of design filled in most fairway bunkers–negating the design strategy. | **Comments:** Raynor developed the hole from a prizewinning submission to the contest in *Country Life* magazine prior to the construction of the Lido G.C. It immediately became a feature hole on all future Seth Raynor designs. Aside from Raynor's prototype at Lido's 6th, a prime example was built at T. Suffern Tailer's nine-hole Ocean Links (1919-1920) as its 9th hole.

Hand-drawn version of the first rendition. (George Bahto Graphics)

The 15th at National Golf Links. (*Skyshots*)

Narrows

Origin: Portion: Second shot: 15th Muirfield, East Lothian, Scotland. | **Length:** Mid-length par 4 averaging 400 yards. | **Bunkering:** Greenside bunkers: Heavily bunkered left, right, and to the rear. | **Approach Bunkers:** In purest form (National), 75-yards short of green are the so-called "Muirfield Twins," flanking each side of the fairway; most identifiable is the bunker in the middle of the fairway, 50 yards before the green. | **Green:** Sloping fairly severely back-to-front; moderately undulating; steep falloff to rear. | **Best example(s):** 15th at the National—prototype Macdonald / Raynor version. | **Comments:** National's 15th has the most beautiful bunkering on the course from tee to green. Pure versions of this genre are few and far between, but the hole is best identified by the "narrowing" of the approach area from about 100 yards in to the green. The bunker in the middle of the fairway short of the green is often removed by golf clubs not fully understanding the hole's strategy.

The 8th at Piping Rock. (George Bahto Collection)

Road Hole

Origin: 17th, St. Andrews Old Course. 461-yard par 4. Originally played as par 5. Architect: Allan Robertson. | **Length:** Various lengths of long par 4s or short par 5s. | **Bunkering:** Deep and notoriously "gathering" pot bunker guards the front of the green. Macdonald and Raynor versions normally installed bunkering beyond the green to represent the road behind original. Pot bunker, though deep, rarely as treacherous as the one at the 17th at St. Andrews. Fairway bunkering often used at corner of dogleg to represent tee shot over railway sheds (now a hotel). | **Green:** Abrupt rise to the green along the right portion, triangular in shape with shallow depth. Green rejects overly bold approaches to rear bunker. It is possible to putt the ball into the pot bunker on some versions. | **Approach:** Drives correctly placed in right side of fairway, leaves best approach to a green oriented at a severe angle to the centerline of play. Many golfers bail out short right of the green to avoid Road bunker, hoping to get up and down. Drive to left, away from hazard directly confronts pot bunker. | **Best example(s):** 7th at the National; 8th at Piping Rock; 3rd at North Shore C.C. (NY). Many other fine versions remain. | **Comments:** Technology-proof hole. As maddeningly difficult today as it was when built by Robertson in 1842.

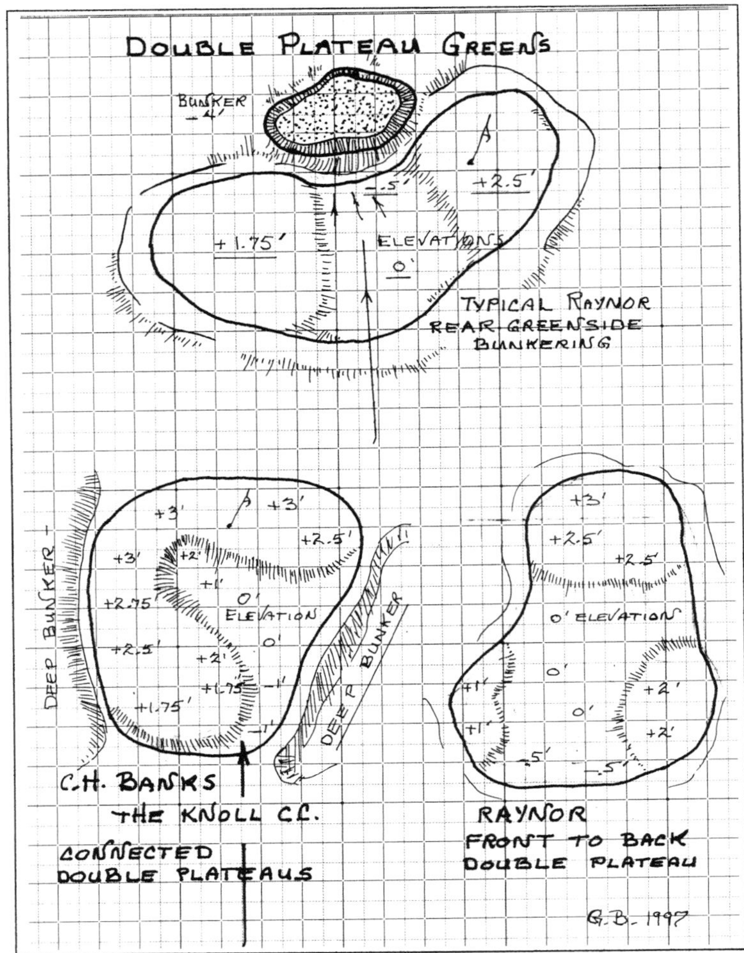

The 11th at National Golf Links. (George Bahto Graphics)

Double Plateau

Origins: Impossible to determine. Design likely based on many natural plateau greens in the British Isles. | **Length:** Long par 4s, often the longest two-shot hole on the course. | **Bunkering:** Moderate fairway and greenside bunkering, often with Principal's Nose-type bunker set 70 yards in front of the green. | **Green:** Stubby L-shaped green. Good renditions feature three levels. Location on putting surface usually front-left and right-rear, though there are many exceptions. Early versions would funnel aggressive approaches through the green to a deep bunker beyond. | **Approach:** Generally open in front of green except for Principal's Nose bunker in fairway short of the green to visually obscure portions of the target. | **Best example(s):** National's 11th green; Chicago Golf's 6th; Fishers Island's 18th; North Shore's 14th. Most renditions still in their original form. | **Comments:** Great variety of single plateau greens in both Raynor's and Banks' s designs, but true representation of this style contains at least two separate plateaus. Most renditions feature very large greens.

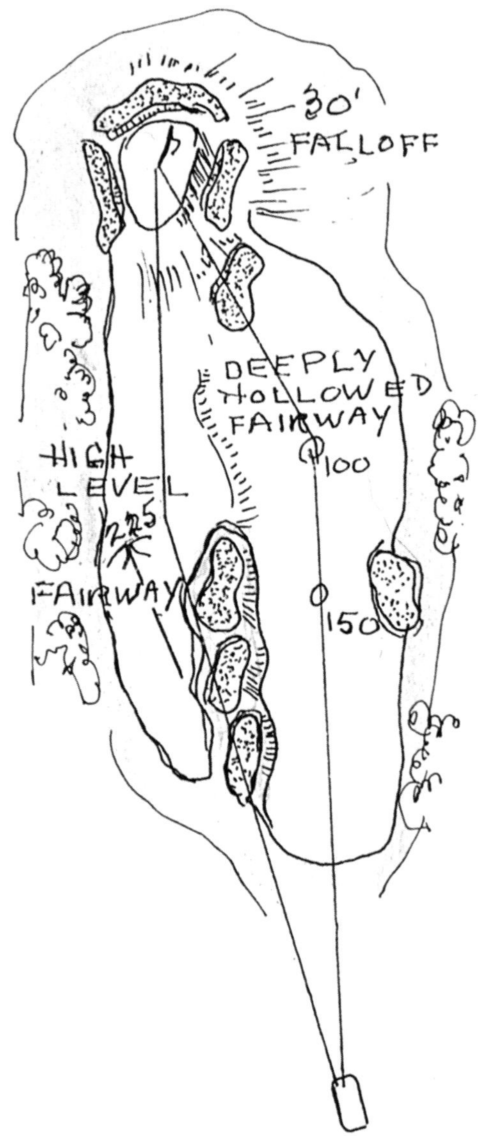

Bottle Hole

Origin: C.B. Macdonald modification of original 12th hole at Sunningdale's Old Course, Berkshire, England (NLE). Architect: Willie Park Jr. | **Length:** Varied lengths of par 4s. | **Bunkering:** Features a dramatic set of fairway bunkers placed on a diagonal to the line of play, separating a two-level fairway. Green site well bunkered with Principal's Nose complex beyond fairway bunkers. | **Approach:** The narrower fairway segment (set on the upper fairway level) offers a less hazardous approach shot. Conversely, the wider and more accessible fairway segment leaves more of a treacherous approach. | **Green:** Elevated and tightly bunkered approach. In its purest form, Bottle Hole requires full carry into green due to a sloping false front at entry point to the putting surface. | **Best example(s):** 8th at the National Golf Links (everyone's favorite). | **Comments:** Though many were built, most have been lost as club committees eliminated one of the optional fairways. Later Charles Banks's versions of the Bottle Hole occasionally featured pinched-in landing areas rather than a split fairway.

The 10th at Essex County Country Club West Course. (George Bahto Graphics)

The 5th at National Golf Links. (George Bahto Collection)

Hog's Back

Origin: Impossible to determine. Many examples found as natural fairways and greens in the British Isles. | **Length:** Medium length par 4. | **Bunkering:** In purest form, a large bunker obscures the prime landing area from the tee. Later versions eliminated this for an unobstructed view of a semicrowned fairway. | **Approach:** Usually a deep bunker to one side with high lip. | **Green:** Hogbacked spine running along the line of play segmenting the green into two distinct areas sloping away from each other. | **Best example(s):** 5th at National Golf Links is considered the overall best hole; 4th at Knoll Golf Club (New Jersey) has the best green. | **Comments:** Hole places premium on tee shot accuracy. Off-line shots catch slope and bound away from line of play, often into a waiting bunker or hollow. Many renditions that remain are no longer effective due to overirrigation, which negates the turtleback effect of fairway slope, and takes fairway bunkering out of play.

The 6th at National Golf Links. (National Golf Links)

Short

Origin: Suggested by the 5th at Brancaster (now Royal West Norfolk), Norfolk, England. | **Length:** Par 3, 130–140 yards. | **Bunkering:** Deep greenside bunkering surrounds putting surface and creates an "island" effect. | **Approach:** Generous green, usually much wider than deep. | **Green:** Plateau green, generally elevated 5 feet above natural terrain. Putting surface features are usually the most complex on the course. Dished depressions, rear shelves, and false fronts abound and segment the greens. 10,000 (plus) square foot greens not uncommon. | **Best example(s):** 6th at the National; 10th at Chicago G.C.; Banks's version at North Hempsted's 2nd; Raynor's version at Nassau C.C. | **Comments:** Green committees often mistakenly lengthen this hole to add yardage to the course. A Short is designed specifically to examine the short iron and putting skills of the golfer.

The 13th at Piping Rock (George Bahto Collection)

Knoll Hole

Origin: 4th hole at Scotscraig Golf Club, Tayport, Fife, Scotland. Architect: Tom Morris. | **Length:** Short par 4 averaging 300 yards. | **Bunkering:** One moderate greenside bunker—if any. | **Approach:** The play to the green is blind because of the extreme elevation of the putting surface. | **Green:** In pure form, greens were built 8 to 10 feet above the fairway with steep falloffs on all sides. Putting surfaces feature a rear plateau, fronted by a sharp slope to an expansive collection area on lower tier. | **Best example(s):** 13th hole at Piping Rock is the prototype Macdonald/Raynor version. | **Comments:** Can be played in a variety of ways depending on the flagstick position. Back tier placement is the most difficult.

The 4th at The Lido Club. (*Golf Illustrated*)

Channel Hole

Origin: 16th hole (Old) Littlestone, Kent, England, based on an original hole by W. Laidlaw Pervis. | **Length:** Optional fairway par 5. Green reachable in two shots only by taking more treacherous route from tee. | **Bunkering:** Greenside tightly bunkered. Original form features a deep cross-bunker short of green. | **Approach:** At Lido, the fairway swung wide along "safer" route, with water off tee and sand hills along the right side. Water pressed along entire left side of fairway and crossed again on the second shot. Hole featured cross-bunker short of the green. Two-shot option required a direct line to the green over narrow, 30-foot high alternate fairway surrounded by water and sandy waste. | **Best example(s):** No excellent examples exist. | **Green:** Built-up with undulating surface. | **Comments:** Original hole at Littlestone set in the sand dunes along the beach. Best example: First built at Lido's 4th hole (NLE). Many were built, though most were very moderate versions. Few unaltered examples remain because golf clubs often did not comprehend the strategy of the hole. Pete Dye's 18th hole at Harbour Town Links is a version with the optional "island fairway" connected.

The 5th at Mid Ocean Club. (*Golf Illustrated*)

Cape

Origin: Generally ascribed to Macdonald's 14th hole at the National Golf Links. | **Length:** Has been built successfully at a variety of par-4 yardages. | **Bunkering:** Left, right, and rear at greenside. | **Green:** Undulating, often with a banked, high-side approach. | **Approach:** At the National, a short iron approach. Due to fairway undulations, however, the golfer often has (and had) awkward lies. | **Best example(s):** 5th at Mid Ocean (rated one of the 100 best holes in the world); 14th National Golf Links. | **Comments:** A Cape green by strict definition would be one that juts out into a body of water (National's original 14th green). Since they didn't always have the topographic opportunity, Macdonald and Raynor often built a Cape green as a terrace seemingly jutting out into midair (example: 2nd green at Yale). With the elimination of the National's original 14th green in the 1920s, the "Cape" hole has mistakenly evolved into describing a risk/reward tee-shot played over a diagonal hazard.

The 9th at National Golf Links. (George Bahto Collection)

Long

Origin: 14th, St. Andrews. | **Length:** Normally identified as the longest par 5 on the course. | **Bunkering:** Fairway bunkering arranged to force players to flirt with moderate representation of the Hell Bunker complex (St. Andrews' 14th). Greenside bunkering is generally moderate. | **Approach:** In true form, tee shots must negotiate a diagonal carry. Most golfers play these as 3-shot holes. | **Green:** Impossible to generalize as there is no identifiable pattern in putting surface contouring. | **Best example(s):** Although the 9th at the National may be the best remaining representative example, the most literal version was built by Macdonald/Raynor at the lost Lido course (hole #17). Only there were all aspects of the St. Andrews original, including Hell Bunker, faithfully represented. | **Comments:** In the 1920s these were difficult holes—often requiring a midiron approach on the 3rd shot. The Hell Bunker complex (75 yards wide and deep at St. Andrews) was designed to present a clear choice to either lay up or attempt the long second-shot carry. Most versions by Macdonald and Raynor were far less severe to accommodate club players.

The 16th at National Golf Links. (George Bahto Collection)

Punchbowl

Origin: Generic term ascribed to many holes on most early golf courses where greens were located in natural hollows where grasses grew healthier because of moisture retention. | **Length:** Have been built successfully at a variety of par-4 yardages—usually longer lengths. Often combined with the Alps genre. | **Bunkering:** Not applicable unless combined with Alps hill. | **Green:** Usually bowl-shaped with dramatic hilly surrounds on three sides. Most properly the outer edges of many Punchbowl greens were actually on the rise of the Punchbowl. | **Approach:** Varied. | **Best Example(s):** 16th at the National Golf Links is one of the finest examples; St. Louis 5th leads a long list of others. Fishers Island 4th—a pronounced example Alps-Punchbowl combination—clearly leads this category. Interesting example at Montclair C.C.'s 1st hole on 4th nine (Charles Banks). | **Comments:** Whenever the topography "allowed," Macdonald/Raynor/Banks located Punchbowl holes in natural hollows. However, many were engineered to create the desired strategy. The Alps combination is very prevalent. One-of-a-kind example of a par-3 Punchbowl/Eden combination: 3rd at Westhampton (170 yards) where only the top third of the flagstick is visible.

The 2nd at National Golf Links. (National Golf Links)

Sahara

Origin: 3rd hole at Royal St. George's at Sandwich, Kent, England suggested the 2nd hole at National Golf Links (Macdonald). | **Length:** Short par 4. | **Approach:** Green defended by huge expanse of sand, sand hills, or sandy waste area often plated with sea bents where applicable. At the National, one-half acre of sand is what is seen on the horizon of fairway. The green is blind to the golfer. | **Best example(s):** 2nd hole at the National Golf Links. | **Comments:** Sahara was a "dinosaur" hole Macdonald could not resist characterizing as one of his "Ideal Holes."

The 1st at National Golf Links. (National Golf Links)

Valley

Origin: Generic term ascribed to many holes where topography dictated a severe downhill fairway. | **Green Complex:** Usually on naturally high ground. | **Best example(s):** National Golf Links 1st. | **Comments:** Fairway bunkering, approaches, and green complex vary and have no specific bearing on this style hole.

Garden City *(Not shown)*

Origin: Original 5th hole at Garden City before lengthening (Devereux Emmet design). | **Length:** Very short par 4 barely over 300 yards in its original form. | **Bunkering:** Large cluster of small mounds and fairway bunkering (usually along the left) with a green fishhooked or tucked in just beyond the hazard area. | **Green:** Nothing specific. | **Best example(s)**: 1st hole at extinct Ocean Links course (NLE); 7th hole at North Shore C.C. (NY). | **Comments:** Macdonald was a member of Garden City men's club before he built the National and he revered the 5th hole on the course. Although he did not use the hole's strategy at the National he, and Raynor later, sparingly inserted it into various courses as the situation dictated. Often green committees lengthened this very short hole to a "normal" length drive and pitch, not understanding its historical significance or origin. This was justified as equipment improved, rendering the hole inappropriately short.

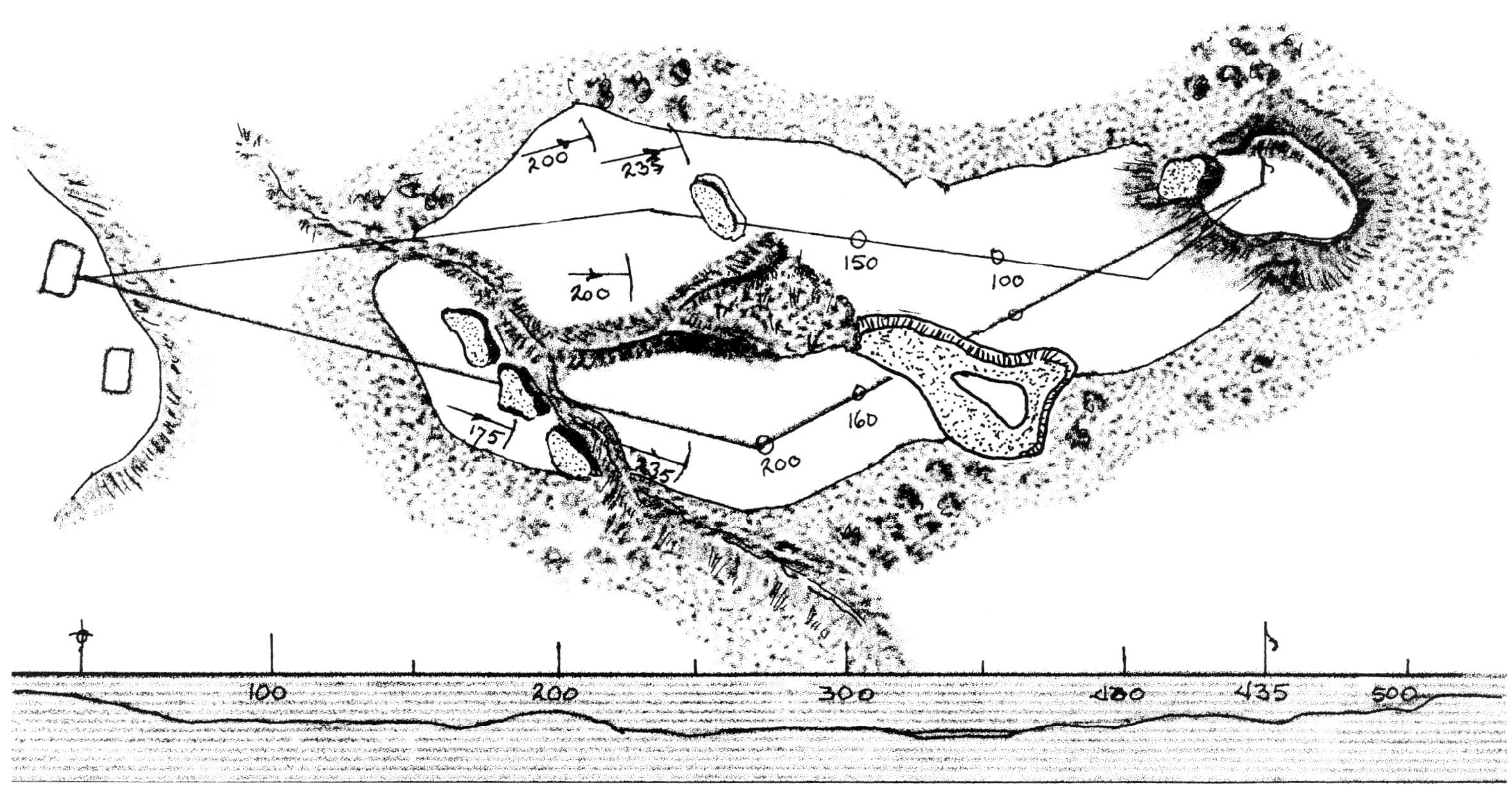

Design submitted by British architect Tom Simpson. (*Country Life*)

Strategy

Origin: 15th at the Lido (NLE). | **Length:** Medium length par 4. | **Bunkering:** Fairway bunkering literally a minefield. | **Approach:** In true form, tee shots must negotiate a risk/reward carry. Most golfers play these as 3-shot holes. | **Green:** Not definable at Lido. Westhampton's 9th green, however—one of Raynor's best—is more than moderately tilted and strewn with subtle and many not so subtle undulations and switchbacks. | **Best example(s):** 15th Lido; 9th Westhampton (option fairway no longer exists). | **Comments:** The drive is played to either side of a string of ridges or mounds separating the very wide fairway; one route is more risky to play than the other (usually over a scattering of bunkers). The reward for this play optimizes the approach to the green while the other option is forced to play over greenside hazards and at an angle considerably more difficult. "Strategy" was all but forgotten by Raynor in later years because it required a fairway area nearly three times the normal width.

Charles Blair Macdonald—founder/architect of the National Golf Links of America. (National Golf Links of America)

CHAPTER SIX

NATIONAL GOLF LINKS *of* AMERICA

There were many who thought my idea was a pipe dream, and even some of my friends felt I was throwing away my time and my friends' affections and money by trying to build an ideal golf course. I remember well when in the autumn of 1907 with little or nothing to show but a weary waste of land with a beautiful sunset and stretches of water and meadow I was enthusiastically declaiming to a few friends whom I had asked for luncheon at the Shinnecock Hills Golf Club the possibility of the future classic course, an intimate friend of mine, Urban H. Broughton, left the table. Later he confided to John Grier that he feared, because of his affection for me and believing that I would be so much disappointed, he would drop a tear.

—C.B. Macdonald

Following a lengthy search for the perfect location to build, Macdonald set his sights on the existing Shinnecock Hills Golf Club, where he was a member. A union of 70 members, each subscribing $1,000 was formed. Such were the persuasive powers and influence of Macdonald that the original membership read like the "Who's Who" of American aristocrats: Horace Harding, William D. Sloane, the Harrimans and Hunts, Harry Payne Whitney, his close friend and companion Judge Morgan O'Brien, Charles Sabin, James Stillman, the ultrawealthy Clarence Mackay, Willie Vanderbilt (William K. II), J. P. Grace (another future son-in-law), President Abraham Lincoln's son Robert, Johnny Bowers, building architect Jarvis Hunt, and his friend and fellow course architect Devereux Emmet.

With $70,000 in hand, Macdonald offered to purchase the Shinnecock property from the Peconic Bay Realty Company on behalf of the consortium. The National Golf Links of America was incorporated on March 11, 1908. The incorporators were:

> Charles B. Macdonald, New York | John M. Bowers, New York | James A. Stillman, New York | James Deering, Florida | Robert T. Lincoln, Washington | Daniel Chauncey, New York | William D. Sloane, New York | Washington B. Thomas, Boston | Henry M. Atkinson, Atlanta

Many members at Shinnecock Hills were outraged—and understandably so. *How dare this Macdonald have the audacity to purchase our course out from under us!*

Unconcerned with their animosity, Macdonald envisioned building a masterpiece on this supreme stretch of rolling sand hills. Although a handsome profit could have been made by the real estate firm that controlled the property, Macdonald was unable to persuade them to sell. Under pressure from the membership, the offer was rejected.

Undaunted, Macdonald uncovered a 450-acre tract adjacent to the Shinnecock Hills course. The property had been looked upon as wholly ill-suited for any development—a worthless mess of brambles, swampy areas, and murky bogs. In fact, so little of the land could be explored on foot it was necessary to use ponies.

It was here that Macdonald, who had no background in surveying or construction, first hired a local surveyor/engineer named Seth Raynor to produce a detailed map of the property. To say the least, the land was by no means perfect, but it was almost entirely sand based. Macdonald envisioned that once the swamps were drained and the underbrush cleared, they would find a site with natural undulations perfect for building his ideal course.

There was a secondary reason the tract had caught Macdonald's eye. This piece of land included a gorgeous stretch of waterfront along Peconic Bay, something landlocked Shinnecock lacked. There would be ample room for a yacht dock, which was an important consideration in that era. Many wealthy founders had huge yachts; at the National they would have the best of both worlds.

From the survey, Macdonald made a rough sketch of the holes he planned to build, and with Raynor, located potential sites and elevations for greens, tees, and turning points in the fairway. Macdonald tinkered endlessly with the routing plan. Finally, after months of planning, he was ready to move to the next step.

Macdonald was impressed by the ability with which Seth Raynor—a nongolfer—was able to reproduce his modified renditions of classic holes on the ground. At the outset, Raynor had no intention or interest in building golf courses. This was just another job to him and Macdonald was just another client.

Raynor had planned to return to his engineering practice in Southampton. Macdonald, however, recognized that his newfound assistant had skills crucial to the success of the National. After weeks of cajoling, Macdonald finally persuaded Raynor to reconsider.

Doubtless with some reservation, Raynor accepted, agreeing to stay on for the duration of the project. He would become Macdonald's chief engineer and problem solver as well as his faithful friend. Macdonald was at best difficult, and at worst, impossible to contend with. Yet, in time they developed the closest of relationships.

What began as a short-term surveying job led to an association lasting nearly 20 years until Raynor's untimely death in 1926. Prior to the golf boom of the Roaring Twenties, Raynor—along with the great Donald Ross—were probably the two architects most in demand.

Macdonald and company purchased the tract in November of 1907. He also purchased 117 acres across Bull Heads Bay for himself, on which he would build a home. As he would later do with the Atlantic Ocean at Mid Ocean in Bermuda, Macdonald built his house facing away from the ocean and toward the golf course.

C.B. next asked Henry Whigham and Walter Travis, each golf champions and course architects in their own right, to assist him in implementing his plan. Though Travis soon bowed out of the project, C. B. and Whigham continued on with assistance from Joseph P. Knapp. Also closely involved were banker James Stillman, Devereux Emmet, financier/Southampton landowner Charles Sabin, and a few others. C. V. Piper of the United States Department of Agriculture was later engaged for agronomic advice. Piper was also connected to the USGA.

Left: A copy of the original blueprint routing plan of the National Golf Links of America by C.B. Macdonald. (George Bahto Collection)

Opposite: C.B. Macdonald, circa 1922
"In 1919 Pine Valley was considered the chief rival of the two outstanding Macdonald creations, the National and the Lido. Nothing would annoy Charlie Macdonald more than mentioning these three in the same breath. He maintained Pine Valley was too difficult and had too many trees for one of the cardinal points of his faith was that a good golfing hole should be equally interesting and playable for the average duffer and the champion. He indeed was so jealous of the National's reputation that he even disliked listening to praise of his own Lido."

–H.J. Whigham, *Town & Country Magazine* 1939

Below: Macdonald's home, Ballyshear, was set on 115 acres on a hill across Bull Head's Bay. The house overlooked 15 of the National's holes. (George Bahto Collection)

Original 10th hole at the National—now hole #1. (George Bahto Collection)

The Alps (# 3) was originally the 12th hole. (George Bahto Collection)

Present Cape hole #14—originally hole #5. There was a beautiful lake on the property, and although Macdonald did not have a classic hole that required water, he introduced a new strategy that caught the attention of the golf world: the "Cape," a Macdonald original with a green jutting out in the bay. (George Bahto Collection)

View of the original 7th green—presently the Punchbowl 16th hole. (George Bahto Collection)

Using Raynor's survey maps and Macdonald's personal drawings as a guide, they forged ahead.

Once cleared, the site was visually striking. Knolls, hills, and basins furnished the topography. They also found natural ponds and uncovered a portion of Sebonac Creek which could be used for water hazards.

Macdonald and company located fairly natural sites for a Redan and Eden, as well as a site for an Alps, requiring only a slight modification. The location for a Sahara hole was selected, as well as spots for a few original Macdonald creations suggested by the terrain. The routing of the course was beginning to take form, and although Macdonald later claimed the majority of the holes were on natural sites, in reality he manipulated a huge amount of soil.

A number of strategic and aesthetic innovations took place at National, yet often overlooked is the seminal influence Macdonald and Raynor had on early course construction. Macdonald was not afraid to move massive amounts of earth in order to achieve a desired artistic effect, and Raynor had the engineering skills to blend it together.

Macdonald eventually admitted to importing 10,000 truckloads of soil to recontour and sculpt areas to fit his diagrams. A meticulous planner, Macdonald knew precisely what he was trying to achieve, and if he could not find an appropriate site, one would just have to be created! It is true that natural sites were located for his Redan and Eden, but to build other replications to his exacting specifications required extensive movement and importing of soil. Heavily influenced by this philosophy, Seth Raynor—and later Charles Banks—would later take earthmoving to new dimensions. Banks, who became known for his highly stylized, cavernous bunkering, was dubbed by fellow course builders as "Steamshovel Charley."

The planning stage did not always go smoothly. Macdonald's reputation for bullheaded stubbornness was well founded, and by his own words he affirmed that there were many heated discussions about the placement of bunkers, greens, and tees. True to his nature, he felt these contentious disagreements were a natural outgrowth of the evolution of golf. In his book, *Scotland's Gift—Golf*, he wrote:

> *I became convinced that any hole warranting warm or acrimonious discussion over a term of years must be 'worth while,' otherwise it would have been consigned to oblivion with far less comment.*

Macdonald had carefully recorded the size and contour of the best green sites in Britain, yet there was still a need for creating putting surfaces at the National to go with his original composite holes. Finding it difficult to achieve the

Top: C.B. Macdonald standing in a massive unfinished bunker at the National. (Mike Tureski family)

Bottom: An early view from the tee of the 6th ("Short"), a par 3 of 141 yards. (National Golf Links of America)

"Disaster *on the* Greens"
1907-1908

Much of the turfgrass knowledge so basic to superintendents today began with an embarrassing setback at the National, after the course's greens were seeded.

When Charles Macdonald began building the course in 1907, little was known about proper seed mixtures on putting greens—in particular about growing fine grass on the sandy soil such as at Southampton.

It was said at the time that, "no one with the possible exception of Herbert Leeds of the Myopia Hunt Club and Herbert Windeler at Brookline, had the remotest idea what sort of seed should be sown on a putting green." Seed purchasing was haphazard at best, and golf committees and course builders were left to the mercy of the seed merchants, few of whom were knowledgeable themselves. One of the primary duties of early green committees was to procure supplies for the course builder, and to be at the beck and call of the architect and construction crew.

Seed merchants at that time went by the principle that if many types of grass seed were incorporated in the blend, something was sure to grow. Consequently the putting mixtures of the day were a blend of "every sort of seed, from fine fescue to rank meadow grass." Naturally, the coarsest grasses germinated first, eventually turning the planted areas into ugly, unmanageable clumps.

Macdonald, trusting the knowledge of the seed merchant, used this mixture for the first seeding ... with disastrous results. Robert White, the eminent golf course architect and close friend of Macdonald wrote in 1914:

At end of the year's time the greens [at the National] resembled cabbage patches. What grasses they contained grew in thick tufts with bare spaces between. Most of the National's greens had to be made all over again. Those that were not ploughed up had bad grass in them for several years afterward.

As a result of this debacle, according to White, the opening of the National was thrown back 18 months. Macdonald was flabbergasted. During the ensuing months, he initiated a thorough study and established an extensive turf nursery. He even went so far as to build a second nursery at his home, Ballyshear. C.B. spent a lot of time experimenting with various grasses in hopes of developing better turf. Eventually, he wrote and published a treatise on his findings titled, *The Growing of Fine Turf Grass on the Sandy Soils of Long Island.* Those findings became the basis for modern greenkeeping, and ushered in a new era of using science and experimentation to improve the turfgrass quality of American golf courses.

He discovered there was far less loam in the sandy soil of Long Island than there was in "similarly situated areas in Scotland and England." A seedbed needed to be established to properly germinate rather than just dispersing seed on the ground. The light sandy soil on Long Island was "ideal for playing the game," but was much more difficult for growing fine grasses than that of similar situations in the British Isles.

He reached two conclusions that—though appearing basic today—were a great revelation in 1907.

First, the soil had to be properly prepared. In order to preserve moisture in the turf, he had blocks of "meadow sod" turned into the ground. Limestone, with a quantity of sandy loam, was added to sweeten the soil. Then came the problem of seed mix. According to Macdonald, Rhode Island Bent, the natural grass on Long Island, was similar to Creeping Bent. Unfortunately, pure seed was nearly impossible to find and it was difficult to differentiate between these two and Redtop, a much cheaper but similar grade. It was very tempting for an unscrupulous seed merchant to substitute quantities of cheap seed.

Because not all greens needed to be plowed under, there were originally several varieties of grass on some of the greens. "Some were seeded with Rhode Island Bent, others with Creeping Bent, while others sprung up with New Zealand Fescue."

Through trial and much error, Macdonald developed a custom mixture of fine grasses that established consistent putting surfaces throughout the golf season. Though primitive when compared to the lightning-fast modern green speeds, the putting surfaces at the National Golf Links set a new standard for quality on American country club courses.

By the middle 1910s, seed mixtures became even more refined. According to Robert White, "the same formula held good for most any climate in the United States at least as far south as

White Sulfur Springs, West Virginia. So much change has come about in seven years [by then 1917] through experimentation and research along scientific lines. Greenkeeping is becoming almost an exacting science. Putting greens were hand-watered in Macdonald's era, but little thought was given to maintaining consistent—yet firm—fairways. In the summer, baked golf courses played hard and fast, and in the winter they were lush and green.

After a year of battling the porous soil of Long Island, it was evident that a complete watering system would be needed. Out of this necessity, Macdonald designed and installed America's first golf course irrigation system; one capable of delivering 300 gallons per minute to the putting greens and approach areas.

The gravity-fed water was delivered from a tower between the 2nd and 16th greens—now the site of the landmark windmill.

natural look he sought, he turned to his close friend and British golf champion, Horace Hutchinson. They spent a few days at the National studying the course together, with Hutchinson offering his advice for the arrangement of bunkers and contouring of the putting surface undulations. Macdonald's recollections of the conversation:

I know he impressed on me that the human mind could not devise undulations superior to those of nature, saying that if I wished to make undulations on the greens to take a number of pebbles in my hand and drop them on a miniature space representing a putting-green on a small scale, releasing them, and as they dropped on the diagram, place the undulations according to their fall. This I did for some of the National greens where I had no copies of the original undulations which nature had made on the great greens of the world.

This was to be the last puzzle piece in creating his ideal golf course. Macdonald fashioned plasticine models of each hole and putting green, Raynor engineered the calculations, and construction began in earnest.

Mortimer Payne, a local contractor, assembled a team of workers, mules, and dragpans. Under Raynor's direction, the course was graded in the hope it would be opened for play within two years. Macdonald continued to make modifications and refinements throughout the construction phase. After seeding the course, an obstacle that even Macdonald had not considered quite literally grew from the ground. Macdonald envisioned a flawless carpet of springy turf to adorn his golf course. What he got instead—and how he attacked the problem—led to the beginning of modern irrigation and turfgrass agronomy.

The National Golf Links of America Opens for Play

The following picturesque description of National Golf Links appeared in the fall 1912 issue of *The Southampton Magazine*:

Throughout the course the scenery has been superb, ever

Above: Prince Troubetzkoy sculpting the Macdonald statue. (*Scotland's Gift–Golf*)

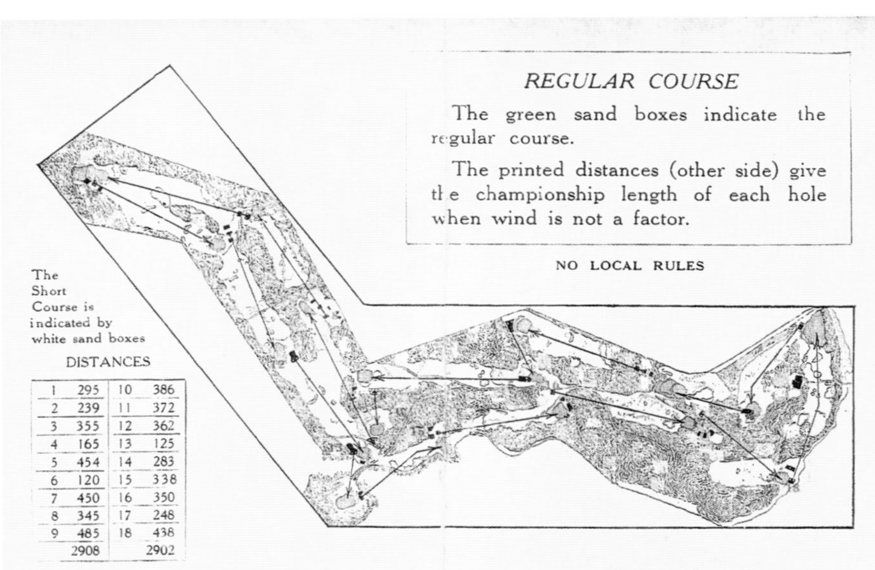

1	295	10	386
2	239	11	372
3	355	12	362
4	165	13	125
5	454	14	283
6	120	15	338
7	450	16	350
8	345	17	248
9	485	18	438
	2908		2902

NATIONAL GOLF LINKS
OF AMERICA

Self ________ Op'nt ________

HOLE	YARDS	PAR	NAME		SELF	O'PT	
1	315	4	Valley . . .	11			
2	261	4	Sahara . . .	13			
3	376	4	Alps . . .	5			
4	185	3	Redan . . .	15			
5	467	5	Hog's Back . .	3			
6	125	3	Short . . .	17			
7	456	5	St. Andrews . .	7			
8	380	4	Bottle . . .	9			
9	525	5	Long . . .	1			
	3090	37		OUT			
10	416	4	Shinnecock . .	8			
11	405	4	Plateau . . .	4			
12	385	4	Sebonac . .	14			
13	160	3	Eden . . .	18			
14	305	4	Cape . . .	10			
15	358	4	Narrows . .	12			
16	410	4	Punchbowl . .	6			
17	311	4	Peconic . . .	16			
18	484	5	High . . .	2			
	3234	36	IN				
		37	OUT				
		73	TOTAL				

Red numerals indicate order in which strokes are given.

Date ________

changing at every step with the continually varying panorama of land and water, furze and sedges, hillsides and tideways, putting greens and playing launches, white sand pits and green islands, grassy vales and whitecapped waves, sere, brown slopes and bright blue bays, a mass of rolling rollicking upland and a maze of creeks, bays, channels and harbors.

Fully 10 years after the idea of an ideal links first came to its designer and four years after initial construction began, the National Golf Links of America finally opened to membership play in 1910. There were still adjustments and refinements to come, but those would never cease until Macdonald's death.

The formal opening of the course was officially celebrated in 1911 with the Macdonald Invitational Tournament, one of many played at the National.

The First Invitational

On July 2, 1910, 14 months before the official opening, the course was finally ready for a test run. An informal Invitational Tournament was held for a select group of founders and friends invited to participate.

A qualifying round was played on the first day, followed by two days of match play. The course was still rough with temporary tee boxes, and a few bare spots on fairways and greens. Macdonald was still altering and refining the course. In fact, a new 9th (current 18th) green was already under construction before the course ever opened.

The National was played in the order as originally designed, beginning from the present 10th. When the course first opened, the yardage was fairly short by modern standards, listed as 3,194–2,967, totaling 6,161.

The top eight qualifying players and their scores were:

82	Max Behr—(38-44)	Morris County / *New Jersey State Champion*
83	Walter J. Travis	Garden City
83	Fred Herreshoff	Westbrook / *Metropolitan Champion*
84	Louis Livingston	Westbrook
87	Charles B. Macdonald	National
89	John M. Ward	Westbrook
89	Devereux Emmet	Garden City
90	Joseph P. Knapp	Lakewood / *Florida State Champion*

Besides the 9th (current 18th), soon expanded by 60 yards, Macdonald changed his mind and stretched the Sahara hole (current 2nd) from a short 215 yards to 261 yards uphill over an extended sandy waste area.

It was noted the tournament served the purpose of revealing any design shortcoming that needed correcting. All holes received high praise, except the Road hole "which did not play as anticipated." Apparently the corner hazard in the driving area was not what it would later become.

Fred Herreshoff survived after two days of match play, winning the first flight (eight players), 2-up over Walter Travis. Of special note was the astounding play of John Ward. During the first round of match play he posted a back nine of 32!

Both Ward and his opponent Max Behr were even at the turn with 42. Ward started the final nine holes in sensational fashion by winning the Valley hole (then the 10th—325 yards) by holing a mashie from the fairway for an eagle 2. At the next hole, Sahara (then 215 yards), he drove the green and ran

Above left: Macdonald and caddie, from a painting by Gari Melchers. (George Bahto Collection)

Above right: A "Who's Who" of American golfers at the time participated in a 1910 tournament to see how good the course really was. (National Golf Links of America)

Opposite: The only known surviving example of the National's first scorecard, circa 1910. This was the first time a course map appeared on a card. (George Bahto Collection)

down a putt for a second consecutive eagle 2. Ward made his par 4 at the Alps hole, following it with a 2 once more on the Redan (then the 15th, today's 4th).

Interestingly, in the qualifying round, on these very same holes, Ward posted 7, 5, and 4—the 7 on the Valley hole "without getting into any trouble" on that short par 4!

Macdonald's creation was the initial effort of what was to become the so-called "strategic school" of golf architecture. The trumpeted opening of the National Golf Links of America served notice on the golf world—particularly in America—that the days of crude and mundane penal designs were over.

Of special interest is the following article published in *American Golfer* magazine, written by the preeminent sportswriter of the era, Grantland Rice. The piece, about Charles Blair Macdonald, was written many years after the construction of the National when C.B. was nearing the age of 70. By this point, with the exception of the Yale University course, he confined his architectural activities to that of an advisor only. In many ways, it was the summation of his feelings and philosophy from a lifetime of experience:

On Making Golf Courses Great and Popular

In Which Charles B. Macdonald, Designer of the National, Lido and Others Gives His Ideas

by Charles Blair Macdonald as told to Grantland Rice

It is no difficult assignment to lay out a golf course that will be a hard championship test—and fit for only the stars to tackle. It is no crushing burden to lay out a golf course that will give the average golfer his chance, regardless of any lack of test for the star.

But there is a big problem in between these two pieces of golf construction work. This job is to build golf courses that will be championship tests and at the same time give the average player his chance to live, breathe and spend a few minutes each round outside of a trap or a bunker. And another section of the job is to build such a championship test under 6,400 yards.

Charles Blair Macdonald, who designed the National Golf Links at Southampton, Lido at Long Beach, The Links on Long Island and the Mid Ocean in Bermuda, among others has distinct and artistic ideas along these lines. Mr. Macdonald believes in obtaining all the beauty that is possible from any given tract, in giving the average player proper chance to play and at the same time punishing pride and lack of control as he makes the star work for his par.

Macdonald's Basis

"The object of a bunker or trap is not only to punish a physical mistake, to punish lack of control, but to punish the pride and egotism. I believe in leaving a way open for the player who can only drive one hundred yards, if he keep that drive straight. But the one I am after is the golfer who thinks he can carry (the ball) one hundred and eighty yards when one hundred and sixty is his limit. So I believe one of the best systems of trapping or arranging bunkers is to let the player make his own choice, from either the shorter or the longer route, and go for that.

"This helps to make the man know and study his limitations, and, if he is inclined to conceit, he will find his niblick has drawn a hard day's work. I can see no reason of running a trap across the course one hundred and fifty yards away when a great number of golfers can't possibly carry that far. For that same reason I rarely believe in putting traps across the front of the green where the second stroke is more than a pitch.

"A bunker or a trap," continues Macdonald, "is supposed to be a place that calls for a stroke penalty, not a shallow dip where the golfer can walk in with an iron or a spoon and get one hundred and seventy yards, or where anyone can use a putter.

"If I had my way there would be a troupe of cavalry horses run through every trap and bunker on the course before a tournament started, where only the niblick could get the ball out and then but only a few yards.

"I have seen a number of traps and bunkers that afforded better lies and easier strokes than the fairway. This, of course, is ridiculous.

"There should be a reward for a golfer who can hit a long, straight ball or else there is no premium upon skill and control. This doesn't mean that the shorter player is to be hopelessly handicapped, he must be provided a shorter route. The diago-

nal effect will nearly always take care of this, but the one who can make the longer carry should have the easier carry shot to a green."

On Building Courses

"In building a golf course there should be beauty, interest and variety as well as a first class test for first class golf, yet a fair test for all who play. There must be variety for general interest. For this reason I am against an endless succession of rolls, bumps and dips.

"I believe each course or each links should have at least four or five greens, well distributed, that are practically flat after the nature of the ground with less artificial build up. One gets extremely tired of putting on nothing but mounded greens with sudden dips and rises to work out. A few of these, when not overdone, are well enough, but there should be variety.

"There should be, also, variety of distances. Some of the best holes at the National are under three hundred and twenty yards. And they are testing holes, too, calling for as much real golf as those over four hundred. Nothing could be more monotonous than a stretch of long holes from four hundred to five hundred yards in length. Three of the first five holes at the National Links are under three hundred yards. There are six holes on the links under three hundred yards, yet I have heard of few who looked upon the National as an easy spot for low scoring.

"Fine short holes and drive-and-pitch holes are nearly always most interesting to play, for skill is a greater factor here than mere physical power. I am also against the two hundred and ten or two hundred and twenty and two hundred and thirty yard type of short hole, except on rare conditions. This type hole is rarely interesting. For short holes I like the range of distances from one hundred and thirty to one hundred and eighty yards, calling for a mashie iron or spoon—depending on the wind—and not a full shot with a driver or brassie.

"I don't believe in pampering any class of golfer, nor yet in forcing average players to attempt impossible strokes with no other outlet. For example the National is hard to score consistently in low figures, yet it is extremely fair and an extremely popular spot for golfers who play between 90 and 105 or 110. For here each player can name his own medicine and take only as much risk or attempt only as long a carry as he thinks he can handle.

"There must be variety, and variety without too much length. How many golfers care about tramping around a 6,700-yard stretch? And what is the need of this when testing courses can be built from 6,100 to 6,300 yards?

"This brings me up to an important point - the number and placement of tees. I believe in at least three sets of tees for every hole, where the idea is practicable. In the first place the direction and the force of the wind can change the entire character of the hole, if there is but one tee to play from. In the second place, with variety of the tees, it is possible to have variety of tests for all classes, to run the distance from 6,000 to 6,400 yards. You can have then a simple course and a hard one, or a moderately hard one as you may select. This is quite an important point, a point that doesn't receive near the attention and consideration it deserves."

These are all valuable suggestions from one of the greatest of all links architects for those planning changes or those planning new courses. Here you will find the answer to the old question as to whether the average golfer prefers a hard course or an easy one. He prefers a fair course that gives him his chance, yet a course that calls for golf. He doesn't want a croquet lawn to play over nor yet to be called on for impossible carries where there are no open ways to play for.

Soon the golf world was buzzing about a revolutionary golf course in America designed by this Macdonald fellow. As friends and visitors the world over came to marvel at it, even Macdonald's worst critics had to concede that his work had broken through to a new level of excellence.

The following is from an article written by Horace Hutchinson that was published in a 1910 issue of *Metropolitan Magazine*:

This National Golf Course of which the world on both sides of the Atlantic has heard a good deal, and of which my friend, Mr. C. B. Macdonald, is the architect. What has been said and what has been written of that course is that it was to make itself a replica and compendium of the best eighteen holes to be found in the whole world of golf. That heroic council and Titanic idea may have animated Mr. Macdonald at one time; and in point of fact, several of the best and most victorious holes on the other side are reproduced here with a faithfulness which is testimony to the scientific care, the labor and the money which have been lavished on it. There is a Redan Hole, an Alps Hole, a Sahara—very reminiscent of the various holes that have these names at North Berwick, at Prestwick, and at Sandwich respectively. There are also two holes representing, respectively, the eleventh hole and the seventeenth hole at St. Andrews. But the larger number, and possibly the best character, have been planned out by the designer's brain with such suggestions as his experience, gathered in Europe, and the natural trend of the ground he had to deal with, supplied to it.

[He continued in part:]

This is a course that is well up to date in all its ideas. It has bunkers guarding the green all carefully placed ... It has its lengths very carefully considered...Variety has been introduced...The diagonal principle on the placing of bunkers through the green has been regarded...Blind shots have been reduced to a minimum...Undulating ground has given opportunity for the introduction of much variety...At one moment we are playing up to a green on a rather perilous terrace; at the next you are driving from a height down toward the plain and the shore of the beautiful Peconic Bay.

"My own opinion of the qualities of this course is so high that I am afraid of stating it too strongly...It has no weak point.

Ben Sayers (1857-1924), the diminutive and much-respected golf professional from the North Berwick Links in Scotland had much to say about the National. His home course contained the original "Redan" as well a "Point Garry," which in some part suggested the National's home hole. After visiting America in 1913 and spending time with Macdonald at the National, he wrote the following review in the July 1913 issue of *Golf Monthly*:

Having traveled and visited all the leading course on this side of the Atlantic, I have stood and sworn by old St. Andrews as the finest course I have ever played on, but after visiting the National course, the links designed by Mr. Macdonald, with touches of St. Andrews, Prestwick, and other British links in it, the famous course of the premier club, in my estimation, must take second place. What a place! And you have got to play the right stuff to get around in a respectable score. The National, in my opinion, is the course of the world. That sounds high praise for a professional who has lived practically all his life at North Berwick and played often at St. Andrews, but I am just saying what I think.

Bernard Darwin also heaped much praise on the course in an article in the September 30, 1910 issue of *The London Times*:

Everyone has heard of the National Golf Links of America, that monument more enduring than brass which Mr. C. B. Macdonald has raised for himself by Shinnecock Hills on Long Island, so that it is with perceptible thrill that one catches one's first glance of the course...How good a course it is I hardly dare trust myself to say on a short acquaintance; there is too much to learn about it and the temptation to frantic enthusiasm is so great, but this much I can say: Those who think it is the greatest golf course in the world may be right or wrong, but certainly not to be accused of any intemperateness

of judgement...If there is one feature *of the course that strikes one more than another it is the constant strain to which the player is subjected to; he is perpetually on the rack, always having to play for the flag itself, never able to say to himself that 'anywhere over the bunker will do.' He is mercilessly harried all the way around from the first tee to the eighteenth hole, and there is not one single hole that can be called dull; one may not think equally highly of all of them, but there are assuredly no obvious lapses from such as the eighth, ninth and tenth holes at St. Andrews. Now and then one fancies that an easy-going hole would be rather a relief...The National Golf Links is truly a great course; even as I write I feel my allegiance to Westward-Ho!, to Hoylake, to St. Andrews tottering to its fall.*

That C.B. Macdonald was focused primarily on the building of his landmark golf course is no surprise. Yet, the club members wanted more than merely a tract of land with a golf course on it.

All of the founders were not as devoted to golf as Macdonald, and joined primarily to have a place for rest, refreshment, and sociability.

Their first home was the old Shinnecock Inn hotel near the current 10th tee. Macdonald's routing and pacing of the course was originally designed with the intention of starting the course on the far end of the property—straight into the teeth of the prevailing wind.

That a clubhouse of suitable elegance was not built immediately can be chalked up to nothing more complicated than a lack of funds. Macdonald spared no expense in building the golf course, and had spent most of the money raised by the founders.

Fortunately for the members who were less than enthusiastic about an aging hotel serving as a clubhouse, their residency at the Shinnecock Inn was short-lived. Soon after the official opening of the course for play, the old hotel burned to the ground.

The club then voted to build a first-class clubhouse on the bluffs overlooking the Great Peconic Bay, turning the project over to Jarvis Hunt—a nationally recognized building architect and founder of the National. The three-story stucco building that stands today was opened in 1912.

At first the only access to the clubhouse was over an old, uncared-for, rough, rutted and sandy road, over which the farmers of the former day had carted seaweed and sedge, when those things were considered valuable. The services of Mr. Seth J. Raynor were again called into requisition and he laid out a beautiful drive, which has been graded and oiled and placed in first class condition and now is ready access to the clubhouse at full speed over one of the best and pleasantest roads in the vicinity. What would those old seaweed haulers say if they should appear some day and see this road and the new, speedy vehicles that are used on it.

Today, reaching the grounds of the National Golf Links is an experience in itself. The approach road bisects the course at the 8th and 11th holes, offering brief glimpses of fairways and greens until you reach the Macdonald Gates. Here, to the rear of the 17th green, the drive up is inboard the 18th fairway—with the blue waters to your right, green fairways to the left, and the imposing clubhouse waiting atop the bluffs overlooking the Atlantic. It is one of golf's most mesmerizing visions.

Above: The original gate and entry to the National Golf Links of America. (George Bahto Collection)

Opposite: Englishman Bernard Darwin is considered by many—including Herbert Warren Wind—to be the greatest golf writer of them all. (*Golf Illustrated*)

Above: Following the completion of the clubhouse, the old wooden gates that marked the entrance to the clubhouse were replaced. After Raynor built a new access road to the club, a new and imposing entranceway was donated by member William K. Vanderbilt. In order to achieve this, the original version of the storied Cape hole was changed from a peninsula green jutting out into the water to the current ninety-degree dogleg hole. (George Bahto Collection)

Below: In 1927 Charles Blair Macdonald wrote his memoirs *Scotland's Gift–Golf*. A well-worn, autographed copy, number "1" is part of the Macdonald memorabilia at his club, the National Golf Links of America. (George Bahto Collection)

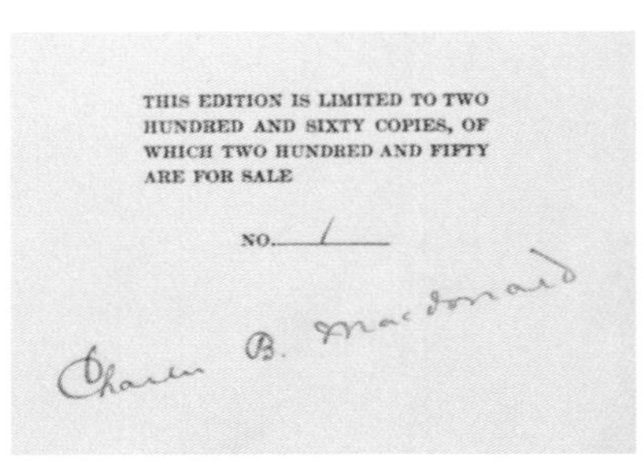

THIS EDITION IS LIMITED TO TWO HUNDRED AND SIXTY COPIES, OF WHICH TWO HUNDRED AND FIFTY ARE FOR SALE

NO. 1

Charles B. Macdonald

The National's Famous Lunch

The traditional lunch at the National is nearly as famous as the course itself. Normally clad in jacket and tie, diners are treated to courses of cold lobster, clam chowder, beef pie or shepherd's pie with veal of beef fillet. All this before dessert of rice cakes in cinnamon or maple syrup.

The Library

The pine-paneled library is replete with bookcases, fireplace, traditional overstuffed leather chairs, and a bronze statue of Macdonald, whose spirit still seems firmly in control of the course, clubhouse, and the members.

Over the fireplace hang three large oil portraits. In the center is Macdonald. On his right is son-in-law Henry Whigham. On his left is his close friend Judge Morgan O'Brien.

In a corner, no longer in use, is the club's telescope. A relic from a bygone era, it was once used by club employees to identify approaching yachts.

Along with Macdonald's golf clubs and various medals from years of competition, is his personal book collection, dating back to the 1800s. The centerpiece is a well-worn version of *Scotland's Gift—Golf*. Macdonald's first-edition personal copy is signed and numbered #1.

The library is, in some measure, a record not only of the history of National Golf Links but also a time line of the early history of golf in America, and Macdonald's seminal role in shaping it. Visitors will find a photo of Macdonald accepting the trophy as first national amateur champion as well as a record of the first Walker Cup matches, where a young Robert Tyre Jones Jr. represented America.

The Collectible Tiles

The peculiar club logo has always aroused curiosity, seemingly incongruous with the traditional tone of the club. A learned historian, when it was time for Macdonald to dream up a lasting symbol for the National Golf Links, he dug deep into the often confusing and esoteric roots of golf.

Figures etched onto early Dutch tiles suggested a game

Henry James Whigham
1869-1954

To describe the legendary Henry Whigham simply as the second national amateur champion and Macdonald's son-in-law does not adequately describe this erudite Renaissance man who wrote and lectured on a variety of subjects.

C.B. had played with Whigham's father while he attended St. Andrews University as a teenager, and knew the younger Whigham from the early days at the Chicago Golf Club.

An Oxford graduate but a Scot by birth, Henry Whigham came to America in 1895 and was hired by the *Chicago Tribune* as a drama critic while also teaching at Chicago's Lake Forest University. A very fine golfer, in 1896 he won the U.S. Amateur and successfully defended it.

A multitalented man, Whigham served for 12 years as war correspondent for the *Tribune* and *American Standard* newspapers —all while assisting Macdonald first at Chicago and later in planning the National. In 1912, he began an illustrious 25-year career as editor-in-chief of both *Town and County* magazine and *Metropolitan* magazine.

In the 1890s, he assisted James and Robert Foulis and H. J. Tweedie in building a course for the Onwentsia Club in Lake Forest, just north of Chicago.

H. J. Whigham was not a course builder. But because of his knowledge of the game and keen understanding of the essential elements of strategic design, he was consulted in the design and construction of a number of courses in the early days of golf.

Aside from his assistance in helping Macdonald at the Chicago Golf Club and the National, he lent his efforts in the planning of Piping Rock, Sleepy Hollow, and the Lido project. At Morris County Country Club in New Jersey, Whigham was also involved when Seth Raynor redesigned that course in 1919-1920.

He was held in such esteem by Macdonald that Henry and Frances Whigham are buried in the same plot with C. B. and his wife.

Judge Morgan O'Brien
1852-1935

O'Brien was Macdonald's closest friend and one of New York's leading citizens. After graduating from Fordham University and Columbia Law School, O'Brien enjoyed an illustrious 50-year career as a member of the New York bar. In 1872, he became the youngest person ever to be appointed to the New York supreme court. He served in that capacity until he retired from public service in 1906. He then became a senior partner in the law firm of O'Brien, Boardman, and Platt in New York City.

O'Brien and his wife Rose lived on Park Avenue with their large Irish family of six girls and four boys. The couple spent much of their time at their estate in Southampton, Long Island, surrounded by their children and grandchildren.

Judge O'Brien was a regular at the National and frequently in the company of Macdonald—either out on the course or holding court in the clubhouse bar. For many years he and C.B. made up the Membership Committee. All nominees had to pass muster under the stern gazes of those two men.

A long-time philanthropist, O'Brien was honored for his good works by both President Coolidge and President Hoover. The judge also served as a board member for several corporations and educational and charitable institutions.

Judge Morgan O'Brien is remembered for his good humor and love for socializing with his many friends. No gathering at the National was complete without him singing his two favorite songs—"A Fine Old Irish Gentleman," and "Never Take the Horseshoe from the Door."

Above: Judge Morgan O'Brien (1852-1935): "A gracious gentleman of the old school." (George Bahto Collection)

Above: Early Macdonald medals from Chicago Golf Club. The earliest date is 1892. (National Golf Links of America)

using sticks and a ball (although it may have been more similar to an early form of hockey). Macdonald had collected these artifacts from the British Isles and became enamored with their crisp symmetry, patterning the club insignia after these so-called Delft tiles. A collection of 41 tiles hangs in the library at the National.

Delft tiles were special fixtures dating back to the sixteenth century and used ornamentally both indoors and out. Delft, named after the Dutch town where they originated, also includes oriental-style decorations, usually in blue or white. It has been suggested that the oriental influence of the designs has its roots in artifacts brought along the Dutch silk trading routes imported originally from Asia.

Macdonald was well aware that these Dutch Delft tiles did not truly depict the game of golf, but rather a winter game played on ice with a post used as a goal. However, the clubs used for this game did, in fact, resemble crude golf clubs. Macdonald purchased the collection of Delft tiles and plates from noted Scottish golfer, Dr. W. Laidlaw Purves, who founded the Royal St. George's Golf Club in Sandwich.

NATIONAL GOLF LINKS OF AMERICA

SOUTHAMPTON NEW YORK

In addition, the collection included some 40 pictures of Dutch golf scenes, some of which hang on a wall in the library of the National Golf Links clubhouse.

The National's logo is not an exact copy of what's on many of the tiles, but one of the figures was adapted with a pair of crossed clubs and two golf balls. Following tradition, a similar set was later used as the insignia of the Links Club.

Official Opening Day Invitational Tournament

On September 11th, 1911, festivities for the official opening of the National's clubhouse included an invitational tournament for a blue-ribbon panel of guests and close friends. In attendance were the following men, many of whom were founders or associate founders of the club:

- Max Behr of Morris County
- William C. Fownes from Oakmont Country Club in Pittsburgh
- Harold Hilton from Royal Liverpool Golf Club, England
- Chick Evans Jr., then from Edgewater Golf Club (Chicago)
- William Watson from Baltusrol Golf Club
- Phillip Carter from Nassau Country Club
- Fred Wheeler from Apawamis Club
- Robertson and Rogers from Shinnecock Hills Golf Club
- Fred Herreshoff from Ekwonok Golf Club
- Joseph Knapp and W. R. Simons from Garden City Golf Club

Fred Herreshoff, who nearly always played the National well, won the qualifying medal with an 84. In the match-play finals, Harold Hilton—at the top of his game and seemingly invincible the last year—defeated Chick Evans 3 and 2.

Hilton had recently won both the British Amateur and U.S. Amateur held at Apawamis, defeating Fred Herreshoff. To the *New York Herald*, Hilton wrote of the National:

> *I had heard so many varied accounts of these links that I really did not know what to believe. Some had told me that I*

would find it merely an unfinished dream of Charlie Macdonald's. Others were loud in its praise and its possibilities. The only thing they seemed to agree on was the fact I would still find it in a very rough condition...I anticipated nothing but iron play through the green. I played there for four days and only once did I get a lie on the fairway to which I do not think it advisable to take a wooden club if required.

Hilton went on to publicly praise the course, its condition, and its routing. "I have seldom come across a course in which greater ingenuity has been exhibited in arranging the holes so that one has an infinite variety of strokes to play...No two holes are in any way alike...In particular I am in love with the short holes...To Charles Blair Macdonald and to those who have helped him in the task I take off my hat. You have accomplished wonders and will eventually have a course in every way worthy of American golf, and just about as good as any in the world."

The Walker Cup

Given the prestige of the club, it is strange that the most noteworthy tournament ever held there was the 1922 Walker International Cup. George H. Walker, retiring from the presidency of the United States Golf Association, presented the trophy and invited the Royal & Ancient to participate in the first international team event against Britain.

The inaugural Walker Cup was played at National, switching the next year to St. Andrews. American clubs hosting subsequent events were Garden City in 1924 and Chicago Golf in 1928. Macdonald had belonged to both.

Legendary golf writer Bernard Darwin, an excellent golfer in his own right, was on site covering the event for the *London Times*. Designated an alternate should one be needed, Darwin was pressed into service when British Team Captain Robert Harris fell ill just before the matches began. In a book of essays titled *Golf Between Two Wars*, he wrote:

In 1921 there was played at Hoylake the first amateur international match between Great Britain and the United States, with disastrous results and a considerable jolt to our (British) complacency. In the following year Mr. George Walker gave his cup, a British team went out to America to play for it, and the series of Walker Cup matches began. It has been a calamitous series for our side, and but for the fact, so infinitely reviving to the spirits, that at least we did win the match at St. Andrews in 1938 I could hardly have endured to write about it. As we did at long last break the spell it is now possible to look back at the nine matches that have been played in a more cheerful frame of mind, admitting the unquestioned superiority of the American side frankly and without excuses but not despairingly, and remembering that however gloomy the aggregate results have been for us, the regular interchange of visits between the amateurs of the two countries has been productive of nothing but friendliness and pleasantness, which is by far the most important thing of all. If it is said, and occasionally with truth, that

Above: Macdonald, always dapper, dressed in plus fours and tie. (*Golf Illustrated*)

international matches do more harm than good, the Walker Cup series can always and with entire truth be cited to the contrary.

I said I would make no excuses but I think I may be allowed to say this much: the Americans had much the better sides but they were not always quite so overwhelmingly superior as the scores seem to show. We never had a chance of winning in the United States but over here we had chances and did not take them. There is no doubt at all that for some years our tails were permanently between our legs and our players seemed incapable of doing themselves justice on the day. They might or might not play their game and they generally did not, while the Americans apparently had the power of rising to the occasion. Too often we began deplorably and by the time the first round of the foursomes were over—we were supposed to be able to play foursomes—our hopes were shattered. Now that Todgers has shown it can do it, I will not say when it chooses, but at least in a long while, it may be permissible to say these things, which would otherwise appear too 'defeatist.' When the match will be played again and what will happen when it does I do not profess to know, but at least we have turned over a new leaf. When once that is done, the old black pages can be re-read without too unbearable pain.

Any account I can give of these matches must be partial and fragmentary, because apart from the first, in which I chanced to play, I have not been present at any of the matches in America, and apart from the briefest references do not propose to tell them second hand. All the matches played here I have seen. I am naturally tempted to say most about the one in which I played. I will try to resist as far as I can, but if I fail, at least it may convey some notion, by analogy, of the other matches, and particularly of the endless kindness and hospitality of American hosts.

Robert Harris (captain), C. J. H. Tolley, R. H. Wethered, J. Caven, C. C. Aylmer, W. B. Torrence, C. V. L. Hooman, Willis Mackenzie; such was the team which sailed from Liverpool on the "Carmania." I went out to describe the match for The Times, *traveled with the side and was to be spare man, if one were wanted. Ernest Holderness, the Amateur Champion, could not come but otherwise it was about as good a team as could be raised. The match was to be played on the National Golf Links at Southampton on Long Island on August 29th and 30th, and we reached New York some considerable time beforehand. Perhaps we got there too soon and stayed too long in New York. I do not suppose that, pleasant as they were, the many good dinners and the excursions to different courses in the neighborhood involving long motor drives and big lunches in blazing weather constituted the perfect preparation. I am very sure, however, that, if we had retired into our shells and gone at once to the National we should have been poor guests and that Mr. C. B. Macdonald would have never forgiven us. Moreover in the end we did quite as well as we could have had any right to expect.*

After these preliminary entertainments and a dash to Philadelphia to see tremendous Pine Valley, we settled down at the National and our golf began to improve, though one or two of us took a long time over it. I will not describe that delightful spot again, it is one of the best and most enchanting of courses, ideal for a match from the player's point of view, but rather too remote for the spectators'. A few days before the match our opponents began to drop in, and they were a truly formidable lot. There are some people who have never lost a match to anyone who took over 69 to a round, and it is human and natural to think our conquerors uncommonly good. Still I must be allowed to say that at least on the evidence of their individual records there has never been such a side as that first American one. Here are their names, written with an awe-stricken pen, and in the order in which they played in the singles: Jesse Guilford, Bobby Jones, Chick Evans, Francis Ouimet, R. Gardner, Jesse

Right: Bobby Jones at National Golf Links 1924. (National Golf Links)

Sweetster, Max Marston, W. C. Fownes. Every single one of the eight has at one time or another won the Amateur Championship of his country; three of them, Ouimet, Evans and Jones, have won the Open; two of them, Jones and Sweetster, have won our Amateur Championship; and one, Jones, our Open. Granted that the extraordinary capacity of Bobby Jones swells the total, it is a record such as I prophesy no other side will ever approach.

We knew all about them and have no very high hopes. At the last moment Robert Harris fell ill; I had to take his place both as a player and captain and was, I fear, a sad encumbrance to Cyril Tolley in the foursomes, though to be sure Ouimet and Guilford played horribly well against us. One foursome, and a very good one, we won; Wethered and Aylmer beat Evans and Gardner 5 and 4. The others we lost. It was a most insufferably hot and steamy day and the ground was wet and heavy after one of those American thunderstorms that does not get it over like a burst of temper but comes sullenly back and back again. It was hard on that noble course and the ball occasionally stuck where it pitched. I remember watching the end of a foursome between Bobby Jones and Sweetster, Torrence and Hooman. On the fifteenth green the end seemed certain, but Bobby's ball though quite close to the hole had stuck firm, and when he tried to dislodge it jumped back briskly and hit him in the foot, thus staving off defeat for us for the length of one hole.

I did not see much of the singles since I had my own match to play and came last on the list. For a long time there was no ray of brightness, for after Tolley had just lost a fine match to Guilford on the thirty-fifth, there followed four more American wins in a row. By that time the whole match was more than over but the last three did a little face-saving. Our hero was Hooman. He played very, very well to beat Sweetster at the thirty-seventh and within a few days Sweetster was destined to win the Amateur Championship at the Country Club, trampling his way through the strongest part of the draw like some all-conquering Juggernaut. Inspired by his example Willie Mackenzie and I managed to win too, he by a considerable and most meritorious margin, I more modestly at the thirty-fifth. This was certainly a curious circumstance for Willis will not, I think, resent the statement that neither he nor I could or had hit a ball before the match. However we made the score sheet look a little prettier.

One odd little fact shows with what a pleasant casualness that first match was played. Nobody had considered what was to be done in case of a halved match. When Sweetster and Hooman halved, the two captains, Fownes and I, were away in the dim distance; so Fritz Byers, as President of the U.S.G.A., sent them off to the thirty-seventh, which Hooman won in a sparkling three. Since then more humane counsels have prevailed and heaven knows that when two men have halved a 36-hole match in the Walker Cup, they have earned an immediate drink with no further demands on them. It was a point which I made clear to Bill Fownes when I was two up on the thirty-fifth teeing ground.

The First Professional Tournament at the National

Six years after hosting the Walker Cup, Macdonald became interested in how his golf links would hold up against the top professionals. He created a 72-hole stroke-play invitational, held in October of 1928 for a total purse of $3,500.

The professionals arrived, and on a clear and windy day Macdonald got the answer he had hoped for as his golf course bared its teeth. A sampling of the participants, their recent victories, and their 72-hole scores:

Player	R1	R2	R3	R4	Total
Tommy Armour	75	73	77	77	302
1927 U.S. Open Champion					
Joe Kirkwood	73	80	74	76	303
Jack Burke	78	74	77	75	304
Bob Cruickshank	76	73	80	75	304
Johnny Farrell	74	73	81	86	314
1928 U.S. Open Champion					
Bill Mehlhorn	80	72	79	78	309
Gene Sarazen	78	74	77	81	310
1922 U.S. Open Champion					
Walter Hagen	79	80	75	78	312
1928 British Open Champion					
Craig Wood	78	79	78	79	314
Joe Turnesa	80	79	74	81	314
Harry Cooper	80	80	74	81	315
Jock Hutchinson	76	78	80	83	317
Alick Girard	84	87	NC	NC	

Others on hand were Cyril Walker, 1924 U.S. Open Champion; and Willie MacFarlane, 1925 U.S. Open Champion. Despite boasting some of the top players in the nation, the field averaged 78.925 strokes per round!

A noted author and contributing editor of *Golf Illustrated* stated:

> *"It may be said of the National Links that its building caused the reconstruction of all the best known golf courses which existed in the first decade of the century in the United States and caused the study of golf architecture which resulted in the building of so many meritorious courses in recent years."*

PLAYING *the* BALL *as* IT LIES

AN AMUSING INCIDENT that became part of the club's folklore involved a high-powered foursome consisting of John Cleveland (Chairman of the Board of Guaranty Trust), W. Alton Jones (President of City Services), Niles Trammel (Chairman of the Board of NBC) and Charles Stewart (New York Trust).

While playing the 18th hole in a club event, Trammel, an 18 handicapper, badly pulled his third shot from a fairway bunker onto the roof of the clubhouse. Unfazed by the laughter of his playing companions, Niles took a niblick from his caddie and strode into the clubhouse. Climbing the stairs to the second floor, he inadvertently walked into an occupied bedroom. He apologized, then climbed out one of the windows onto the roof.

A first swipe with the short iron was not successful; the ball was lodged in a gutter. Niles took another mighty swing and managed to extract the ball back toward the fairway.

Once again apologizing to the bedroom's occupants, he left the way he had come, finished playing the hole and holed out for an 11. Word of Niles Trammel's escapades soon made the New York City papers. Incidentally, he finished 3rd for the day's event.

FINDLAY S. DOUGLAS
1874–1959

BORN IN ST. ANDREWS in 1874, Findlay Douglas was a pupil of Madras College and a student at St. Andrews University. Before immigrating to the United States in 1897, he captained the university golf team in 1895-96.

Newly arrived in America, Findlay Douglas captured the United States Amateur Championship in 1898, beginning a distinguished career in American golf spanning five decades.

A founding member of the National Golf Links of America, his father was a frequent golfing companion of C.B. Macdonald in the 1870s when C.B. himself was a student at St. Andrews.

As a prominent businessman and noted ambassador to golf, Findlay Douglas was honored as a member of the Royal and Ancient in 1920. He went on to serve with distinction as president of the New York Metropolitan Golf Association (1922-24) before being elected vice-president of the USGA in 1926. Douglas went on to become the USGA president between 1929 and 1930.

In the latter capacity, he presented Robert Tyre (Bobby) Jones Jr. with the United States Open and Amateur trophies in 1930, the year Jones also won the Open and Amateur titles in Britain.

Findlay S. Douglas died in New York City in 1959 at the age of 84. He left no surviving relatives, and his ashes were eventually interred in the Eastern Cemetery in St. Andrews.

Ironically, a few months before his death, Findlay Douglas was presented with the Bobby Jones Award for Distinguished Service to Golf.

Photo courtesy *Golf Illustrated*

Devereux Emmet
1861–1934

Devereux Emmet was a noted aristocrat, huntsman, and golfer who eventually turned his course design hobby into an occupation. Born into a prominent New York family whose name is listed in Ward McAlister's First Fifty Families in America, Emmet was a man of leisure who regularly trained hunting dogs in the summer, sold them in Ireland in the fall, and spent the winter golfing and hunting in the British Isles.

It was on these yearly visits that he had the opportunity to play and study the greatest courses of Britain. At the time (with the exception of C.B. Macdonald), there were few Americans who understood the game well enough to lay out a functional course. In 1899, Emmet designed a short nine-holer on Long Island known as Island Golf Links, which he soon remodeled and expanded to 18 holes. The new course was formalized into a club and renamed the Garden City Golf Club.

No doubt influenced by Macdonald's Chicago Golf Club (1892), the Island Golf Links course differed greatly from the overly-penal designs scattered about the country. Though crude by comparison to what was to follow, this remarkable first attempt earned high praise for its natural feel and varied routing that took full advantage of the shifting breezes.

In 1900 Charles Blair Macdonald moved east from Chicago and became an influential—and controversial—member of the Garden City Golf Club. Macdonald and Emmet soon became close friends and during the planning stages of the National Golf Links of America, Devereux spent a winter in the British Isles measuring holes and documenting designs for Macdonald. He later asked Emmet to assist in the design of National with his son-in-law H. J. Whigham. Emmet eventually became a founding member of National Golf Links.

Garden City Golf Club counted as one of its prominent members the great amateur player Walter J. Travis. It was Travis who in a 1906 magazine article analyzed the deficiencies of Emmet's design at Garden City and suggested some improvements. The club eventually took heed to his writings, and undertook a remodeling of the greens and rebunkering of the course. A combination of the talents of these two men produced what is widely held to be one of the finest golf courses in America.

Garden City was constructed on an enormous loam deposit atop a base of gravel and sand—an ideal situation for growing fine turf. Though Emmet managed to build the course for less than $2,000, cementing his reputation as a fine course builder, it nearly contributed to his downfall.

Despite the fact Devereux Emmet went on to build such notable courses as Congressional C.C., Leatherstocking and Wee Burn in Connecticut, he never again was able to recreate the quality of Garden City so inexpensively.

Emmet and his son joined with architect Alfred Tull in 1929 to form the firm Emmet, Emmet & Tull. In reality, Emmet's son did little or no actual work for the firm, and following the death of Devereux in 1934, Alfred Tull continued on his own.

Photo courtesy *Golf Illustrated*

The National Golf Links—hole by hole

Hole #1

VALLEY

310 | 300 | 290 yards (circa 1920)

Par 4

Original yardage: 315

Present yardage: 322

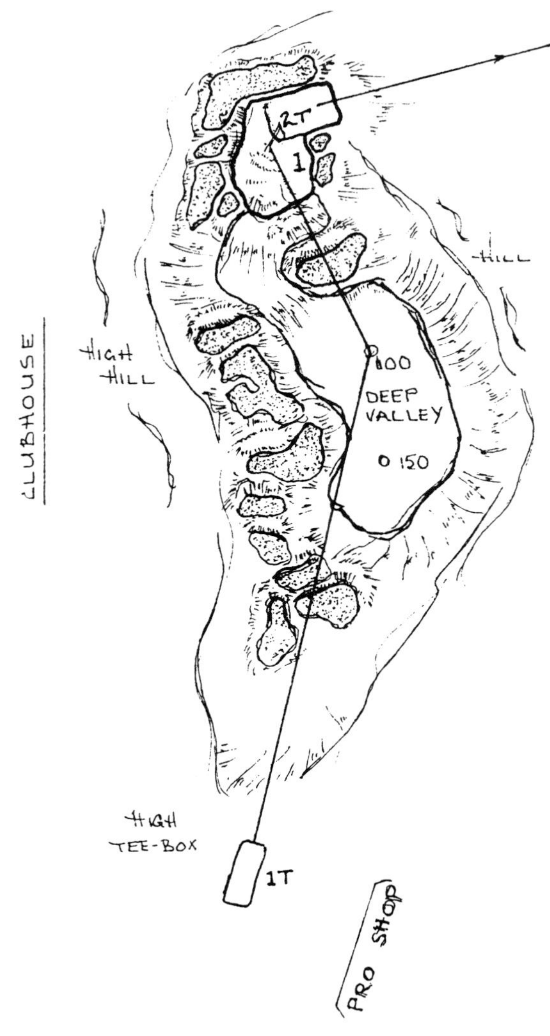

Standing on the first tee at National Golf Links, most first-time players are taken aback by its rather short yardage—a mere 310 yards. Looking toward the green beyond the valley below, a shot directly for the green is an inviting prospect from this lofty perch of a tee box. The fairway lies in a natural depression, 30 degrees to the line of play and sloping upward to the surrounding sand hills on all sides. The "Valley" is an elongated bowl that feeds slightly sprayed tee-balls safely inward before rising steeply to the putting surface.

The built-in temptation, or course, is to fire your tee ball directly at the green just over 300 yards away. The elevated tee deceptively foreshortens the perspective, giving the golfer a false sense of the true distance. It is a theme that Macdonald returns to again and again from the very first shot to the last—tempting the ego of the golfer.

A direct line to the green requires a substantial drive over a series of some dozen bunkers and sand mounds, set into the left hillside along the fairway from 175 to 245 yards. Macdonald deliberately hid one bunker, lurking just beyond what appears to be the last of the hazards, specifically located to catch the tee balls of long hitters who dare to be too close to the left.

The temptation to play straight to the green is strong, but a bit foolhardy even with a helping wind. The safer play, of course, is a bit to the left of center, leaving a wedge to the green. However, the farther right your choice of line from the tee, the more troublesome and blind the approach becomes. Macdonald arranged a couple of small mounds—cunningly positioned just before the green in the right fringe—that must be carried. One tick too timid on the approach and your ball will likely carom right or left off the green into trouble. There are severe falloffs left and right into deep bunkers. The putting surface is partially hidden from the fairway, so judging the second shot on this short opening hole is a bit trickier than it appears. Following tradition, there are no yardage markers at the National.

The green, with its daring and complex undulations, is the heart of the hole and one of Macdonald's most intricate. From the fairway, it resembles nothing so much as a large turtle sitting atop the crest of a sand hill. The putting surface measures a shade over 6,000 square feet and is contoured with a myriad of elaborate undulations surround-

ing a large mounded area through the right-middle portion of the putting surface. All sides slope away from the center, some sharply, so golfers should not be too aggressive in putting or on approach. Putts struck with a tad too much bravado can easily wander off the front of the green or into the deep bunkers that flank the sides. There is little, if any, fringe to hold the ball on the green.

The restoration at the National in recent years by Karl Olson and green chairman David Mullen is an attempt to take the course back to a period in the middle 1920s, about the time the International Matches (the original Walker Cup) were held at the National. This ongoing restoration process is at times slow and tedious. Macdonald made many changes in the course, so it is often difficult to determine if a newly rediscovered fairway bunker, for example, is the correct one for the time or one that Macdonald discarded. The key to the restoration process is the enlargement of the putting greens and the short cropped fringe areas around them. The overall effect is intended to reinitiate a "ground game" at the National where possible. This is very difficult to accomplish in this day of lush fairways and greens. In Charlie Macdonald's era, he insisted his superintendents keep the fairways and greens hard, in spite of much objection by the membership. He fully understood the ground-game, especially on a links course where the wind is such an important factor.

Above: Although the golfer is tempted to play down the left side, that play is fraught with danger. (National Golf Links of America)

J. Peter Grace, of Grace Steamship Lines fame, Charles Macdonald's grandson, was considerably more interested in polo than he was in golf, but occasionally played with his famous grandfather. Peter loved to tease his grandfather Charlie, usually about his golf course and knowing full well it was sure to get a rise out of him. Macdonald believed he had the greatest course in the world and Peter knew any reference to the contrary would have Charlie steaming. Peter Grace had been somewhat critical of portions of the layout, singling out the short first hole as a prime example. He openly scoffed at the hole's quality, claiming it far too short.

As is common with golfers, arguments about the virtue of a given hole or course design is bound to get lively. We can be sure any discussion with Macdonald about golf in general would have been contentious, but criticism of his course, right there in the clubhouse, must have been downright exciting.

One evening at the club, Grace persisted in taunting Macdonald about first hole, loudly boasting that he could drive it. Of course Charlie vehemently disagreed—"The feat is impossible" bellowed Macdonald. A heated argument ensued and a bet was offered: Peter would attempt to drive the green. The two walked to the first tee with three balls and a driver. The wager would be for $20 (a pretty paltry sum for a couple of rich guys). With a slight tailwind, Peter's third attempt just barely crossed the fringe onto the green. Charles Blair Macdonald was livid with rage. Grace's gleeful request for payment of the wager landed on deaf ears—Macdonald was steaming—he ignored the issue. Peter Grace continued to gloat and insisted loudly in the clubhouse before some members that the lost bet be paid. Finally, an infuriated Macdonald threw the money at his feet and stormed from the clubhouse. The next morning, he promptly phoned his attorney and had Peter removed from his will.

Peter Grace, winner of the $20 bet, lost an estimated $4 million dollars of inheritance. It was an expensive golf shot, but let us not feel too sorry for him. The heir to the Grace Shipping Lines fortune had more money than his grandfather.

In speaking with people who played the course prior to the installation of a modern irrigation system, they often recall the firm surfaces and dormant grasses during the summer months. It is a different course in those conditions.

It is difficult to imagine playing out of the Valley under original conditions. Even with today's technologically advanced equipment, it is difficult to hold a ball on the first green. Imagine playing the shot with a smooth-faced niblick.

Looking back toward the tee, the thought that was put into the opening hole is remarkable: the cluster of bunkers nesting along the hill, the bunkering propped up on the front left of the green, and the little rejection mounds. This brilliant arrangement of hazards and strategic options is a prime example of how tasteful and sophisticated a short par 4 can be. Weighted with abundant variety, Macdonald's opening salvo is an architectural masterpiece.

<u>Hole #2</u>

SAHARA

262 | 252 | 228 yards (circa 1920)

Par 4

Original yardage: 262

Present yardage: 330

The strategy of the second hole at the National, though not a replica, is that of the original Sahara, the 3rd hole at Royal St. George's at Sandwich, England. Bernard Darwin eloquently described the original:

> *When a name clings to a hole we may be sure there is something in that hole to stir the pulse, and in fact there are few more absolute joys than a perfectly hit shot that carries the heaving waste of sand which confronts us on the third tee (Royal St. George). The shot is a blind one, and we have not the supreme felicity of seeing the ball pitch and run down into the valley to nestle by the flag (the original hole was a par three). We see it for a long time, however, soaring and swooping over the desert, and, when it finally disappears, we have a shrewd notion as to its fate. If the wind is fresh against us we must play away to the right for safety, and the glorious enjoyment of the hole is gone, but even so a good shot will be repaid, and every yard that we can go to the left may make the difference between a difficult and an easy second.*

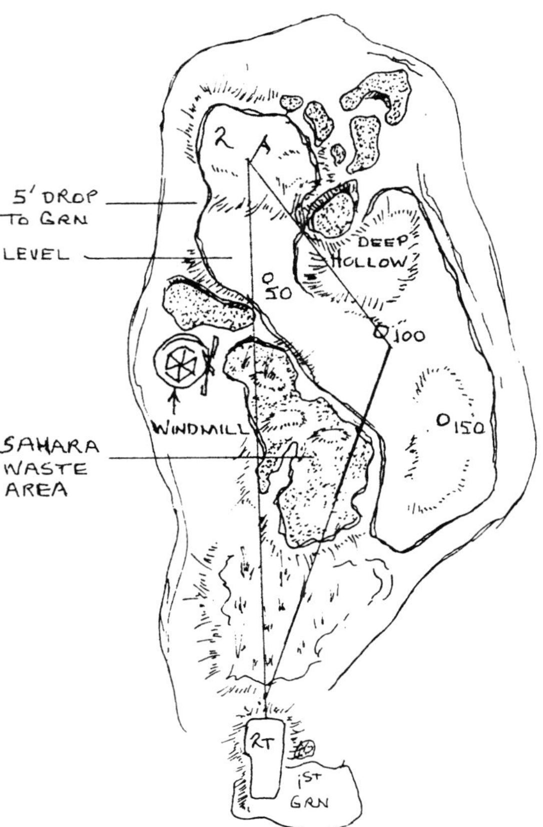

At Royal St. George, the original hole was a shortish, blind par 3 over a huge nondescript sandy waste area. That hole fell victim to the ball change when the gutty was replaced by the Haskell. It was changed in 1975 when Frank Pennick turned it into a middle-to-long-iron play of 214 yards.

At the National, the Sahara was originally built at 261 yards (1996 yardage: 330). Like the first hole, it appears to be a fairly simple 4 on the card. Charles Blair Macdonald did not design simple holes. Ever. A look the scorecard is deceptive; one would think that the hole can be driven by a long hitter. The risks of an attempt, though, are totally out of proportion to the reward.

Sahara's green is blind to the golfer from the tee box. A third of an acre of sand hills and bunkering—a total waste area—tempts the player to drive over its right-to-left, echelon carry. Choosing the line is a matter of feel and experience. The left side is similar in strategy to the first, where you are faced with a taxing carry along the left side if you forge directly toward the center of the green. The hidden landing area is disturbing and provokes many players to involuntarily bail out to the right. Extreme cowardice at the last moment with a driver usually proves disastrous—well-struck balls to the right of the centerline invariably end up at the bottom of a deep grassy basin in the fairway, leaving a blind shot at the green from an awkward angle.

Players must pick a specific line from the tee and carefully choose the proper club. The further right (and safer) the intended line, the shorter the club to the narrow landing area.

The main bunker complex on the hill, for which the hole is named, runs diagonally, right to left. A carry of just over 200 yards was required when originally built by Macdonald, but in recent years the length has been adjusted for more modern equipment by simply extending the tee. Unlike many clumsy attempts to "restore" holes by modifying hazards, National's Sahara illustrates that often the simplest solutions prove to be the best. The regular tee still retains its original feel of simply being an extension of the 1st green—a representation of the traditional architecture of St. Andrews. The "Olson Tee," a championship tee-box named after its creator, has been added on slightly different sight lines on a narrow promontory behind the original tee.

The key is the tee shot and the player's intimidation level, which under adverse weather conditions has a tendency to escalate. Avoiding the Sahara bunker is crucial. Like at the first hole, there is an additional pot bunker just beyond where the main complex of bunkers appears to end. This often catches the golfer who is hoping to overpower the hole. To fire over the waste area requires courage to avoid the basin, though if you frankly choose to lay up you must carefully select where to land the ball. For today's player, clumps of love grass have been planted in the hazard to help define target lines. It is doubtful, however, that Macdonald would approve.

By 1988, the Sahara green at National had shrunk to 8,700 square feet. Careful study of the original maps and photos led to the green and surrounding area being reexpanded to 12,500 square feet. The undulations are moderate and subtle; the green readily accepts a crisply struck approach. However, there are sharp falloffs to the left, right, and rear waiting patiently to penalize an overaggressive short-iron.

In an article that he wrote (with amateur champion H.J. Whigham) for the May 1914 issue of *Golf Illustrated*, Macdonald perfectly summed up the hole:

> *"The second hole at the National Links is called the Sahara, because it carries out the principle of the Sahara or*

Above: Hole 2: A blind shot over a sandy wasteland—perhaps the most confusing tee-shot at the National for the first-time player. (National Golf Links of America)

Right: Sahara at the National Golf Links—a line drawing by Franklin Booth from an article written by H. J. Whigham—"The Ideal Golf Course." (*Town & Country Magazine)*

third hole at Sandwich. Otherwise the name is a trifle misleading. For whereas at Sandwich a sandy waste stretches in front of the tee for a distance of nearly two hundred yards, at the National the chief bunker is more circumscribed, and therefore less reminiscent of the African desert. But the principle in both cases is the same; and is the basic principle of all the best full-drive holes. The distance from the middle tee to the middle of the putting green is about 270 yards. The large bunker is so placed that a ball played straight on the flag must carry about 185 yards. The edge of the bunker runs diagonally so that the extreme right is only 118 yards from the middle of the tee; the small pot bunker which is at the extreme left of the main hazard and is just a little to the left of the straight line to the hole is 200 yards from the middle of the tee.

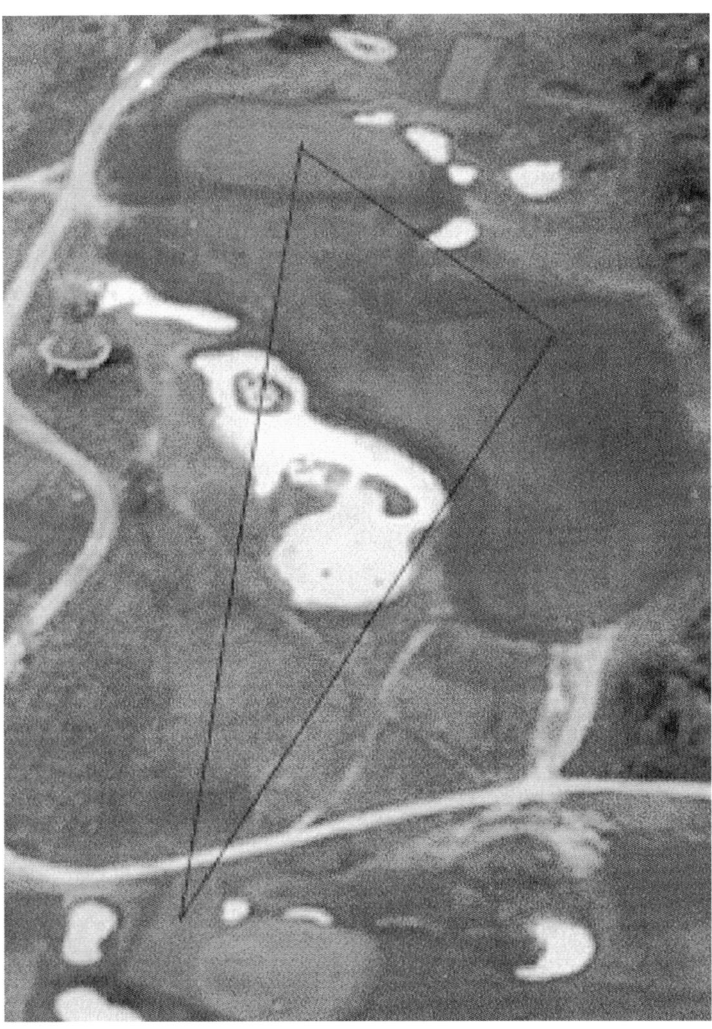

When the player steps to the tee therefore he has a choice of carries from 148 yards to 200 yards. If he wants to be absolutely sure of avoiding all hazards he must carry 200 yards; if he plays perfectly straight on the flag he must carry at least 185 yards; if he cannot do that he can take a shorter carry by aiming more to the right, and then if he puts a little hook on his ball he can still reach the green; if that shot is beyond him he can make a safe carry to the right of about 150 yards and leave himself a short but rather difficult approach from the hollow to the right of the green. All these carries at the National are uphill so that they really represent a little more than the actual figures would seem to indicate.

The short player who cannot even carry 150 yards must avoid the waste area altogether by aiming to the right. He has a perfectly open fair green there, but he cannot reach the brow of the hill and is left with a blind and extremely difficult second. The principle of the hole is to give the player on the tee a great number of alternatives according to his strength and courage. If he plays for the green and succeeds he has an advantage of at least one stroke over the opponent who takes a shorter carry to the right, and probably more than one stroke over the player who avoids the carry altogether. But if he fails he is bunkered and may easily take a five or six and lose to the short player who goes round."

Blind tee shots have fallen out of vogue, so a hole of this type is bound to be controversial. It is uncomfortable to many players, yet it is old-style and traditional, and Macdonald's creation is a museum piece of traditional golf. Sahara has a charm of its own—not easily duplicated. In earlier days the blind shot was the rage, and most great British courses had a few. Although Macdonald often strongly opposed blindness, he never let go of his fondness for both the Sahara and Alps holes. Though Macdonald and Seth Raynor continued to produce Alps holes after constructing the National, this was to be the first and last rendition of the classic Sahara they ever built.

Left: Aerial photo of the second hole at the National. (George Bahto Collection)

Hole #3

ALPS

418 | 398 | 357 yards (circa 1920)

Par 4

Original yardage: 376

Present yardage: 426

How a golfer feels about the relative merits of the Alps hole speaks volumes not only about personal tastes, but ultimately how he views the game itself. Stern, no-nonsense types who desire a challenge to be frankly spelled out with no element of chance are likely to hate this hole. However, for the adventurous types, who have not forgotten that golf is a whimsical and sometimes beguiling game, this might be the most entertaining hole at the National.

The hole deliberately confuses from the outset, confronting the player with a minefield of bunkers in the wide landing area, and with a wooden bell tower poking out atop an enormous hillside in the distance. Players who successfully finish the hole give a satisfying clang to signify the green is clear, and the challenge has been met.

But what to do? The shorter hitter must first negotiate the diagonal cross-bunker standing sentinel at the gates of the landing area; the longer hitter must carefully choose a line of play and stick to it. Placing the tee shot near the base of the towering sand hill is the first order of business—a base camp from which to regroup before the final charge up the steep and fiercely defended hillside There is a narrow ribbon of fairway to the right, placed perhaps to give weaker players an alley to hit their second shots, or to tempt the bold driver looking to shorten the approach. The crack player who declines the longer carry to the right over the cross-bunker, and fearfully pulls his drive, will find two deep pot bunkers patrolling the bailout area. Macdonald, always in character, leaves no direct route or correct answer. Only choices.

The origin of the National's Alps is the 17th at Prestwick Golf Club in Ayrshire, Scotland. Not only is the green blind to the second shot, but the huge, deep cross-bunker guarding the front of the green is also hidden from view. The fascination with the Alps hole is the unknown result of the shot over the high hill. Will it be long or short? Will it be found in the front bunker, or will it be found at all? Yet, hope springs eternal in the game of golf. Regardless of yesterday, today is a new day and we are forever convinced that this time, our ball is destined to sit proudly upon the green.

Macdonald's distinctive style often synthesized two classic holes into one; National's Alps actually combine a rendition of Prestwick's 17th with a punchbowl green in a hollow. This "catcher's mitt" motif was a favorite of Macdonald and Raynor, and it was often used more than once on the same golf course. Frequently, like at the National, they contoured a ridge through the putting surface to further segment the sizeable green. Good shots are rewarded by the ball feeding toward the center of the green. The contrary problem is that

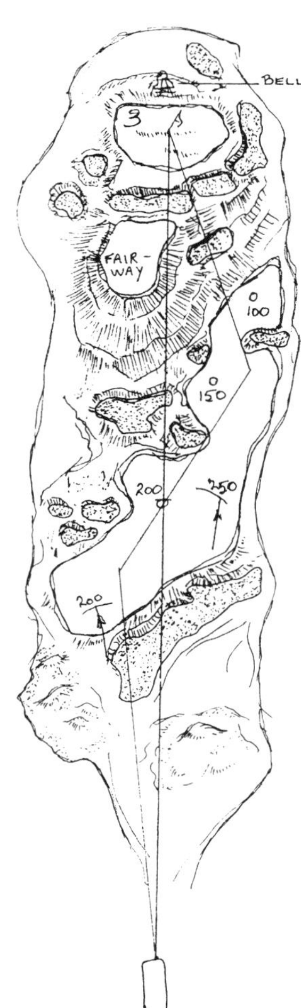

a stray shot is punished with a downhill chip. Although the necessary topography was often not available, this ingenious combination was sometimes simulated with an abrupt rise in the fairway followed by a steep drop-off at its crest to a punchbowl.

Worthy of special note and discussion is the cross-bunker fronting the green, an essential ingredient in the original. Many people quarrel with the fairness of pinpointing a bunker just short of the ideal landing area, and yet it is this element of luck that provides the hole with much of its thrill. Sadly, at many of Raynor and Macdonald's courses, this "Alps bunker" was often filled in by green committees unable to comprehend the design's fascination. Happily, years later under the direction of more knowledgeable committees and superintendents, the bunkers are often restored to their rightful place on the hole.

Again we turn to the eloquence of the great Bernard Darwin for a description of the Alps at Prestwick Golf Club. The following is from his 1910 book, *The Golf Courses of the British Isles*:

> *The 'Alps,' one of the finest holes anywhere, and the finest blind hole in golf. The drive must be hit straight and true down in a valley between two hills, and then comes the second, over a vast grassy hill, beyond which we know there is a bunker both deep and wide. The ball may clear the hill and yet meet with a dreadful fate, but there is a glorious compensation in the fact that if we do clear the chasm we should finally be near the hole and may possibly be putting for a three... Old Willie Park wrecked his chances of yet another [British Open] Championship in 1861, owing to a daring attempt to cross the Alps in two, which brought his ball into one of the worst hazards of the green, and cost him three strokes... Truly the 'Alps' is a hole with a great history.*

With the exception of daring modern-era artists like Pete Dye, classic blind holes like the Alps have gone the way of persimmon woods. With the explosion in golf's popularity, fewer and fewer players appreciate the sporting challenge of these wonderful museum pieces, and we are poorer for it. This element of chance is one of the essentials that draws us to the game and hastens our coming back for

Above left: Looking back toward the 3rd tee. Note the alternative route along the left for those golfers to hit it over the Alps mountain. On top of the hill is a small landing area that's blind from the fairway and short of the cross-bunker that's in front of the green. (George Bahto Collection)

Above right: From the original "Alps" the view of the famous undulating green of Prestwick's 17th as well as the infamous, sleeper-faced cross-bunker that must be carried on the approach. It's been the scene of many disasters. (*Golf Illustrated*)

Opposite: View from the tee of the 3rd at the National. (George Bahto Collection)

more. It is a shame that so few architects have the courage to dust off this classic piece of history and display it for new generations to enjoy.

A long tee shot played directly on the flag or anywhere to the left leaves the ball at the foot of the Alps hill. The second shot is then extremely difficult, for the ball must be raised abruptly yet still have a long flight. The best line is to the right, where the hill slopes down to the level, making the next shot much easier. But to reach the landing area, a long carry must be taken from the tee.

> *Therefore although the Prestwick tee-shot has to be placed rather more exactly, the National tee-shot is more spectacular. And at the National the second shot is more difficult on account of the extra length and the higher position of the green. In other words the third hole at the National is an improved Alps, and as a test of golf it is beyond reproach. It is impossible to reach the green in two unless both the tee-shot and the second are real big golfing strokes, hit in the middle of the club, and that can be said of very few holes with a maximum distance of only 413 yards ... But there is also another reason why the second shot at the Alps is such a good one, and that is because to make sure of getting on to the green and staying there the player must make a high shot with a long carry and very little run which is perhaps the most golfer-like stroke in the game.*
>
> *—Country Life Magazine*

Hole #4

REDAN

185 | 172 | 143 yards (circa 1920)

Par 3

Original yardage: 185

Present yardage: 195

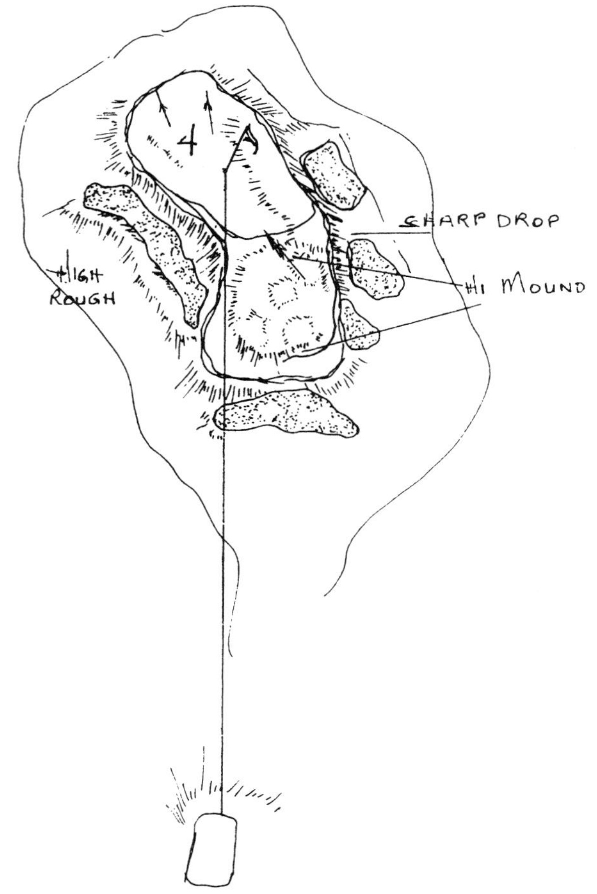

Of all the pure strategies in golf course design, the Redan hole is perhaps the finest. Much in golf has changed since Davie Strath created the original Redan while serving as Keeper of the Green at North Berwick (1876-1879), yet no hole has better stood the test of time in its purest form than this monument to strategic genius. Located on a windswept corner of East Lothian, Scotland, the hole's name was taken from the famous redoubt the British troops unsuccessfully stormed during the Crimean War in 1885.

More importantly, the design demonstrates the virtue of strategic architecture so well that it has become the single most emulated green complex in golf. To many who have been ensnared in its bunkers, the Redan is the most complex par 3 in the British Isles. Other golf architects recognize the value of the design, and not only copy the original but utilize its timeless concept on par 4s and 5s as well.

The Redan demands a thorough reevaluation of how best to attack its defenses with every shift of the wind—and seldom is there complete agreement as to the most effective route. Unless the circumstances are just right, a direct frontal assault will be cruelly dispatched to the deep bunkers that surround and defend the fortress. So what is the secret?

Historically, most players prior to the advent of the Haskell were unable to carry a ball the distance required at North Berwick. Often the best approach, then and now, was to utilize the front-right contour to funnel the ball onto the green between the hazards. The shot must be crisp and true, however, for an indifferent offering will be shouldered away through the green into deep sand pits. A dangerous approach? Indeed. In fact, there is little about the Redan that is not dangerous.

Another alternative was to play the ball short of the Redan bunker, hoping for steady nerves on the difficult pitch. The timid are not spared, either. Approaches that are left short and right are dealt a slippery downhill chip into the throat of the green with little hope of stopping the ball—the putting surface falls off 6 feet from right to left.

Although the Redan retains its complexities despite equipment advances, confronting an equivalent challenge in the era of the gutty would require a hole of at least 230 yards today. The option of laying up the tee shot no longer exists; like at the Road hole at St. Andrews, players feel compelled to ignore the risks and fire for the green.

On the more accurate renditions of this genre, the putting surface of a Redan is not visible from the tee-box—just a suggestion of the green barely visible along its front ridge. Many golfers, unaware of the Redan`s design concept, label the hole "unfair" or "too difficult." Over the years some ver-

sions were modified in length, usually to make the hole easier to play. The complaint was often that balls were too easily rejected to the rear and off the green. Club members who never bothered to decipher its mysteries would whine that the front Redan bunker was overly penal and demanded that it be softened or removed altogether. However, once the genius of the hole was comprehended and its place in history acknowledged, the Redan suddenly becomes a favorite hole. Members can then be heard espousing its virtues and origins to their friends and guests—a hole they hated not long before.

National television exposure during the U.S. Open at Shinnecock Hills in 1995 gave the Seth Raynor-built Redan on that course considerable recognition. America watched the world's touring professionals struggling mightily to comprehend a hole they simply could not overpower. Well over a third of the tee balls of the world's greatest players rolled into the front bunker, or kicked off the back of the green. It was a fitting tribute to the original concept.

Above: Redan at the National. (*Golf Illustrated*)

Below: An aerial photo of the green complex of the 4th at National. (Karl Olson)

Comparisons can be misleading, but the fact remains that while visiting America, Ben Sayers, North Berwick's resident professional, was moved to state unequivocally that the National Golf Links version was better than the original—a shocking admission, considering the source.

Here, Macdonald and Whigham explore the Redan's many options in their own words:

Take a narrow tableland, tilt it a little from right to left, dig a deep bunker on the front side, approach it diagonally, and you have a Redan. At North Berwick, of course, all these things were done in the beginning by nature. The only original thing that the greenskeeper (Strath) did was to place the tee so that the shot had to be played cornerwise, instead of directly down the tableland...The tableland is long and narrow, sloping from right to left, there is a deep bunker in front and a smaller bunker at the back. It would be almost impossible to drop the ball on the green near the flag and keep it there if the green were not banked a little beyond the hole. The distance is 180 yards from the center of the tee. With a head wind of one coming a little from the left a wooden club may be used and the shot played straight at the flag, for then the ball will drop dead on the green. But it is a long carry over the deep bunker in the face of the green; and because the direction is diagonal the carry gets longer to the left, so that the least bit of a pull will put the ball into the bunker. With no wind at all the same kind of shot can be played with a mid-iron; but it must be a high shot that will drop dead, the most difficult shot in golf. With the wind behind, the direct attack becomes impossible; and then the player must aim for the right of the green where he does not have to carry the deep bunker in the face. The ball landing on the high end of the tabletop will break to the left and be kept going more to the left by the fact that the green is banked like a circular bicycle track; and so a shot played twenty yards or more to the right of the hole may end up within a foot of the flag. But it has to be played just right. The least bit of a

Above: The Redan today, the famous fourth hole at the National. (George Bahto Collection)

pull will take it into the bunker in front of the green, and the least bit of a slice will prevent it getting the break to the left and will carry it into the bunker beyond the green. With a strong wind behind the hole is still more difficult; for it must then be played with a lofted club, or else with a running shot which must carry a large bunker to the right which as a rule, hardly enters into one's calculations, and get pulled up on the side of the tableland. Either shot admits of all kinds of error.

In the same article, they go on to explain that the essential ingredient of the Redan is the tilt of the tableland—the green itself. When he routed the National, the Redan green site was said to have been completely natural. The construction crew only dug out the front left bunker and set the tee-box position.

The National's Redan is rather more difficult than the North Berwick hole, because the bunker at the back of the green is much deeper and more severe. Some people think the hole is too difficult altogether. But anyone who gets a legitimate three there, especially in a medal round, is sure to say that it is the finest short hole in the world. There is no compromise about it. Whichever of the various methods of attack is chosen, the stroke must be bold, cleanly hit and deadly accurate. At the ordinary hole of 180 yards it is a very bad shot that does not stay on the green. At the Redan it takes a exceedingly good shot to stay anywhere on the green; and to get a putt for a two is something to brag about for a week.

By 1914, when they wrote the article, there were only a few Redan holes in America. Macdonald termed Seth Raynor's version at Piping Rock "simplified." At Sleepy Hollow Macdonald and Raynor built their first "reverse Redan." There was also one at the Hugh Wilson-designed Merion Cricket Club. Wilson wrote an article on turfgrass in December of 1916. When writing of his construction of the Merion Club, he made an interesting reference to Charles Macdonald:

Our ideals were high and fortunately we did get a good start in the correct principles of laying out the holes, through the kindness of Messrs. C. B. Macdonald and H. J. Whigham. We spent two days with Mr. Macdonald at his bungalow near the National Course and in one night absorbed more ideas on golf course construction that we had learned in all the years we had played. Through sketches and explanations of the right principles of the holes that formed courses abroad and had stood the test of time, we learned what was right and what we could use. May I suggest to any committee about to build a new course, or to alter their old one, that they spend as much time as possible on courses such as National and Pine Valley, where they may see the finest type holes and, while they cannot hope to reproduce them in entirety, they can learn the correct principles and adapt them to their own course.

Shortly after, George Crump constructed a hole that Macdonald described as "a beautiful short hole with the Redan principle on the new Philadelphia course at Pine Valley." It was Pine Valley's 3rd.

The great 2nd hole at the Walter Travis-designed Garden City Golf Club, with its "Bottomless Pit" front-left bunker complex, has Redan bunkering and length but lacks the severe tilt of the green. George C. Thomas Jr., having observed Wilson, Crump, and William Flynn, took the Redan to the West coast and used it for the 4th hole at the Riviera Country Club.

Sir David Baird, a former British Guards officer and a member at North Berwick, remarked that the escarpment Strath used at the 15th hole reminded him of the fortification he had stormed in Crimea 20 years before—the hole was immediately christened the "Redan."

Memorialized for his inauspicious experiences in the so-called 'Strath' pot bunker fronting the Eden hole at St. Andrews, Davie Strath was nevertheless an exceptional golfer. Sadly, the name Strath remains attached to the bunker that brought him so much grief, rather than the golf hole that spread around the world.

Strath and Young Tom Morris were contemporary competitors, playing many memorable challenge matches throughout the British Isles. Strath left North Berwick in 1879 in poor health, traveling to Australia in search of a milder climate. Unfortunately he never reached his destination, passing away aboard ship.

In 1915-1916, Macdonald and Seth Raynor redesigned Shinnecock Hills and built an extraordinary version with a severe right-to-left tilt to the green. When William Flynn redesigned the course in 1930-1931, it was one of the holes he retained—a huge tribute.

Charles Blair Macdonald concluded the 1914 article with this statement:

> *The principle (of the Redan) can be used with an infinite number of variations...In reality there are only four or five kinds of good holes in golf. The local scenery supplies the variety. Here is one of the four or five perfect kinds, the principle of the Redan.*

Most subsequent Redan holes built by Macdonald, Raynor, and/or Banks were a bit less formidable than those at North Berwick and the National. The maddening knob guarding the run-up area was replaced in later versions by a smoother shoulder, and the bunkers were never as exacting nor severe again. The spacious green site at National's 4th measures 80 feet wide and 35 feet deep. It was not the largest rendition they ever built, but it was certainly the boldest and most perilous. Although most later versions were excellent renditions in their own right, it seems that Macdonald never wished any Redan hole to rival his original version at the National.

Hole #5

HOG'S BACK

478 | 460 | 420 yards (circa 1920)

Par 5

Original yardage: 467

Present yardage: 478

Hog's Back, hole #5 at the National Golf Links, is an interesting example of Macdonald`s use of deception off the tee. The hog-backed fairway is a natural design encountered often in golf, most notably on courses in the British Isles. Macdonald recognized the brilliant simplicity of this strategy, and recognized how seamlessly it could be incorporated into his repertoire.

In general, the term hog's back refers to a turtle-backed landing on which the sides are sloped away. Both tee balls and approaches, if not properly placed, bound away from the optimum line of play into hazards or difficult areas. The design strategy is a useful tool for both landing areas as well as the green sites themselves. Though Macdonald was possibly the first to introduce this idea to American courses, Donald Ross became famous for his artistic fallaway green complexes at Pinehurst #2. Like Macdonald, Ross brought his original inspiration from Scotland, more specifically his birthplace in Dornoch.

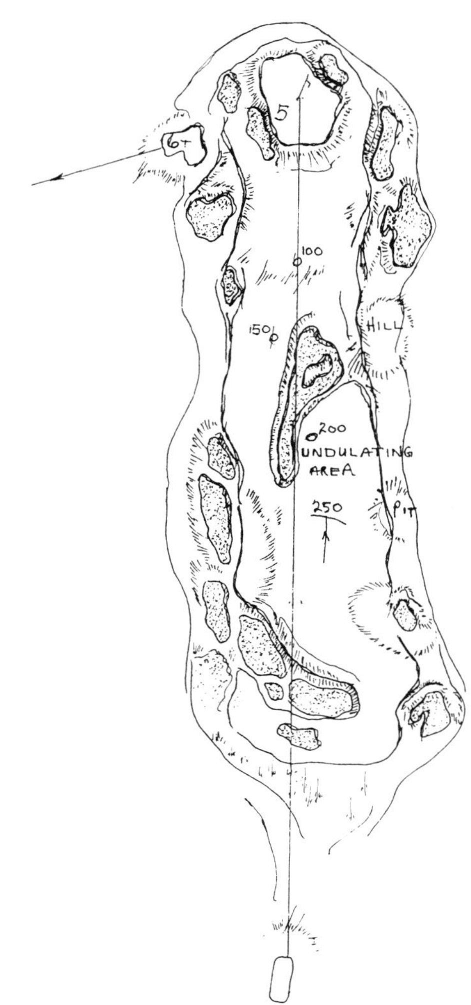

The photo above presents the perspective from the tee box at National's 5th. Players are challenged with a visually uncomfortable tee shot, further complicated due to a crescent-shaped bunker ridge that obscures a clear view of the landing area. The essential strategic element here is the visually confusing clues as to the optimum line of play. A formidable bunker stretches diagonally across all but the most conservative line—a familiar and very effective gambit by Macdonald. The blind carry often has a tendency to quicken the tempo of a player's swing, suggesting doubt as to the proper line and a disruption of concentration.

Deep hollows, 25 to 30 feet in places, patiently wait on both sides of the landing area to collect errant drives that fail to find the center of the hogback. These collection areas, though closely mowed at fairway height, greatly complicate the second shot, making the choice of intended line difficult. It is an interesting deception from the tee, because when you turn around and look back from the landing area, the fairway seems to have widened, as if there were ample room all along.

At about 260 yards off the tee the landing area divides, bisected by a 120-foot-long bunker parallel to the line of play. To the left of the bunker is a narrow tongue of fairway of a few precious yards that represents the optimum landing area. To the right of the bunker, the fairway opens up and looks to be inviting, but the rolling, tumbling ground leaves uneven lies to contend with. The angle from there is favorable, but the lie of the ball is ultimately left to providence. Or Macdonald.

Macdonald contoured a distinct downslope to the fairway from roughly 100 yards out from the green, feeding the ball in before rising to the putting surface. The green is slightly built up and slopes to the left and in from the right. A bunker guards the left front, harassing the approach from the left fairway.

The green is small when compared to others at the National—a bit less than 5,000 square feet. The putting surface contours are gentle by Macdonald's standards, as the

Above: The tee shot at the National's Hog's-Back (# 5) is a prime example of Macdonald's clever use of deception. There is a deep hollow to the left and an undulating area to the right of the optimum fairway-landing zone. The crescent shape of the cross-bunker at the crest of the hill is very intimidating from the tee box. (George Bahto Collection)

green rises less than three feet from the back. It is interesting to note that Macdonald, ever the perfectionist, redid the green several times until he was satisfied with the result.

Macdonald's protégés, Raynor and Banks, were so enamored with the idea that they incorporated the Hog's Back into virtually all of their designs. Seldom did they use the cross-bunker off the tee but rather hogbacked the fairway to create a more exacting target, often orienting the fairway diagonal to the line of play. On the putting surfaces Raynor and Banks sometimes modified the idea by installing a sharply rising spine through the green, front to back with fallaway contours on either side. Bank's versions are particularly noteworthy for their boldness, sharply shouldering balls away from the centerline. This segmentation forces players to play quadrant of the green, reducing the margin of error.

This short par 5, though reachable, should be played with a bit of caution. Thoughtless play, on what is a breather hole, can instantly change a potential birdie to a card-wrecker. Once again, careful placement off the tee is the key to the hole. In short, keep out of the hollows and bunkers and your chances of reward will be greatly improved. Choose your line wisely though, for Hog's Back is designed to tempt and ensnare the golfer who ignores his limitations.

Hole #6

SHORT

135 | 125 | 100 yards (circa 1920)

Par 3

Original yardage: 125

Present yardage: 141

The 6th hole at National Golf Links is the shortest of a group of three par 3s on the course, but is by no means the easiest. From its elevated tee, you look down across a rough area to an expansive undulating green ringed with intimidating bunkers. The green looks long and wide, an inviting opportunity to perhaps regain a shot. That is, until you closely examine the putting surface. With every change of the flagstick, the fierce contours present an entirely different challenge to the player.

In the early days of the National, sand areas framing the green suggested a more natural appearance. Wood planking held up its banks and the sand blended naturally into the surroundings. Over time, the appearance has evolved into a sharper, more neatly defined look. Modern golfers, not accustomed to fuzzy-looking, unkempt edges, wrongly equate rough-hewn bunkering and brown grass to poor maintenance. Although there is no right or wrong, what was there in Macdonald's day was a bit more in keeping with the traditional look.

Where he had no prior model on which to base his putting surface contours, Macdonald found inspiration in a piece of advice he received from the great English champion Horace Hutchinson. In trying to simulate the random nature of linksland contours, he was counseled to take a few pebbles in his hand and drop them on a piece of paper drawn to the shape of the intended green. It was then a simple matter of contouring the green to match the pebbles. Macdonald

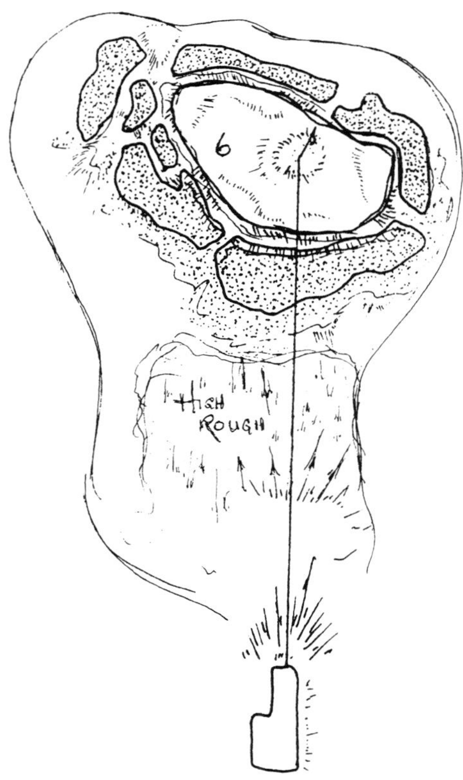

firmly believed the most important part of a golf course lay in the greens, likening them to a portrait. Here, in his own words, Macdonald describes his philosophy:

> *The right length of holes can always be adopted; after that the character of the course depends upon the building of the putting-greens. Putting-greens to a golf course are what the face is to a portrait. The clothes the subject wears, the background, whether scenery or whether draperies - are simply accessories; the face tells the story and determines the character and quality of the portrait - whether it is good or bad. So it is in golf; you can always build a putting-green. Teeing grounds, hazards, the fairway, rough, etc., are accessories.*

Above top: This early photo shows the boarded-up face of the greenside bunkering, the early lack of segmentation of the bunkers and the broad expanse of sand to the right. This photo appeared in an early seed company advertisement that often showed pictures of greens during the construction phase. (National Golf Links of America)

Right: Shoreacres' 135-yard 12th hole is played down into a 50-foot deep ravine, one of many ravines on the course. The front bunker was once a large triangular sand-filled waste area much like the National's 6th when it was first built. Seth Raynor, design and construction: 1916–1921. It's one of his finest courses. (George Bahto Collection)

The green at the 6th is an example of the portrait Macdonald tried to create; the bunkering is the portrait's handsome frame. In a 1909 article in *Scribner's* magazine, Henry Whigham described the hole as it was growing in:

> *On the National links the shortest hole is about 140 yards. The shot is played from high ground across a wide bunker on to a small plateau which is entirely surrounded by bunkers. Where the hole is so short it should be made as difficult as possible; consequently the little plateau is undulating and slopes off on every side toward the bunkers. The nicest accuracy is necessary in order to keep the ball on the green. With the wind*

behind the shot must be played with a good deal of back spin. The bunker in front of the green is deep and sheer, so that it is quite impossible for a topped ball to run through. The bunkers round about will not be so severe because even a well played shot may just run over the green and a recovery should be possible, though difficult. Lastly, the fact that the tee is a good deal higher than the little plateau green makes the distance deceptive, and calls for the most careful judgement."

The dramatic undulations of this green rival that of National's 1st. They are certainly the two most difficult greens on the course to putt, and particularly play havoc with poor lag putters who leave the ball far from the pin. There is a doughnut-shaped depression at the high point with slippery falloffs radiating out in all directions. National's superintendent, Karl Olson, has expanded and restored the green near to its original size of 11,000 feet. Balls flirting with the edges once again trickle into the surrounding bunkers. The hazards are definitely in play, even when putting.

The Short is really Macdonald's refined composite of many Short holes in the British Isles. Because of Macdonald's love for St. Andrews, for years it was believed that he used the 8th hole there as the model for his Short at the National. Macdonald's bunkering and contours are far more complex and unnerving; at St. Andrews there is really only one bunker guarding the approach.

In truth, Macdonald augmented the design partially from the original 5th hole at Brancaster, a hole of 130 yards. In his article of February 1907 entitled "The Ideal Golf Course," his shortest hole was described as, "Similar to 5th at Brancaster, with raised tee so player can see where pin enters the hole."

Brancaster is in Norfolk, England, a low-lying course requiring many formidable, forced carries over sandy wastes and salt marshes. During the highest tides, the course is

Above: Low sunlight accentuates the undulations on the National's 6th green. (George Bahto Collection)

nearly cut off from its surroundings. Macdonald seemed enthralled with the forced carries at Brancaster and probably tried to emulate some of its features at the National.

Bernard Darwin describes the 5th at Brancaster as "where you pitch from one height to another across a sandy gorge that stretches between." He offered the following description of Macdonald's 6th at the National: "...a most terrifying little hole, the green fiercely guarded by a timbered bunker and the hole cut in a hollow shaped like a horseshoe...a little paradise to which the roads from all other parts of the green are beset with shocks and switchbacks worthy of Coney Island."

So it was during the early days at the National, where the front waste area was ill-defined, intimidating, and stretched considerably closer to the tee. The Short hole at the National is possibly the best example of this concept, which despite its length, presents an intricate challenge for both the short irons and the putter. Although Seth Raynor and Charles Banks went on to create some excellent renditions of Macdonald's holes, the Short is where they consistently did their finest work. The common trait they share is expansive greens, which as a practical matter are a synthesis of many smaller target areas blended together, yet individually distinctive in contour.

Hole #7

ST. ANDREWS (Road Hole)

Par 5

480 | 465 | 410 yards (circa 1920)

Original yardage: 456

Present yardage: 478

The 17th at St. Andrews needs no introduction. Anyone who has played or followed golf for any length of time is acquainted with the "Road Hole," golf's ultimate examination of strategy and nerve.

This dogleg-right 461-yard par 4 begins with a blind drive over a building on the property of the Old Course Hotel (drying sheds in the early days). It immediately demands to know how much risk the player is willing to take in an effort to cut the corner. A slight miscue to the right of the intended line is out-of-bounds; a loss of courage to the left makes one of golf's most terrifying approach shots that much longer.

Central to the Road Hole's difficulty is the fearsome "Road Bunker," which must be skirted to reach the clubhouse safely with score intact. With few exceptions, the hazards at St. Andrews can be avoided by players with less lofty expectations by laying up, or simply playing around them with perhaps the loss of a shot. Not so on the Road

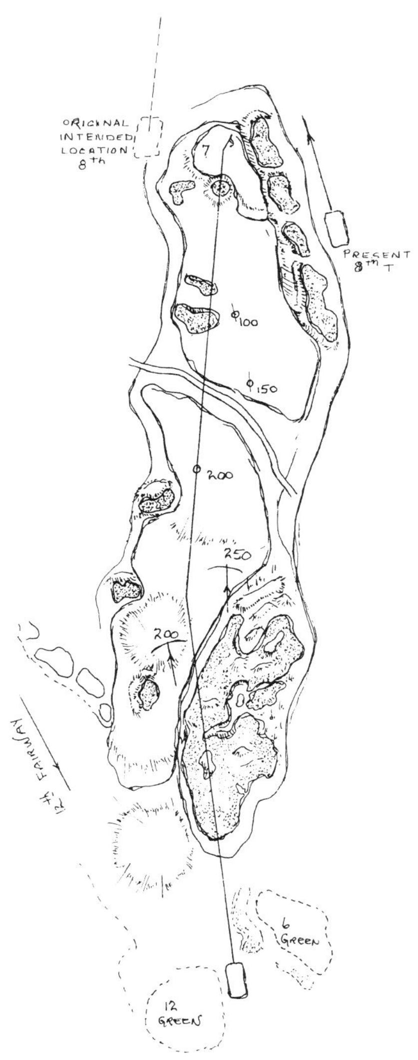

Hole, where even a simple pitch to the crowned green—which slopes severely toward the massive collection bunker—is perhaps the most nerve-wracking and dangerous shot in all of golf.

Picture a player with a long iron in his hand and in need of a four in the British Open and it is easy to understand why the grandstands adjacent to #17 always fill up first during the championship. Even during regular play, townspeople can be found milling about near the green, watching the fun. The rare approach shot that finds the putting surface is met with hearty applause, while the unfortunate soul who finds purgatory is met with deafening silence.

First built in 1842, the Road has withstood every era and generation of golfer, immune to the radical changes in golf equipment and styles of play. Ben Crenshaw has pointed out that "the reason the Road is the hardest par 4 in the world is because it is really a par 5."

At first glance, the 17th green does not appear as visually intimidating as some that have been built in recent years—just a pushed-up putting surface set near an access road bordered by a stone wall. Yet, the hole cannot be completely appreciated until a golfer stands in the fairway and contemplates the tiny margin of error between the cavernous Road Bunker and the pavement. It may not be attractive but it is effective; the green repels away all but the perfect approach, frequently undoing 16 holes of good work with one unfavorable bounce.

It must be remembered, however, that golf in the British Isles is normally contested at match-play. The 17th hole on any course is extremely pivotal and quite often the conclu-

Above and right: The Road Hole pot bunker at the St. Andrews 17th is one of the most feared bunkers in golf. It serves as one of the key ingredients of strategy in the Macdonald / Raynor / Banks renditions of this most difficult and revered golf hole. (Above: GOLFWEB Internet site–courtesy: Ed Pattermann, below: Iain Macfarlane Lowe)

sion of a match. The Road Hole lends itself perfectly to match-play competition, daring the aggressor to put himself at risk or providing the (relatively) safer option to protect a lead, hoping the opponent will find ill fortune here.

In match play, the last hole is frequently anticlimactic as the match has often been concluded. Perhaps this is the reason so many 18th holes on Britain's older courses seem uninspired when compared to their penultimate holes. The modern architect, on the other hand, is oriented toward a medal-play finish, with each hole building to a crescendo. In this day of professional golf's obsession with medal play, Americans overlook the strategic and sporting dimension of traditional match play.

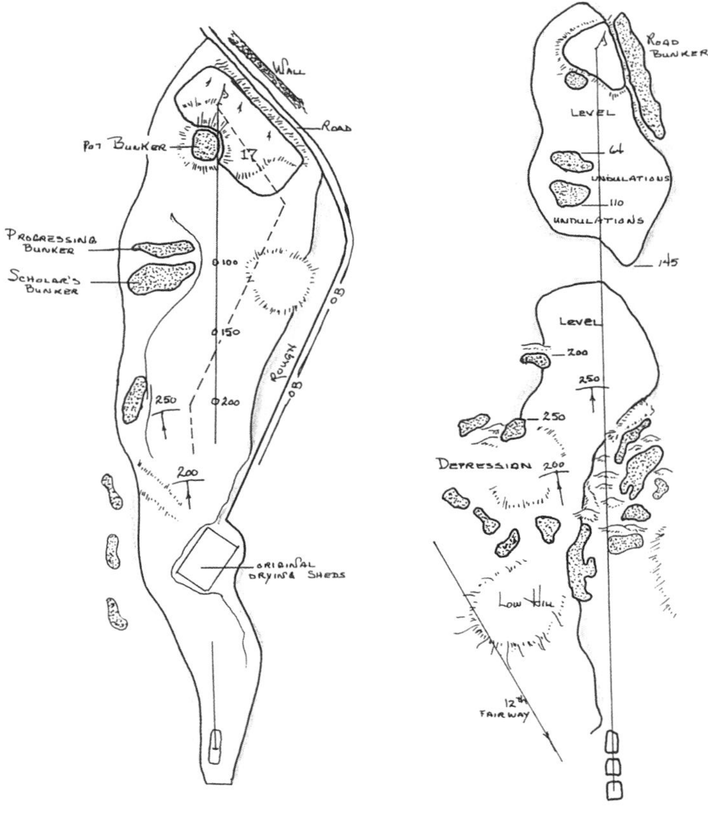

Above: Comparison of the original Road Hole at St. Andrews and C. B. Macdonald's at the National **Left:** 17th St. Andrews, Allan Robertson: architect. | **Right:** 7th The National, Charles Blair Macdonald: architect. (George Bahto Graphics)

Like most one-of-a-kind architectural creations, the Road Hole has provoked contentious debates since the beginning, usually over the fairness of its unorthodox hazards. Yet even its most vocal detractors do not have the temerity to suggest it be changed. It is what it is, and if golf has one signature hole, this is it—to touch it would be sacrilege.

The origin of the Road begins with Allan Robertson, the third generation resident professional and preeminent featherie ball maker in the British Isles. In the 1840s, as part of a citywide upgrading project, Robertson was asked to modify and update the then 22-hole course. St. Andrews then had 11 holes out and 11 holes in, using 12 greens. Two holes had their own "single" greens. The Society of St. Andrews Golfers (later the Royal and Ancient) felt the first four holes of the course lacked sufficient difficulty and decided on modifications that would combine several holes. This reduced a round at St. Andrews to 18 holes, setting the standard for the future.

Using the precepts of today as a measuring stick, the Road Hole borders on absurdity. Imagine a modern designer purposely laying out a hole with a blind tee shot over the corner of a building! If that wasn't enough to set off howls of protest, Robertson dug out a deep pot bunker directly in the line of play and beveled the approach area and putting surface in order draw balls into misfortune.

Sand play from the straight-faced bunker required utmost touch or balls would skittle across the green toward the road and wall. This intentional placement of the Road Bunker by Robertson is generally recognized as the earliest expression of planned golf architecture.

An unfair hole? Perhaps. But unlike many modern designers, Robertson cannot be accused of designing a hole to suit his particular game. Despite being the best player of his era, even the great Allan Robertson never made a 3 on the Road Hole.

With no drying sheds or hotel building as an obstacle to drive over at the National Golf Links, Macdonald reproduced the driving strategy of the Road Hole with the use of a mostly blind diagonal carry over a waste and bunker area. This simulated the dogleg and landing area at St. Andrews. It is unclear exactly where he derived the inspiration for the waste area at the corner of the dogleg. However, Macdonald often expressed his admiration for the compulsory carry over sand hills at (Royal West Norfolk) Brancaster's 9th hole. Macdonald also praised Brancaster's similar 5th hole as an

Left: To simulate the driving problem of the tee shot on the Road hole, Macdonald created a semiblind hazard at the corner of the dogleg. It is unclear, but the feeling is this hazard was influenced by the vast waste hazards he saw at Brancaster (Royal West Norfolk), England that was built by his close friend Horace Hutchinson (and Halcome Ingleby) in 1891. (George Bahto Collection)

excellent hazard. Thus, National's Road hole is conceivably a synthesis of several different design influences.

To stand on National's 7th tee is to be sorely tempted to dare the corner, yet the carry is further than it appears—and the price of failure is high. Macdonald's continuing theme of forcing a player to weigh choices is all the more evident when considering the safer route. Directly on line of a conservative tee shot is a deep bunker that waits patiently in a crook of the fairway to ensnare players who decline the more challenging route.

The green complex is a larger but less severe hybrid of the original, with more traditional representations of St. Andrew's hazards. The "road" is represented by a long bunker guarding the right and rear of the angled green. For the Road Bunker, Macdonald installed an 8-foot-deep pot bunker slightly left of the green's centerline. Over the years the bunker has been gradually filled in, but it still remains a formidable hazard.

Like the original, this 480-yard par 5 requires a bump-and-run approach from the bailout area to the right of the green. Macdonald felt the abrupt rise in the original Road green unfairly penal, so he softened his version at the National considerably. This subtle, yet distinct rise suggests countless short approach options without sacrificing playability. Historians have never ascertained whether the original putting surface extended down the rise to fairway level. Some of the later renditions by Macdonald (as well as Raynor and Banks) did away with the rise in the fairway altogether.

Despite its apparent difficulties, the 7th green will accept a properly played golf shot, tempering the sharp delineation between safety and complete disaster found at the original Road Hole. The green is medium-sized, but the surrounding cropped collar has been reexpanded to 10,000 square feet as part of the club's efforts to reemphasize and encourage the ground game. The shallow putting surface approximates the original shot value in a friendlier form. It is 90 feet long, tapering off from 40 to 20 feet on the right side.

Raynor and Banks invariably built at least one version of the Road Hole green complex on each course that they designed. While often visually diverse, the designs maintained the Road Hole's basic strategic elements. Some earlier versions required driving over the corner of a dogleg, but many times did not present too penal a hazard to negotiate.

Yet there are examples of Road holes with no diagonal fairway. Strangely, several had a tee along the centerline of the fairway with no hint of a dogleg. The reason for the omission of this integral component in depicting the hole by Raynor and Banks remains a mystery. The greens were consistently drawn on the route plan and blueprints as triangular shaped, which gives clubs interested in restoration some clues about a hole's intended origins. However, their greenside bunkering contains as many variations and diverse arrangements as could be imagined. Equally puzzling, the pot bunker guarding the front of the green was often omitted entirely—though at times a large shallow bunker was installed in its place.

On their more literal versions, most clubs have softened

their Road Bunker (despite the protests of better players in the club). Although not strictly correct, it is understandable in private club play.

Seniors, who normally wield a large influence in the manner in which a course is presented, frequently are in agreement about their desire to be challenged but not frustrated. Oddly enough, the great paradox is that the same members who prefer watered down versions of classic holes on their own course, are often the first ones to return from Scotland and expound on the virtues of the original hole!

Notably, many of Raynor's and Banks's better versions of the Road Hole on their other courses were designed as long par 4s rather than par 5s. There were exceptions, but few were short, even by modern yardage standards (usually in excess of 430 yards). In reality, the accepted par of these holes makes little difference in the hole's strategic interest because Raynor and Banks remained mostly faithful to the basic design strategy. Such is the brilliance of the Road Hole.

Above: Aerial of the 7th green with its "Road Hole" bunker. (Karl Olson)

Hole #8

BOTTLE

386 | 366 | 286 yards (circa 1920)

Par 4

Original yardage: 380

Present yardage: 424

In Macdonald's 1907 article entitled "The Ideal Golf Course," he stated that he originally envisioned the 8th as the first hole: "370 yards, similar to the Bottle hole at Sunningdale, placing deep graduated bunkers in place of the ditch and bunker the green properly."

The reference is to the 12th at Sunningdale's Golf Club in England, which consisted of a gradually narrowing fairway crossed by a diagonal hazard through the line of play. Macdonald modified the original concept by arranging the 8th at the National so that the hazard would have to be negotiated off the tee instead of on the approach.

This reversal proved to be a stroke of genius, for the Bottle hole at National Golf Links is recognized not only as one of Macdonald's most fluid interpretations but one of his most strategically complex. Macdonald originally designed the hole at 386 / 366 / 286 yards, though the present yardage measures 424 / 404 / 286. The measured length of the hole, however, does little to articulate the exacting bunkering scheme, which makes the Bottle a rather formidable and intimidating challenge. It is also a hole of stunning beauty, owing to the texture of the terrain and Macdonald's artistic arrangement of hazards. When pressed to name a favorite hole at National, players familiar with the course almost invariably name the "Bottle."

The basic strategy of the hole lies in the choice of two distinct fairways from the tee. The left fairway, though narrow and fraught with trouble, is the most desirable because it affords the golfer a more advantageous angle into the green. The right-side fairway is far wider, and though it is certainly a more inviting prospect, the safe tee shot leaves an awkward approach from a challenging angle. Regardless of the selected line, the shot must be correctly executed. At the onset of each fairway, there is a five-to-seven-foot hollow waiting to catch the short or timid drive.

A tee ball down the left side calls for a fade to gain the best advantage in hitting the ever narrowing and diagonal tongue of fairway. The landing area is fiercely guarded by bunkers on both sides, so precise distance control is also a must. The right side is a bit more forgiving target, yet an intimidating grass wall fronting the putting surface is oriented specifically toward drives in this section.

Cross-bunkering in front of the plateau-type green forces the player into a heroic carry, and a miss to the right begets an abrupt falloff of 30 feet to the floor of a grassy hollow. The pitch back must be perfect to have any chance of clearing the nearly vertical barrier and controlling the ball on the slippery green.

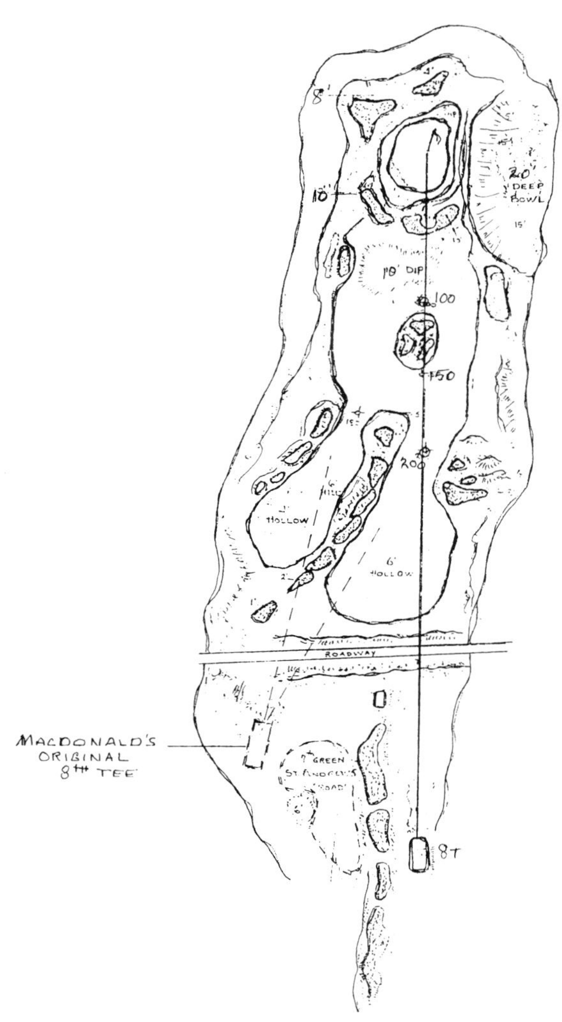

Right: A severe fall off to the right of the 8th green punishes missed approaches by calling for a near-perfect recovery shot to the slippery putting surface. (National Golf Links)

Below: The 8th hole. Echelon bunkering off the tee to a split fairway, Principal's Nose bunkering 100 yards short of the green. A heroic shot must be carried deep into this dramatically bunkered, undulating plateau green. Short left on the green may result in the ball rolling back into the left front bunker. (Skyshots)

Golfers who decline the challenge altogether are forced to lay up to the left and contend with a replica of the "Principal's Nose" bunker about 100 yards from the front of the green—again, St. Andrews was never far from Macdonald's thoughts. The bunker serves the dual purpose of hiding a

There were a number of split fairway holes built on the courses of Macdonald, Raynor, and Charles Banks. Sadly, few of their original creations remain unaltered. Some were drastically changed or removed as a result of maintenance and financial problems during lean years, but many were destroyed by club green committees unable or unwilling to grasp the basis of the hole's strategy. The same fate befell nearly all of the bunkering complexes that emulated the Principal's Nose bunkering at St. Andrews. Often during pointless redesign phases in later years, the original intent of the architecture was not recognized and the alternate fairway was allowed to grow in—eventually falling victim to ill-advised tree planting programs. Many clubs just planted trees in every open area available, not understanding the necessity and importance of these areas for play. With the holes permanently altered, succeeding generations of members became accustomed to a single, defined route to the green, and the charm of the original design was lost forever.

deep catch basin extending to the front of the green while also obscuring the true distance of the approach.

The strategic elements found in the Bottle hole were a seminal influence in much of the work produced later by "Golden Age" architects. George C. Thomas Jr., designer of Riviera, described the essence of strategic golf course design in his 1927 classic work, *Golf Course Architecture in America*:

> *The spirit of golf is to dare a hazard, and by negotiating it reap a reward, while he who fears or declines the issue of the carry, has a longer or harder shot for his second, or his second or third on long holes; yet the player who avoids the unwise effort gains advantage over one who tries for more than in him lies, or fails under the test.*

In C. B. Macdonald's world, the object of a bunker was not simply to punish a golfer's physical mistake or lack of control, but rather to punish his pride and egotism. One favorite gambit involved placing a bunker at 180 yards off the tee for golfers who feel they can carry the ball 180 yards but in reality can only carry 160 yards.

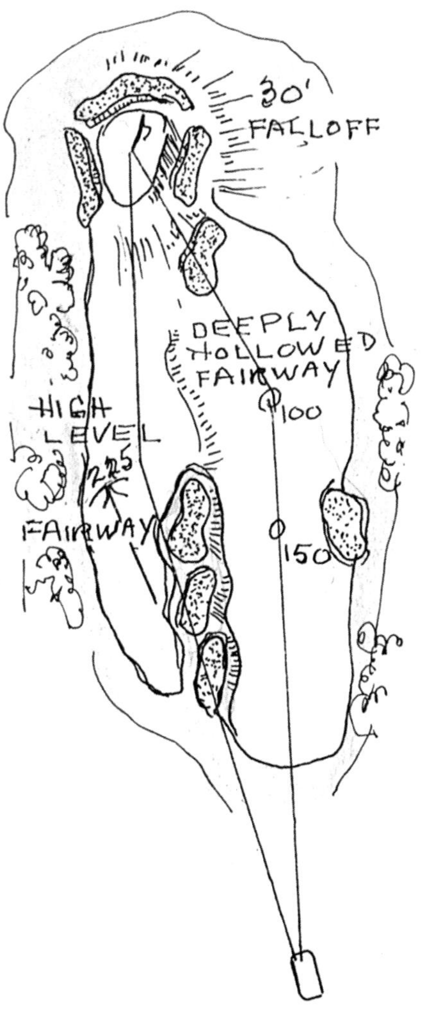

True to Macdonald's architectural philosophy of risk and reward, the 8th green presents an inviting target only for those who dare to challenge his ever-narrowing fairway to the left.

Above: Bottle hole strategy at Essex County Country Club's West Course in New Jersey—presently the 10th hole at Francis Byrne Golf Club. Hole designed by Charles Banks in 1926-27. The strategy is lost on many courses due to lack of understanding—many examples no longer exist. (George Bahto Graphics)

<u>Hole #9</u>

LONG

542 | 527 | 505 yards (circa 1920)

Par 5

Original yardage: 525

Present yardage: 540

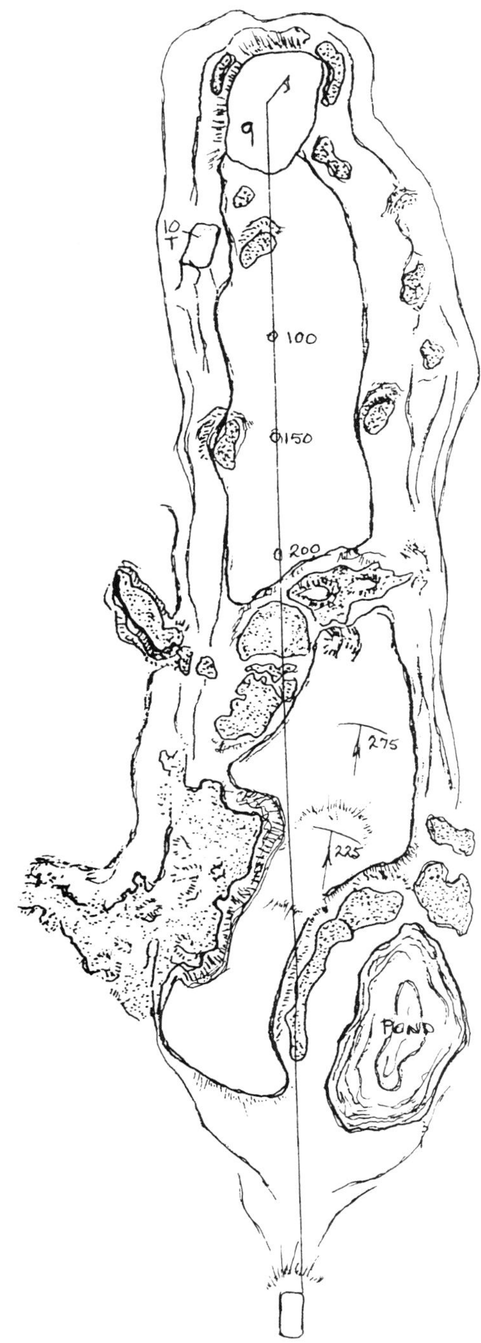

The 9th hole at the National Golf Links, again named for a hole at St. Andrews, is the third par 5 on the par-37 front nine. The hole was initially designed at 525 yards, and although only 15 yards have been added since then, it continues to be an exacting challenge. Beginning from an elevated tee box with a commanding view of the hole, the 9th is a representation of the great 14th at St. Andrews—known as "Elysian Fields" or the "Long." Macdonald's "Ideal Golf Course" article referred to it by calling for "a likeness to the 14th St. Andrews, making green larger and run-up less fluky."

Again, Macdonald returns to the theme of a diagonal carry from the tee, this one from left to right. A pond will catch a topped tee ball and a diagonal bunker short of the fairway will entrap a weak drive. Tee balls that seek the safety of the left side must negotiate both a bigger bunker and a cluster of pot bunkers that ensnare the long hitter who fails to find the narrow corridor of fairway to the right.

Carries off the tee at the National are a bit unforgiving and the echelon carry is one of the common threads that form the tapestry of Macdonald's design. The second shot must carry another left-to-right diagonal hazard that looms near the halfway point to the green. Two accurately and well-struck shots will leave the player near the green for an inviting pitch to the 10,000-square-foot, moderately undulating putting surface. However, if the wind is unfavorable it is necessary to execute three well-struck full shots.

The midway bunker complex, a representation of Hell Bunker at St. Andrews, is not nearly as difficult as the original—Macdonald apparently chose to moderate his interpretation. He did install, however, three staggered bunkers in the landing area of the second shot to emphasize the necessity for accurate placement and to again compress the landing area on a diagonal. Surprisingly, the complicated strategic options of St. Andrew's 14th, including the green site configuration, were not fully articulated at the National. The most literal version of the hole was constructed by Macdonald and Raynor at the 17th at Lido Country Club,

which included a properly placed Hell Bunker complex (sadly, now defunct).

Before reversing the nines when the new clubhouse was built near the beach, this was originally the finishing hole of the course. Macdonald followed the traditional design of many courses in the U.K. by providing an opportunity to take advantage of the prevailing wind and finish the round with a birdie. Providing, of course, that the golfer was not greedy or careless.

For reasons that remain unclear, with the exception of Lido, Macdonald, Raynor, and Banks never appropriately placed a Hell Bunker on any version of the Long hole that fully simulates the shot values of the original. Conceivably, they felt that forcing a choice of laying up and leaving a very long third shot or risking a heroic carry over Hell was too much to ask of the average club member who would play the course on a regular basis.

What is certain is that the name "Long," when used on an early scorecard by any of the three architects, was always the longest hole on the course—usually between 530 and 560 yards. As at the 9th at the National, there was often bunkering at the driving zone to be challenged or played safely around. Fairway bunkering, particularly along the edges of the second shot landing area, was used mainly to entrap errant shots, and not so much as a component of an overall

Aleck Bauer compiled an extraordinary, much coveted book in 1913 entitled *Hazards* in which he details the 14th at St. Andrews and referred to the hole "as a most excellent one, two full shots and a difficult approach." Bauer considered the 14th at St. Andrews more dangerous than the Road hole "owing to the tricky shot that follows a bad third. We may play safe at the Road hole ... but if our third is not on the fourteenth, the run up from anywhere is the hardest shot to be found on the course. It is not often holed out in four, and we may breathe a sigh of relief, having secured our coveted five."

One strategy at St. Andrews' 14th is to direct the tee shot to the right center of the fairway on a level area known as the "Elysian Fields." In classical mythology, Elysian Fields refers to the place where souls of the good went after death; a peaceful and beautiful region, full of meadows, groves, sunlight, and fresh air; a place of supreme happiness and bliss. From the Elysian Fields at St. Andrews, a decision must be made whether to risk a play over the Hell Bunker complex or to skirt the hazard and play to the fifth fairway. Much of this decision will be predicated on the length of the tee ball, the wind direction and the skill and player's risk tolerance.

If the choice is be to the fifth fairway, the player must negotiate the "Crescent" and "Kitchen" bunkers, staying left or beyond the borders of "Hell." From here he should be inside 100 yards of the green. Bauer continued: "We now have to play a running pitch over the ridges near the green. These ridges are the essential ingredient in the hole, as the green is not only quite small, but on a distinct slope to the left." The hole requires a long, deadly accurate tee shot between out-of-bounds and a hazard. An errant first stroke will leave the golfer with a continuing problem all the way to the green.

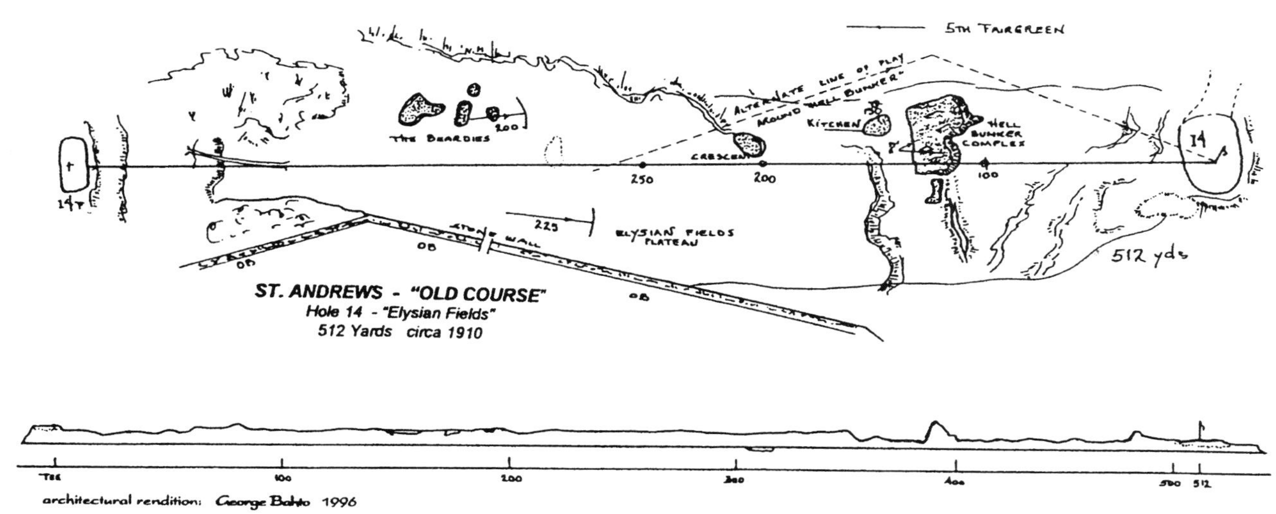

Opposite top: The National's 9th is a replication of some of the strategy of the 14th ("Long") at St. Andrews, although, for some strange reason the strategy of the Hell Bunker complex has not been used. At the National Golf Links there is a huge bunker complex left of the fairway. The photo shows the marvelous use of the diagonal hazard, not only on the drive but on the second shot as well, where a similar strategy segments the latter part of the fairway. Fescue grass frames the fairways. (George Bahto Collection)

Opposite bottom: "Hell Bunker," Old Course, St. Andrews. (*Golf Illustrated*)

Above: The 14th at St. Andrews. (*Golf Illustrated*)

strategic schematic. Going a step further, Raynor and Banks often utilized off-fairway bunkering in their versions of "Long" to frame the fairways, helping clearly define the path to the green.

The 9th green measured about 10,000 square feet, with a gentle back-to-front tilt. This was a brief respite from some of the bolder contouring found on earlier holes of the course. In subsequent designs of his own versions of "Long," Raynor remained faithful to the original in terms of size and slope. In later years, however, Banks deviated from this traditional strategy. In a departure from his mentors, Banks often segmented greens into three or four sections, creating smaller targets for golfers to play to.

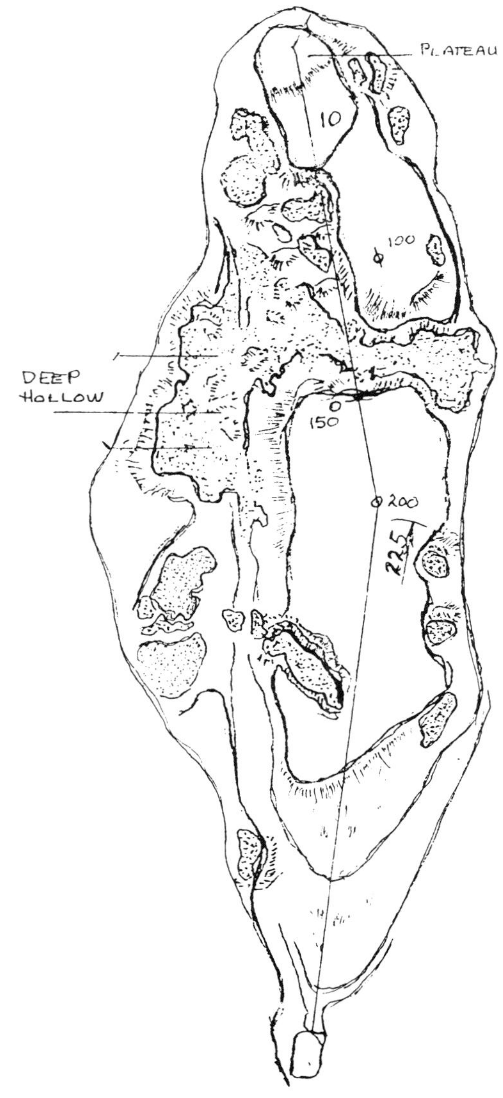

Hole #10

SHINNECOCK

435 | 412 | 371 yards (circa 1920)

Par 4

Original yardage: 416

Present yardage 450

For the second nine, the course turns into the prevailing wind and offers the first of three par 4s in a row. The 10th, originally laid out at 416 yards, was stretched in the 1920s to 435 yards.

The hole is named in honor of the National's famous neighbor, Shinnecock Hills Golf Club, which it borders along the right side of the fairway. During the time frame when Shinnecock was a Macdonald/Raynor design (1916 through 1930), it was not uncommon for members from Shinnecock to play nine holes on their course, cross over to the National and play 10 through 18 up to the clubhouse for the justly famous lunch. Following the refreshments, the golfers would play 1 through 9 at the National and then cross back onto Shinnecock to finish the round—an unmatched 36-hole day.

At first glance, the 10th appears to have an invitingly large fairway. It is only after closer examination that subtle complexities present themselves. An expanse of sand bunker must be carried off the tee, demanding at least a 200-yard-plus carry. A shot too far to the left dives into a bunker that nibbles quietly into the narrow landing area. Tee shots lost a bit to the right are likely to find one of the small collection bunkers lurking on that side of the landing area. Unfortunately, anywhere to the right of center makes the approach to the green considerably longer, as the putting surface is oriented to the left.

Regardless of where the drive ends up, both a bailout area to the right and the green itself are uncomfortably obscured

by the stairstep break between the upper and lower fairways. Even the bailout is complicated by the narrowing gap between greenside hazards and the trio of bunkers looming at the far end of the layup area. The conservative choice at the 10th still demands very accurate placement and distance control without the benefit of visual cues to guide you toward the target.

The origin of the hole is undeterminable with components of several classic elements (it's one of Macdonald's original composite holes). Although the National predates Pine Valley, it is noteworthy that there exists a striking similarity in approach to the famous 13th there–with the omission of the putting surface canting away from the bailout area.

"Shinnecock" was originally planned to be the opening hole of the course. But when an inn near the tee that once served as the clubhouse burned to the ground, it forced a change in Macdonald's thinking.

Commiserate with the difficulty of the hole, the green is enormous. In fact, it is the largest at the National. It includes an elevated plateau along the rear one-third of the 50-foot-wide green, making the task of getting the ball close with a "Sunday" placement an exacting challenge. Prior to the National's restoration of the greens to their original size, the 10th was 8,640 square feet. After restoration, the teardrop-shaped green and its surround totaled an incredible 16,669 square feet. Because it is so difficult to get the ball close, the 10th green is a supreme test of lag putting. The breaks here are not as overt as other greens, but gauging the line and pace is confusing, even to longtime members.

Above: The putting surface on the 10th hole is the largest at the National. (George Bahto Collection)

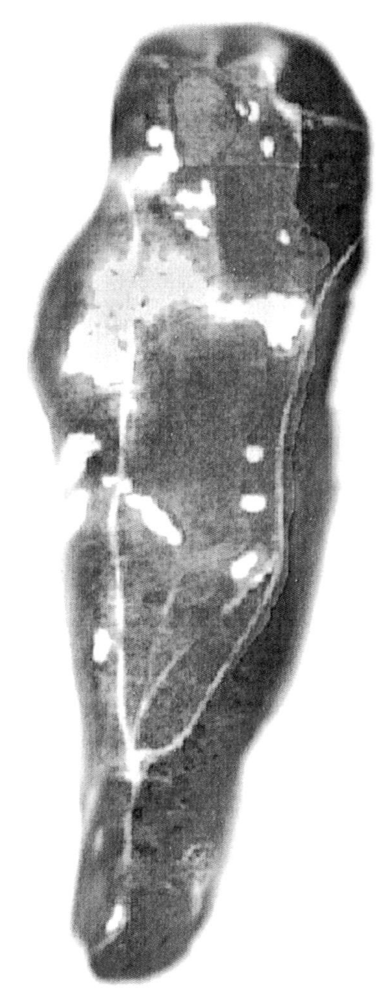

In 1931, many of the best professionals in the world played at the National. The par-4 10th hole had the highest stroke average on the course: 4.79 strokes. Among the players were Tommy Armour, Gene Sarazen, Craig Wood, and Walter Hagen.

After No.10 was lengthened by 34 yards, it became the #1 handicap hole on the back nine. Into the wind, it is truly a rigorous test of skill and strength as the golfer begins the perilous journey back to the clubhouse.

Above: Hole 10. Until the Shinnecock Inn burned to the ground during construction, it was the National's first hole. (*Golf Illustrated*)

Hole #11

PLATEAU

432 | 405 | 383 yards (circa 1920)

Par 4

Original yardage: 405

Present yardage: 432

The "Plateau" hole design was used on every golf course built by Macdonald, Raynor, and Banks at least once, and often twice. The dramatic green and classic bunkering make it a favorite of fans of the three architects.

"Plateau" at the National Golf Links was originally built at 405 yards but was lengthened by 29 yards over the next decade in response to improved golf equipment. Macdonald felt that the added length would maintain the hole's design integrity. Today it plays to a strong 432 yards and is rated the second most difficult hole on the back nine.

The drive is blind, up and over a hill and then down to a more level area short of where a local road bisects the fairway. (The roadways that cut across the course in various places—and the vehicles that travel on them—cannot be seen. Embankments were built so that vehicles and their occupants would not be in danger and so the roadways would not detract from the aesthetics of the course.) Following the drive, the approach is to a three-tiered green. Seventy-five yards short of the putting surface is an artistic Principal`s Nose bunker complex that stands guard in the middle of the fairway and partially obscures the approach. This bunker complex originally had wooden ties shoring up its sides, but they were removed after a number of ricochet accidents.

Which Plateau green in particular caught Macdonald's fancy during his research overseas is uncertain, so to identify a single green as the origin of the one at the 11th would be impossible. What's possible is that it may have been the greenside bunkering of a hole that made an impression, because in his and Raynor's early designs, they left a slot on the lowest level of the green on which an overly aggressive approach can easily run through the green into the rear bunker beyond.

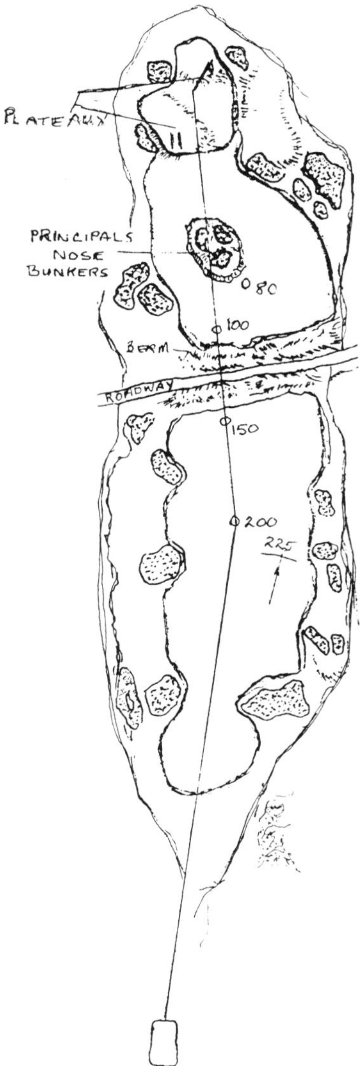

The kidney-shaped "Plateau" green could have been called "Double Plateau"—there are three distinct elevations, dramatically segmenting the putting surface. There's one at the left front, two feet higher than the center, and one at the right rear, about one and one half feet higher than the center. The lower level feeds through the middle of the green.

The second shot on the 11th requires a long approach that must carry the Principal's Nose bunker and sneak through a fairly narrow opening to the green. The putting surface had been allowed to grow in over the years, especially the rear plateau area. Superintendent Karl Olson, however, has overseen the restoration of this area to near its original configuration. At its maximum, the green is nearly 100 feet long and about 50 feet across. Including the wide fringe area, the green measures about 13,000 square feet.

Putting up to a plateau presents intriguing angles of play, a unique challenge for those used to less daring contouring. Shots played from the greenside bunkers require great finesse and distance control when played to one of the raised areas. Recovery shots struck timidly or a tad too strong are shouldered away, making par possible only by sink-

Below: Often Seth Raynor had more than one Double Plateau green on a course. The two levels were in different positions on a green and were at times side-by-side along the back of the green. Another variation was to have a simple rear shelf. Shown are typical examples of three of the most common configurations. (George Bahto Graphics)

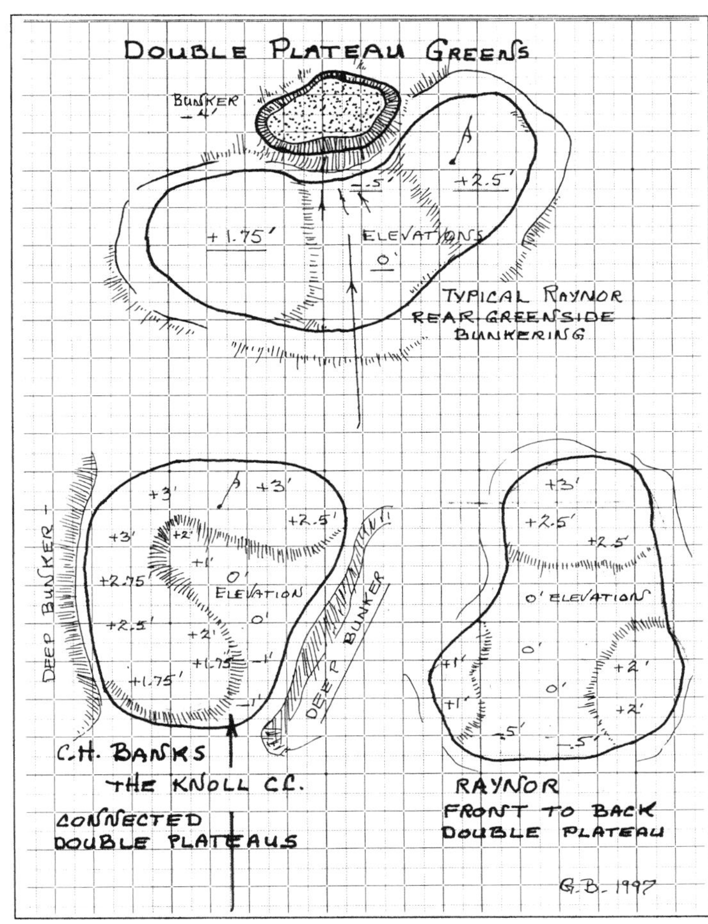

ing a long undulating putt. So exceptional is the Plateau concept that the simple addition of this type of green to even a mundane generic hole immediately elevates it into a noteworthy challenge.

On most Macdonald/Raynor/Banks courses, these greens were among the largest. Sadly, it was common that these greens were the first to be allowed to grow inward due to savings in maintenance. This left many of the plateaus partially off the green, compromising the integrity of the design. There was often more than one plateau hole on a course, but these secondary ones were normally less severe. More complex green designs such as Westhampton, the National, Yale, and Chicago Golf, offered a series of minor plateaus. Additionally, the plateaus were not always positioned the same in relation to each other.

Top: The approach to the 11th green is partially obscured by a Principal's Nose bunker complex in the middle of the fairway. (George Bahto Collection)

Bottom: Seth Raynor checking elevations on the 11th green, circa 1925. (George Bahto Collection)

Hole #12

SEBONAC

385 | 374 | 348 yards (circa 1920)

Par 4

Original yardage: 385

Present yardage: 435

Sebonac is another of the Macdonald composite holes whose features are difficult to assign to any particular hole in the U.K. The 12th hole derives its name from the view of Sebonac (Bull's Head) Bay laying directly beyond the line of play.

The general topography of the hole is moderately rolling. It's played from a slightly elevated tee box toward a hollow area that then rises to the green. The optimum drive is directly at the diagonal bunkering that runs up the right side some 225 yards from the tee. This will leave the desirable angle into the green. Players must either work the ball right to left, or exercise precise distance control to place the tee shot between that bunkering on the right and a low hill on the left side.

Although the hole has lost some of its former intricacy to modern irrigation (see sidebar, p. 116), it is still very easy on a breezy afternoon to find the right-side hazards. Playing directly to the green from there is nearly impossible. The massive expanse bunkers wander to the left all the way to the green and demand an insurmountable carry.

A secondary option from the tee is to toe the line along the echelon bunkering to the left, leaving an unimpeded approach (although a hanging lie off the low hill makes the shot more difficult). A drive that finds the bunkers to the left is tantamount to a stroke lost. The bunkers are deep, and frequently a play out sideways is the only option.

The fairway narrows considerably 40 yards short of the green, pinched in by mounding and bunkering. The traditional run-up shot is very difficult to play successfully due to an abrupt four-foot rise from the fairway to the putting surface—severely crowned along the sides and set at a slightly oblique angle. Approaches slightly off line are often shouldered away into the greenside bunkers, leaving a touchy chip or sand shot.

Sebonac tends to play long, normally into a quartering

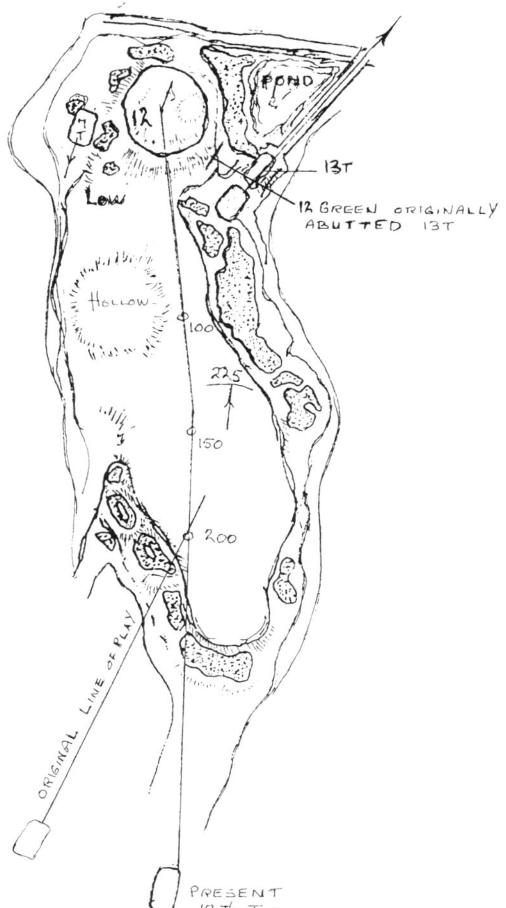

wind off the Bay, and it is a test of will and a golfer's strength. Macdonald believed the wind was a great equalizer, particularly with firm fairways.

As an interesting side note: the tee was originally situated to the left some distance to introduce a more pronounced diagonal carry from the tee. Sometime in 1931, during one of his last major revisions, Macdonald repositioned the tee from where it was next to the 11th green to its present location. In doing so, he straightened the hole. While this was necessary for safety issues, the challenge of the tee shot over a set of yawning bunkers was compromised. The slope of the fairway from the original angle under typically firm conditions shouldered seemingly good tee shots toward a strategically placed bunker far down the right side of the fairway. Those who landed in that hazard were faced with a long shot over a string of sandy waste.

The green complex at the 12th is a daunting target owing to extreme falloffs on all sides. Only a perfectly judged shot will stay on the green. However, the putting surface itself is unremarkable, lacking the rolls and folds that characterize Macdonald's work.

Interestingly, a 1911 photograph of the large plasticine model (built by Raynor) of the National shows a pronounced doughnut feature similar to the one found at the 6th green. The model also shows that the 12th green originally extended on the right and abutted the 13th tee, a situation that ultimately required an adjustment for safety reasons as play increased. Undoubtedly the loss of the green's doughnut feature was also a result of the safety alteration to the green.

Below: "X" in the lower left corner indicates the original tee-box versus the present tee, lower right corner. The new tee negates Macdonald's original tee-ball strategy. (George Bahto Collection)

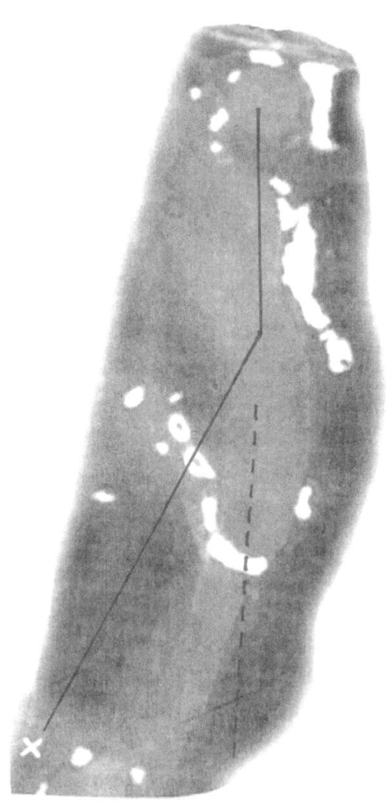

Macdonald's interpretation of the correct playing characteristics of a golf course was quite different than on today's courses. The improvements in turfgrass varieties and irrigation, while cultivating more consistent playing surfaces, have precipitated an undesirable alteration of the original architectural intent of many classic golf courses.

"Sebonac" is an example of a fairway bunkering schematic becoming in some measure irrelevant by the desire of a membership to maintain lush turf. The bunkering that appears to be far removed from the line of play was actually placed to entrap shots that ran far off the fairway on the firm and fast surfaces.

Soft and lush fairways that limit the roll of the ball require the game to be played mostly through the air. This gives a tremendous advantage to the long hitter, while severely limiting the options of shorter hitters—often reducing the game to a slugging contest. This is particularly prevalent in some of the modern designs that demand approaches be struck to elevated greens surrounded by hazards—with no options or alternate entry.

Much of the time, these one-dimensional and overly penal designs are the work of ex-professional golfers who have lost touch with the principle that courses must be also be playable for the average golfer as well as the scratch man.

To architects of the golden age, it was a basic precept of the game that players should utilize the contours of the ground to direct their shots to the desired target. Sadly, on the majority of clubs in America, this understanding of the essential characteristic of links golf has been lost on green committees.

By directing the superintendent to maintain a lush cosmetic appearance, without regard to the negative effect overwatering has on the strategic elements of the holes, an essential component is literally being drowned out of the game in America.

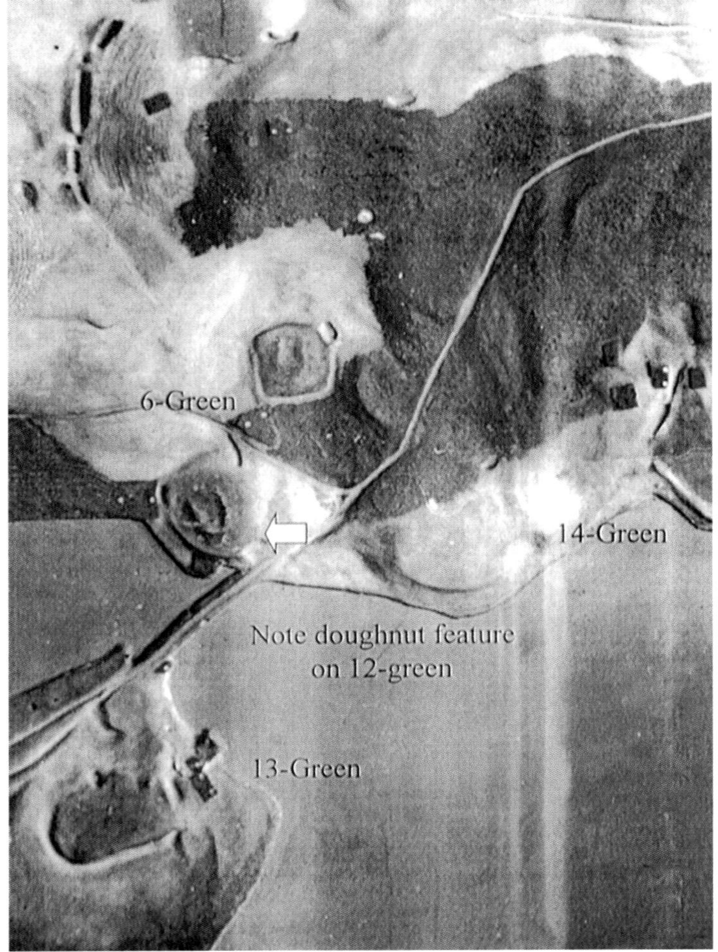

Above: Rare aerial photo of the 6th, 12th, 13th, and 14th greens. (National Golf Links)

Below: The 12th green lacks the slopes of other greens at the National, but does feature falloffs on all sides. (George Bahto Collection)

Hole #13

EDEN

170 | 162 | 125 yards (circa 1920)

Par 3

Original yardage: 160

Present yardage: 174

The 13th at the National is C. B.'s version of the great 11th at the Old Course (basic yardage: 172). Also known as "High Hole In" and the "Eden Hole," owing to its proximity to the Eden estuary directly behind the green, this par 3 is recognized as one of golf's premier one-shotters. To fully grasp the idea behind Macdonald's version, it is important to first understand Bernard Darwin's reference to the 11th at St. Andrews as "by common consent...the most fiendish short hole in existence." In the famous "Great Hole Discussion" that helped prod Macdonald into building his Ideal Golf Course, the Eden hole was voted the best one-shot hole in the British Isles.

The basic premise of the hole is, in actuality, very simple. The Eden presents a mid- to short-iron tee shot to a long and narrow teardrop-shaped green that is severely canted toward the player, with a high rise to the rear. The green is guarded on the left by a "Hill Bunker," named simply for the hill it creates on the putting surface, and to the right by a "Strath Bunker," named for the fine player Davie Strath and his lifelong confrontation with the bunker that now carries his name. The challenge of either bunker can be likened to being thrown down a well with a niblick and obliged to somehow play out. The Strath is the smaller of the two, a deep pot that gathers any shot daring to flirt within its territory. The Hill Bunker is over 10 feet deep with a sod-faced wall.

The gap between the two bunkers on a calm day seems reasonable enough for those who wish to bounce the ball up, but the opening is crowned at the sides, nudging all but perfect shots into one of the deep sandpits. The natural tendency, though, is to use plenty of club to avoid the front of the green. Shots that end up over the back of the green, however, leave the player with a straight downhill putt or chip with no fringe area to slow the ball down. A breath too strong and there it goes into one of the bunkers. Worse yet, a pitch back from the edge of the estuary can be the beginning of a maddening game of Ping-Pong between the bunkers and the rear of the green.

Complicating the issue (or adding to the challenge) is the wind, which changes from day to day—sometimes hour to hour. Eden is at its most dangerous when played directly downwind, and the list of world-class players bloodied in battle here includes the greatest amateur of them all, Bobby Jones. After recording a double-digit score here in 1921, the young man who would later win the 1927 Open Championship at St. Andrews tore up his card and stalked off the course. Ted Ray, another Open champion, once took an 11. One year, Gene Sarazen left three shots in Hill Bunker before escaping—ruining his bid for the title.

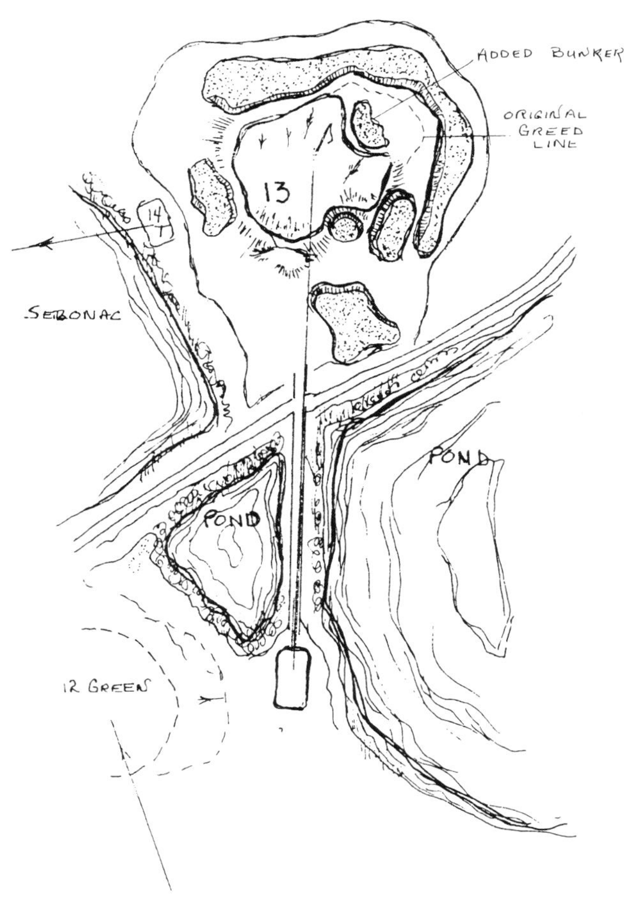

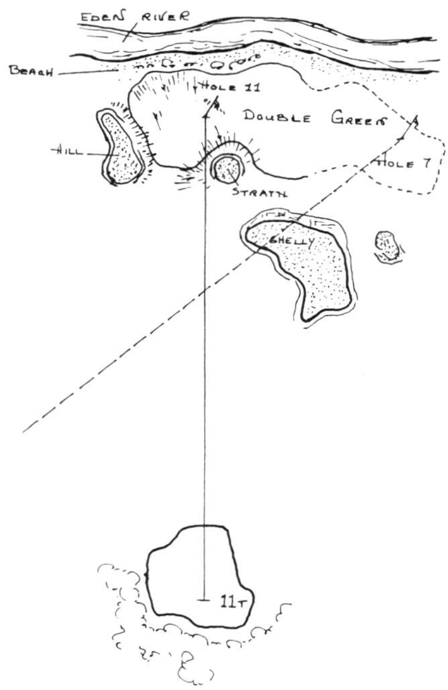

THE "EDEN" has always been considered one of the best one-shot holes in the world. It served as the model strategy for C.B. Macdonald's medium-length par 3. A version of the "Eden" was used on every course built by architects Macdonald, Raynor and Banks. The "High Hole, In" at St. Andrews has a diabolical green—balls coming to rest above the hole risk being putted completely off the front of the green and into the "Strath" pot bunker. The disasters witnessed at this hole on the "Old Course" are the stuff of legend. Macdonald found a "flaw;" it was the fact that a player could use a putter off the tee to advance the ball near the green from where the player could chip for his par or at worst a bogey. With this play, he would hardly ever be above the hole. On a Macdonald's "Eden" there would always be a hazard directly in front of the tee box to nullify any attempt to bounce the ball to the front of the green. (George Bahto Graphics)

A description of the Eden hole at St. Andrews appeared in the British version of *Golf Illustrated* in 1901 by reigning Open Champion J. H. Taylor. It was a reply to the Best Hole discussion that had much to do with Charles Macdonald's dream of building the Ideal Golf Links:

> *The 11th Hole at St. Andrews is the most difficult single shot hole I know. I do not say it is the best, as well as the most difficult as there exists a diversity of opinion as to whether it can be properly considered a fair hole.*
>
> *Perched as it is in the little plateau, that nasty bank just a few yards away has, I feel convinced, spoilt more good strokes and ruined more scores than any other obstacle in the whole realm of Golf.*
>
> *For it be remembered, it is not the bank itself that is to be dreaded, that is only a link in the chain, for the ground just below the bank falls somewhat in towards two of the very worst bunkers that it is possible to conceive, with steep faces. It is no uncommon sight to see a perfectly played high dropping ball strike the said bank full in the face, break back and be drawn into the crater-like mouth of one or the other flanking bunkers, and if the player can extricate himself in one stroke he will have every reason to congratulate himself.*
>
> *Besides all this there is the Eden (River), not a great many yards beyond, to catch the unwary player who rather exaggerates the well-known dictum, that one should always play boldly at the hole. One of the strongest arguments that the unbeliever adduces, to point out the unfairness of the hole, is the manner in which a great number of players negotiate it; that is, by not playing the hole at all, but by simply knocking the ball up short of the bunkers—a putter has even been known to be used for this stroke, thereby ensuring a safe four, and a possible three.*

The hole was so penal that eventually frightened competitors often began using a putter to roll up to the front of the hole and chipping on, in hopes of salvaging a par or bogey, or at least keeping double-bogey or more off their card. The fact that a putter was being used off the tee infuriated many British golf fans. It so disturbed Macdonald that when he built his version at the National, he selected a site with water in front of the tee box, nullifying this absurd strategy. In fact,

Opposite: One of the great strategies in golf. Eden, whose origin goes back to the 11th at St. Andrews, is used by many architects. (Karl Olson)

every Eden hole constructed by Macdonald, Raynor, or Banks included some type of hazard—be it pond or ravine—between the green and tee. Yes, a short iron can be played just short of the green at the National's Eden, but a putter cannot. Charlie added to the difficulty by inserting two small hogback mounds in the opening to divert running shots off line, and by placing an additional pot bunker to the right.

Here's an eloquent description of the St. Andrews 11th by Bernard Darwin from his 1910 book *The Golf Courses of the British Isles*:

The only consoling thing about the hole is that the green slopes upward, so that it is not quite so easy for the ball to run over it as it would otherwise be. This is really but cold comfort, however, because the danger of going too far is not so imminent as that of not going straight enough. There is one bunker called 'Strath', which is to the right, and there is another called the 'Shelly Bunker' [Ed: called Hill in later days] to the left; there is another bunker short of Strath to catch the thoroughly short and ineffective ball. The hole is as a rule cut fairly close to Strath, wherefore it behooves the

careful man to play well away to the left, and not to take undue risks by going straight for the hole. This may sound pusillanimous, but trouble once begun at this hole may never come to an end til the card is torn into a thousand fragments. With a stout niblick shot the ball may easily be dislodged from Strath, but it will all too probably bound over the green into the sandy horrors of Eden. From there it may again be extracted, but as it has to pitch on a down slope, it will most certainly trickle gently down the green till it is safely at rest once more in the bosom of Strath. This very tragedy I saw befall Massy in the Championship of 1910, and he took six to the hole. Many a good golfer has taken more strokes than that, and, indeed, it is a hole to leave behind one with a sigh of satisfaction.

The Eden hole at the National is not as severely sloped, nor as exacting as is the original, though a ball left above the hole still requires only the gentlest of strokes. Like his versions of the Road Hole, Macdonald never built an Eden as frightening as the original, no doubt to accommodate the average club player. Nobody, not even the mighty C.B., was ever able to muster the courage to construct a duplicate faithful to the severity of the St. Andrews hole.

Despite the disparity in difficulty, the 13th at the National is certainly still a par 3 to be reckoned with. Representations of Hill Bunker to the left and an eight-foot-deep Strath bunker to the right are joined by another pot bunker to the right of Strath as well. There is also a "Cockleshell" bunker just over the water. The Eden estuary is depicted in the form of a long crescent-shaped bunker at the back of the green.

In contrast to the original, Macdonald's 13th green has over 10,000 square feet of putting surface, with enough depth to present a reasonable if not inviting target. The back-to-front tilt is pronounced, yet Macdonald chose merely to make it difficult, not terrifying. As originally intended, the areas adjacent to the actual putting surface extend to the very edge of the greenside bunkering, often over the edges of the falloffs into the bunkers. There is no 2- or 3-inch wide fringe to stop the ball from wandering into the sand. At Macdonald's masterpiece, hazards are not for decoration.

Additionally, there is some question as to the original size of the Eden green at the National. Incredibly, it may have been even larger than the present sprawling putting surface.

It seems that Macdonald, Raynor, and Banks developed individual versions of the Eden design. Though increasingly divergent from the original, most still captured the basic essence of this classic design. With each succeeding year, however, newer versions of Hill and Strath featured shallower and shallower bunkering. Strath, in many cases, was repositioned to the right of the green—essentially removed from the direct line of play.

Hill Bunker evolved into a moderate left-side hazard and the opening to the green became larger and easier to negotiate. The golfer was no longer rejected into the side bunkers on short shots. Many Edens had fairway landing areas short of the green, usually framed by a pair of small bunkers, simulating "Shelley Bunker" of St. Andrews.

Of all the famous holes represented over the years, the Eden (as well as the Road) were designed with the most artistic latitude by Macdonald's two protégés; still fine holes, but deviating considerably from the original design.

Like the Redan, the Eden hole concept has evolved into a basic cornerstone in the work of American architects. Further proof that regardless of the era and changes of style or equipment, the basic genius of these classic holes is timeless.

The long crescent-shaped strip-bunker identifies the location of the original right edge of the green. Presumably, Macdonald felt the green was too large a target for the length of the shot and chose to reduce its width and position two more bunkers inside of the crescent bunker.

The evolution of the Eden hole in the design work of Seth Raynor, and later Charles Banks, is a gradual softening from the dreadful finality of a missed shot found in the original. Neither Raynor nor Banks ever saw the 8th at St. Andrews, having only Macdonald's description of the strategies and his surveys for their basis. Their later versions of Eden featured greens with various mounds and spines running through them—almost a composite of the Short hole at the National. It is interesting to note that while many of these holes seem quite tame from the tee, their putting surface contours present an awkward approach with pin positions that are difficult to challenge.

Hole #14

CAPE

355 | 337 | 236 yards (circa 1920)

Par 4

Original yardage: 305

Present yardage: 365

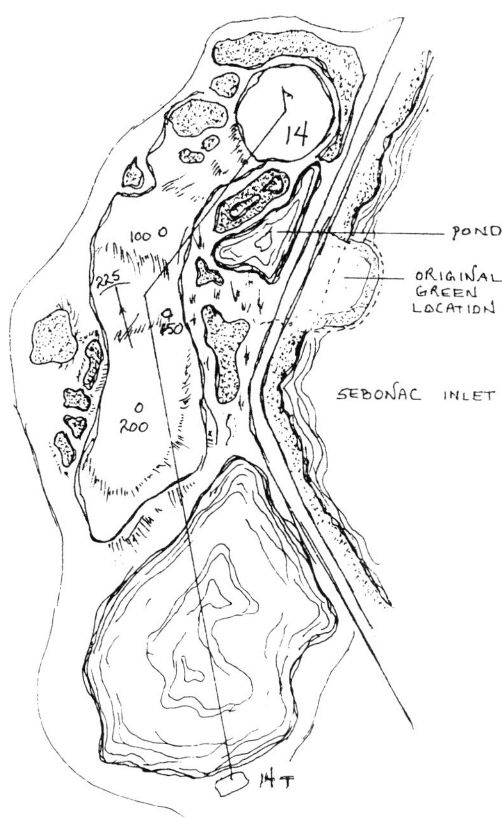

Over the years, a major misconception about the strategy of the Cape hole has evolved in part because of the evolution of the original at the National. The definition of the word "cape" refers to a "point of land extending into water." This is a far cry from what we consider it to be in today's golf terminology.

Most golfers, students of golf architecture, even golf course architects, believe the fundamental principle of a cape design is a tee ball carry over a diagonal hazard.

In an article written by Macdonald and Henry Whigham for a 1914 issue of *Golf Illustrated*, the first sentence states:

> *The fourteenth hole at the National Golf Links is called the Cape Hole, because the green extends out into the sea with which it is surrounded upon by three sides.*

Later, the article makes this claim:

> *It is today one of the most individual holes in existence and there is probably not another like it anywhere.*

The original 14th green at the National was subsequently moved for two reasons. Macdonald's original design was a slight dogleg-right of 305 yards. On a straight line from the tee to the built-up green, it was 296 yards. As equipment improved and the players became more skilled, Charlie feared that the hole that had received so much acclaim might be driven one day with a helping wind. His grandson, Peter Grace, had driven the first hole; Macdonald didn't want it to happen at the 14th. In 1924 and 1925, in conjunction with a number of other changes taking place at the National, he decided to move the green and lengthen the hole.

As a matter of practicality, Macdonald was forced to relocate the green to its present position. He simulated the original approach shot by surrounding the new green with expansive greenside bunkering, and by digging out a new pond inside the right elbow of the dogleg.

Despite the change in the fundamental strategy of the hole, the 14th continued to be called "Cape." Over the years, the diagonal drive has become the hole's dominant feature. The original green—the real reason for the hole's name—was all but forgotten.

Macdonald considered the green concept an original. The diagonal carry over a hazard was certainly not an original idea, but this positioning of a green surrounded by water was unique in golf. The most famous Cape, Mid Ocean's 5th, partially extends into water. However, there are other Cape holes that do not.

One example is the 2nd green at Yale University Golf Course. It's considered a Cape green, described that way in writings by Charles Banks, yet there isn't any water near the putting surface. Greens positioned in this manner have dra-

matically built-up escarpments, some seemingly suspended in space. There are actually more Cape greens built in this manner than ones jutting into a body of water. A Cape green could also jut into a marsh, sand, or another hazard.

National's Cape hole as we know it today uses the Sebonac Creek as a diagonal hazard off the tee box to a turbulent fairway set at a severe angle to the line of play. A player may cut off as much of the hazard to the green as he dares. However, the more conservative the line from the tee, the longer and more exacting the approach becomes. Because of the shallow curve of the fairway, a long straight drive will likely bound through the landing area into bunkering beyond. Though Macdonald tempts the golfer to cut the corner to gain an advantage, the limitless body of water to the right is a compelling invitation to slice. Constant temptation is a repeating theme at the National. At the 14th, though, the penalty for a serious misstep is not sand but the finality of water. (In light of Macdonald's habitual and incur-

Above: Although the 14th at the National is short, it is difficult. The angled fairway facing the player off the tee affords an uncomfortable looking drive zone; the second is played into a beautifully bunkered green. (National Golf Links of America)

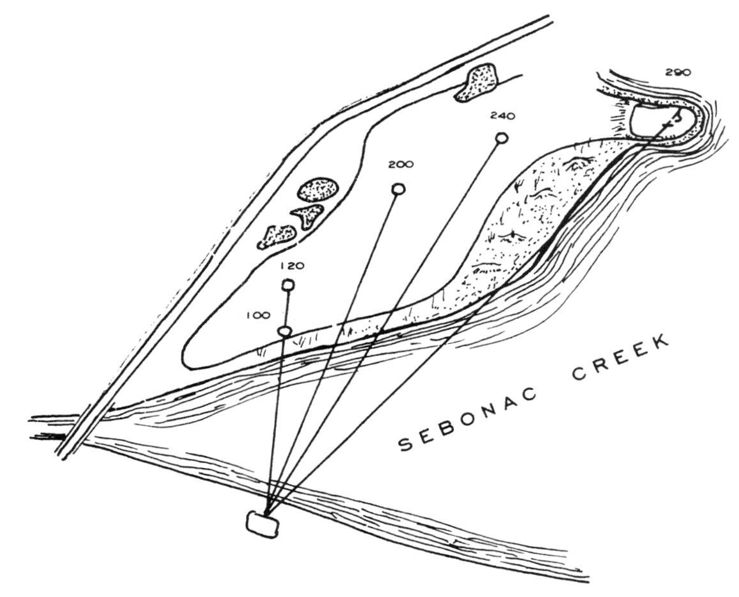

Right: As seen in the drawing, C. B. Macdonald originally designed the "Cape" hole green as jutting out into Sebonac Bay; the true definition of the word. The green was later relocated considerably further to a new location, adding some yardage to the hole. The reason was twofold; Macdonald had a fear the hole would be driven; a new access road to the clubhouse looped around the area and prevented the green from being placed in that type of location. (George Bahto Graphics)

Opposite top: A golfer from earlier times hoping to reach dry land with his drive at the National's "Cape Hole," the 14th (circa 1910). (*Golf Illustrated*)

Opposite bottom: The original Cape green at National. (*Golf Illustrated*)

able slice, it's odd that he would create such a dangerous dogleg-right!)

A drive flirting too close to the Sebonac might also end up in the formidable bunkering complex to the right of the fairway—leaving a dangerous but direct play to the green. Even today, with modern equipment, it is very easy to underestimate the difficulty of successfully skirting the hazard. Balls that carry the diagonal over water, but do not reach the fairway, land into the bunker/waste area. From here, the approach must cross the pond and more bunkers before reaching the putting surface. Aggressive approach shots that fly the green find deep bunkering as well.

Macdonald, who strongly believed that uneven lies are an essential part of the game, deliberately contoured the fairway at National to introduce awkward lies, especially downhill lies for short irons. Hitting the fairway was no guarantee of a par, particularly when the wind was up.

Yet with all the compelling golf features of the National's Cape, the most important may lie in the stirring beauty of the hole. In the late afternoon, with shadows draping across landscape, the combination of the blue water, green fairways, and the colorful landmark windmill in the distance cannot help but uplift even the heaviest of hearts.

Hole #15

NARROWS

355 | 337 | 236 yards (circa 1920)

Par 4

Original yardage: 358

Present yardage: 397

Arguably, the most artistic arrangement of bunkering at the National can be found on the par-4 15th, known as the "Narrows." From the tee, players are presented with a shot between two ponds to a landing area pinched by bunkering. The fairway hazards act as a gateway, clearly directing the path toward a shallow gathering basin in the center of the fairway. From there, the approach is another echelon carry to a green completely surrounded by sand.

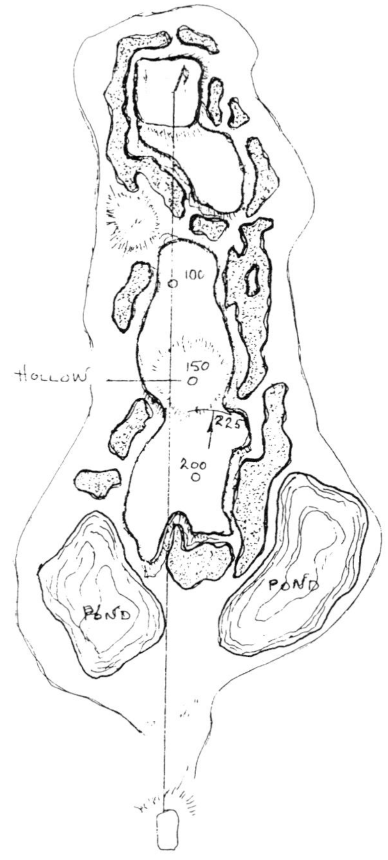

The approach, with the green tucked to the left and partially obscured by bunkers, has an unsettling quality about it. At first glance, the impression is that of an awkward approach across a diagonal carry. In truth, the danger is more psychological; there's a bit more room to the right than it appears.

The 15th was clearly designed as a challenge to the tee shot; because of all the sand, accurate placement is crucial. Macdonald's concept required a drive to the left side of the fairway. By doing so, the natural contours will direct the ball back toward the middle and possibly down a helpful slope. Drives to the right or down the center with a hint of fade will often find a fairway bunker, leaving a long sand shot that's often played into the wind.

Opposite top: The 15th at the National is very long but it's bordered by trouble all the way to the green. (Skyshots)

Opposite bottom: 15th Hole. (*Golf Illustrated*)

The Boston Sprinkler Man

While firm and fast ground is certainly a more desirable playing surface than the often overwatered bogs littering the American landscape today, the opposite problem of dry and rock-hard fairways often plagued otherwise fine tests during the game's formative years. The answer to the quandary of how to make drought ravaged courses playable came in the form of a mysterious man who appeared at the National Golf Links one afternoon, asking if it would be possible to meet the famous C.B. Macdonald.

His real name, lost in the march of golf history, may never be known, but this "Boston Sprinkler Man" had in his possession a new invention used to irrigate public parks in the New England area. It was 1912 and the art of greenkeeping was in its infancy.

New and sometimes radical techniques were being tested in an effort to increase the quality of the nation's golf courses. Incredibly, almost no one had conceived of the idea of using, of all things, artificial irrigation of greens. Sound silly? Perhaps, but it is true. It was not until about 1912 that this "revolutionary" idea was first suggested.

On the British links, it was the 1890s before the first mowing machines were used on their putting surfaces. Golf in that era was mostly played in the spring and fall when the grasses were naturally short. Sheep kept the courses cropped in the summer for those who wished to play in those off months–although only on busier courses like North Berwick and St. Andrews. Foot traffic provided enough wear to keep the courses playable, and rabbits cropped the finer grasses on the greens along the linksland.

Golf's migration in the late 1890s spread like wildfire to every conceivable climate and terrain, quickly illustrating the profound disparity between our manufactured courses and the natural layouts which had evolved on the linksland in the British Isles. Artificial irrigation was expensive, and spending vast sums of money on maintenance in the era was inconceivable.

On America's greens, rollers and mowers soon replaced sheep. In order to establish a fine and durable turf for putting greens, artificial irrigation was needed. Charles Blair Macdonald immediately recognized the possibilities brought by this salesman from the Boston Sprinkler Company and seized the opportunity to pioneer a revolution.

Macdonald designed and constructed a gravity-fed irrigation system from the existing water tower near the 16th green when he first built the National. The results were immediately successful. The greens and approach areas at the National were immeasurably better, and soon became among the best in the nation.

Prior to the implementation of artificial irrigation in 1913, summer golf at both Shinnecock Hills and the National was often in poor condition. Excluding an occasional thunderstorm, drought conditions began annually around the middle of May and usually lasted until the middle of August. The ground was often rock-hard and virtually barren as fairway grasses turned dormant.

The hole strategies Macdonald labored so hard to reproduce were nullified as the ground baked from three months of sunshine and wind. The result was drives of incomprehensible length. Average golfers were often hitting balls nearly 300 yards. Worse, golfers often saw their well-laced shots careen at uncontrollable angles into off-fairway and greenside bunkering—even nearly perfect approaches were impossible to keep on the greens. Each fall, thousands of dollars were spent top-dressing and reseeding the greens.

Credit for this revolution really belongs to this mysterious Boston Sprinkler Man who convinced Macdonald that it was perfectly possible to keep the whole course green throughout the entire three months of dry, scorching weather.

Another piece of the puzzle involves the great landscape architect Frederick Law Olmsted. A close friend of Macdonald, his genius at transforming nondescript land into aesthetically balanced and picturesque parklands using artificial irrigation no doubt influenced his decision. Macdonald was the first to utilize the Boston Sprinkler, and noting his success, several other courses soon adopted similar plans. Most notable was the Garden City Golf Club, where 4-inch piping was laid in 1913.

Garden City, previously highly criticized for inconsistent turf, was immediately transformed from a dusty and dry golf course during the summer into a properly conditioned golf course. Drivers could suddenly be used off the tee where previously there were a dozen holes that required an iron in the summer. Despite the enormous $10,000 cost, it proved a huge savings. It was no longer necessary to budget for the cost of yearly reseeding and top-dressing.

The Boston Sprinkler Company was ultimately responsible for much of the proliferation of golf across the inland areas of America. Their invention showed the world that high quality golf could be brought anywhere there was water.

The origins of the Narrows concept at the National has never been established for certain. However, there is evidence that the hole finds part of its genesis at the 15th hole at Muirfield. The description below, taken from *Championship Courses of Scotland* by Sandy Lyle, is nearly identical to the 15th at National Golf Links:

> *Another fine par 4, the 15th is a good deal less intimidating than it looks from the tee. You may even find it almost recreational before you tackle Muirfield's powerful finish, which starts at the next hole.*
>
> *This one is reasonably straight, and slightly downhill... The fairway beyond is quite wide, slopes left to right and beyond... The real test of the hole is concentrating on the second shot and this emerges not so much from the hazards you see as the impression they make on you.*
>
> *A real good drive might put you about 150 yards from the green. Look up the fairway and you will see, yet again, the Muirfield twins—bunkers on either side of the fairway about 60 yards short of the green. But this time, about 20 yards on and smack in the center of the fairway, is a third bunker, quite big.*
>
> *This may give you the feeling that the entire area up there is cramping and narrowing. It isn't really. The central bunker is the culprit. It looks very close to the green, but in fact there is a good 30 yards of fair ground between it and the front of the putting surface. You must carry this trap. If you do, and your shot is straight, you have a fair chance of running on.*
>
> *The green itself is quite heavily trapped with one-third sloping off to the left, one-third sloping off to the right, and the central third then slopes upward to the back of the green.*
>
> *The at 15th Muirfield is a perfectly fair hole which needs just a little thought on the second shot.*

Hole #16

PUNCHBOWL

419 | 380 | 360 yards (circa 1920)

Par 4

Original yardage: 410

Present yardage: 404

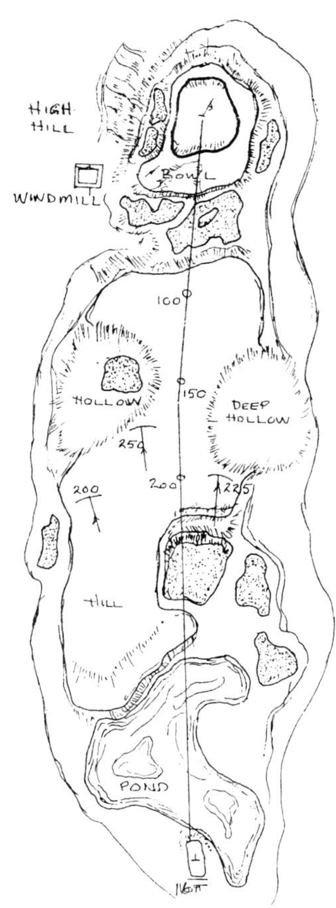

In the early days, with only rain to irrigate a golf course, the better conditioned greens were usually those located in natural depressions—"Punchbowls" as they were called. These natural catch-basin sites retained the moisture from normal rainfall and lent themselves well to growing and maintaining richer turfgrass. So remarkable was the success of these Punchbowl greens that virtually every course in the British Isles included at least one. More than likely these courses were on linksland, where there was a naturally sandy base. Once golf courses began to be built inland on less porous soil, however, Punchbowl-style greens frequently became muddy and disease-prone due to a lack of drainage. As greenkeeping evolved, techniques such as trenching, surface

contouring, and drain tiles to divert water helped to solve these problems.

Generally speaking, the Punchbowl-style green was popular because it was more accepting of an approach shot than, say, a turtle-backed green. The natural contours of a Punchbowl green—low in the center, higher on the sides—create a "catcher's mitt" type situation that gathers in approaches and even deflects wide shots toward the middle of the putting surface. Although this kind of green is a comforting target, players who prefer their golf to be free of the vagaries and whims of providence often point to some of the shortcomings of Punchbowls. A flaw that is frequently mentioned is a blind approach, with only the flagstick marking the line.

On the other hand, to the adventurous there is something devilishly exciting about a Punchbowl green. Often it comes down to how a player views the game of golf, and, perhaps in a larger sense, the game of life: as a cold and objective examination, or as a great adventure filled with uncertainties.

The 16th at the National is a combination of a Punchbowl green nestled snugly beyond the peak of a rising Alps fairway. Macdonald seamlessly synthesized these two classic elements together to create an original rendition that is testing of skill without being gimmicky. The line of play from the tee carries over a brackish pond that Macdonald converted from swampland. To reach the ideal landing area, the drive must be long enough to carry a bunker on the right side of the fairway, a formidable carry into the wind. Regardless of the drive's position, though, all approach shots to the 16th hole are blind. The only directional cue is a pole at the top of a hill in back that marks the center of the putting surface.

Though the landing area is nearly 75 yards wide, it has a hogback quality that tends to deflect off-line shots into 20-foot-deep hollows on both sides of the fairway. From here the blind approach shot is even more daunting—not even the directional pole is visible from the bottom. Thirty yards before the green are imposing cross-bunkers that segment most of the fairway (a rare forced carry approach at the National).

These deception bunkers are one of the most interesting aspects of the hole's design—located in such a way as to create the illusion from the ideal position in the fairway that they are directly in front of the green.

Similar to how it is at the famous 8th at Muirfield in Scotland, Macdonald left a 20-yard area between these hazards and the green to give players the opportunity to still bounce up a shot. Though this tactic often works even today, overirrigation sometimes leaves a correctly played bump shot hanging on the slope in front of the green.

The five-thousand-square-foot putting surface is surrounded by an equal area of closely mowed fringe. Eight- to ten-foot-high hills rise sharply along the left side of the green near the National's landmark windmill. The area behind the green also rises but less sharply.

Macdonald's trademark undulations adorn the green, although they have been dramatically softened over the years from his original design. Early photos show a very distinct spine running through the green, a pattern that Macdonald and Raynor nearly always used on greens of this style.

Above right: The National's famous windmill stands on a hillside facing the Atlantic. Inside is a water tower. (George Bahto Collection)

Opposite: 16th Hole. (George Bahto Collection)

The National Golf Links' Windmill

Dan Pomeroy, president of publishing giant Condé Nast, and one of National's original associate members, remarked to Macdonald one day in the bar that rather than the rudimentary water tank then in place, how much more aesthetically appealing it would be if a windmill were built over the water tower.

"Excellent suggestion," replied old C.B., who in short order had the new structure designed and built.

To a man, the membership was thrilled with this stately new 50-foot windmill, sitting proudly atop high land between the 2nd and 16th holes. It could be seen for miles around, and faced toward the yacht harbor where members frequently sailed in for an afternoon of golf.

The day following the windmill's completion, Dan Pomeroy found an example of Macdonald's autocratic rule waiting in his locker: a bill for his bright idea.

Hole #17

PECONIC (also "Leven")

360 | 338 | 323 yards (circa 1920)

Par 4

Original yardage: 311

Present yardage: 375

Any discussion about favorite holes at National inevitably comes around to the 17th, "Peconic." The high tee, perched on a hillside shelf in the shadow of the windmill, offers a panoramic ocean view so breathtaking that the golfer must labor to remain focused on the business at hand: choosing a line on the broad expanse of fairway cascading down the hillside. Yet while the 17th is visually arresting it's also littered with a collage of hillocks, bunkers, and a yawning waste area that tumbles toward a pond.

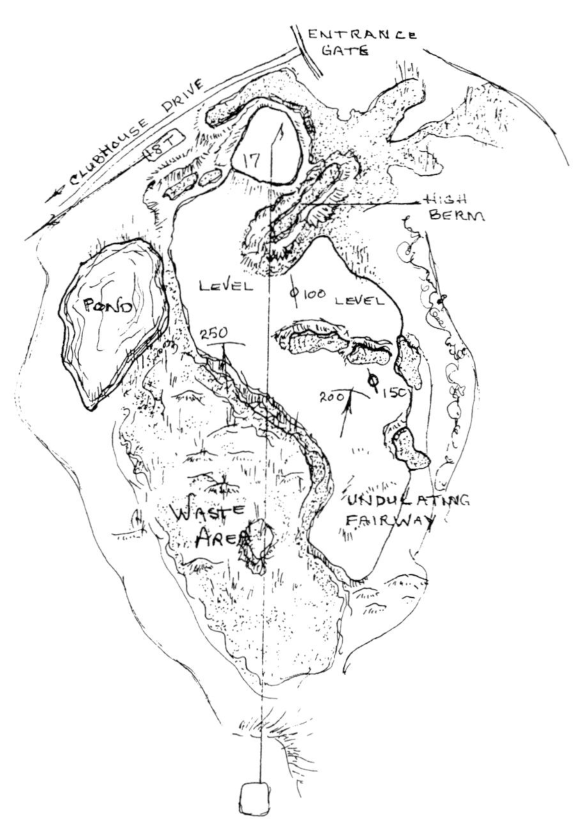

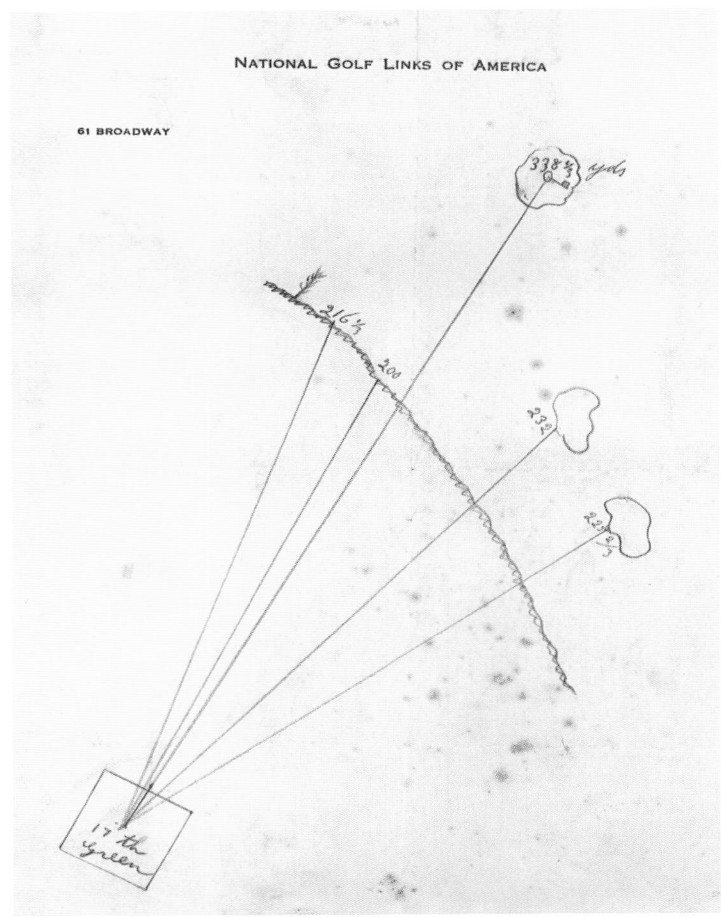

The epitome of strategic golf, "Peconic" offers the golfer the chance to play directly at the green or to take a safer route to the right. The choices pit the player against his talents, ego, and the frequently swirling breeze off the water. Although the green is overly wide—even for the National—Macdonald cleverly segmented the extremely wide fairway with bunkers. A waste area of sand, mounds, and native grasses waits in a right-to-left diagonal off the tee.

The basic premise of Peconic is fairly simple; Macdonald set up the hole to require a long and precisely struck tee shot flirting the left side of the fairway, carrying and avoiding the enormous waste area. Using the contours of the fairway to direct the shot, a correctly aimed drive will feed down the fairway to a narrow alley of fairway short and left of the green.

Peconic becomes complex, however, the moment you stray from the ideal line of play. A pulled shot is disastrous, and

although a drive to the right is less risky, it brings into play a pair of fairway bunkers that will result in a blind approach over a set of 15-foot-high hillocks and more sand in front of the green.

In his 1907 list of holes on his "Ideal Golf Course," Macdonald included a 300-yard hole that suggested the strategy of "the 7th at Leven [pronounced 'leave in'], which is only 240 yards, with burn running at a bias, and green guarded by sharp hillocks."

A particularly picturesque description of the 17th hole appeared in *Southampton Magazine* in the fall of 1912:

> *The seventeenth hole is 311 yards and is named 'Peconic'. Throughout the course the scenery has been superb, ever changing at every step with the continually varying panorama of land and water, furze and sedges, hillsides and tideways, putting green and plying launches, white sands and green islands, grassy vales and white capped waves, sere, brown slopes and bright blue bays, a mass of rolling, rollicking, upland and a maze of creeks, bays, channels and harbors; but the scene almost reaches its climax as the player steps up to the tee of the next to last hole. He is on a high elevation with the sail-dotted blue waters of Great Peconic Bay spread out before him, while beneath him lie the white sands of Sebonac beach*

Above: The first priority on the 17th is to avoid a long waste area running down the left side of the hole. (George Bahto Collection)

Opposite top: This is a color copy of an original C. B. Macdonald sketch on a pad from his New York City office. It indicates one of the changes in the length of his great 17th hole. The hole was originally built at 311 yards; this sketch shows the green on a direct line from the tee box at 338 and 1/3 yards—quite precise was Mr. Macdonald. The brown spots on the paper are mildew marks. (George Bahto Collection)

and the peaceful, landlocked waters of Bull's Head Bay lie spread out alongside him. In addition to its entrancing scenery, this hole is a modified copy of the famous seventh hole at Leven. It is downhill all the way but is very exacting in its requirements. Sandpits, mounds and natural gullies and sand beaches are lying in wait for the unskilled and the unwary before his ball safely reaches the green down by the shore of Peconic bay.

—Charles A. Jaggar [Editor]

The shorter or more conservative player wishing to decline the challenge altogether has a bit of a minefield to dance through in order to reach the green unscathed. Although at least a small portion of the waste area must be carried no matter which route is chosen, the upper section of the fairway is riddled with rolls and folds that may kick the ball into a pair of bunkers backing up the fairway just over 200 yards from the tee. From this awkward position, the next shot must either skirt the greenside mounding–hopefully stopping on the narrow tongue of safety short of the pond–or go blindly for glory directly at the green. Too short lands in the bunkers or hillocks, too aggressive bounds over the green into more sand.

The best play for a skilled player from the tee is directly at the left corner of the green, leaving only a portion of the hillocks to deal with. With the expanse of fairway up ahead, the better player often tries to work the ball off the tee to gain an advantage, rather than just pick a line and play straightaway. It is often this temptation to press for a bit more that spells disaster at Peconic—the specter of Charles Macdonald always lurking.

Even a seemingly simple short approach can be testing, because there are no trees or yardage markers at the National to help with perspective. Under ideal firm conditions, a bump and run is the best play for a straight-in approach, but any flirtation over the hillocks with a lofted club in the wind can be adventurous. If it's set up as originally designed, the firm putting surface will reject shots into the bunkering beyond.

Like all of Macdonald's short par 4s, the basic question remains the same: How much to risk? The choices are as simple as they are complex at the National's penultimate hole, for everything is visible. It's a pure articulation of Macdonald's basic strategy, and one presenting a different challenge for every class of player.

Opposite top: Mounding, sand, wind and a firm putting surface is more than enough protection for the green at the 17th. (George Bahto Collection)

Opposite bottom: When a new access road to the clubhouse was built in 1925, Macdonald's gates were added and the green was moved from its original location where the hillocks are today. Charlie felt the hole was, in effect, too short and insufficiently defended for the penultimate hole on a course with a history of match-play events.The original green was much larger than the present one, as were the bunkers around it. The hole is also 65 yards longer today, due in part to the addition of a rear tee. Peconic's present green and fringe area have been restored from a total of 4,276 square feet to the 7,200 square feet found in the mid-1920s. (*Golf Illustrated*)

Seth Raynor used many variations of the Leven concept in his course designs. Often incorporating the hillocks in the earlier days to block visibility to portions of the green, his later variations utilized bunkering with a high hill in back to change the appearance at greenside.

The premise was the same; the use of some sort of hazard off the tee to direct less risky shots wide. By constraining the landing area, Raynor forced players choosing a more conservative line to contend with greenside hills and bunkering, introducing a progressively blind approach. Yardage seldom was over 360 yards. In his earlier versions the yardage was often as short as 325 to 335 yards. Insufficient acreage at many sites curtailed the use of the Macdonald-style, super-wide fairway with all the various options.

Following Raynor's death in 1926, Charles Banks (Raynor's partner at the time) began to depart from their traditional interpretations of the Leven hole when completing their unfinished work. Perhaps sensing the need to inject a new feel for future courses, the drive and pitch holes became longer and more treacherous. Instead of utilizing just a berm or rampart to obscure much of the green, "Steamshovel" Banks often dug out a cavernous bunker, sometimes as deep as 15 feet. Banks used the excavation to pile up the face of the bunker, creating a similar strategy, but one with a more menacing appearance.

Hole #18

HOME

484 | 467 | 468 yards (circa 1920)

Par 5

Original yardage: 484

Present yardage: 502

Finally there is, I think, the finest finishing hole in all the world. The tee shot must first be hit straight and long between a vast bunker on the left which whispers 'slice' in the player's ear, and a wilderness on the right which induces a hurried hook. Then if the drive has been far and sure there is a grand slashing second to be hit over a big cross-bunker, and at last comes a little running shot at once pretty and terrifying on to a green of subtle undulations backed by a sheer drop into unspeakable perdition.

—Bernard Darwin, 1913

The last leg of the journey begins on a terraced tee, with the Great Peconic Bay on the right and the clubhouse in the distance, presiding over the fairway which charges up the hillside to the Sebonac Bluffs.

The 18th at the National can be played one of two ways, each with an element of risk, reward, and perhaps a bit of chance. The short way "Home" must directly confront the defiant bunker on the left side of the hole that stares unblinkingly back at the tee, challenging the long driver to risk the carry to the peninsula of fairway. Success brings a clear line to the green and a birdie opportunity, but a stumble on the assault leaves a difficult shot from a high-lipped bunker–often into the wind, and directly toward a cluster of bunkers that pinch the fairway to a narrow sliver.

A common thread stitching together the National Golf Links is that trouble, if not dealt with respectfully, invariably begets more trouble. Those who resign themselves to the loss of a shot and take their medicine will likely find safe passage. It is the foolhardy attempt to extract oneself, particularly here at the last hole, that may lead to a card-wrecking march from sand trap to sand trap.

For those with less ambitious goals, declining the carry from the tee presents another challenge not unlike the 14th at St. Andrews. Like a sailboat fighting the wind, you must tack to and fro around the bunkers, being careful to avoid both the cliffs (which steadily climb with the fairway) and the clubhouse (which is in bounds and has seen more than one shot played from its roof).

A flagpole, flying the flags of the United States and National Golf Links, marks the extreme edge of the cliff, 100 yards from the green. It also presents an obstacle, as Arnold Palmer discovered many years ago when he attempted to hit a big hook out over the water and around the pole. He was not successful.

Those finally reaching the green are rewarded with a nearly unguarded target, except for a small cluster of bunkers short and left. There is also sand to the rear, but this may merely save the aggressive play from falling off the bluffs. The area around the green has been expanded from 4,200 square feet to over 7,000 square feet as Macdonald designed it. The Home green is more subtle than dramatic, relatively

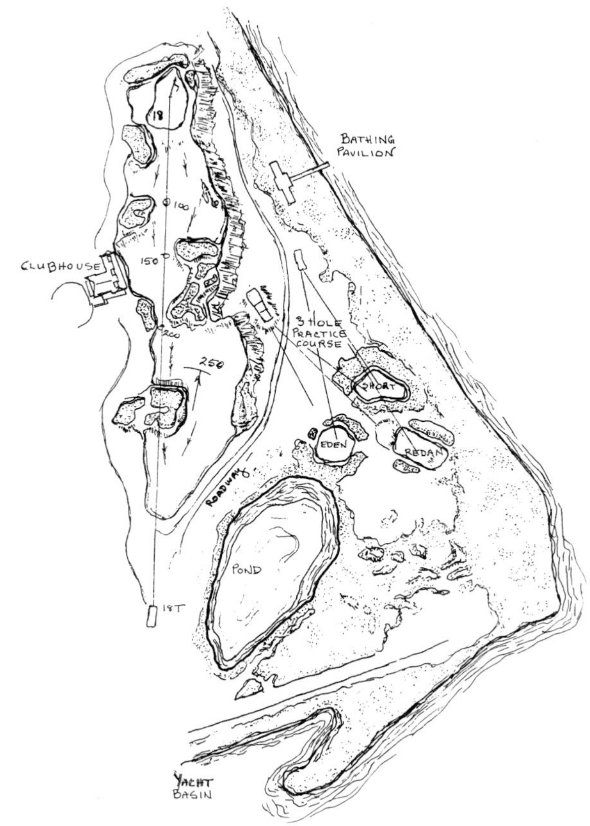

flat through the middle, but crowned at the edges.

In the beginning the 18th was known as "High" hole, owing to its geographic place on the property. Before the clubhouse was built it was also the original 9th, with a yardage of 440 yards. The green was planned to be nearly 100 yards long, although the present green was soon laid out at the crest of the hill, adding 60 yards to the hole that we know today.

In 1914, Henry Whigham wrote of the 18th hole:

> *The last hole, the 18th, is named 'High.' It is the second longest on the course, being 484 yards with a par of 5 and a bogey of 6. This is another new hole, an original one, peculiar to this course, born on the ground and unexcelled elsewhere. It is a hard one and it is all uphill. It is a fitting climax to the course. Having reached almost tide level at the seventeenth hole, the player must now mount to the top of Sebonac bluffs just west of the club house, where the view in all directions is unparalleled and beyond all power of adequate description. Roads and ravines, cliffs of caving sand are among the difficulties that require both skill and caution, but the green is an enormous one always ready to welcome the successful golfer to its great bosom with a smile.*

For those who hold the game closest to their hearts, there are few sights to match the windmill in the distance, standing sentinel over the Atlantic, and the late afternoon sun casting shadows on the 18th green. As you look to the sea, and turn back toward the sand hills, rolling across the horizon outlining the links, there is an overwhelming awareness of being in a special place, walking in the footsteps of golf history. Perhaps it is the overpowering presence of Macdonald, still watching over his masterpiece—a magnificent golfing tapestry that hangs on the eastern wall of our nation: The National Golf Links of America.

Above: The 18th, from the green looking back down the fairway. (Skyshots)

Opposite: In the early days of the course, Macdonald and Raynor designed a revolutionary practice course on a lower terrace below the fairway that simulated the approaches golfers would find in real playing situations using classic holes.

From two elongated tees at different angles, golfers could play to either a "Short," "Redan," or "Eden" hole from the same position, sharpening the skills necessary to meet the challenge of three exacting approach shots.

It was an ingenious arrangement of options that both Macdonald and Raynor would later build on the private estates of clients and friends. This was a particularly efficient way to provide good golf holes to those who lacked the sufficient acreage or malleable land to build a full-sized course. (George Bahto Collection)

Seth J. Raynor
May 7, 1874–January 23, 1926. (Princeton University)

Seth J. Raynor was born in Manorville, Long Island (NY). After receiving his primary education locally, he was enrolled in Princeton Preparatory School for a year before moving on to Princeton University in 1894. At the university he received his formal education, graduating with a degree in Civil Engineering and Geodesy with the class of 1898.

CHAPTER SEVEN

SETH *the* SURVEYOR

Initially, Seth Raynor was employed only to map the land and assist in plotting holes on the property that would become the National Golf Links of America. Following the initial survey, Macdonald recognized his talents and retained him to oversee construction according to his detailed drawings. For Raynor it was an easy transition from documenting the features of existing terrain as a surveyor, to the engineering calculations necessary to carry out Macdonald's plans. Raynor's education at Princeton was in both disciplines—a perfect combination for golf architecture.

> *Employing him to survey our Sebonac Neck property, I was so much impressed with his dependability and seriousness. I had him make a contour map and later gave him my surveyor's maps which I had brought from Scotland and England, telling him that I wanted those holes laid out faithfully to those maps. For three or four years he worked by my side. He scarcely knew a golf ball from a tennis ball when we first met, and although he never became much of an expert in playing golf, yet the facility with which he absorbed the feeling which animates old and enthusiastic golfers to the manor born was truly amazing, eventually qualifying to discriminate between a really fine hole and an indifferent one.*
>
> *When it came to accurate surveying, contours, plastic relief models of the land, draining, piping water in quantity over the entire course, wells and pumps, and in many instances clearing land of forests, eradicating stones, finally resulting in preparing the course for seeding, he had no peer.*
>
> —*Scotland's Gift—Golf*

The relationship that developed between the reserved Raynor and the volatile Macdonald was a study in contrasts, yet one filled with respect and trust—perhaps even mutual devotion. Raynor was an observant and studious pupil, and working with Macdonald, obviously a patient listener. Having no preconceived ideas on how a course should look or be constructed, he absorbed and implemented Macdonald's philosophy with detailed precision—once commenting that he wished he possessed "the ears of a donkey or an ass" so as not to miss a single word from his mentor.

Despite a close relationship, working month after month with a personality as overwhelming as Macdonald's sometimes wore out even Seth Raynor. Elizabeth Johnson, Seth Raynor's grandniece, once spoke of how on the weekends, Seth and his family would escape Macdonald for a day, taking to the campsites across Bull Head's Bay for a brief respite—a few hours of peace and quiet away from his obsessive boss.

At this time, Macdonald brought in another local resident, Mortimer S. Payne (and his team), to implement the major construction. Payne had previously been employed in the same capacity at neighboring Shinnecock Hills and the Maidstone Club in Easthampton. Being very familiar with course construction, and having easy access to local men and equipment, he worked for Macdonald off and on for many years—much of it reconstruction as Macdonald tinkered endlessly with National.

As the scope of Raynor's responsibilities quickly grew, he soon became immersed in orchestrating the planning and construction of what was to become the National Golf Course (its original name). To him, golf course design was a natural extension of his landscape design business, and Raynor found the work fascinating—it appealed to his aesthetic creativity and knack for clearly visualizing the intended final product. Having less and less time to devote to his engineering and landscape practice, and absorbed in meticulous preparations (which included an enormous plasticine model of the course), Raynor's attentions became focused nearly full time on what had become an apprenticeship.

Though he kept his landscape architecture practice open for several years while remaining in Southampton, eventually the demands of his newfound occupation during the golf boom dictated a move of his business to Manhattan in the early '20s.

Unlike the wealthy Macdonald, who never accepted a fee for his work, Seth had to run his business to earn a profit. Macdonald had an inflexible view of the definition of "amateur" (one of many inflexible views), and steadfastly refused to profit in any way from the game. If C.B. underestimated the cost of a job, he would merely ask for more funds from the founders or would kick in funds on his own—untold amounts of his own monies were spent at the National and Mid Ocean. C.B. was usually fortunate to have selected the land himself. Raynor, on the other hand, was obliged to use what each club gave him. Often that land proved to be a trying challenge.

It was here, in difficult circumstances, that Raynor's brilliance shone brightly. On courses like Chicago's Shoreacres, his gift for visualizing routings and adapting classic strategies on awkward terrain helped create some of his most enduring work. Expensive? Often it was, but never unnecessarily so. Raynor was a frugal man whose designs simply embellished the natural paths suggested by the land. Though Seth had a kind heart, and there were times he charged little for his work, like all great craftsmen, he was sensitive about his credibility. If he felt the integrity of his design would be compromised, Raynor would quietly reject the commission and remove his name from the project. During the golf boom in the '20s when many of his competitors intentionally understated construction estimates, Raynor maintained his reputation for honesty.

The former Mary Araminta Hallock was born in 1876. She married Seth Raynor in 1903. Little is known about her. There is no record of the couple having children, yet in a 1923 Princeton alumni profile, Raynor is quoted as saying "his son expects to attend Princeton about the year 1934." This would suggest a boy 10 or 11 years old. However, Princeton shows no record of any "Raynor" attending the university in that time frame, and none of the many obituaries following his death made mention of a son.

Araminta Raynor never remarried after Raynor's death in 1926, living until 1949. She is buried in Southampton with her husband across the pathway from C.B. and Frances Macdonald and H.J. and Frances Whigham.

Ironically, Raynor never actually played golf until the completion of his fourth course, St. Louis Country Club, and then with only passing interest. Throughout his career he played little, only learning the basic rudiments of the game. Raynor purposely avoided becoming a frequent player for fear his course designs would tend to deteriorate to his level of play. He felt "the golfer should learn to play the ideal links and that the ideal links should not come down to the playing ability of a lesser skilled player."

More importantly, he was one of the first to meticulously plan his greens to the inch, with layers of different material similar to the techniques used in modern construction—this he learned from his mentor. Even today, course superintendents marvel at the engineering and drainage of his courses, most of which still work beautifully 75 years later.

During the First World War, course construction came to a virtual halt as the nation turned its attentions to the war effort. Raynor was 44 years old, and though too old to serve in the armed forces, he assumed responsibility to the war effort by raising Liberty Bond funds, and working with the Red Cross and YMCA fund drives. He worked on the New York City Draft Board, assisting returning veterans with legal problems. Raynor was also active in the New York Bar Association, serving on various Wartime Committees helping veterans and their families.

Once, while addressing the Board of Directors at the Essex County Country Club in West Orange, New Jersey, a club considering several different architects to design their course, he was asked how much the job would cost exactly. His answer was, "I don't know." Given the terrain of the site, after due explanation from Raynor, he and Banks were hired. Macdonald convinced Seth to strike out on his own in 1914, passing the torch, but continuing the Macdonald concept of using the strategies of the great holes of the world as models. Charlie reminded Seth that he would be available for help as needed. Taught well, confident of his talents, and a man of personal pride, Seth seldom asked. Occasionally Macdonald became involved in design work, usually at the specific request of a club, though he would often get the project under way and leave the rest in the capable hands of Raynor. Now past 60 years old, Macdonald was more interested in refining National and spending time with his cronies.

By this point, Raynor had become a virtuoso of sorts, a master of seamlessly integrating classic strategic elements to existing land.

It is important to note that Raynor never ventured to the United Kingdom to see the authentic holes that served as the original prototypes. His influences began and ended with C.B. Macdonald—only rarely did he deviate far from the pathway laid out by his mentor. While others tried, in essence, to reinvent the wheel, Raynor never allowed his work to be contaminated by the whims of current fashion - clinging to the belief that classic ideas never go out of style.

If any observation can be made on the differences between a Macdonald and Raynor course, it would be that their tendencies mirrored their personalities. Many of Raynor's interpretations of Redan, Alps, or Cape were more understated, with a smoother and less of a defiant appearance. Macdonald's work, like the man himself, tended to be more theatrical, often intimidating players with brooding hazards, leering back as if to dare the golfer.

Above: This locket contains two rare photos of Seth Raynor. The family shot on the left includes Seth, his wife Araminta (on his left), and the owner of the locket (to the right), his grandniece Elizabeth Johnson. The photo of Raynor on horseback was taken in Bermuda. (George Bahto Collection)

Opposite top: Seth Raynor looking out at the Atlantic, circa 1924. (George Bahto Collection)

Opposite bottom: Seth Raynor with wife Araminta in Bermuda during the construction of Mid Ocean Golf Club. (George Bahto Collection)

Seth's reputation began to grow during construction of the massive Lido project in 1914. The huge landfill operation continued for years at the Long Beach site and because of its immensity, the project caught the attention of the golfing world. An operation of this scale had never been attempted before—the creation of a golf course on tidal marsh was unprecedented. It took many months to pump out the 2,000,000 cubic yards of fill from the bowels of Reynolds Channel.

Raynor

Though Macdonald was involved in the early stages, it was Raynor who executed the plans and directed the placement of bunkers and fairway and green contours. Lido was his detailed thesis—the culmination of Raynor's mastery of engineering and architecture. Upon completion, it was immediately recognized as one of the finest courses in the world—mentioned in the same breath as National and Pine Valley. Sadly, this masterpiece was to become the Atlantis of American golf, lost to financial hardship during the Great Depression. During Lido's construction there were lulls when Raynor's attention could be turned elsewhere (requests for new Macdonald/Raynor style courses were pouring in), beginning with the construction of Westhampton Country Club. Soon after, because of the apparent success of Lido, a similar landfill operation began at the Country Club of Fairfield in Connecticut.

It was the beginning of his meteoric rise as a golf course architect, coinciding with the start of the coming golf craze in the '20s. Next came Blind Brook, Gardiner's Bay, Bellport, and Greenwich—all nearby the Lido construction. The Macdonald/Seth Raynor redesign of Shinnecock followed, a response to the membership's dissatisfaction with their course, which paled by comparison to their next-door neighbor (National Golf Links) in Southampton. Soon after, even Maidstone called, wishing to retain Raynor's firm to make some modifications. All the while, the Lido construction continued.

Macdonald traveled in the toniest of circles, and the founders of the early clubs were the wealth of the Northeast; the Whitneys, the Rockefellers, Vanderbilts, Sloanes, Stillmans, Otto Kahn, bankers, investment brokers and industrial barons.

As requests came in to Macdonald, he would explain that Mr. Raynor was well adept at designing and constructing Macdonald-type golf courses, and that he, C.B., would be available for consultation. Raynor would give them courses using the "famous hole concept" for which they had become known.

From the beginning, virtually all their courses were built for the elite of each area. On Long Island and New Jersey, it was the major industrialist and financiers who operated out of New York City. In the northern states it was an outgrowth of Newport Country Club and Ocean Links, a course built for T. Suffern Tailer. Minnesota/St. Paul checked in with a group of courses headed by the wealth of the area, notably the Somerset Country Club.

In Pittsburgh, the coal and steel barons in the northern suburbs also wanted courses. In wealthy North Chicago, retail magnate Marshall Field and his son Stanley were instrumental in the founding of Shoreacres. At the Canadian border, multimillionaire George Boldt was a driving force in the development of the Thousand Island area. It was the

SETH J. RAYNOR, C. E.

Landscape Engineer and Surveyor

Grounds, Formal Gardens, Golf Courses laid out according to approved designs to conform with surroundings

Plotting and Subdividing of Tracts

Title Surveys

OFFICE AT RESIDENCE ON BOWDEN SQUARE, SOUTHAMPTON
Telephone 89-J

Top: Raynor family coat-of-arms. (J.J. Raynor)

Bottom: Magazine advertisement for Raynor's firm, circa 1914. (*Golf Illustrated*)

same story in the South—Chattanooga, Tennessee; northern and southern Florida; Charleston, South Carolina.

Working with America's upper crust came easily for Seth Raynor. His placid demeanor was instrumental in solving conflicts that arouse at Piping Rock and Sleepy Hollow - when the volatile Macdonald had problems with their administrations. He was a well-educated man who carried a confident air about him, and rightly so—his work spoke for itself. Dealing with wealthy clientele did not intimidate him in the least—he was quite comfortable with it.

When the volume of work became overwhelming, Raynor enlisted the help of two academicians, Ralph Barton from the University of Minnesota and Charles "Josh" Banks, a Yale graduate and professor at the prestigious Hotchkiss Preparatory School where Raynor was designing a course. Banks stayed with it until Raynor's death and carved out a career for himself.

Seth and Josh soon became involved with the Olmsted Brothers and as result, with Frederick Ruth. These men were the most influential land developers and landscape designers of the day. They worked with Raynor and Banks on projects like Fishers Island, Yeamans Hall, Gibson Island, Country Club of Charleston, Mountain Lake, Whippoorwill and others.

The same held true with the clubhouse designers—Macdonald's old friend Stanford White; Charles Wetmore of Warren & Wetmore; Jarvis Hunt; and later, Cliff Wendehack. All were top men in their field. In Florida Raynor was involved with the group initially responsible for the development of Florida as a major resort: Henry Flagler, John D. Rockefeller's business partner, Addison Mizner, whose architecture still defines the look of Palm Beach, and wealthy dilettante Paris Singer, heir to the sewing machine fortune.

On Raynor's second visit to California, through connec-

Above: MacKenzie teeing off on the par-3 16th hole at Cypress Point. (Sleeping Bear Press)

tions originally established in the East, he was chosen as the original architect of choice for the Del Monte land development of the Monterey Peninsula. Raynor had established an early relationship and gained the respect of Marion Hollins, the great amateur and a driving force behind development of the Pebble Beach area.

It was Hollins who attempted the innovative idea in 1922 of establishing a club and course designed specifically for women—the Women's National Golf & Tennis Club in Glen Head, Long Island. Though the course is credited to Devereux Emmet, Hollins insisted on input from both Macdonald and Raynor. In fact Raynor drew up the blueprint for Women's National—close inspection of the Emmet plans indicate a heavy Raynor/Macdonald influence.

This contact would prove invaluable. In the early 1920s, when Miss Hollins undertook the enormous task of developing the Monterey Peninsula, she awarded Seth Raynor (and his partner Josh Banks), the contracts for the Dunes and Lake courses at the Monterey Peninsula Country Club. The pair was rewarded for initial work on the Dunes course with a contract for three other courses, beginning with Cypress Point.

Ceaseless travel was beginning to take its toll on Raynor's health. In November of 1925, he routed Lookout Mountain in Georgia then immediately took the train to California to design Cypress Point.

Raynor left California and sailed to Hawaii for what, sadly, were to be his last two designs. After laying out Waialae and Mid Pacific, weakened from travel and overwork, Raynor returned to the United States. He immediately ventured by train across the country to the Everglades Club in exclusive Palm Beach for the opening of the course's second nine. An exhausted Raynor had finally pushed his failing health to the limit. Falling ill shortly thereafter, Raynor passed away of pneumonia in January of 1926 at age 51.

With the death of Raynor, and Macdonald well in his 70s, Charles Banks completed as many of the projects as possible given the difficulty of travel in the era. The Cypress Point job was then awarded to the great English architect Dr. Alister MacKenzie.

Given that the courses built by Seth Raynor were recognized as top-level golf courses, it is surprising how little is known of the man, and how little recognition he has received from golf historians. Certainly he was at the top of his field, and received the acclaim in his day, yet two World Wars and the great depression obscured his memory as a generation passed. Much can be attributed to Raynor himself—a reserved man who passed away long before his flamboyant mentor.

While other architects of the era were adept at self-promotion, and often penned books and magazine articles on the subject, Raynor felt no need to express himself beyond the courses he built. He never sought to reinvent golf architecture, but instead honored the past by anchoring his work firmly in time-honored themes. Like a great symphony conductor, Raynor's masterful interpretations of classic compositions were ever new and ever fresh, yet grounded firmly in timeless genius.

> *Sad to say he died ere his prime at Palm Beach in 1926 while building a course there for Paris Singer. Raynor was a great loss to the community, but a still greater loss to me. I admired him from every point of view.*
>
> —*Scotland's Gift—Golf*

Above: "It is but proper, too, that I should say a word of thanks to those outside of our organization who have aided to the undertaking. I cannot speak too strongly of the work of Mr. Seth J. Raynor, civil engineer and surveyor, of Southampton. In the purchase of our property, in surveying the same, in his influence with the community on our behalf, and in every respect, his services have been of inestimable value, and I trust that the club will extend to him the courtesies of the clubhouse during his lifetime."
—Charles B. Macdonald, 1910-1911
(Olympic Club)

Raynor was commissioned to design a course in 1918 for the Olympic Club in San Francisco, who had purchased the foundering Lakeside Country Club, and planned to superimpose a new course over the existing Wilfrid Reid layout. Though the club later elected to divide the property, and build 36 holes to accommodate the membership's growing interest in golf, a feature article on Raynor appeared in *The Olympian*, the club's monthly magazine.

To document the commission, a professional photographer was called in for a studio-type portrait of Mr. Raynor, who agreed to sit for the photo later used on the cover of the magazine. As Raynor's correspondences with clients were notoriously short and to the point, *Olympian* writer Theodore Bonnet thought this would be a perfect time to write about Raynor, who normally shunned interviews. What follows, courtesy of the Olympic Club, is the article in its entirety:

The World's Most Distinguished Golf-Course Designer Talks of Lakeside

By Theodore F. Bonnet

"He's a good sitter." This was the verdict of the photographer who had made the picture for the cover of this month's magazine.

Nobody had asked him for his judgement. Nobody cared what he thought of Mr. Seth J. Raynor's quality as a poser in front of the camera. He was only a volunteer, this photographer, a man of more than three score years, who doubtless judges all men in terms of his profession. He was not interested in Seth Raynor as a designer and builder of golf courses, but he appreciated the man's patience and the ease with which he did precisely as requested. In truth he knew nothing of Mr. Raynor's profession. It never occurred to the photographer that Mr. Raynor has other marked characteristics as, for instance, reticence. Here is a man whom you might say if ever you knew Seth Raynor that he could play golf all day with John D. Rockefeller without either of them provoking a foozle. He's a good deal like John D. in temperament.

So while the photographer appreciated one salient quality of the man's personality I lamented another; for fancy interviewing a man so reserved that like a person with a passion for a shut-in life he seemed deliberately concealing the best part of himself lest I might get something out of him. In truth I was eager to get something out of him, something about the Lakeside golf course which Mr. Raynor came to San Francisco to reconstruct. I was in a hurry too, for Mr. Raynor was on his way to a transcontinental train. This was to be a hurried interview, but I'd like to see the man able to hurry this designer and builder. One needs a corkscrew to penetrate Mr. Raynor's shell.

"I suppose," said I by way of inducing him to loosen up on a subject in which he was interested, "I suppose you play a lot of golf."

"No, not a good deal," he said in a tome of indifference, and then he straightened up in his chair as though about to defy me to extract the slightest bit of information.

I paused, bewildered. But presently I suggested that doubtless he had had a world of experience at golf before becoming an expert designer and builder of links. As this observation involved no inquiry Mr. Raynor by his manner gave me the impression that he was not going to make a reply. In desperation I asked him bluntly how he came to take up the business.

"Well, you see," he said, "I'm a civil engineer and Mr. C.B. Macdonald hired me to lay out a course at Southampton." By dint of prodding I learned that sixty men joined a club and contributed a thousand dollars apiece to build a golf course. After writing (Author note: visiting is correct) all over England and Scotland for suggestions and for opinions as to what were the best eighteen holes individually considered and getting quite a collection of models and maps and profiles, they selected a course for the National Golf Club which Mr. Raynor was employed to duplicate.

"Since then I have built about sixty courses," he said. And then he volunteered the information that in recent years people's ideals in golf have been revolutionized. Presently Mr. Raynor found himself discussing Lakeside, and he was quite eloquent for a little while.

"The beauty of Lakeside," he said, "is that nature has done so much for it. Conditions lend themselves so, to the kind of improvements that may be made that The Olympic Club can get a great deal for very little."

"How does it compare," I asked, "to other courses you know of?"

"In some respects," he said, "it is like the Lido Club links chiefly in the matter of soil, and that course is considered an ideal course for golf. In my opinion, Lakeside can be made the equal of any course that I know of anywhere, abroad or in this country."

Mr. Raynor is a man with imagination who already has the new and finished Lakeside in his mind's eye. Indeed when he left here he was prepared to sit down and make maps. The holes he sees precisely as a musician sees the notes as they are written in the sheet music though there is no sheet music before him.

"That first hole," he said, "I'd leave as it is now with some alteration in bunkering. The second hole as I plan it will be like the sixth at the National Club, a hole that (Harold) Hilton says is the best short hole he ever played." Not to know Hilton, I suppose, is to be like one benighted or at least to be pitied for lack of the knowledge that every man ought to possess.

Urging Mr. Raynor I extracted a dissertation on Lakeside and its potentials.

"The third hole," he said, "will be an Alps hole like the 17th at Prestwick, the most famous golf hole in the world. The fourth will be a drive and a pitch across a ravine, similar to the seventeenth at the National course, the Leven hole." My education in golf was getting on.

All through this discourse as it progressed was interlarded golf history. Mr. Raynor was always looking far into the distance at other links that he knew of, and of which he was reminded by the landscape at Lakeside which seems so restful to his mind's eye.

I learned that on the Lido course at Long Beach is a hole that must be reproduced out here—they are so much alike. Now that is a prize hole; that is to say, it won a prize in a contest held under the auspices if England's *Country Life* in which the contestants submitted designs of what they regarded as the best golf holes.

As designed by Mr. Raynor the sixth is a short hole—160 yards—an exact reproduction of the eleventh at St. Andrews, the most famous short hole in the world. The seventh is a 540-yard hole to be bunkered to the character of the ground. The eight and ninth are drive and pitch holes of decided character; the tenth a 440-yard hole, a fine two-shot hole to carry from the tee taking you across the road that runs up to the Club House. The eleventh is a drive and pitch hole "like the thirteenth at Piping Rock—a Knoll Hole." The twelfth is a two-shot hole right in front of the Club House. "This is one of the best two-shot holes I know of," said the famous artist of the links.

Mr. Raynor became really ecstatic when he reached the fourteenth hole on the ocean bluff. "A punch-bowl with fine possibilities, "was the way he described it. "The fifteen hole—a 220-yard hole—along the ocean bluff is a duplicate," he said, "of the famous Biarritz hole in France. In order to get a similar hole the Lido Club went to a great expense, paying as high as $160,000 for the land required."

Again Mr. Raynor grew enthusiastic when discussing the seventeenth hole, a reversed Redan, which has been constructed in many courses. The eighteenth hole he told me is one that lends itself in bunkering to the model of the eighteenth at Lido, which was one of the prize holes of the *Country Life* contest.

The Lido course, by the way, which is what Lakeside will be like eventually, cost $1,350,000. But that is wholly an artificial course. The hills were imported on trains. Even the fairways were not native to the site, and the soil, which is the same as the soil the ocean swept into Lakeside in the course of centuries, was pumped out from the depths at Long Beach. No wonder the course cost more than a million. And now agreeable to learn that Lakeside may be made equal to the best courses at a cost not to exceed $25,000 which sum will be repaid at the end of two years if we conclude not to exercise our option.

Mr. Raynor made known to me at the wind-up of our interview by way of summary that we have four short holes ranging 130 to 220 yards; six drive and pitch holes ranging from 310 to

375 yards; eight full shot holes ranging 400 to 540 yards. This division of a total of 6,200 yards is what Raynor pronounces an ideal arrangement; especially so, he said, considering that both nines end at the Club House and there are three different ways of playing nine holes.

This course as planned by Mr. Raynor would lend itself to the average golfer's playing as well as to the expert's. In its construction he plans to cut out all unnecessary climbing by following the contour of the ground, and also to eliminate all blind holes.

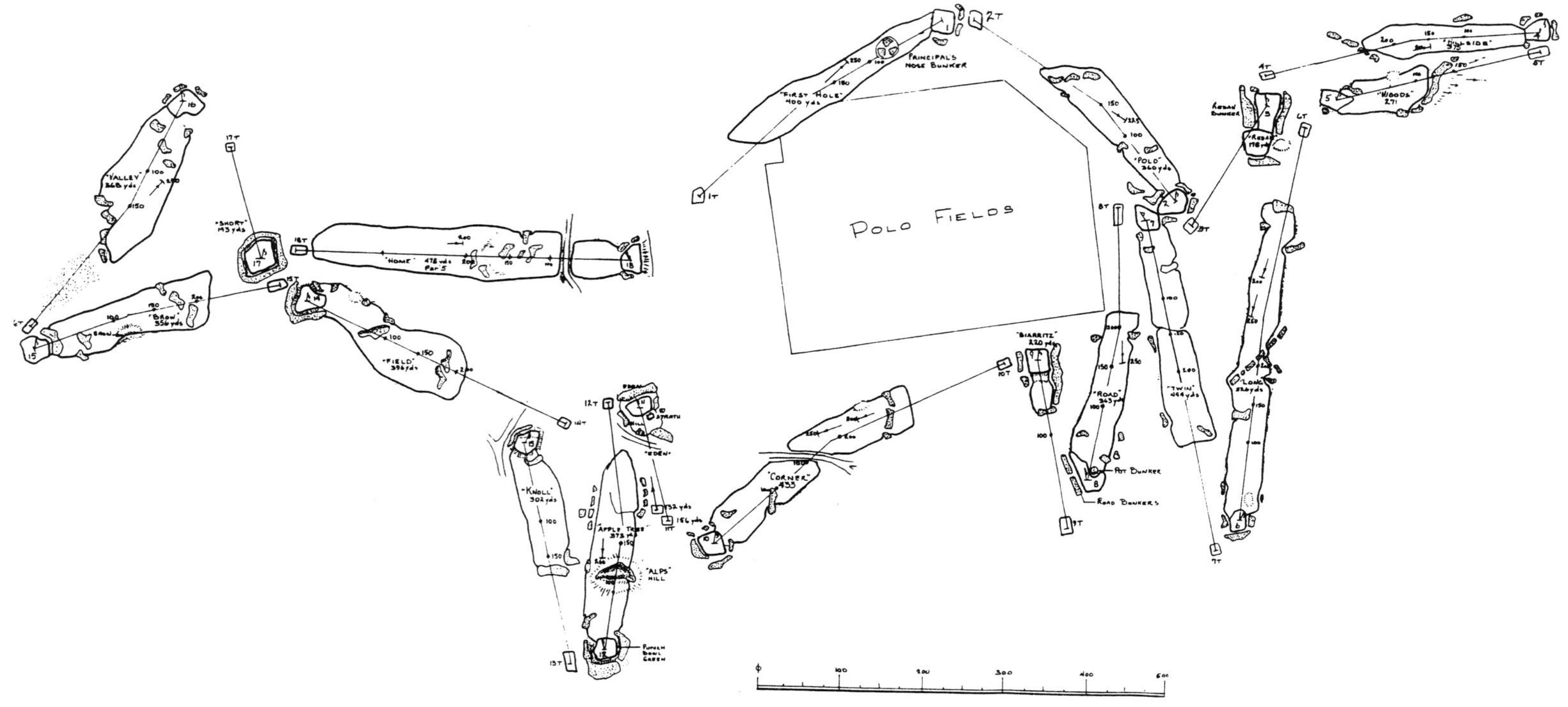

1911–1912 (original contact 1909)
Locust Valley, New York
Charles Blair Macdonald: architect
Seth Raynor: construction
Club founded: June 1,1909
Clubhouse and grounds: Guy Gowell, Boston
Clubhouse interior: W & J Sloane, New York
Revisions: R T Jones, 1950s
Pete Dye (Tom Doak & Woody Millen), 1985
Richard Spear (superintendent)

Piping Rock

1	400	First Hole	10	455	Corner
2	360	Polo	11	156	Eden
3	178	Redan	12	373	Apple Tree
4	375	Hillside	13	302	Knoll
5	271	Woods	14	396	Field
6	526	Long	15	358	Brow
7	444	Twin	16	368	Valley
8	363	Road	17	143	Short
9	220	Biarritz	18	440	Home
	3137			2991	
				6128	

CHAPTER EIGHT

PIPING ROCK CLUB

In his classic novel The Great Gatsby, *F. Scott Fitzgerald immortalized the 'Long Island Set,' the fabulous wealthy denizens of Long Island's North Shore, which is known as the 'Gold Coast' while it glittered. Their time was one of elegance and splendor, private yachts, formal gardens, and castles surrounded by polo fields. A typical summer's day on the Gold Coast started with a morning round of golf, then lunch on the terrace at the Piping Rock Club. In the afternoon, it was off to a game of polo at the Meadow Brook Club, then to a dinner party that more often than not would last to the wee hours of the morning.*

—Dr. William Quirin, golf writer/historian

The time was 1911, and following the opening of National Golf Links, interest in golf was slowly catching on with the social elite of New York, many of whom lived in a secluded, wooded area of Long Island known as the "North Shore."

The trek to Southampton in the early part of the century was a choice between a two-hour train or an arduous three-hour adventure over bumpy roads by car. Either option made a round of golf after work unappealing. With the exception of Garden City Golf Club, there were few courses of real quality within a short distance of Manhattan.

There were a number of private clubs in the North Shore area, but most were devoted to polo and hunting. One of those clubs was Piping Rock, founded in 1909 as a polo and hunting club with plans for a turf racing course to encircle the vast polo fields. The Piping Rock name was taken from a large stone located along the ancient trail between Glen Cove and Oyster Bay. Legend has it that Indian tribal leaders conferred and smoked their legendary peace pipes at this site.

Wishing to obtain a course of comparable quality to National, the membership of Piping Rock, led by Roger Winthrop, approached Macdonald about the possibility of laying out another golf course. Already a wealthy man, Macdonald had never intended to make a career of golf architecture. But it was difficult to turn down his friends. In his book he wrote:

In 1911 Roger Winthrop, Frank Crocker, Clarence Mackay, and other Locust Valley (Long Island, New York) friends wished me to build the Piping Rock Golf Club course....I was content with the knowledge that I was really contributing something to American golf and at the same time had the pleasing sense of gratifying my more intimate friends.

Opposite: Macdonald's routing plan for the exclusive Piping Rock Club on Long Island. (George Bahto Graphics)

Neither did Seth Raynor have any intention of continuing to build courses, intent as he was upon returning to his landscape design and surveyor practice in Southampton. The construction of the National had taught Raynor much about golf, but it had also taught Macdonald how crucial a good engineer and surveyor is in building top quality courses. He simply did not have the energy or patience to handle the endless details and calculations, and convinced Raynor to help him build one more. Again from Macdonald's book:

I employed (Seth) Raynor on this job. It would have been difficult to accomplish it without him. There was too much work and too much interference...I was content with the knowledge that I was really contributing something to American golf and at the same time had the pleasing sense of gratifying my more intimate friends. In accomplishing this end it was imperative I secure an associate, one well-educated with engineering capabilities, including surveying, companionship, with a fine sense of humor, but above all, earnest and ideally honorable. Such a man I found in Seth Raynor.

Above: The Biarritz is sometimes known as the "Chasm Hole." Macdonald came upon the original on a Willie Dunn course at the resort/spa of Biarritz, France. The 220-yard par 3 stretched cliff to cliff between an eight-foot high tee at one edge, and a fifty-foot high green on the other. It was a carry of 175 yards over a portion of the Bay of Biscay. (George Bahto Collection)

When Macdonald and Raynor first inspected the property, they found an expanse of gently rolling land, surrounding a spacious field used for polo beneath the clubhouse veranda. Perfect, Macdonald must have thought. Unfortunately, that was where the trouble began.

Told by the club that he could not use the fields but must route the course around it, Macdonald was apoplectic. He could not fathom why a club devoted to equestrian pursuits would want to keep their polo field! It was explained to him that golf was a secondary sport at Piping Rock, and that the membership might not share his singular enthusiasm for this new game with balls and sticks.

> *I found they wanted a hunt club as well as a golf club. Some of the leading promoters thought golf ephemeral and hunting eternal. Consequently, I had my troubles. The first nine holes were sacrificed to a racetrack and polo fields.*

Macdonald was ready to renounce the whole project, but luckily Raynor's patience and even temperament helped smooth everyone's ruffled feathers. It was finally agreed to reroute the course around the polo field and racecourse, though a miffed Macdonald stepped away after the plans were finalized, leaving Raynor to build the course.

As they would eventually include in nearly all their designs, Piping Rock was built around the positioning of the par 3 holes. At National, Macdonald built only three par 3s—a "Short," "Eden," and "Redan"—chiefly because he did not have a suitable site to showcase a fourth hole he had long

THE BIARRITZ was at that time quite controversial, referred to by detractors as "Macdonald's Folly."

Most Biarritz holes feature the swale in a closely mowed run-up area, though some, most notably Yale's 9th hole, are entirely putting surface. In recent years, many Biarritz putting surfaces have been expanded to include the entire landing area.

Below: Biarritz hole (9th) at Piping Rock. (George Bahto Collection)

admired. Here, he also included variations of the three, plus what is now identified as a "Biarritz," which added significant balance to the set of par 3s.

Like at National, there were no spectacular cliffs at Locust Valley. But because he was determined to incorporate the long wood shot he felt made the hole, Macdonald built a representation of a Biarritz for the 9th at Piping Rock. It had a 225-foot-long green and closely mowed landing area bisected near the center by a deep swale (often referred to as the "Valley of Sin"). It was to be a mainstay in nearly every course Macdonald and Raynor built.

The *American Golfer* magazine had this to say about Piping Rock's 9th just after the course was completed in 1912:

> *There is a Biarritz hole of about 220 yards which is new to this country and is one of the best one-shot holes in existence. There is a hog's-back extending to within thirty yards of the green and a dip between the hog's back and the green. Under normal conditions the hole has to be played with what is now known as the push-shot, a low ball with plenty of run which will land short of the dip and run through it onto the green. But the push-shot must be very straight, otherwise it will land on one side or the other of the hog's-back and break off into a bunker. This is the ninth hole at Piping Rock.*

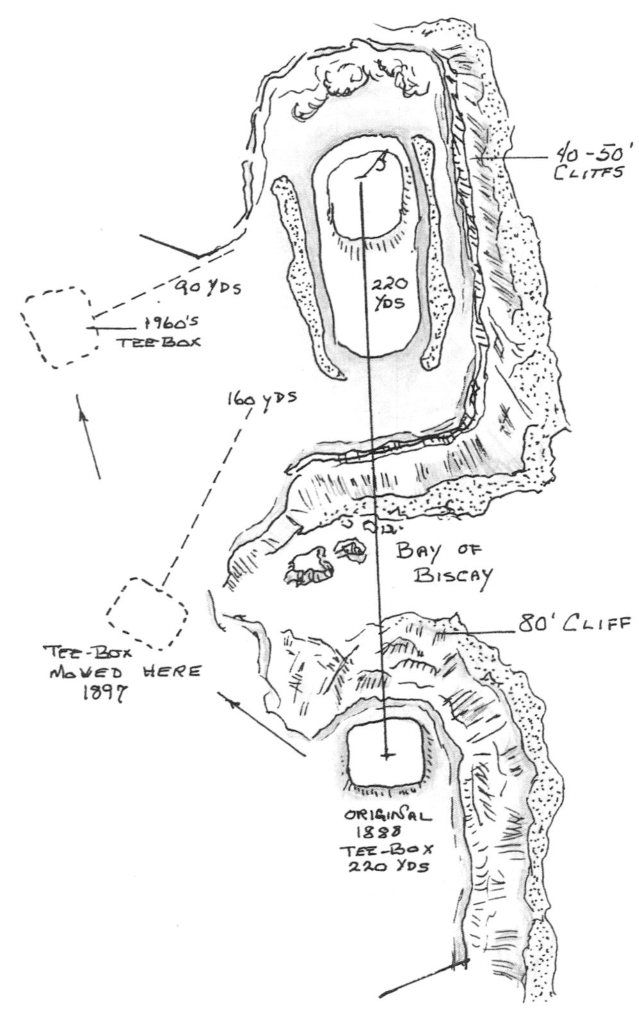

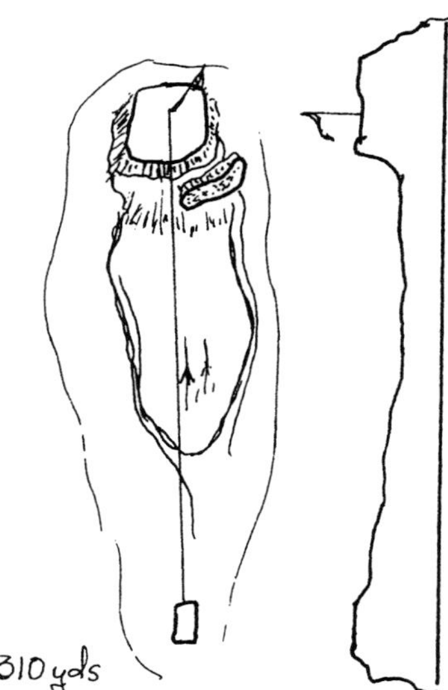

Left: Piping Rock's "Knoll Hole," the 13th. (George Bahto Graphics)

Above: The original Biarritz in France. This drawing shows the changes over the years. Because the hole was so difficult, it lasted only a few years. A hotel was built on the cliff. (George Bahto Graphics)

Opposite top: 4th hole at Scotscraig Golf Club, Scotland. (Scotscraig Golf Club)

Opposite bottom: The 13th hole at Piping Rock. (George Bahto Collection)

Macdonald also added for the first time what has come to be known as the "Knoll" hole, inspired by the devilish 4th hole at the Scotscraig Club in Scotland. Rarely longer than 330 yards, the Knoll requires a well-placed drive and an approach to a severely elevated plateau green with steep fall-offs on all sides. The putting surface features a plateau along the rear that require a perfect short iron to get near the pin. This hole is another of Macdonald's renditions that is often copied by modern architects without a clue as to its origins.

In the mid-1980s, after some ill-advised tinkering had diminished the course's strategy and aesthetics, the club brought in Pete Dye and his then assistant Tom Doak, both admirers of Macdonald and Raynor. Their superb restoration brought the club back into prominence.

Of particular note is the 8th, Piping Rock's Road hole. Originally a shortish, rather lackluster rendition, the hole was conspicuous for its lack of strategy. Dye, Doak, and superintendent Richard Spear, took a straight hole and constructed a new tee, creating a sweeping dogleg over high grasses to the fairway. This improvement, while not original, is a much clearer articulation of the Road hole principle—Macdonald would doubtless approve.

Piping Rock boasts the full measure of classic Macdonald/Raynor holes including a fine Alps and standout Redan—a must-see for fans of their work. Macdonald's first course after National is still viewed as both an elite course and club, though things have changed since 1911.

Only the barest of remnants remain of the horse track the club once held so dear. As for the polo field that caused all the fuss? Macdonald would be amused to know that it is now the driving range, one of the largest practice areas in New York.

Opposite: Piping Rock's Redan bunker is one of the deepest and one of the best. The Redan green here is among the very best built by Seth Raynor. (George Bahto Collection)

Above: Although considerably shallower than it was when built, Piping Rock's Road Hole bunker commands considerable respect. Piping Rock's version of the famous 17th at St. Andrews is one of Macdonald's and Raynor's best versions. Piping Rock was the first course built by this two-some after the National. (George Bahto Collection)

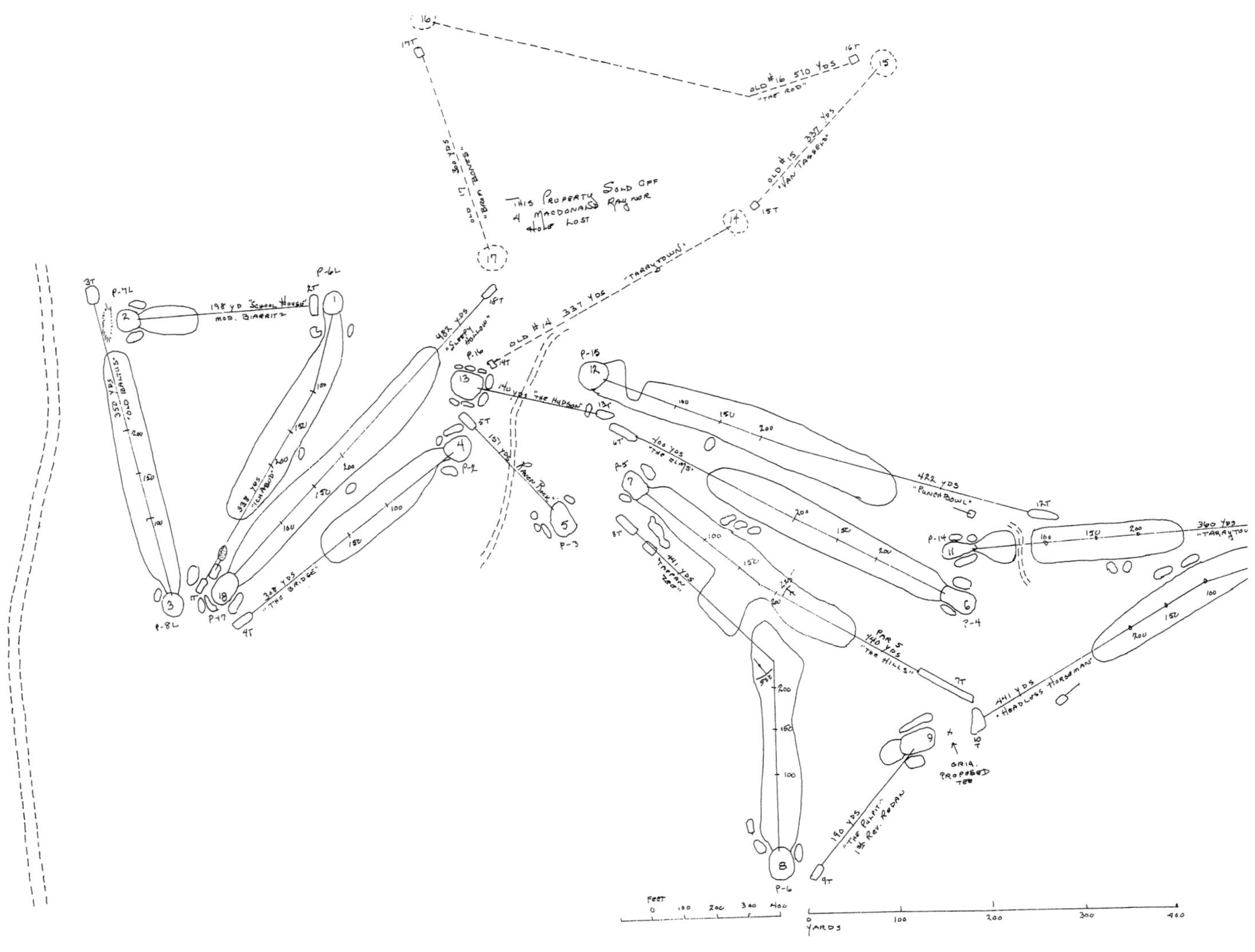

1911–1914
Scarborough-on-Hudson, New York
Charles Blair Macdonald: architect
Seth J. Raynor: construction
Club founded: 1911
Clubhouse: McKim, Meade & White
Revisions: Tom Winton, 1929;
A. W. Tillinghast; R, A-7 new holes to 27, 1933;
R.T. Jones, 1966
Rees Jones

CHAPTER NINE

SLEEPY HOLLOW COUNTRY CLUB

The Sleepy Hollow course would be next, with its commanding view of the Hudson River and its ghosts and legends quietly observing the proceedings of Macdonald and Raynor.

Sleepy Hollow was not originally meant to be a championship layout. After years of redesign, however, it has been the host of many championship events. The original construction of the course was under Macdonald's supervision with Seth Raynor as the foreman.

Sleepy Hollow's founders and members trace their beginnings to 1911 and the muster reads like a *Who's Who of America*: William Vanderbilt and his son Percy; John Jacob Astor; James Colgate; James Stillman; Franklin Vanderlip; Oliver Harriman; V. Everit Macy; A. O. Choate; Cornelius Vanderbilt...the list seemed endless. It was a powerful group of men.

According to Macdonald, he was "lassoed by James A. Stillman's friends to lay out a golf course in Sleepy Hollow." But it was not without problems. Macdonald called it "an almost impossible task to carry through." He and Raynor were told that William Rockefeller was not going to allow Macdonald to cut down or remove any trees on the property. Still seething from similar problems encountered at Piping Rock, he "was almost inclined to throw up the task."

Many of the original Macdonald and Raynor golf holes were named after characters and sites of the story: "Ichabod," "School House," "Headless Horseman," "Brom Bones," "Pumpkin," "Van Tassels," and even "The Bridge."

The present clubhouse is the second of two buildings that were used. The first, "Woodlea," was located near the present first green. During lean times the cost of operating two sites became prohibitive and the present "clubhouse" became the primary building. And what an imposing structure it is. The estate was purchased by Col. Elliot F. Shepard and his wife, who then hired Stanford "Stanny" White of McKim, Meade & White to design a 75-room summer home, a White-adaptation of Italian design. Landscaping was done in sunken gardens and viewed from the "Italian Terrace."

The grounds and building were hardly a golf clubhouse, but "they would have to struggle through it all." Completed in 1893, it was the largest and most expensive building up to that time for an individual. But alas, Mr. Shepard did not live to see his 2.5 million dollar home completed. In just over ten years the home was sold to William Rockefeller and Frank Vanderlip, who sold it to the membership of the Sleepy Hollow Country Club.

It is the scenic valley, so vividly described by Washington Irving, that is the overpowering feature. Its rolling terrain is

Opposite: Sleepy Hollow hand-drawn routing plan. (George Bahto Graphics)

ideal for golf, and Macdonald and Raynor built a fine course in this atmosphere. But the Macdonald course design of Sleepy Hollow was nearly lost from the very beginning because of Mr. Rockefeller's insistence that no trees were to be removed. Macdonald was furious, but in the end cooler heads prevailed. "...at a meeting with Cooper Hewitt, Jim Whigham and I had with William Rockefeller and Frank Vanderlip, I was given a free hand." The soil was good and once the disagreement about tree removal was ironed out, construction began. The initial summer was torrid, prompting Macdonald to remark: "This was a hard task for Raynor in appalling heat." Evidence suggests that Macdonald did more observing than laboring.

In the late 1920s, A.W. Tillinghast and his crew were called in to build seven new holes, expanding the course to a twenty-seven-hole layout. The signature hole of the course, however, is patterned after the 6th ("Short") at the National. It began as the course's 5th but because of various reroutings, it has been the 11th, the 12th and today is the 16th. The elevated tee offers a view of the tabletop green, which in the beginning was totally ringed with bunkers with the usual steep falloff off the back of the green. The tee shot is over a gully, and there is a beautiful view of the Hudson beyond.

At Sleepy Hollow, Macdonald designed his very first version of the so-called "Reverse Redan," where the green sits on a left-to-right tangent to the line of play and requires a slightly different strategy. He and Raynor used this configuration on occasion when dictated by the topography, but they rarely built Reverse Redan holes when the land had to be manipulated.

Research has uncovered an early scorecard (one of three different early versions) and descriptive text from 1922, which provides the routing, original yardage and a short but accurate description of the original Charles Blair Macdonald /Seth J. Raynor golf course at Sleepy Hollow.

THE MOST FAMOUS OF MANY LEGENDS surrounding Sleepy Hollow is that of the "Headless Horseman." According to the story, the ghost of a Hessian soldier who was beheaded during the Revolutionary War had possessed the body of Brom Bones,a local schoolteacher. Bones and another townsman named Ichabod Crane were vying for the hand of wealthy heiress Katrina Van Tassel. One fateful night, Crane was confronted by the ghost and chased toward a nearby bridge. As Crane frantically tried to get away, the "Headless Horseman" suddenly stopped and threw his head at him. Crane was never seen alive again. The story gained even more popularity after Washington Irving wrote his classic "The Legend of Sleepy Hollow" in 1820.

Above: Sleepy Hollow's magnificent clubhouse. (George Bahto Collection)

Left: The unequaled opulence of the clubhouse (*Golf Illustrated*)

Brief, picturesque, 1922 hole *by* hole description *of the* Macdonald design

Hole	Yards	Par	Hole Name	Handicap	Description
1	338	4	Ichabod	10	"a facile starter until woods are reached which bound the green"
2	198	3	School House *(a "Redan")*	15	"over a knoll, between two traps, to a banked green"
3	350	4	Old Baltus	8	"on gently side-swiping ground into a tree-bower"
4	308	4	The Bridge	12	"up and up (seems the ground climbs and catches your ball at top flight, an eerie sensation)"
5	151	3	Raven Rock	18	"a perilous short-shot between trees that are trying to get together to talk it over"
6	400	4	The Elms	6	"straight ahead past an outreaching tree-and-bunker convention, if bravery is in you"
7	440	5	The Hills	4	"up and down and up again"
8	441	5	Tappan Zone	5	"a dogleg, down and around a corner past trees that ought to be put in a fireplace"
9	190	3	The Pulpit *("Eden")*	17	"a side-sliding downhill trek to a green about the size of a card table but not so flat and simple to pitch on"
	2816	**35**			
10	441	5	Headless Horseman	5	"over a road, over some peaked bunkers, and, probably, over a high green into some bulrushes"
11	360	4	Tarrytown	9	"kitty-corner downward and similarly upward"
12	422	4	Punchbowl	7	"a long trip which eventuates all right if you get by a certain tree that has lost its folks"
13	140	3	The Hudson *("Short"—present 16th)*	16	over the Grand Canyon of the Colorado
14	337	4	Pumpkin	11	"uphill until you find the green, or something else"
15	323	4	Van Tassels	13	"likewise while you knock heads upon the sky and you play a star for your ball"
16	510	5	The Rod	1	"a fair trial to an orchard-edge with desultory implements in the way, placed there by men who never play the course"
17	300	4	Brom Bones	14	"diagonal up into the clouds"
18	482	5	Sleepy Hollow	3	"straight down out of them again, if possible. But a lot of the boys stay up in the air the rest of the evening."
	3315	**38**			
	6131	**73**			

Descriptions by Ralph Knight—*Golfer's Magazine*—Chicago 1922

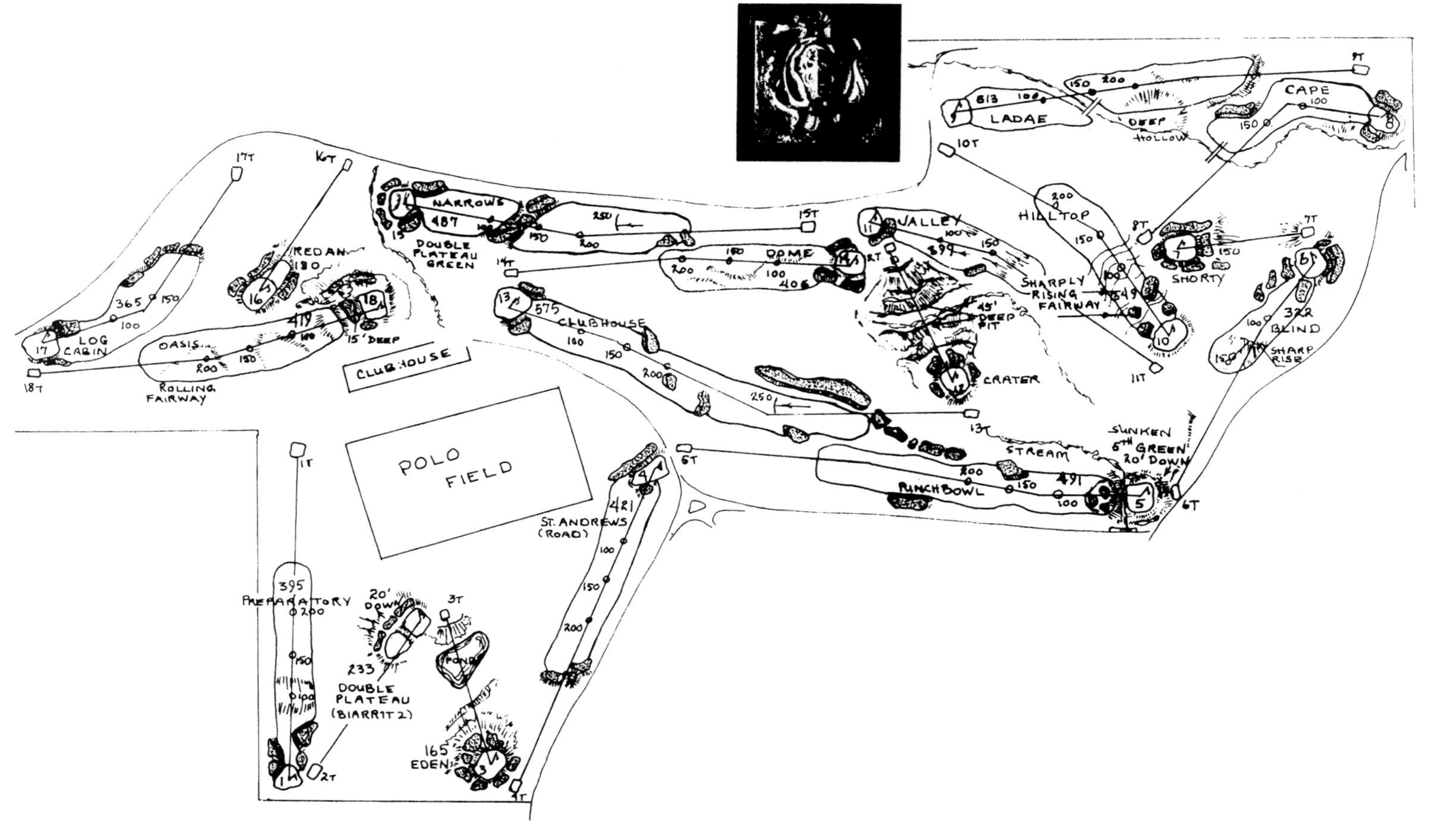

1913–1914
Clayton (Ladue), Missouri
Charles Blair Macdonald: architect
Seth Raynor: construction
Club founded: 1892
Clubhouse architect: Mauran, Russell & Crowell
Landscape architect: Henry Write
Revisions: R T Jones, 1952
Other revisions: in-house

St. Louis Country Club

Hole	Name	Yards	Par	Hole	Name	Yards	Par
1	Preparatory	395	4	10	Hill Top	349	4
2	Double Plateau	233	3	11	Valley	399	4
3	Eden	165	3	12	Crater	170	3
4	St. Andrews	421	4	13	Club House	576	5
5	Punch Bowl	491	5	14	Dome	406	4
6	Blind	322	4	15	Narrows	487	5
7	Shorty	150	3	16	Redan	180	3
8	Cape	340	4	17	Log Cabin	365	4
9	Ladue	513	5	18	Oasis	419	4
		3030	35			3351	36
			35		**Total**	6381	71

CHAPTER TEN

ST. LOUIS COUNTRY CLUB

By 1912, the Macdonald revolution in course design had taken a firm hold on the East Coast, this despite the fact that only three first-class courses had been constructed—all in the New York area.

Macdonald knew America had a long way to go in developing the game, particularly in the Midwest. His hometown of Chicago had the only notable courses, so when a request from the prestigious St. Louis Country Club came to lay out a course on land the club had recently purchased, Macdonald and Raynor boarded a train and headed west to spread the gospel of golf.

Founded originally in 1892, St. Louis Country Club records show that the club later two years later acquired a 200-acre parcel in nearby Clayton where the members "could enjoy golf, polo, tennis, and the fellowship of Kindred Souls." The course was rudimentary at best, with play crossing back and forth across local trolley lines, but it was still golf.

St. Louis held its first tournament in late 1897, introducing formal golf to the area, just as it had done with polo the year before. The affair was greeted with enthusiasm by the membership and spectators, but the caliber of golf could have been better. Early club records recall a smitten membership: "So tempting was the day that before the opening tournament quite a number of society women present played a round on the links, an invigorating cross-country jaunt of about one and one half miles."

The major problem, of course, was that very little was known about the game and how it was played - the members needed direction and instruction. This was supplied when the club hired Willie Anderson as their first club professional. Willie became their mentor and instructor, lending considerable stature to the club. He showcased his golfing talents quickly, winning the National Open four times in five years, 1901, 1903, 1904, and 1905. His successes brought so much fame and exposure that President Theodore Roosevelt paid the club a visit while visiting the Louisiana Purchase Centennial Exposition in 1904.

By 1912, the center of town had expanded dramatically and the Clayton property was no longer the pastoral setting it once was. Finding that it needed more breathing room, the club purchased some land from the Roman Catholic Church and moved to the Ladue section of St. Louis where the club is today.

It was agreed a new golf course would have to be built to modern standards, and C.B. Macdonald was America's premier architect. Though there was much discussion of

Opposite: Layout of St. Louis Country Club, circa 1913-1915. (George Bahto Graphics)

Macdonald's eccentric behavior, it was, after all, his architecture that had raised the bar. That was reason enough to choose him and Raynor to do the job.

Arriving in St. Louis, the pair found the Ladue site nearly perfect, with rolling terrain and many natural green sites on which to build their trademark holes. Free of the kind of interference from the club's board that they had encountered on their two previous projects, Macdonald and Raynor went right to work.

Though their first contact with the club was in 1913—when plans were formalized—Raynor had the par-72, 6,542-yard course ready for play the next year.

Along with their customary inclusion of a Short, Cape, Redan, and Alps, the property had a deep ravine shaped much like a crater that demanded to be used in one form or another. Macdonald had already positioned his four par 3s, and most of the basic routing was in place, yet he was determined to somehow incorporate this natural piece of ground. Breaking form, he built a fifth par 3 across the deep crevasse, perching the green precariously at the opposite edge and calling it "Crater." It remains a most noteworthy hole at St. Louis.

The par-5 5th hole is also unique. A medium length three-shotter with a green sitting in a deep hollow guarded by a rambling brook, it's a fine example of a Punchbowl/ Alps strategy and one of St. Louis' more memorable holes. In the 1950s, thinking that eliminating the blind green would improve the hole, the club relocated the putting surface onto high ground beyond. The change displaced the 6th tee box

Prior to Lindbergh's historic trans-Atlantic flight, the famous aviator set a coast-to-coast record by flying from San Diego to New York in less than 22 hours. En route, young Lindbergh stopped overnight in St. Louis. Seeking some financial assistance for his upcoming ocean crossing he was introduced to St. Louis club members Harry Knight and Harold Bixby. The pair rounded up eight investors—five of whom were fellow members—and raised $15,000 for the flight. Bixby's suggestion for a name for Lindbergh's airplane?

"The Spirit of St. Louis."

and shortened the 6th hole. Today, thankfully, the green has been returned to its original position and even improved upon. With the addition of a Principal's Nose hazard at the crest of the hill and short of the sunken green, the club reestablished the Macdonald/Raynor design.

Fortunately, that is also the case on much of the course. It remains a largely unaltered creation in the career of two men whose ideas and style were still evolving. In reality, St. Louis offers some of their best work, particularly the par 3s, which jump out as striking examples of their classic strategies. Some of the credit must go the topography, of course, but their bold routing took full advantage of the site without unnecessary or artificial embellishments.

Above: Note the built-up sides of the 9th green. Much depends on length and direction from the tee. (*Golf Illustrated*)

Opposite top: St. Louis finished with a rolling par 4 that ascended a hillside and ended in a natural amphitheater. The green was fiercely guarded in front by a cavernous sandpit, a final hurtle on this largely unsung–and unacknowledged–piece of architectural history in this quiet corner of St. Louis. (*Golf Illustrated*)

So what makes reclusive St. Louis Country Club exceptional? Pressed for an answer, visitors inevitably cite the pacing and absence of weak or ordinary holes. It has been described as a course a man could play the rest of his life and never grow weary of. And yet, in the final analysis, the merits of the course are best defined on a more subtle, visceral level: it just feels special.

The first major event held at St. Louis was the 1921 U.S. Amateur. Jesse Guilford won the title by holding his own over a field of legendary amateurs such as Bobby Jones, Chick Evans, Cyril Tolley, and Francis Ouimet. The Women's Amateur followed in 1925 and was won by Glenna Collett.

In 1947, the U.S. Open visited St. Louis CC for the first and only time. It was also the first time an attempt was made to show the Open on television, even though few people in America had a set. Some 25,000 spectators attended the event. Sam Snead, tied with Lou Worsham at the end of regulation play, shockingly missed a two-and-a-half-foot-putt to lose the play off by one shot, 69 to 70.

The U.S. Amateur returned in 1960, with Deane Beman defeating Bob Gardner for his first championship. The last major event held at St. Louis CC was the 1970 Women's Amateur. Mary Budke defeated Cynthia Hill.

Eschewing any more high profile events, the club inaugurated the "Charles Blair Macdonald Cup Matches" in 1992. The competition between St. Louis, Creek Club, Mid Ocean, National, Piping Rock, and Sleepy Hollow, rotates among clubs designed by Macdonald. Chicago GC was invited to attend, but declined, citing a limited membership. They did, however, host the first event.

"Old White"
1913–1914
Charles Blair Macdonald: architect
Seth Raynor: construction
Revisions: moderate, in-house

Past tournaments include:

1922 U.S. Women's Championship (Glenna Collett)
1938 PGA Tour event—White Sulphur Springs Open (Sam Snead)
1979 Ryder Cup
1985-1987 Senior PGA Tour event—Greenbrier/American Express Championship
1994 Solheim Cup Matches

CHAPTER ELEVEN

THE GREENBRIER RESORT

White Sulphur Springs, in a beautiful valley tucked amidst the towering Appalachian Mountains, was originally a Shawnee Indian settlement. Drawn by the deer, elk, and buffalo that roamed there, the Shawnee found the mineral springs were a natural "lick" for wildlife. They also discovered that the springs contained a strange curative power for many types of physical maladies—a kind of magic panacea bubbling from the rocks of the valley floor.

White settlers came in 1778, and soon they, too, were bathing in the mineral springs. Most famous of all was an early settler known only as Mrs. Anderson. The woman suffered from rheumatism, but found great relief from the springs after several weeks of treatments. Word soon spread to nearby cities and the sulphur springs became the destination of choice for scores of travelers who came to "take the cure."

The Legend of White Sulphur Springs

Ancient Indian myth has it that two young lovers, who came to the valley to escape the notice of tribal elders, were discovered by a chieftain who shot two arrows at the couple, the first piercing the heart of the young boy. The second, narrowly missing, stuck deep into the earth. When the young girl pulled the arrow from the ground, a sulphur spring began to flow. The Indian legend concludes that the young boy will be brought back to life only when the last drop has flowed from the ground.

In 1850, by virtue of a government grant, the Greenbrier Land Company was formed. The grant stipulated that the company would not only have to survey the land but settle on the site. The legendary powers of the sulphur spring water continued to spread, and resident physician Dr. John Moorman began earnest investigations as to what diseases, if any, the spring water actually cured.

As part of his research, he prescribed its use for a varied assortment of diseases ranging from rheumatism, neuralgia, and scurvy, to "derangements of functions in the organs of digestion." Many visiting "believers" claimed it even cured ugliness, for it seemed to them an elixir of eternal youth; others claimed it cured everything except "smoking, spiting and swearing."

The sale of the water from White Sulphur Springs blossomed into a full-fledged industry, with sales agents in most major cities up and down the East Coast. The price? Five dollars for a case of 24 bottles. In later years, the water was promoted as a natural laxative.

Opposite: Original poster from 1883. (Courtesy Greenbrier Hotel)

The Old White Hotel was built in 1857. Following the end of the Civil War, General Robert E. Lee lived there from 1867 to 1869. In time, nearly every president and important dignitary visited this isolated outpost in the mountains of West Virginia.

The trip from Washington, D.C. that previously had taken four or five days by stagecoach, was shortened considerably when railroad magnate C.P. Huntington expanded the Chesapeake and Ohio rail line across the Appalachians. Having recently purchased the resort, Huntington literally laid the tracks to the front door of the hotel. It then became a mere 15 hour trip for the nation's elite who flocked there, often arriving in their elaborate private railroad cars.

The Old White Hotel had outlived its day by 1913, so the new 228-room Greenbrier Hotel was opened. The once sleepy valley had grown from a mysterious, illness-curing spring to a grand resort.

Golf takes Root in Sulphur Springs

Golf in the area had a humble beginning in 1884. About two miles from the Old White Hotel, a small group of Scotsmen took their long-nose woods, solid brass irons, and gutta-percha balls and laid out a crude nine-hole course (to the amusement of most guests who happened by). Routed over the estate of one Russell Montague, the "course" would become the Oakhurst Club, believed by many to be the first golf course in America. One local was quoted as saying, "I did play marbles as a kid, but by gad this is the first time I have seen men play it." The Oakhurst Club and course was disbanded in 1897.

Golf returned to the area in 1910 when the original Lakeside course was built at the Greenbrier by Alex Findlay (it no longer exists). Like the Oakhurst layout, it wasn't much —described as a rudimentary nine-holer "hacked out across

The Old White course was described this way in 1915:

The situation, in a narrow valley flanked by wooded mountains, is one of great natural beauty, reminding the traveler of the golf links at Pau in France which has long been celebrated as one of the most beautiful in Europe. The holes will embrace many of the features which are associated with the National Golf Links in Southampton, L.I. Mr. Macdonald, the founder of the National who is recognized as the greatest authority on golf architecture in the country, has kindly lent his assistance, and his advice has been carried out by Mr. Seth Raynor, who did a great deal of work on the new Piping Rock course on Long Island. As might be expected, many of the holes will be reminiscent of the National and Piping Rock. The short holes, by which a golf course generally stands or falls, are all first class. They include a "Redan" and an "Eden" hole, and a full drive hole taken from Biarritz in France which has also been used at Piping Rock.

The longer holes are well conceived, and they include two or three of the "dog's hind leg" variety without which no modern course is complete. The ground is naturally undulating, presenting many natural features which will give individuality to the course, while the river makes a splendid water hazard in four holes. It would be difficult to imagine a more fortunate combination of circumstances.

It was calculated that the work of laying out the new course will cost at least $40,000. But the money will be well spent, since the climate of White Sulphur Springs is such that it can be made a golfing center all the year round. The putting greens of the "Old White" course are one of the fine features of the new course and one of the few courses in the south with real grass on the putting surfaces.

The architects of the course have not forgotten that White Sulphur Springs is a pleasure resort, and while they have got as far away as possible from the regular type hotel course, they have not made it too severe for the average golfer.

Above: The view from the golf clubhouse, overlooking what is now the Lakeside and Greenbrier Courses. (*Golf Illustrated*)

Below: Driving over Howard's Creek from the first tee of the Old White course. (*Golf Illustrated*)

Opposite: The Greenbrier Hotel, White Sulphur Springs, West Virginia —1913-1931. (Courtesy Greenbrier Hotel)

some pastures." Eventually noticing the success of Piping Rock, Sleepy Hollow, and St. Louis, executives of the C & O Railroad Company summoned Macdonald to construct a new championship test at the resort. It was originally called the "Number One" course when it opened in 1915, but it was soon being referred to as the "Old White."

At 6,250 yards, the new 18-hole layout offered the usual Macdonald holes, including an array of classic par 3s. There was a Punchbowl and a Road Hole design as well. Mindful that many of the resort's guests would be playing the game for the first time, Macdonald provided ample room so that the less skilled could take an easier route to the greens. "Old White" would go on to garner more than its share of recognition in the years to come.

The Greenbrier Course

1923–1924
Seth Raynor: architect
course demise: 1977
new Greenbrier course architect: Jack Nicklaus

In 1922, the U.S. Women's Amateur Championship was played on the "Old White" course. After it was won by Glenna Collett, a few vocal competitors—unfamiliar with a traditional links design—criticized the course for its often unpredictable bounces in the run-up areas fronting the greens. Though the course had clearly identified the best player of her era, the owners still asked Macdonald and Raynor to come back and make a few modifications. Macdonald was otherwise occupied, but Raynor returned to tweak the course in spots to "offset the element of luck, penalize poor shots, and secure proper advantage and result for well played shots."

Once he arrived, it became apparent to Raynor that the owners also wanted another course built to accommodate the increasing amount of play. Raynor set to work in 1923 and the new #3 course (the old nine-holer was still in use) was opened the next year. Although Old White remained the marquee layout in the minds of guests, many locals felt that the new 6,313-yard, par-72 course was a superior test of golf.

In order to lay out the new course, Raynor found it necessary to encroach on the old nine-holer. Following the completion of the #3 course, he redesigned and rebuilt the old Findlay course.

The Ryder Cup Comes to the Greenbrier

In 1977 Jack Nicklaus was brought in to strengthen the #3 course in anticipation of the Ryder Cup Matches. An entirely new course, longer and less forgiving emerged—sadly eliminating Raynor's original work. The new Greenbrier course impressed the PGA however, who selected it to host the Ryder Cup matches in 1979.

Above: Out on the Old White course in the 1920s. (*Golf Illustrated*)

Opposite: Advertisement placed in the *New York Times* on September 4, 1942, three days after the sale of the resort to the U.S. Army. Apparently no one needed 600 rooms of furniture at the time (note that the offer was for a one-transaction sale), because there were no takers. (Courtesy Greenbrier Hotel)

Lakeside

Alex Findlay: original design—1,971 yards—par 30
Seth Raynor: total redesign, 1923
Dick Wilson: expanded to 18 holes in 1962

For beginners, corpulent old gentlemen, and for a short practice round, the 9-hole No. 2 course is recommended.

—*Golf Illustrated*, 1920

In 1962, the old nine-holer was redesigned and expanded to 18 holes by architect Dick Wilson. The par-70 layout was also renamed the "Lakeside Course."

When the Greenbrier hired a young assistant golf professional in 1936, there was no way of knowing that he would become one of the legends of the game. Twenty-three-year-old Samuel Jackson Snead was hired for $45 per month, plus room and board. His career at the Greenbrier, however, was almost over before it started.

From Golf Resort *to* Military Hospital

Shortly after the outbreak of WWII, the Greenbrier was contacted by the U.S. State Department and asked to house ambassadors and certain citizens from newly hostile nations. President Franklin D. Roosevelt immediately ordered the removal of all Axis diplomats from Washington, D.C. and sent them to the Greenbrier until exchanges could be made for captured U.S. diplomats. Within a year, there were over a thousand "guests" at the hotel.

Invoking the War Powers Act in 1942, the federal government bought the facility from the C&O Railroad for $3.3 million (it was worth far more) and converted it into a 2,000-bed military hospital. It was then renamed Ashford General Hospital. Over the four years that it was utilized as a hospital, nearly 25,000 patients came through, including Generals Dwight Eisenhower, Jonathan Wainwright, Mark Clark, Matthew Ridgway, and Omar Bradley.

After the war ended, the resort lay empty and unused for a time. It was also for sale. Fortunately, President Harry Truman signed a bill "allowing the former owners first priority in purchasing surplus military property." Through the efforts of C&O Board Chairman Robert R. Young, the railroad bought back the Greenbrier for slightly less than the 1942 selling price. The company then set about restoring the property, and carte blanche was given to noted decorator Dorothy Draper who purchased 30 miles of carpeting, 45,000 yards of fabric, 15,000 rolls of wallpaper, and nearly 35,000 pieces of furniture and decorative items.

Three years and 12.5 million dollars later, the hotel reopened with an enormous celebration. Chairman Young invited what he referred to as "300 of the biggest wigs he could find." The guest list included the Duke and Duchess of Windsor, John Jacob Astor, Rose Kennedy and her children, William Randolph Hearst, Malcolm Forbes, and members of the Vanderbilt, Biddle, DuPont, and Pulitzer families.

Never one to miss a round of golf or a fancy party, crooner Bing Crosby took part in the celebration. Afterward he remarked, "I had to wash and iron my shirt before sending it to the laundry."

Thus was the stature—and still is—of the Greenbrier Resort in White Sulphur Springs, West Virginia.

One day not long after Snead was hired, a director of the club named Alva Bradley—owner of the Cleveland Indians—was putting out on one of the shorter par 4s. Suddenly, a golf ball bounded onto the green and whacked Bradley in his backside. Infuriated, he demanded to know why someone in the group behind had hit into his foursome with an approach shot. To his great surprise, Bradley was informed that the ball had actually been a tee shot that had been launched by the new assistant professional—a 335-yarder!

Impressed with the awesome power of the new employee, Bradley became a great fan of the young golfer. "Slammin' Sam" eventually became a fixture at the Greenbrier. In 1959, Snead added another incredible feat to his long list of accomplishments by firing an 11-under-par 59 on the Old White course. It was the first time a sub-60 score had been recorded during a PGA sanctioned event.

FOR SALE

for immediate removal

ENTIRE CONTENTS OF

The Greenbrier Hotel

White Sulphur Springs

west va.

Total contents and equipment must be sold in one transaction (offer for partial contents cannot be considered). An unusual opportunity is offered to those who can handle entire lot. Sale necessitated by preparation of property for occupation by the U. S. Government for hospital purposes.

Telegraph or Telephone

L. R. JOHNSTON, *General Manager*

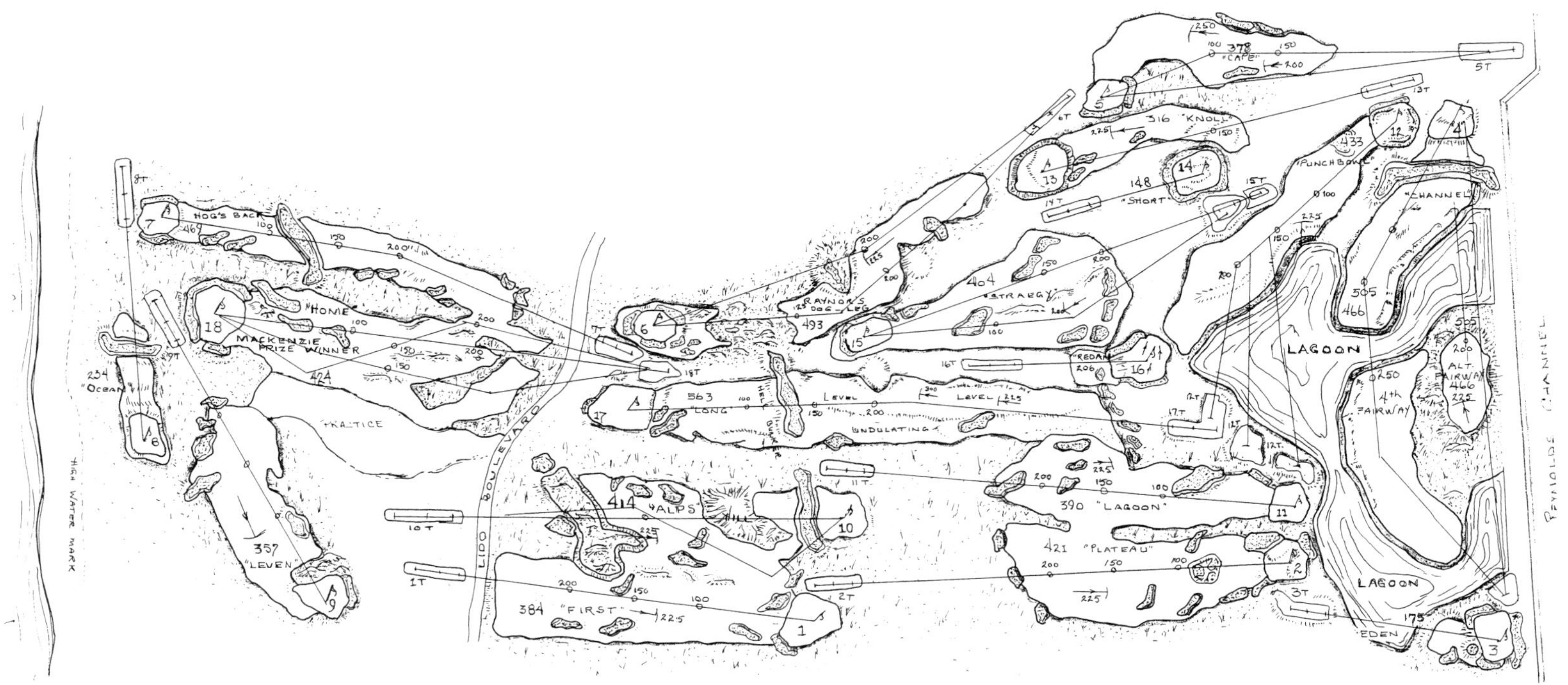

The Lido Club

1914–1918
Long Beach Island, Long Island, NY
Charles Blair Macdonald and Seth Raynor: architects
Seth Raynor: construction foreman
Peter J. Lees: turf expert—Keeper of the Green
W. Albert Swasey: Lido Club clubhouse architect
Club founded: 1914
Official opening: spring 1918

Hole	Par	Name	Yards	Hole	Par	Name	Yards
1	4	First	384	10	4	Alps	414
2	4	Plateau	421	11	4	Lagoon	408
3	3	Eden	175	12	4	Punchbowl	433
4	5	Channel	505	13	4	Knoll	316
5	4	Cape	278	14	3	Short	148
6	5	Dog's Leg	493	15	4	Strategy	404
7	5	Hog's Back	469	16	3	Redan	206
8	3	Ocean	234	17	5	Long	563
9	4	Leven	357	18	4	Home	424
	37		**3316**		**35**		**3316**
							6632

CHAPTER TWELVE

THE LIDO CLUB

THE GROWING REPUTATION OF THE National Golf Links gave rise to a demand for more high quality courses in less remote areas. While Macdonald was putting the finishing touches on his beloved masterpiece in Southampton, he and Raynor designed and built Piping Rock, Sleepy Hollow, St. Louis Country Club, and White Sulphur Springs at the behest of friends.

Eventually tiring of devoting so much time to the endeavor, Macdonald's intention of taking a break was sidetracked by an offer to build one more course on a lonely stretch of land on Long Island known as Lido Beach.

By the time the Lido project was in the planning stages, Macdonald was recognized as the leading golf course architect in America. Nearing 60 and no longer interested in new projects, Macdonald preferred just to play the game, while continuing to finetune his beloved National. He had encouraged Raynor to go out on his own and Seth was becoming more and more comfortable with the idea. Unless a special project or problem arose, Macdonald was perfectly content to pass on to Raynor any contacts for course building that came his way.

Routing plan of the Lido Club, Lido Beach, Long Beach Island, New York, 1914-1918. (George Bahto Graphics)

While designing and constructing Piping Rock in 1909, Macdonald had become friendly with Roger Winthrop, then president of the club. Five years later, Winthrop headed a group of wealthy investors that approached Macdonald with an idea. The hope was to lure him out of semiretirement for what they believed would be one of the most daring and innovative projects in golf history: The Lido Club.

The plan was to found a club with amenities of the highest standard that would attract a wealthy, international membership. It would be the finest and largest facility of its kind in the world. There would be a grand hotel with hundreds of rooms, a world-class golf course, and tennis, equestrian, fishing and shooting facilities. All of it would be located on a beach—a feature no other club at the time could boast about—and it would be within a short distance from Manhattan. It was to be the supreme social club for sportsmen.

The National was considered by many to be the premier golf course in the nation but it took time to get there. Some of the members, many of whom were also members at Piping Rock, wished for another choice to enjoy during the week—one that would be closer and much more opulent. The question, however, was how to interest Macdonald.

The investors were certain that only a Macdonald/Raynor creation would ensure the success of the project. And they had lots of money to spend. Included among the group of investors were Winthrop, Paul Kravath, Thomas Cuyler, Cornelius Vanderbilt, Robert Goelet, Charles Sabin, Henry Bull, W. Forbes Morgan, James Stillman, Harry Payne Whitney, and Otto Kahn. Eventually, however, they became equally certain that money was not the key to pulling Macdonald into the project—since he hadn't charged a dime for any of his previous design services, he clearly had plenty of his own.

Being both shrewd and observant, Winthrop soon realized that the only way to hook C.B. was to play to his enormous ego. If the idea was big enough, the challenge big enough, he knew that the architect could never resist.

So they made a simple proposal:

Build us a course that would have on it, your greatest holes ...and you can have complete freedom...

Any kind of golf hole he wanted? No monetary restrictions? It was too good to be true!

While building Piping Rock and Sleepy Hollow, Macdonald had felt restricted because of land constraints and a more diversified country club atmosphere (the members felt their existing polo fields were more important than their new golf courses). Now, though, his hands would not be tied. Many examples of his ideal holes could be featured, plus composite holes in different combinations. He also had some original designs that he had never used because they did not fit the contours of previous sites. Best of all, with a blank canvas and a blank check, he could create a links course.

At the National and other courses, Macdonald and Raynor had rearranged considerable soil to achieve the desired effect. Here, they would start from scratch. Knowing that Raynor would be at his side to solve the myriad of problems of this enormous undertaking, Macdonald could not refuse.

Later, Macdonald wrote, "To me it was like a dream. The more I thought it over the more it fascinated me. It really made me feel like a creator. "

But, oh, the site on which Lido was to be built.

Swept up in the opportunity, without seeing the site, Macdonald conditionally agreed to the plan. This sequence of events was exactly what the investors had hoped for because (1) they knew he was a man of his word, and (2) they knew perfectly well what his reaction would be when he saw the site.

The property was on Long Island's south shore at Lido Beach, just over the dunes at the shoreline. Like many other areas of Long Island, it was barely above sea level and nearly untraversable by foot. Someone described the land as "a bogged filled marsh-lands along Lido Beach's sandy beachfront...a vast morass, consisting of sand, reeds and brackish water, where croaking frogs held in high revel...a virtual no man's land."

When Charlie was shown what he called "this horrible 115 acres of sea-swamp and quagmire," he was furious. Bellowing that the entire idea was preposterous, he recanted and adamantly refused to accept their offer. Citing that although there was a possibility that the land could be filled at considerable expense, it "could not be constructed without water hazards and with a variety of undulations resembling the real thing." The answer was absolutely NO!

The community of founders assured him that at his disposal would be more than sufficient funds to build "anything you want to build." They would guarantee it.

Winthrop gently reminded Macdonald that he had, after all, already agreed to the project, and set out to convince him how they proposed to eventually turn this quagmire into a golf course.

The plan was to accomplish it through a complicated process of dredging, pumping and redistributing the sand from the bottom of nearby Reynolds Channel, and filling the swampy lowlands along the beachfront. This was a complete reversal of normal course-building procedure. Instead of sculpting the land to suit his design, Macdonald could first design the course topographically, then fill the land in as required.

Even the great Macdonald was a bit intimidated by the scope of the undertaking. Raynor, however, who had solved impossible construction problems before, knew that if properly supervised, the plan could work. To everyone's relief, Macdonald finally relented. Lido would be built.

"The construction of the Lido course was probably the most daring experiment undertaken in the world of golf course construction to that time," he wrote in his memoirs.

The year was 1914 and rumblings were coming from the other side of the Atlantic - the beginnings of World War I. By contrast, though, in the United States, it was still business as usual.

At Lido, hole designs and routings, dredging plans, hiring of laborers, locations of topsoil for import, site surveys, and irrigation issues were the problems of the day. Raynor could handle that, but the most worrisome problem still looming was how to grow grass on sand. Macdonald had been through this once before at the National with disastrous results.

Everyone, including the founders, understood that the enormous project would take years to complete. Macdonald wanted his fairways at least five feet above the high water mark, fearing encroachment by the sea would wash away his work. Massive amounts of fill would be needed to accomplish this. In addition, the plans called for a special hole requiring enough fill to construct "an eminence some fifteen to twenty feet above the fairway."

Grass could not grow on sterile sand, so huge amounts of topsoil and manure for fertilization would be needed. Macdonald and Raynor were quite well versed in turfgrass culture by now, but this project was different. The sand from the bottom of the channel was totally devoid of nutrition. Though he had learned much at the National about growing turf in sandy soil, Macdonald felt there was one more important person still needed; someone who understood course construction, to be sure, but someone who also could solve the difficult problems of growing fine turf grasses on seaside links. This was an absolute necessity if they were to have a great golf course.

Not to anyone's surprise, Macdonald sought out the person who was considered the best in the world: Peter Lees, Keeper-of-the-Green at the Royal Mid-Surrey Golf Club in England. Lees had been recommended to Macdonald by five-time Open Championship winner J.H. Taylor, and Lees was eventually retained by the Lido Country Club as their course superintendent.

The Brits were outraged.

Lees' defection across the Atlantic touched off a major scandal, as furious readers sounded off in *Country Life* with a chorus of condemnation. First this arrogant Macdonald had sailed over and plagiarized their country's finest golf holes, and now he was stealing Peter Lees from their shores to grow grass for a new course. In America yet.

But the transition was anything but smooth, as related by Horace Hutchinson in an article in *Country Life* in 1914. According to Hutchinson, golfer and writer James S. Worthington was on hand when Peter Lees was shown the would-be construction site for the first time. He related that:

> *It was a strange sight to see the famous Peter Lees, when on one bleak day, escorted to the spot by some of the bold pioneers of the Lido Club, he first cast eyes on the veritable desert. Arriving at Long Beach (Island) the party proceeded by slow stages through the sand and bent to their destination. The wind whistled about their ears and blown sand hit into their eyes.*
>
> *Eventually a halt was called. Peter looked at his companions and they looked at him. The situation looked gloomy in the extreme. An impasse was at hand. Feeling something was expected of him, Peter in gentle accents, inquired, "Where is the course goin' to be?"*
>
> *One of the founders, a bit sheepishly, waved his arm out towards the panorama of sand and mostly water. "Oh, all around here," he replied.*
>
> *Peter couldn't believe his eyes. A dour man, he had been offered some silly propositions in his time. But this was the limit. Had he come clear across the Atlantic to see this?*
>
> *"Oh, is that so?" Lees retorted. "Well then, if that's the case, I am goin' 'ome!"*

Now it was Macdonald's turn to do the convincing. Sorely needing Lees' expertise for this project, he lobbied furiously to convince the famous greenkeeper to stay. After additional cajoling from Roger Winthrop and a few other members, the reluctant Lees finally agreed—at least long enough to inspect the hole designs and elevations of the proposed course.

Once the concept of this radical construction was explained in detail, his stand began to soften and eventually he agreed to stay. It was a long trip home to England, and undoubtedly he knew that getting involved with Macdonald

Above: Scotsman Peter W. Lees became the greenkeeper at the Lido after it was built. (*Golf Illustrated*)

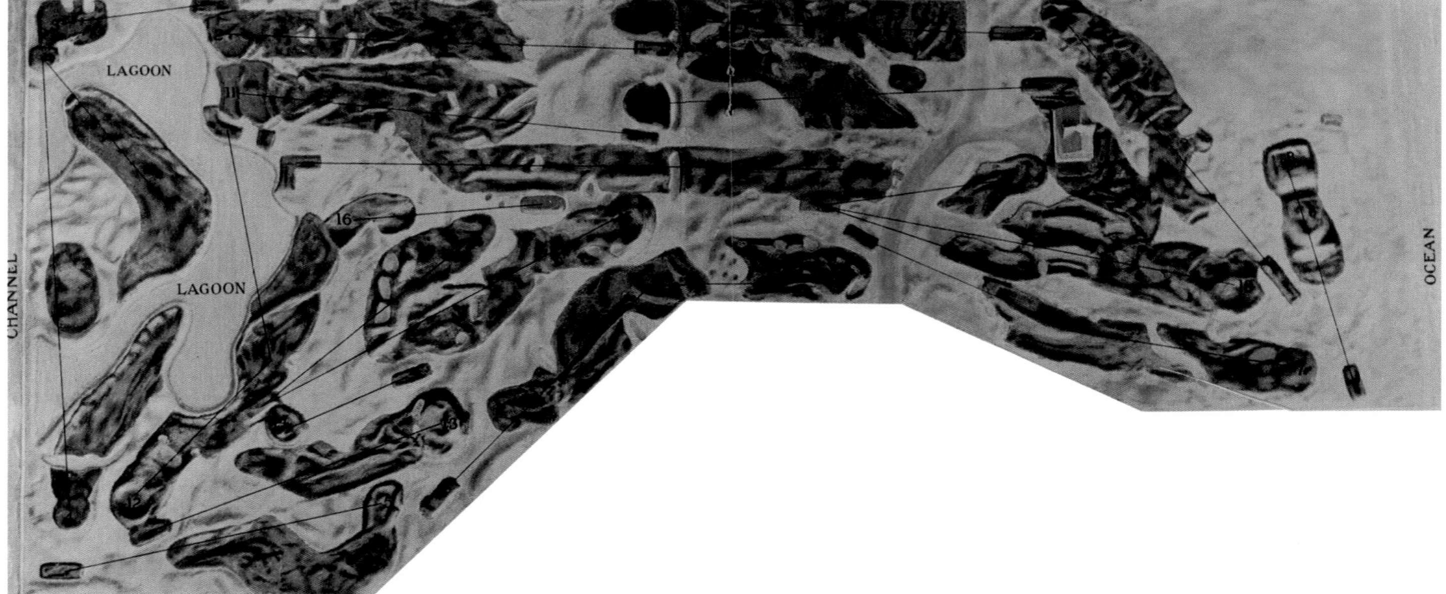

and this illustrious group of millionaires could only help his reputation. Besides, the challenge of raising a golf course from the bowels of the sea was something he should be a part of.

In all, 200 acres were purchased. The course itself would occupy 115 acres, the rest used for building sites. At the time of purchase, much of the land was literally underwater. A lagoon had to be dug with sea gates installed to control the tides. This lagoon also served as a major portion of the water hazards included in the Macdonald design. Indeed, because of Lido Beach's angle to the sea, stone jetties would have to be built beachside to help protect the shore from erosion.

After the basic routing and design work was complete, Macdonald had Seth construct a large-scale model of the entire Lido course from plasticine, even indicating all of the intricate undulations they had planned for the fairways and greens. This served two purposes: it was helpful for the client, and it enabled Macdonald and Raynor to view what would be the finished product.

If necessary, it would easier to make alterations to the model rather than through trial and error on site. It also afforded the construction foreman and crews a visual guide while shaping various portions of the course, freeing up the course architects to pursue other projects. In fact while Lido was under construction, Macdonald and Raynor at various times worked on or planned a dozen more courses. These included Westhampton, the Country Club of Fairfield, Bellport, Gardiner's Bay, Blind Brook, a redesign of Shinnecock, and Somerset Country Club in far-off Minnesota. Meanwhile, Lido's construction continued.

The landfill operation soon began and, according to

Top: Photo of the Raynor-built model of the Lido layout. (*Golf Illustrated*)

Left: To fill in the wasteland that was to become the golf course, sand was sucked out of nearby Reynolds Channel and piped over scaffolding to the proper locations. (*Golf Illustrated*)

Macdonald, "2,000,000 cubic yards of sand (costing seven cents a yard)" was sucked out of the bottom of nearby Reynolds Channel. This was pumped through miles of large diameter pipe to various locations of a slowly emerging golf course. Enormous scaffolding was erected to support the cumbersome dredge piping, through which flowed "a slurry mixture of 15% sand and 85% water that breathed life into this swampy wasteland."

Lido required over 100 acres of sand filled to an average depth of nearly eight feet, a difficult job even with modern equipment.

The problems incurred during the construction phase were endless: scaffolding buckling under the tremendous weight, broken pipes, jammed and leaking pumps wearing out as the abrasive mixture moved through their veins, all transported around the course by manpower and mules. In time, a small railroad was built on site to help expedite the massive movement of sand and soil. At the time, it was normal to have two or three hundred immigrant workers on a golf course construction crew. At Lido there were many more.

> *On top of the sand fill, to form the foundation of the fairway and the topsoil, was placed meadow bog five inches thick in blocks 15 by 30 inches in size, and on this again was placed muck—both meadow bog and muck was taken from adjacent meadow land. A lagoon was to create the island for the fairway of the fourth hole [the remarkable alternate-route "Channel" hole] with gates to let water in and out of the channel.*
>
> —*Scotland's Gift—Golf*

Once the muck was in place, topdressing of lime, topsoil, and manure was spread.

Seth Raynor was invaluable in this work, seeing that the hills, the hummocks, and the undulations would fit in as well as possible with the plans.

The seeding procedure used was to lay out nine square yards and then hand sow and gently rake in predetermined amounts of seed—all under the watchful gaze of Lees, one block at a time.

Work on the Lido project began in 1914, barely a week before World War I broke out in Europe. Given the enormity of the project, work at the site was painstakingly slow. It was not until 1917, as the United States was about to enter the War in Europe, that Lido was finally complete. The course had its official opening the following year.

Below: The rough at Lido Club consisted of over 1,000,000 hand-planted bents, rushes, and "eel grass" plants so penal it usually required a niblick to extricate oneself from it and play was usually back "to some island of land" with the loss of at least one stroke. (*Golf Illustrated*)

The cost of constructing a golf course on a rock-free site, at the time, was roughly $50,000. The cost for problematic terrain was more like $150,000 to $200,000. The cost for the Lido project soared to an unheard-of $1,430,000; nearly $800,000 in construction costs alone.

And remember: Macdonald never took a fee for his work.

The $1.43 million dollars did not include the cost of a clubhouse. With the coming of the First World War, the attentions of many original investors waned, and though the membership role was huge and wealthy, the planned majestic 400-room complex would not be built until ten years later.

Although the fairways were not as wide as those at the National, the holes at Lido included alternative routes to each green. Players were confronted with different carries and hazards commensurate with the approximate skill level of each player—all while judging the swirling breezes on this windy stretch of Long Island. Like at the National, Macdonald and Raynor tempted you to overstep your game... and to pay the consequences for it.

The Par 3s

As always, Macdonald and Raynor inserted their usual assemblage of classic par 3s, the heart of their designs. The 3rd hole was a 175-yard "Eden" that featured Reynolds Channel behind the green, representing the Eden River. The 14th was their "Short" at a modest 148 yards, while the "Redan" at the 16th played to a hefty 206 yards. The much-acclaimed 8th hole along the beachfront was aptly called "Ocean." It was a modified 235-yard version of the Biarritz.

The 8th was terrifying; one of the most difficult par-3 holes in America. The prevailing breeze was off the Atlantic, naturally, moving across the line of play from right to left. Tee shots were often aimed out over the beach to allow for them to drift back toward the green. The putting surface of the original 8th green was literally on the beach, completely at the mercy of the elements.

At high tide the waves often lapped at the borders of its elevated green. It was visually stunning but, in the end, totally impractical. High surf often threatened the green, where keeping a good stand of grass in the salty mists was impossible even for Peter Lees.

Sadly, storm damage eventually undermined the green. This forced the hole to be shortened one year, then moved entirely twice several years later.

The Par 4s

With little to constrain the architects but their imaginations, the par 4s were bold tests of skill and courage. All their of favorite strategies were there: "Punchbowl" with a carry over water; a double-plateau with a Principal's Nose bunker directly in the line of play; and the 15th, called "Strategy"—a hole reminiscent of the "Bottle" hole at the National but

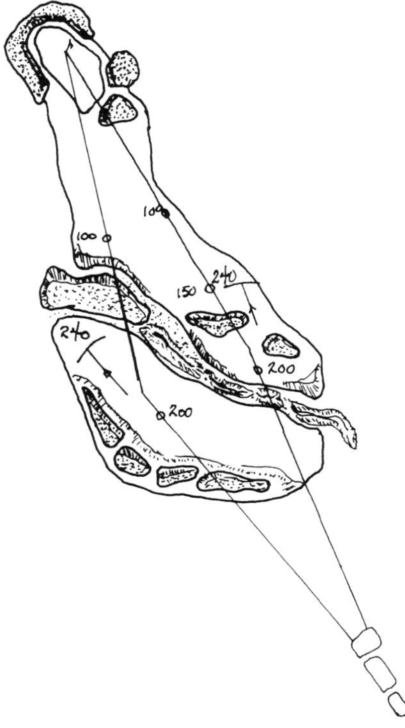

adapted by Raynor from a *Country Life* contest selection.

The 378-yard Cape hole required precision driving and very delicate iron play over an expanse of sandy waste. This was a bit of a different Cape because the carry was on the second shot. The play was to place the drive as close to the edge of the waste area as possible to gain the advantage of a shorter second. The drive and pitch 13th, called "Knoll," was similar in design to their beautiful rendition at Piping Club, with a plateau across the back of the green.

Long or short, there were no easy holes. At Lido, the player was always "on the rack, and flirting with danger. Shots that were lost to par were seldom reclaimed, even for the scratch man."

The par-4 Alps was hole #10. Even after the best of drives the golfer faced an intimidating second over a hill. The shorter hitter, unable, clear the sharp rise, was afforded a relief route around to the right but was forced to play it as a three-shot hole.

Though the course was a stern test, Macdonald and Raynor never lost sight of the average golfer. There were adequate landing areas for the "handicap player" who flew the ball less than 180 yards. The longer hitter, on the other hand, often faced a much narrower landing area laced with hazards. These bunkers, usually unreachable for the shorter hitter, were part of Macdonald's philosophy of always leaving a less-hazardous, alternative path to the green.

The Par 5s

The par 5s were an accumulation of the best strategic three-shotters seen at the time. Three were on the front, including two in a row—Raynor's prize dogleg was #6; "Hog's Back" was #7. The 6th measured over 460 yards and it tempted the "long man" with two difficult carries.

After a daring drive down the right side to the inside corner of the dogleg, the shot to the green was blind and over an expanse of sandy waste. The longer way around to the outside of the dogleg required three shots to a plateau green that was ringed with bunkers. The hole was a derivation of two entries in the Country Life contest. Seth recognized the genius of the design. With some modification, he used it initially at Lido and then virtually on all of his courses afterwards. (Subsequently, Charles Banks also used it.)

Above left: Lido Club's 15th. (George Bahto Graphics)

Above right: The Punchbowl green at Lido's 433-yard par-4 12th hole. (*Golf Illustrated*)

Opposite: The original Biarritz along the beach at Lido. The original modest clubhouse is in the background. (*Golf Illustrated*)

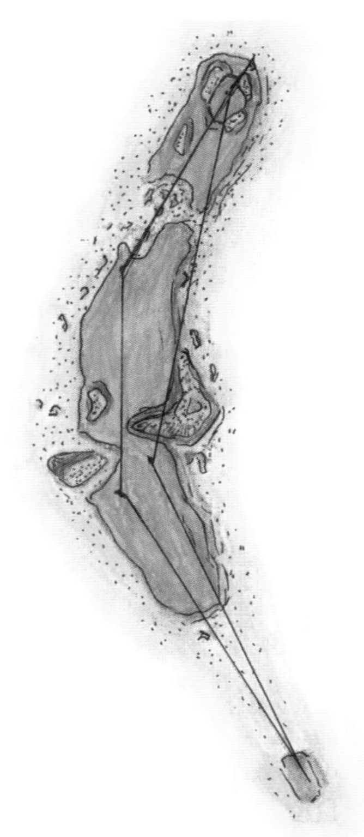

The par-5 17th was the closest approximation of the 14th at St. Andrews ("Long") that Macdonald ever designed, and the only one with the correct placement of a "Hell Bunker" (across the line of play). Most of their renditions placed the famous bunker in a less-threatening position along the side of the fairway, leaving an open avenue of play.

The strategies of those three par 5s would have been enough for any great course. But the Lido also had the "Channel" hole, its most memorable creation. An alternative fairway hole, the 4th was the first of its type in America, and it remains as the most dramatic ever built.

Danger was everywhere—even if the player opted for the longer, safer route to the green. Over this route the player had to negotiate two water carries, squeezing between a lagoon along the left and sand hills on the right. The second was either a layup or a long carry over water. A layup also brought into play a huge cross-bunker some 30 to 40 yards before the plateau green. Three well-executed golf shots totaling 505 yards were required to play along this "safer" route.

The alternative route was the epitome of high-risk golf, tempting the player with an heroic carry to a patch of island fairway that was only 30 yards wide, 100 yards long, and elevated some 20 feet above the rest of the hole. This tempting oasis, between scrub and sand, provided a direct route to the green.

Like everything else about the hole, the "shortcut" had card-wrecking perils—a miss to the left or short found a field of sea bents and eel grass; shots too far right splashed in Reynolds Channel. For whatever reason—sheer accident or pure genius—Macdonald placed this potentially disastrous hole early in the round. This gave players a quick chance to boldly go for birdie. Those who failed, however, found little opportunity at Lido to recoup any lost shots.

Recognizing that his somewhat stereotyped style needed an infusion of new ideas on occasion, Macdonald decided to seek input from his friends Horace Hutchinson and Bernard Darwin, and the editors at *Country Life* provided the vehicle for doing so in their weekly section called "On the Green." It was decided to solicit the public's opinion by running a golf hole design competition of an "entirely novel character" for a "two-shot hole designed for the purpose as one not less than 360 yards and not more than 460 yards in length." The winning design would be incorporated into the layout at the Lido.

Macdonald was no fool; the contest would also serve as a promotional piece to attract membership to the Lido Club and to publicize the quality of course he had designed.

Dr. Alister MacKenzie, a 34-year-old nonpracticing physician who had just begun to dabble in golf course architecture, won the first prize. The multitalented MacKenzie had done some work with renowned British architects Harry Colt and Charles Allison just after the turn of the century. By utilizing his experience as a camouflage expert during the Boer War, he had discovered a passion for golf architecture. He soon left the field of medicine entirely in order to concentrate on course design.

MacKenzie's prizewinner was the apotheosis of strategic

Above: Seth Raynor's prize dogleg at Lido. The 6th was a 493-yard par 5. (George Bahto Graphics)

Opposite: Design submitted to *Country Life* by British course architect Tom Simpson. (*Country Life*)

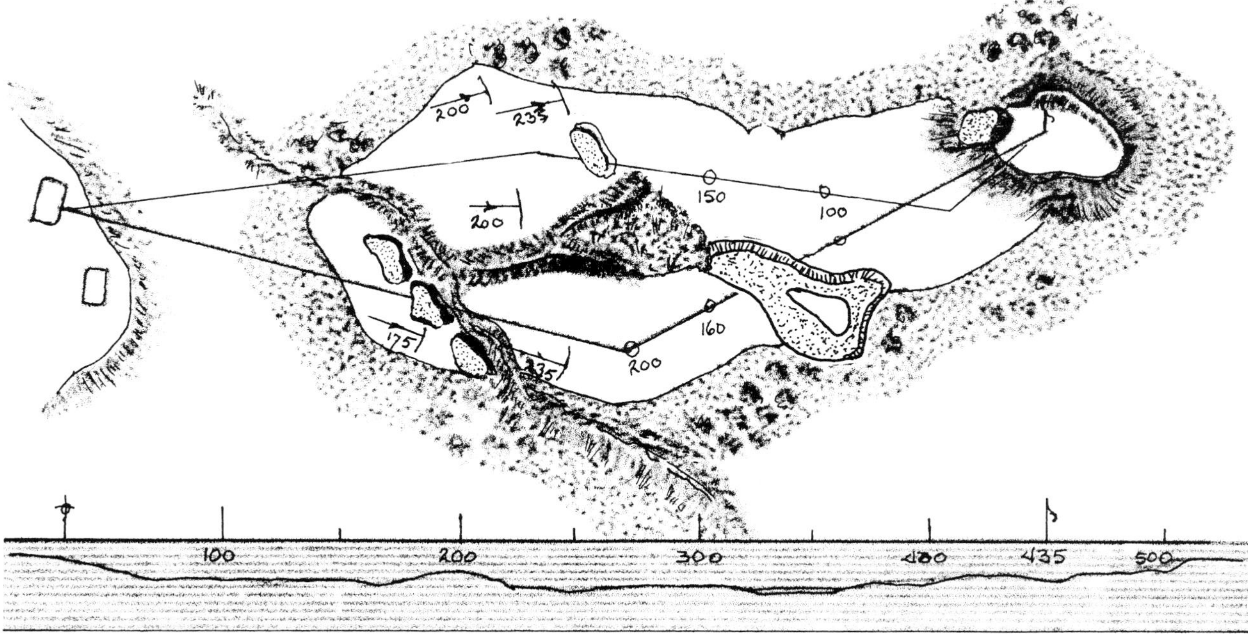

design. It featured five alternative routes to the green, each for players of different skill levels and each with varying degrees of trouble commensurate with the route selected. This complex hole required a fairway width of some 200 yards. Macdonald eventually used a simpler version, one that afforded three alternative routes rather than MacKenzie's five. The final version became the 18th at Lido.

Though Macdonald did not adopt any of the other contest submissions in their entirety, he claimed he "did incorporate certain excellent features from some of them."

When it was finally completed, the Lido Club immediately vaulted to the stature of C. B.'s National Golf Links of America. The two were heralded as the two finest courses in the country and a threat to equal the stature of the great classic layouts of the British Isles. Some British writers referred to Lido as the "Wonder at Lido Beach."

> *Over the many "sand hills" and other undulations in the "rough," 1,000,000 bents and rushes were planted by hand by Peter Lees' crew of laborers. These served the dual purpose of holding the fine sand in place as well as acting as an "off-fairway" hazard.*
>
> —C. B. Macdonald

The one criticism of the course was simply that it was too hard. The rough was deep, and the areas planted with sea bents and eel grass gave the fairways the appearance of isolated islands surrounded by wasteland, similar to the look of many desert designs in the western United States today.

> *Lido is the finest course in the world. It is a standing miracle, the wonder of which will never fade. It is the sandiest of seaside courses, majestic and tremendous, full of variety and interest, but I do think the rough is, in a good many places, too thick. Not only is it tiresome to have to hunt for a ball but is a little monotonous to have to play niblick shots when you find it.*
>
> —Bernard Darwin

Tournament play at Lido

There were many invitational tournaments at highly touted Lido, beginning with the 1922 Metropolitan Open. In the field were reigning U.S. Open Champion Gene Sarazen, Tommy Harmon, Johnny Farrell, and the cream of the club professionals and amateurs of the New York area. They were all anxious to have a go at the highly touted new course at Lido Beach. Despite the brutal setup and high scores, the players were delighted with the course, as were the galleries in attendance.

In the October 1922 issue of *Golf Illustrated*, Arthur Ross wrote:

> *Most tournaments are so common place, as far as the gallery is concerned. The experts drive monotonously straight from the tee, play their irons with deadly accuracy and hole out in one or two putts, and one hole is much like another that the thrills are few and far between. At Lido it is different. The haughty stars were forced to suffer from the ignominy of playing in and out of the rough. How they hacked and hewed, fretted and fumed, and many other things. There was no getting home in the next one at Lido. You took a heavy niblick and played for the nearest island of safety and then thanked your stars that you were lucky to get out in one. The gallery had a great time!*

The surprise winner of the Met Open was Marty O'Laughlin of Plainfield, New Jersey. Carding a disastrous front nine of 45 that included two double-bogies on the first four holes, O'Laughlin righted his ship and tamed the fierce winds, shooting only 3 over for the rest of the way for a 72-hole total of 309 (21 over par). His score was 3 shots ahead of runner-up Johnny Farrell. Sarazen carded 322—34 over par!

Many other local, regional, and invitational tournaments were held at the Lido Club during her glory years.

The Clubhouse

The original Lido clubhouse was, by most standards, a fine building. It stood just off the 9th green along the beach, and housed the pro shop, locker room, and dining and dancing facilities on the upper floor. It was as nice a facility as any private club could hope for.

But nothing compared to what was to come.

During the spring of 1928 there arose from the sand hills of Long Beach Island a five-story Spanish Mission style clubhouse designed by W. Albert Swasey. By that time, Lido's membership rolls had grown to 1,500. The new building, with its 400 guest rooms, put the final touch on this extraordinary sporting facility by making it more of an opulent resort and spa than a traditional "country club." The huge structure, with its large veranda and arched windows, overlooked the ocean and a walkway of colorful umbrellas. The Lido clubhouse was visible for miles around.

Sadly, the Lido Club would not survive. After weathering the stormy years of World War I—saved actually by a resurgence in membership during the Roaring '20s—the palatial clubhouse proved to be a major factor in the club's undoing. Less than a year after the clubhouse was completed in 1928, the stock market crash brought America, and the club, to its knees. The club fell into the hands of real estate people and out of the hands of the founders. The integrity of the Macdonald/Raynor design would eventually be ruined.

Above: After a round of golf, the Eastern elite would retreat to the luxury of Lido's rambling hotel and spa (photo, circa 1932). (*Golf Illustrated*)

Opposite: The five-story, Mission-style clubhouse that was built in 1928 included 400 guest rooms. (*Golf Illustrated*)

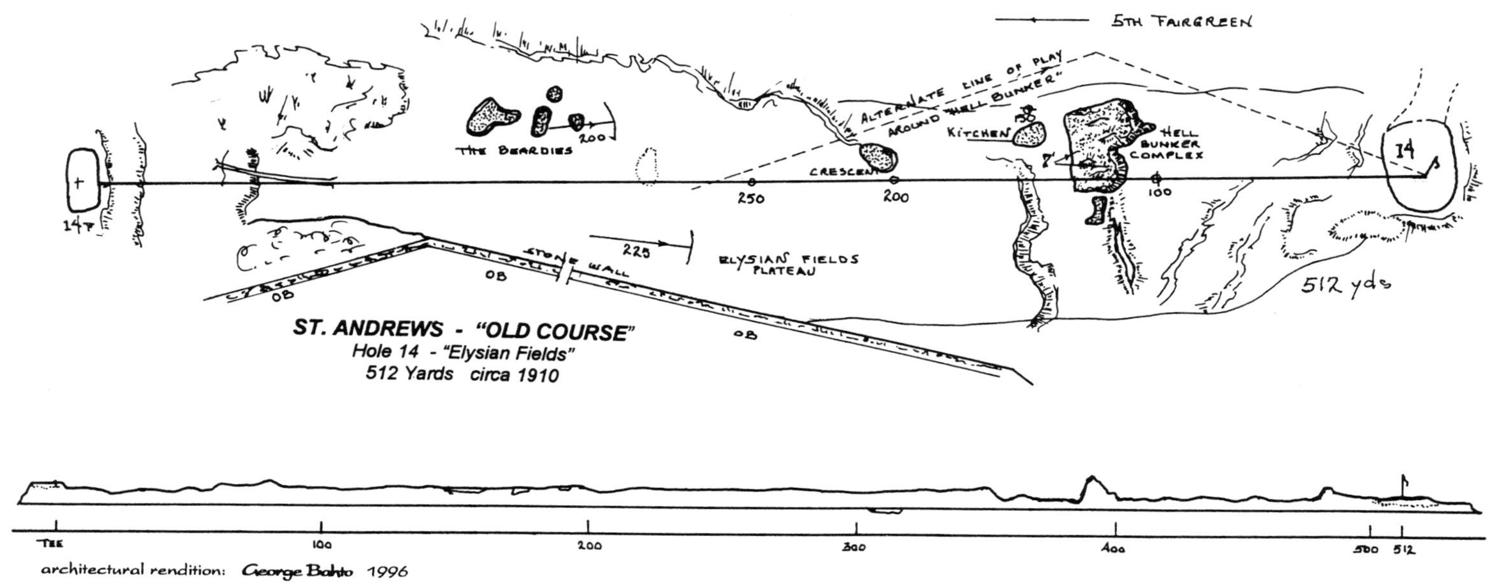

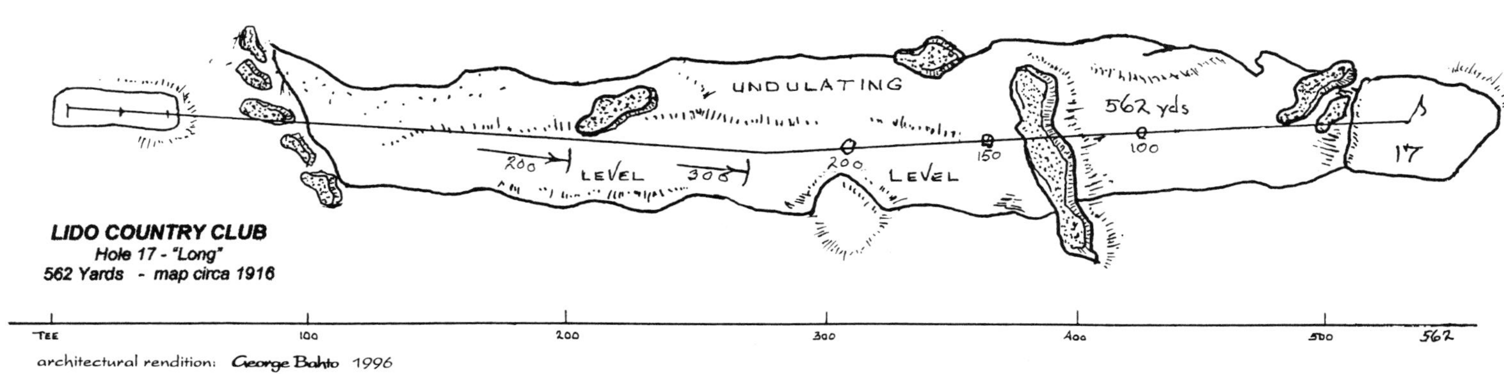

Above: Strategy comparison Top: "Long" at St. Andrews: the 512-yard 14th. Bottom: "Long" at Lido Club: the 562-yard 17th. (George Bahto Graphics)

Seth Raynor had passed away in 1926 so he did not live to see the demise of his greatest achievement. Macdonald was not entirely ecstatic with the end result at Lido. In his memoirs, he stated it was a "pity that toward the end of the fill the company did not carry out exactly the contours of our original map. So the course was not exactly what it might have been." This was partly caused by the astonishing cost of the project.

Several years after Raynor's death, and after the crash on Wall Street, Macdonald made a "pilgrimage to the Lido [that] only brought sadness to me, and I returned home feeling as if it were love's labor lost. To make matters more depressing, it was intimated to me that the present owners of the property intend on abandoning the holes on the ocean front, developing residential sites some sixteen to twenty acres."

The beginning of the end

It was to be a slow and painful death for both the club and magnificent golf course. The enormous cost of maintaining the huge building dragged the club to near rock bottom, forcing a sale of the property. Lido finally fell into the hands of real estate developers with little interest in golf. From there, the slide was inevitable. Waterfront property was ruthlessly sold off for housing without regard for the

Above: The course has been lost for over 50 years but its beautiful Spanish Mission "Clubhouse" built in 1928 still dominates the skyline at Lido Beach. This seaside view shows the sandy beach where magnificent lawns and promenades once were. At one time a swim club, the original Lido Club is now a condominium complex. (George Bahto Collection)

Left: Lido's 17th, "Long." (*Golf Illustrated*)

integrity of the course. Lido Boulevard—once a narrow, little used road close to the beach—became a major thoroughfare. The tees of many holes were moved, shortening the course and leaving the once mighty Lido a shadow of its former glory.

The course and club were a shambles.

Lido would eventually reach its demise during World War II. The United States Government deemed Long Beach Island a strategic defense site and the U. S. Navy took over the entire area in 1942, closing down the Lido facility. To this day, a portion of the area where the original oceanside holes were is retained by the U.S. Navy.

In 1956, a newly designed Lido course reemerged on a site next door. This Robert Trent Jones design continues to operate as a municipal course by the Township of Hempstead. Though a fine layout, it bears little resemblance to the original Macdonald/Raynor classic of the 1920s.

Top: Aerial view of the "Miracle at Lido Beach." (*Golf Illustrated*)

Middle: The fearful cross-bunker 50 yards before the green at Littlestone's 16th. This hole was the inspiration for the Channel Hole at Lido. (George Bahto Collection) (Aleck Bauer's Hazards)

Bottom: The tee shot of the 510-yard, par-5 4th hole at Lido—a hole C. B. Macdonald called the best hole he ever designed. (*Golf Illustrated*)

Opposite top: The Channel Hole at Lido (# 4) was a one-of-a-kind Macdonald design. The "safe" route (505 yards) was over a "C" shaped fairway around a huge sand hill on the right and water most of the way on the left. There were two carries over water plus a carry over a cross-bunker just short of the green. However, the green could be reached if a golfer chose to drive to a 30-foot-high "oasis" measuring 30 x 100 yards, surrounded by water and sand hills with bents and eel grass; the second shot was over a portion of the lagoon and the cross-bunker. (George Bahto Graphics)

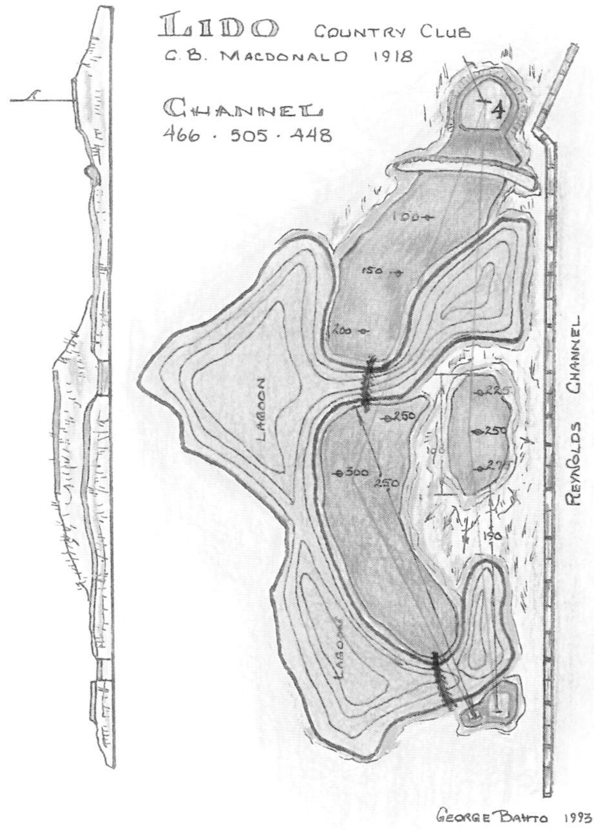

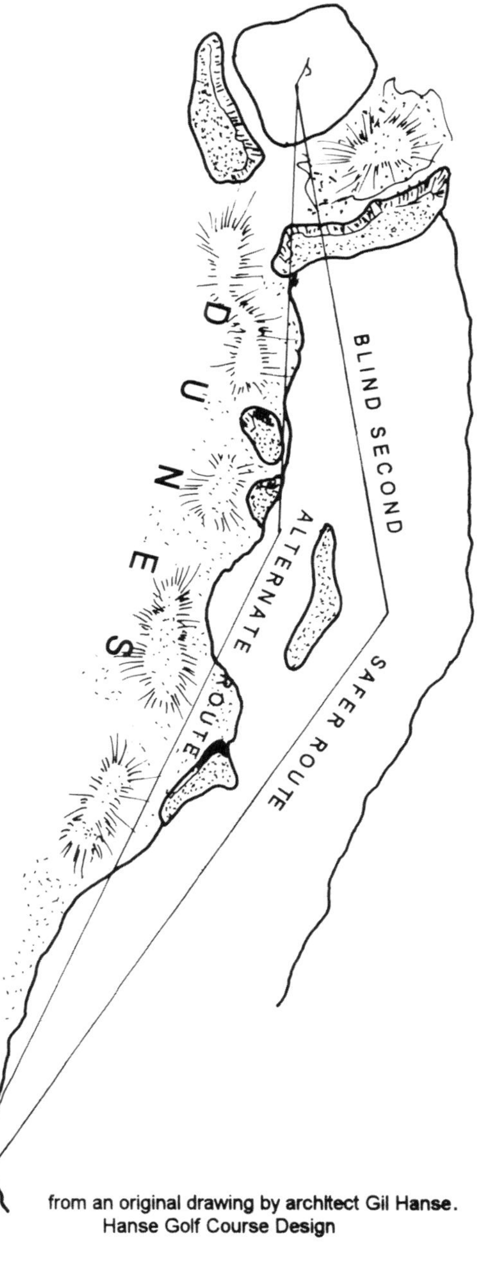

Right: The Channel Hole at Lido Club (# 4) par 5–466/505/448 yards (George Bahto Graphics) Origin: suggested by 16th Littlestone Golf Club

The Channel hole at Lido was the first attempt by Macdonald at this design. The lagoon had to be dug out, the fairway, green, and dune areas on which the "alternate route fairway" was located had to be filled to nearly 30 feet above the original level. The entire area was a morass. More than 2,000,000 cubic yards of sand fill was pumped out of Reynolds Channel to fill the 150-plus acres of the Lido Club.

At Littlestone Golf Club there were times when the area in the dunes was mowed for play and there were times when it was left to the elements. It is unclear if Macdonald ever saw the area while it was being used. If it were not in use, he certainly heard of times when it was and with his genius, he saw the practicability of its potential of being a great golf hole in the proper setting.

The routing changed at Littlestone in 1898. The new green was the old 15th green. The option area remained unaltered. If the regular fairway was used, hardly any player could reach the green.

At Lido, the setup of the hole was the same. The direct route allowed the long, straight hitter a chance to reach the green in two, while the alternate route required a three-shot play.

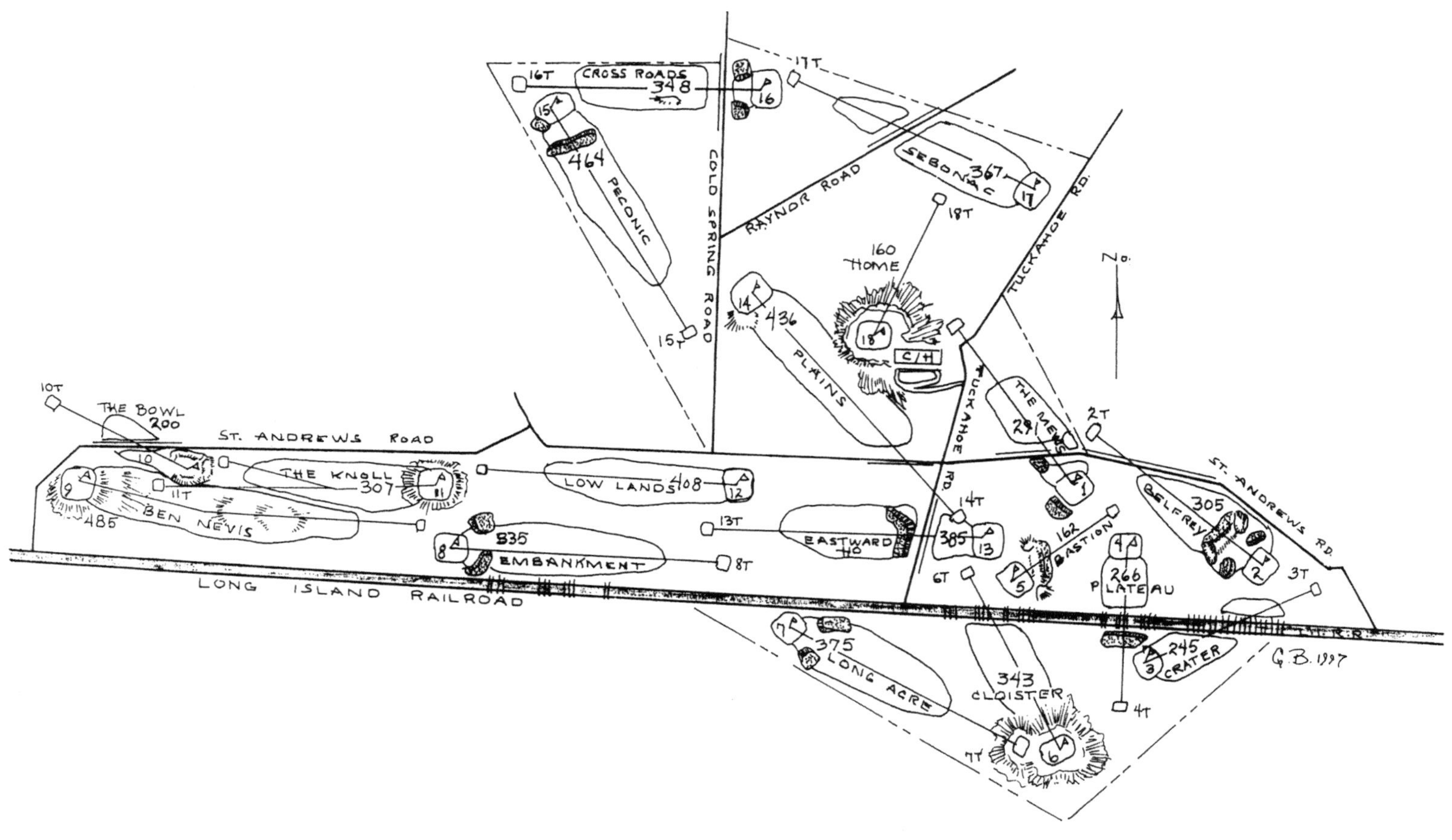

Southampton, Long Island, New York
Charles Blair Macdonald & Seth Raynor: redesign architects (1916); Seth Raynor: construction
Club Founded: 1891
Original architect: Willie Davis Jr., 1895
Other redesigns and renovations:
Willie Dunn, 1899
Macdonald & Raynor, 1916-1929
Wm. Flynn & H. Toomey, 1929-31
Wm. Mitchell, 1967
Clubhouse: Stanford White, 1892

Shinnecock Hills Golf Club

Hole	Name	Yards	Par	Hole	Name	Yards	Par
1	Westward Ho	353	4	10	Lowlands	380	4
2	Montauk	400	4	11	Eden	160	3
3	Short	120	3	12	Long	466	5
4	Eastward Ho!	356	4	13	Peconic	460	4
5	Shinnecock	381	4	14	Redan	160	3
6	Biarritz	200	3	15	Cape	335	4
7	Embankment	461	5	16	Sebonac	375	4
8	Ben Nevis	317	4	17	Roadhole	383	4
9	Knoll	430	4	18	Home	371	4
	Out	**3018**	**35**	**In**		**3090**	**35**
				Total		**6108**	**70**

CHAPTER THIRTEEN

SHINNECOCK HILLS GOLF CLUB

When one stands on the balcony of the historic Shinnecock Hills clubhouse, set on a Southampton hilltop, and looks to the north, the view encompasses not only the rolling linksland of one of the world's great championship courses, but also the landmark windmill in the distance that marks the National Golf Links of America.

These nextdoor neighbors, nudged together halfway between the clubhouses, are an embarrassment of golfing riches for this village on the road to Long Island's Montauk Point. Although the National is forever associated with Macdonald and Raynor, and Shinnecock with William Flynn, there exists a past secret that entwines them together: Shinnecock Hills was once redesigned by Macdonald and Raynor. Six holes of their original work, including the seventh green, remain to this day.

Why this is not common knowledge has as much to do with the later evolution of Shinnecock's golf course as with the complex and mercurial relationship between Macdonald and the club he once called home. There is scant mention of his contribution in Shinnecock's club histories, and in Macdonald's *Scotland's Gift—Golf*, there is nary a word. The only evidence is found in advertisements for Seth Raynor's design firm, which, in later years, listed Shinnecock Hills as one of his credits.

The club was officially founded in 1891, its course roughly 4,500 yards in length. The original 12-hole routing was the work of Scotsman Willie Davis, but it was expanded to 18 holes in 1899 by fellow countryman Willie Dunn Jr. Shinnecock Hills was one of the five founding members of what is now the USGA. During the first few years of the century, the course was gradually lengthened to 5,800 yards. It was a decent length for that era.

All of that changed, however, with the 1911 opening of the National Golf Links. For the first time, mighty Shinnecock Hills found itself rudely nudged from center stage as the golf world flocked to Southampton for a glimpse of the future. Shinnecock was not only no longer the best course in New York, it wasn't even the best course in Southampton. In truth, Shinnecock at the time paled in comparison with its new neighbor. And everyone knew it, especially the membership, which looked like an unabridged version of *Who's Who in America*.

In the tournament program for the 1995 U.S. Open at Shinnecock Hills, Dr. David Goddard, Southampton resident and professor of sociology at New York University, wrote:

Opposite: Hand-drawn map of the pre-Macdonald/Raynor course. (George Bahto Graphics)

Relations between the two clubs were always cordial, but Shinnecock had clearly been upstaged. Even its draughty, unheated clubhouse could not compare to the massive stone edifice, internally opulent, which Macdonald had erected. Shinnecock was a family club where women played a prominent role. The National, while not quite an 'Eveless Eden,' was a men's club par excellence. The food was better, the golf undeniably so, the parties legendary.

It was most certainly not Macdonald's original intention to build his ideal golf course right next door, and in truth he was reticent to do so even when it became obvious it was his best option. He was a member at Shinnecock and counted many close friends there; Macdonald knew that comparisons would be inevitable. In fact, the natural features of the Shinnecock site were so outstanding that Macdonald first tried to purchase that land, hoping to build over the existing layout. But he was turned down by the club.

But comparisons were made, inadequacies identified, and in 1915 a decision was made to drastically alter the historic Shinnecock Hills layout. According to the club history, the opening of the National "had a profound effect" that was to shape the future of the club, which then as now, shared many members belonging to both clubs.

The most glaring issue to address was the fact that the course played four times across the tracks of the Long Island Railroad. The spark-sprouting engines of the trains often ignited fires on the dry grasses of the golf course. According to historian/writer David Goddard: "By 1913, the course was up to about 6,100 yards—the same as National. This course lasted for a scant three seasons. In 1916, lawyers for the Long Island Railroad warned of increasing danger of accidents on the holes that crossed the tracks. They demanded that the club either enter into a $25,000 bond agreement indemnifying the railroad for any liability to players or caddies, or change the course."

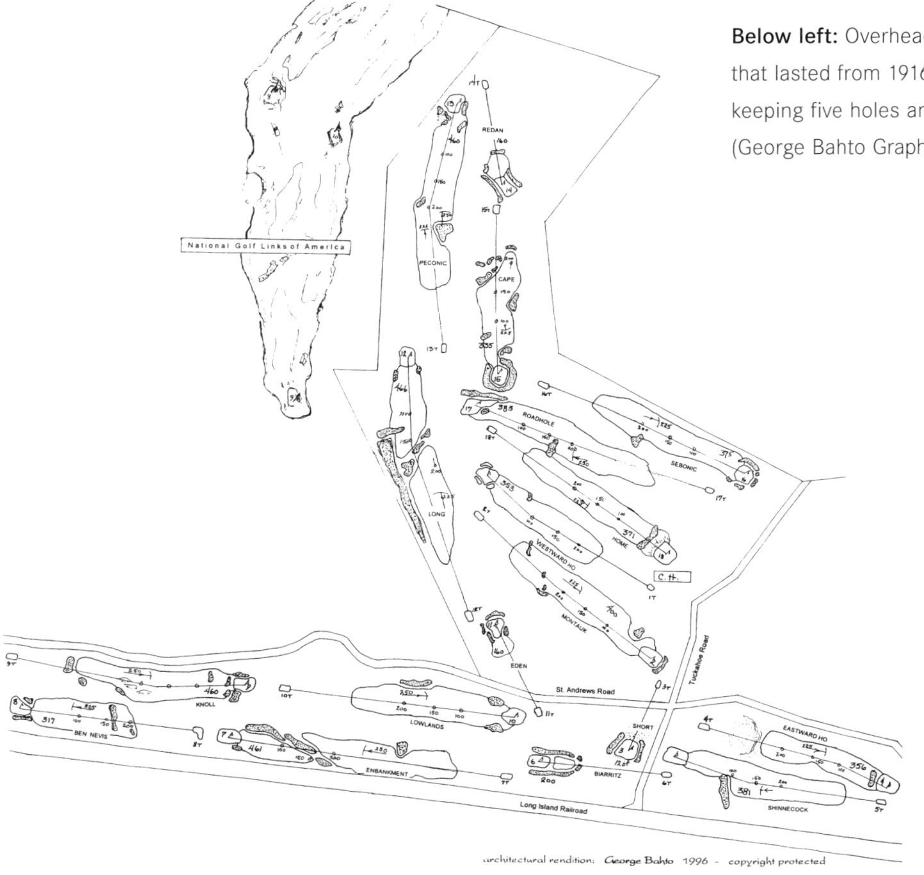

Below left: Overhead drawing of the original Macdonald/Raynor course that lasted from 1916-1931. William Flynn redesigned the course in 1931, keeping five holes and six greens from the Macdonald/Raynor layout. (George Bahto Graphics)

Willie Dunn Jr., the Scottish professional brought to America at the behest of William K. Vanderbilt, will be forever associated with Shinnecock Hills. He expanded the original—albeit primitive— 12-hole golf course with the help of 150 laborers from the nearby Shinnecock Indian Reservation.

Among the workforce was 16-year-old John Shippen, the son of a black Presbyterian minister and schoolmaster who lived on the reservation with John's half-white, half-Indian mother. Over time, Dunn took a liking to Shippen and taught him to play golf.

Shippen got so good at the game that by age 21, he was one of the favorites to win the first U. S. Open (1895). At the time, the tournament was actually an add-on to the nation's first Amateur Championship held earlier that same week.

An unseemly protest by many of the competitors ensued, the complaint being that Shippen and his Indian friend, Oscar Bunn, should not be allowed to compete. The protestors swore to withdraw from the event rather than compete against nonwhites.

USGA President Theodore Havemeyer tersely informed the protesters that if that was the case, the tournament would be played with only the two Shinnecock players in the field. No one withdrew.

After a good start, Shippen found disaster on a sandy road in the final round, taking 11 blows on the 13th hole. Despite this, he still finished 5th. Shippen's performance did not go unnoticed, however, as he was soon hired as the head professional at nearby Maidstone Club in Easthampton, a position he held for many years.

Shippen later served from as a private instructor for millionaires Henry Clay Frick and James Cromwell.The following year, C.B. Macdonald, one of the protestors attempting to bar him from playing in the U.S. Open, entrusted him to take over as greenkeeper at the National Golf Links for a short stint.

Knowing the situation could only worsen in the future, 50 adjacent acres to the northwest of the clubhouse were purchased by the club. Since Macdonald was a member at both clubs, his selection as architect for the redesign of Shinnecock Hills was an obvious choice.

The new course was built in record time. The redesign added 13 new holes, with five of the original Willie Dunn holes left largely in their original form. The course also included renditions of most of Macdonald's favored holes, which made it a perfect complement to the National Golf Links, with its trademark alternative-route holes for less skilled players.

While Raynor's construction crews "gouged out enormous bunkers" and built up their patented plateau greens, the members of Shinnecock enjoyed the hospitality of its neighbors at the National. The members were asked to pay only a dollar to play the National, a practice that continued for a long period after the new Shinnecock Hills course was complete. It was not uncommon to play a few holes at Shinnecock, cross over at the National's 10th hole and play up to the National clubhouse for lunch. Play would then continue down the National's front nine, cross over again, and finish the circuit on the remaining Shinnecock holes.

Macdonald was elected to the board of trustees at Shinnecock, and because of his accumulated research concerning the growing of a fine stand of turfgrass, he was also appointed to head the Green Committee—a position held for a good number of years.

So, what became of the Macdonald/Raynor course at Shinnecock Hills? In the late 1920s, it was rumored that Suffolk County was planning to build a highway that would cut off a portion of the course. Since the club was not in a financial position to buy any more adjacent property, Lucien Tyng, a prominent member of the club, had the foresight to purchase substantial acreage northeast of the course. (He continued to own this land until the club purchased it from him in 1948.)

The choice of an architect was not as clear at the time because Macdonald was no longer associated with the club, and Seth Raynor had passed away in 1926. In addition, Macdonald's brusque demeanor and controversial opinions had caused some rancor among a few members. In the wake

Above: The 7th hole at Shinnecock Hills, the original Redan-style par 3 designed by Seth Raynor. William Flynn thought so highly of the hole that he kept it intact and incorporated it into his 1931 redesign. (George Bahto Collection)

Opposite: The present-day 9th hole was originally Raynor's 18th hole. It was another hole retained by Flynn in his '31 redesign. (George Bahto Collection)

of yet another "incident," Macdonald resigned (or was asked to resign). This precipitated a membership silence about what had happened and, as a consequence, Macdonald and Raynor were basically left out of the club's written history. The silence continued until at least part of the story was revealed prior to the 1995 United States Open.

As noted by Ross Goodner in Shinnecock's 75-year history book, there were other issues that began to fester:

> *Despite the apparent harmony, the sailing was not always smooth. For example, many old-timers claim it was more than coincidence that the Shinnecock club manager, chef, menus and even the flag found the way to the National.*

In 1926, Shinnecock Hills created a class of honorary memberships and gave one to Samuel Parrish, George A. Dixon, Judge Morgan O'Brien (C.B.'s closest friend) and, surprisingly, Charles Blair Macdonald himself.

The club eventually hired William S. Flynn of the Philadelphia firm of Toomey and Flynn to again redesign the course. Included among their past projects were Cherry Hills near Denver and Huntingdon Valley in Philadelphia. At Shinnecock, under the direction of then assistant Dick Wilson, 12 new holes were added to the course and they have scarcely been altered to this day. Flynn retained six of the original Raynor holes: 1, 12, and 13 became Flynn's No. 1, No. 2, and No. 3 holes (Raynor's old 12th was shortened to a par 3). Raynor's 14th, 15th, and 18th became Flynn's No. 7, No. 8, and No. 9 holes, working their way back to the clubhouse. The present 7th (Raynor's old 14th) is a Redan.

So, is Shinnecock Hills a Macdonald/Raynor course or a William S. Flynn course? In truth, one of America's most admired championship venues is really a synthesis of several great artists rather than one visionary. Despite this, Shinnecock Hills gives no hint of inconsistency or conspicuous change from hole-to-hole—just an effortless blending together of the best efforts of everyone who has touched her.

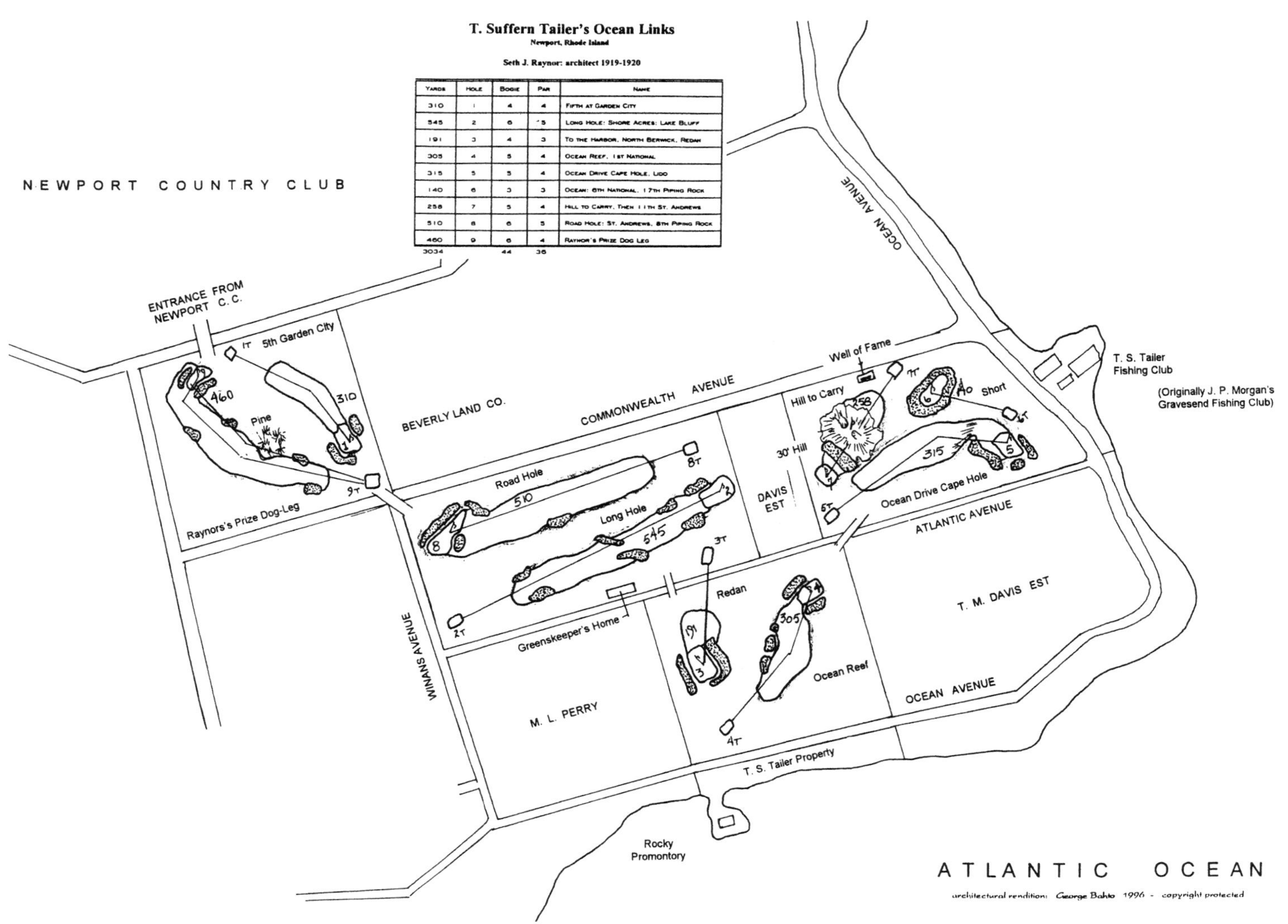

1919 - 1921

Newport, Rhode Island

Charles Blair Macdonald & Seth Raynor: architects

Seth Raynor: construction

Privately owned course of T. Suffern Tailer

Ocean Links

Hole	Yards	Bogie	Par	Name
1	310	4	4	Fifth at Garden City
2	545	6	5	Long Hole: Shore Acres: Lake Bluff
3	191	4	3	To the Harbor, North Berwick, Redan
4	305	5	4	Ocean Reef, 1st National
5	315	5	4	Ocean Drive Cape Hole, Lido
6	140	3	3	Ocean: 6th National, 17th Piping Rock
7	258	5	4	Hill to Carry, Then 11th St. Andrews
8	510	6	5	Road Hole: St. Andrews. 8th Piping Rock
9	460	6	4	Raynor's Prize Dog Leg
	3034	44	36	

CHAPTER FOURTEEN

OCEAN LINKS

IN 1919, LESS THAN A YEAR after the signing of the Armistice agreement that ended WWI, a group of members of Newport Country Club proposed a remodel of the venerable old layout. The group was led by Thomas Suffern Tailer, a wealthy investment banker and noted international sportsman. A member of several clubs, including Piping Rock and Nassau County, Tailer split his time between his homes in New York and Newport. Due to improvements in the golf ball and equipment, the Tailer-led group sensed a growing disparity in difficulty and length and felt that Newport was in danger of becoming obsolete. Despite Tailor's stature at the club, the proposal was rebuffed by Newport's Board of Directors, evidently believing that their historic but short (5,000+ yards) course was quite good enough and in no need of change.

Incensed by the club's inability to see things his way, T. Suffern decided to take matters into his own hands and build a bigger course himself. Although there wasn't enough room for a full 18 holes, Tailor did own four large residential lots at nearby Breton's Point—on land directly adjacent to Newport Country Club.

As might be expected, Tailer brought in his close friend C. B. Macdonald to review the land and determine if it was possible to route a modern strategic course on this checkerboard collection of lots connected only at the corners (see map).

Together they walked the property, as Macdonald offered ideas and suggestions. C.B. marveled at the views along the ocean. The terrain was also exceptional, its sandy base ideal for fine turf. To his way of thinking, "nature had made apt provisions for close approximations at reproducing some of the classic holes of the world."

An excited Tailer apparently wanted exact duplication of some of the great classic holes that Macdonald revered. C.B., however, suggested that, "minutely detailed reproductions are very rarely possible, but here was an opportunity for several finely conceived counterparts."

Because of the war and the recovery period following it, there had been a lull in new course construction. But with a new project in hand, Raynor was brought in promptly and he set about preparing the plans for construction the following year. Tailer, a man of immediacy, would have none of it. He wanted the course completed yesterday. Raynor, by now used to handling demanding men like Tailer, cautioned that it was late fall and that with winter approaching, little could be

Opposite: Suffern Tailer owned four lots on Breton's Point on which he had Macdonald and Raynor build his Ocean Links course. This map was developed through conversations with the son of the original golf professional who grew up on Ocean Links. (George Bahto Graphics)

accomplished over the next few months. Tailer persisted, however, resolving to take all steps necessary to ensure an early completion. It turned out that even Raynor couldn't dream of the lengths that he was willing to go through.

A short time later, when the ground began to freeze, Tailer initiated one of the more radical methods of keeping the soil loose: "Dynamite was used in sufficient quantities and in timely intervals to keep the soil workable." Preliminary construction continued throughout the winter, and the course was completed in record time. There is no record, however, of what his neighbors thought of hearing intermittent blasting throughout the winter.

This was the pair's only new project since the end of the war and since other unfinished projects were creeping along at a snail's pace, Raynor assigned three of his top construction foremen—Arthur T. Arnold, William Edward, and Rocco Nocco—to ensure the job was carried out exactly as Mr. Tailer wished.

The design was a fairly typical Macdonald/Raynor course, albeit squeezed on the limited property. Although most holes were called by a different name than the classics they emulated, the nine holes were still a composite of some of the world's best golf holes.

Dynamiting the course in the winter was not the only innovation by the flamboyant Mr. Tailer. He was unhappy with the "dull color" and texture of the local sand to be used in his bunkers, so Raynor arranged to send men and equipment to Maryland and Virginia to import hundreds of truckloads of "white marble dust" for the bunkers in order to enhance the beauty of his course. The combination of the green turf, the blue of the ocean, and the white marble dust in the bunkers created one of the more visually beautiful golf courses in the country.

When completed, Ocean Links had only one member: Thomas Suffern Tailer. However, members of the Newport Club were invited to play it any time they wished. There was no formal clubhouse, though Tailer maintained a "Greenkeeper's Lodge" on the second hole where he later displayed one of the world's oldest collection of golf clubs and artifacts.

The formal opening of Ocean Links took place on July 9th and 10th in 1921 with an inaugural tournament.

> *Headed by Mr. Macdonald, a party from the Links Club of New York went to Newport for the opening aboard the power boat of Mr. Rickard F. Howe. Included in the party were Messrs. Macdonald and Howe, George Bourne, Ford Johnson, F.L. Crocker, Conde Naste and Bert Walker. And just as if to show that he was master of his creation, Mr. Macdonald then aged 66 at the time showed the rest of the party how the new course should be played, turned in the best card for the two trips over the nine holes with a 42-43-85. Mr. Naste and Mr. Bourne tied for second with 89s.*
>
> —*Golf Illustrated*, 1919

Above and opposite: Watercolor hole paintings commissioned by Mr. Tailer of his Ocean Links course in Newport, Rhode Island. (Photo by George Bahto)

To the chagrin of Newport's Board of Directors, the shortcomings of their course became apparent as their members flocked to play the new nine-hole course next door. T. Suffern Tailer had made his point, and in 1921 Newport C.C. purchased an additional 44 acres and hired A.W. Tillinghast to remodel the golf course. The reason Raynor was not commissioned with the job was largely a matter of club politics, though aside from some disputes involving land ownership and construction delays, the Tillinghast course remains one of the world's best seaside links.

Gold Mashie Tournament

Shortly after completion of Ocean Links, Tailer inaugurated a major amateur event that came to be known as the "Gold Mashie." The event was always held the week before the U.S. Amateur, and it showcased leading amateur golfers from around the nation. Participation in the championship was by invitation only, chosen by Tailer and former national champions Francis Ouimet and Jesse Sweetser. All expenses, including travel to and from the tournament, were paid for by Tailer himself. The first prize? A gold mashie (5-iron) that was said to cost over $3,000 (1921).

The Gold Mashie was contested as a 36-hole stroke-play event. It was followed by two better ball matches, and usually on Labor Day weekend. Following this extraordinary tournament, Tailer normally transported the players to the U.S. Amateur the following week—in his private railroad car.

After six years of successful "Gold Mashie" tournaments, Mr. Tailer decided to add yet another interesting touch to Ocean Links: "a suitable monument to Gold Mashie winners." He commissioned celebrated architect John Russell Pope to design a bronze plaque on which to permanently display the winners of his now famous tournament—"a counterpart of the ancient Grecian practice of carving the names of the mighty in imperishable stone on the architecture of the community well." An appropriate spot already existed because there was an "old fashioned and weather-beaten well" between the 6th green and the 7th tee where players paused for a refreshing drink of cold water.

Gould Martin, a writer for *Metropolitan Golfer* magazine, described the artifact in this manner:

> *John Russell Pope imported an old well-head from Greece which is a work of art and intrinsically something of great value. The entire top, some four feet in diameter, is cast in*

Above right: Photograph of artist Paul Moschowicz's watercolor of the "Short" at Ocean Links. It was a gift from Tailer to C.B. Hand-written on the bottom left of the painting is, "To Charlie Macdonald—Here is a painting of one of your masterpieces." (Mike Tureski family)

heavy bronze, on which is embossed the names of the winners of the Gold Mashie Championship.

The Greek wellhead was said to be over 2,000 years old. Also inscribed were the names of the Silver Mashie winners (tournament runners-up), winners of the Gold Ball prize and Silver Ball prize (best scores for 36 and 18 holes), and course record holders. It all added a significant touch of class to Tailer's amateur event, and it was a reflection of its founder. It was a classic tradition that was meant to perpetuate along with Tailer's innovative championship.

Although he seemed in perfect health, T. Suffern Tailer died suddenly while attending a family Christmas dinner in 1929. He had recently finished planning for another Gold Mashie the following July and had arranged to have a private railroad car for himself and family to travel from New York to Pebble Beach Golf Links in California where the National Amateur would be held the week after his own tournament.

Above: Tailer's son, Tommy, was regarded as one of the premier amateur players in the country at the time. He was the youngest to play in the Masters as an amateur and was an influential member later at The National Golf Links of America. (*Golf Illustrated*)

Top, right: T. Suffern Tailer, his son, Tommy, and his wife. (*Golf Illustrated*)

The Gold Mashie champion that year? His son Tommy Jr., a golf prodigy who not only was low amateur in the 1938 Masters, but also one of the youngest players ever to successfully qualify for the U.S. Open.

During the 1930 Gold Mashie Championship, appropriately 11 former winners and participants of the championship affixed a bronze tablet into a boulder near the "Well of Fame" on which were inscribed their names as well as a tribute "in memory of Tom" for "his sportsmanship and love of golf."

Following Mr. Tailer's death, Ocean Links was run by a management firm for several years but with only moderate success. It was finally phased out in the 1940s when the properties were sold.

After a lapse of over 40 years, the National Golf Links decided to reestablish the tradition of T. Suffern Tailer's tournament in 1971. It lasted for seven years but only had three winners: G. Bostwick Jr. won in 1971 and 1972; George Burns III (before he became a PGA Tour pro) won in 1973, 1974, and 1975; and Danny Yates won the last two in 1976 and 1977.

Above: The Gold Mashie Tournament, sponsored solely by Thomas Suffern Tailer at his Ocean Links course, was held one week prior to the U.S. Amateur. All prizes and expenses were paid for by Tailer. In addition, he would transport all attendees to the site of the Amateur wherever it was held, usually in his private railroad car. **Tournament Format:** 72 holes medal play, Gold Mashie Champions: 1923: Jesse P. Guilford & Jesse W. Sweester / 1924: D. Clarke Corkran / 1925: Francis Ouimet / 1926: Jesse Guilford / 1927: Jesse Sweester / 1928: Tommy Tailer Jr. / 1929: Tommy Tailer Jr. (*Golf Illustrated*)

Tailer was also the proud owner of a collection of eight antique golf clubs that were undoubtedly the finest collection this side of the Atlantic.

In an article published in *Golf Illustrated* in the late 1920s entitled "Fossils from the Past," it was reported that:

> *Mr. Tailer had for some time been angling for the collection when a sudden completion of the deal by cable a few months ago gave him the opportunity to acquire it. For many years these clubs have been in the possession of a famous family of British golfers, and were sold to Mr. Tailer by a well-known architect who for some sentimental reason prefers to remain nameless. They were collected by himself, his father, his grandfather, and great-grandfather during a period of over 75 years. Of the two old leather balls now in Mr. Tailer's collection one was found on the old links at Musselburgh somewhere along in the 1820s and 1830s.*

Tailer's antique clubs are part of the permanent collection of the USGA and are on display at the United States Golf Association Museum in Far Hills, New Jersey. They're listed below in the approximate order of their age.

1. Track Iron: by Willie Park, the elder of Musselburgh, 1770
2. Sand Iron: 1780
3. Wooden putter: the prize of the collection—1807 by Hugh Philp
4. Driving putter: by Allan Robertson about 1815
5. Short spoon: Jamie Dunn, twin brother of Willie Dunn the elder—1824.
6. Long spoon: by McEwan of Musselburgh in 1838—the most famous of McEwan's clubs.
7. Brassie: earliest known brassie—by Tom Morris—about 1840
8. Driver: by Willie Dunn the elder—1840

> *In all* [of Tailer's] *clubs, the shafts are great-heart, and in the wooden clubs the heads are redwood. The handles of the clubs are all noticeably short and thick."*
>
> —Gould B. Martin, *Metropolitan Golfer*, 1928

Also of special interest was an old "feather" ball called a "Gressick." This particular specimen was closer to egg-shaped than round. The ball was made by one of the Robertsons who made balls and clubs at St. Andrews, probably by the father or grandfather of Allan Robertson who made balls in the 1820s. At the time that Tailer acquired it, there were only three known Gressick balls in existence, this being in the finest of condition. The Gressick ball was obtained from the great-granddaughter of Hugh Philp, a Miss Fleming. It had been in her family for 80 years and had been made 40 years before that. A conservative guess places the date of the ball at 1808 and perhaps even earlier.

For years, Tailer's collection was displayed on a wall in the caddie house along the 2nd hole of the Ocean Links course.

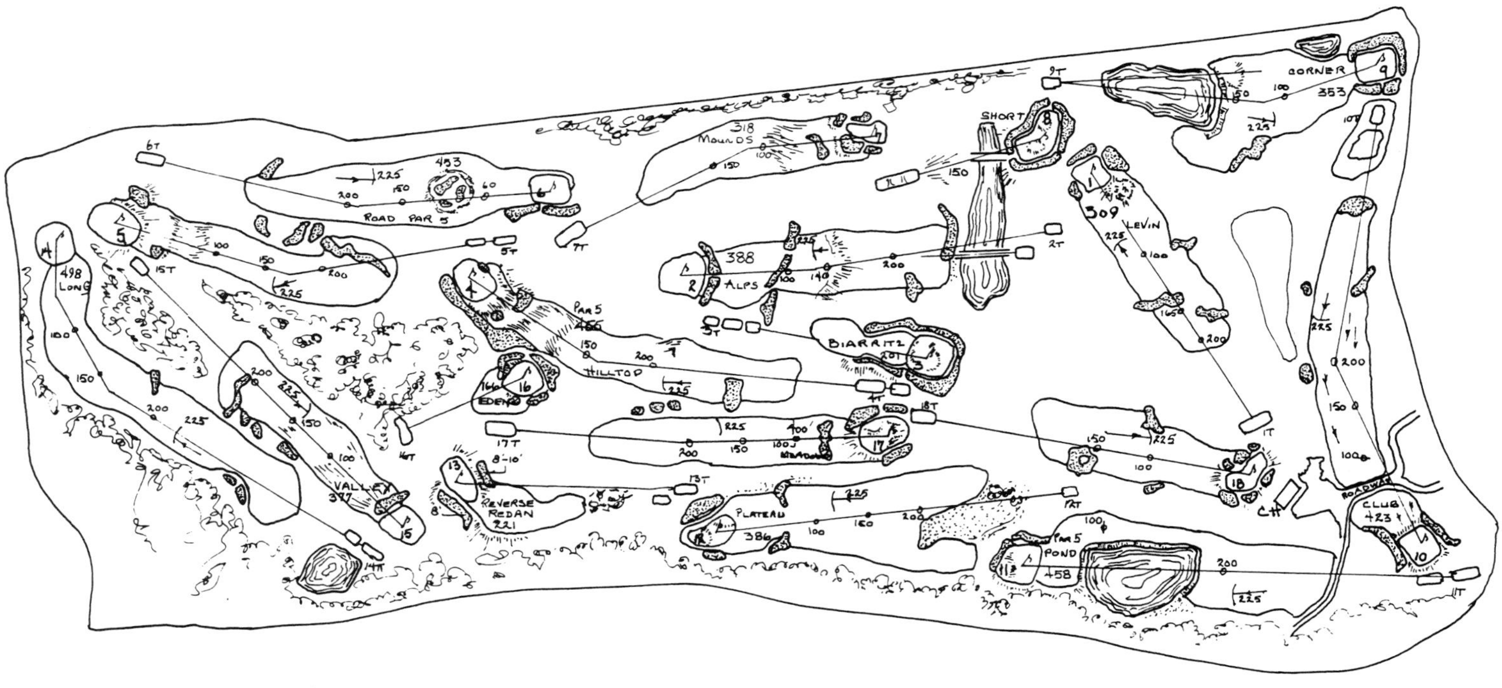

North Hills, Long Island, New York						

North Hills, Long Island, New York
1919–1985 (No Longer Exists)
Charles Blair Macdonald
(& perhaps Seth Raynor): architect
Seth J. Raynor: construction
Revision: Perry Maxwell (minor), 1930s

Links Club

Hole	Name	Yards	Par	Hole	Name	Yards	Par
1	Leven	309	4	10	Club	423	4
2	Alps	388	4	11	Pond	458	5
3	Biarritz	201	3	12	Plateau	386	4
4	Hilltop	455	5	13	Redan	221	3
5	Woods	400	4	14	Long	498	5
6	Road	453	5	15	Valley	377	4
7	Mounds	318	4	16	Eden	166	3
8	Short	150	3	17	Meadow	400	5
9	Corner	353	4	18	Home	357	4
		3027	36			3286	37
					Total	**6313**	**73**

CHAPTER FIFTEEN

LINKS CLUB

The story of the Links Club is above all else a cautionary tale, and how a once great club's reclusiveness—bordering on paranoia—can inflict irreparable damage upon itself. While many stories of historic clubs continue to evolve with the passing of years, the accounting of C.B. Macdonald's Links Club sadly has a definite ending.

Built in 1919, the Links is one of the few courses where C.B. Macdonald was involved in most aspects of construction—painstakingly tending to every detail regardless of how minute. Seth Raynor was surely on hand, but this project was very special to Macdonald and the select few of his close friends for whom the course was built.

The Links property was an intimate refuge from the outside world, covering only slightly more than 100 acres on Long Island. Right up to its demise, any information about the club—even the membership roster—was fiercely guarded. Guest play was frowned upon and required special permission, and no cameras of any type were allowed on the premises. It was as if the club, fearing contamination from the outside world, considered itself under siege for all 66 years of its existence.

Opposite: A hand-drawn map of the Links Golf Club. (George Bahto Graphics)

It is also the story of permanence, however, as exemplified by two men: former Superintendent Benny Zukosky and former Head Professional Joe Phillips. Incredibly, these two men were the only ones to hold these positions from the club's inception in 1919 until its demise in 1985.

Both men—Zukosky especially—worked under Macdonald's watchful eyes for nearly 20 years. Benny, still living on Long Island at the time of this writing, recalls C.B. as a walking paradox, at once an opinionated and demanding autocrat, and at the same time an often kind and generous man with great loyalty to his employees.

Benny also recalled meeting with Raynor on several occasions, commenting that "he was a quiet and rather serious man who attended to business with great attention to detail."

Regarding C.B., the superintendent said:

> *Mr. Macdonald kept us on the edge, he noticed everything. We were always worried about what he might say to us. He certainly knew just about everything there was to know about designing courses, and he was very learned about growing and controlling turf grass. We didn't need to bring in a turf expert to solve problems because Mr. Macdonald could solve them himself.*

Zukosky recalls Macdonald's insistence—over the objections of other members—that the course be kept firm and

fast at all times. He knew that golf was a ground game, and that was the way the course was to play. Period.

Everyone knew exactly who was in command at the Links Club.

In accordance with Macdonald's wishes, the rough was kept high, and there weren't rakes in any bunkers until after his death. His instructions were that no bunker be smoothed out unless it was in terrible condition. Unhappy with this, some members went so far as to bring their own rakes and leave them on the course. Hearing of this, Macdonald immediately had them removed and destroyed.

Macdonald was distressed about the trend to smooth out the sand in bunkers. Many early photographs of golf in America show players in deep and craggy bunkers, trying to extract themselves from purgatory as the rest of the foursome and caddies look on.

Macdonald thought that this was the way it should be, writing, "Errors in play should be severely punished, but now the golfer wants his bunkers raked and the unevenness of the fairway rolled out." But that wasn't all. "If I had my way there would be a troop of cavalry horses running through every trap and bunker on the course before a tournament started, where only a niblick could get the ball out but for a few yards."

Needless to say, at courses Macdonald controlled (National, Links, and Mid Ocean), rakes were scarce.

Despite Macdonald's hard line, the Links Club course was a moderated version of the National Golf Links. That was because the original membership needed a more comfortable and less strenuous version to play over. Many were also members at National and nearby Creek Club and Piping Rock.

In reality, the name "links" belied the true nature of the course. It was more parkland in nature, with trees planted on the perimeter of the property to act as an enclosure to the outside world. There were wooded valleys and intimate ponds along its rolling fairways, with an ingenious routing

Above: Rare aerial photo of the Links Club; this has never been published. The view illustrates the links-style appearance despite its suburban location. (*Golf Illustrated*)

Opposite: A view of the Alps green at the Links Club. (Tom Doak)

that took maximum advantage of what were barely 100 acres of golf course.

So what became of the Links Club? As the original founders began to pass away, the club's membership rolls were replenished almost exclusively with immediate family members only. With the changing era, and the economic realities of high taxes and maintenance costs, those in control of the club were unwilling to either welcome outsiders to this exclusive fraternity or to adapt to the needs of its younger members to update the facilities.

In fact, the quaint and insular clubhouse (actually a converted barn) remained much as it had been since Macdonald's era. Sadly, the sons and daughters gradually drifted away until only 13 or so members remained.

Rather than attempt to overcome their predicament, the club that survived two World Wars and the Great Depression opted instead to die by its own hand. Unable to afford the upkeep of the course, the club's board of directors voted in 1985 to disband the Links Club and sell off one of Macdonald's finer creations to a real estate developer.

The Holes:

#1 "Leven"—309 yards

Much like the 16th at the National, the first hole here was almost driveable but protected along a direct line by a "berm" that had to be pitched over if the player took the direct route. Like at the National, the better route was a longer carry over a waste area to the left side, leaving a more open shot to the green.

#2 "Alps"—388 yards

A drive over 35-40 yards of water to a tee-level fairway. The second shot was a blind one over the "Alps" hill to a green guarded by a cross-bunker in the front. The green was also bunkered right and left and in the rear. The sand in back was eventually covered over.

#3 "Biarritz"—201 yards

The hole could be extended to as much as 225 yards. The teeing ground was high, giving a good view of what was originally a double-mown green. Over the years, due to the hole's difficulty, the front portion of the putting surface was allowed to grow to fairway height and serve as a landing area. The usual swale before the rear green was left intact.

#4 "Hilltop"—455 yards

This short par 5 offered a second shot toward a lower area and onto an elevated green that was guarded by two flanking bunkers some 20 yards in front.

#5 "Woods"—400 yards

A good drive left an approach over a deep cut in the ground. Bunkers on either side cut into the face of an elevated green.

#6 "Road"—453 yards

The "Road" hole was originally a long par 4 that was turned into a 5 by lengthening the tee. There was typical "Road" bunkering greenside. The front "Road" bunker was a wide "pot" style but apparently not overly deep. In later years the green was reduced to about half the original size, the membership not really understanding the original design concept.

#7 "Mounds"—318 yards

A short 4 from a highly elevated tee to a green complex oriented at a 45-degree angle to the right. Bunkering left-front, a larger one at left-rear, and another large one across most of the front and to the right ten yards short of the green.

#8 "Short"—150 yards

A typical "Short" from an elevated tee box. Bunkers surrounded the tabletop green but there was an open walkway right up the center.

#9 "Corner"—353 yards

A "Cape"-style drive with the second shot to a green severely sloped toward the rear. There were right and left front bunkers and a large horseshoe-shaped bunker in the rear that was covered in over the years.

#10 "Club"—423 yards

A long par 4 with an approach that was played over a ravine some 30 yards short of the green.

#11 "Pond"—458 yards

A par 5 with a pond that could be reached off the tee. The green contained a plateau to the right rear.

#12 "Plateau"—386 yards

A blind second to a green that contained a pronounced plateau covering the rear half of the green.

#13 "Redan" (reverse)—221 yards

The yardage to this Redan seems long at 221, so a rear tee may have been added. This appears to have been one of the most difficult of Raynor's Redans. Bunkering in the front seems to have been 12 to 14 feet deep with the rear bunkering somewhat shallower at a 45-degree angle from left-to-right with no shoulder to the left-front.

#14 "Long"—498 yards

A par 5 that went straight with the first two shots, then doglegged to the right with a short third shot. Problems at the corner of the dogleg prevented players from going at the green with their second shot.

#15 "Valley"—377 yards

Straightaway Valley-type hole of moderate length. An elevated tee down to a valley, then back up a hill to the green.

#16 "Eden"—166 yards

Hill and Strath bunkering left and right of the moderately undulating green.

#17 "Meadow"—450 yards

Straightaway to an elevated green complex with moderate plateaus to the right- and left-rear.

#18 "Home"—357 yards

This fairly short finisher featured a front-to-back-sloping green with two rear plateaus. Bunkering included two to the right side, one to the rear, and a strip bunker to the left of the green.

Above: The Links Club's Eden green (#16) with the Redan hole in the background. (Tom Doak)

Opposite top: No. 2–Alps–from behind the green. (Tom Doak)

Opposite bottom: The 8th–Short–was an oasis surrounded by sand. Photo was taken shortly before the course was destroyed. (Tom Doak)

Macdonald's Downtown Men's Club

"The new Links Club Building at Nos. 36 and 38 East 62nd Street, NY, will soon be finished. Plans were filed April 14 by John W. and Elliot Cross, the architects. Charles B. Macdonald is the owner of the property, and he will be president of the club. Charles H. Sabin, president of Guaranty Trust Company; James Stillman, president of National City Bank; and Frank Crocker of the Piping Rock club are some of the members. American golf is again indebted to Macdonald for making such a club where golfers can gather, and a new interesting 'nineteenth hole' will be famous as a luxurious clubhouse."

—*Golf Magazine*, December 1916

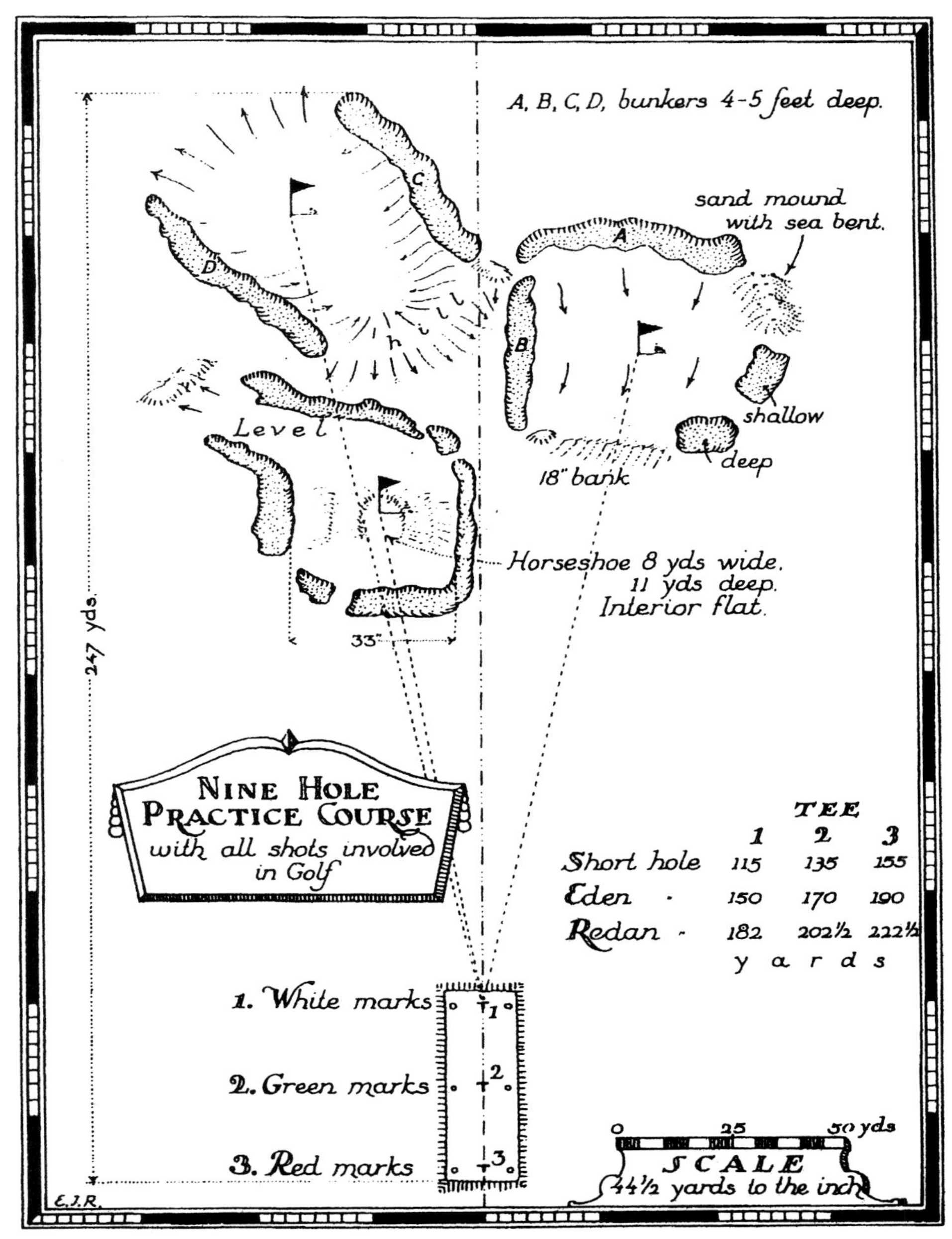

Eddie Moore Practice Course: private estate course

Roslyn, Long Island, New York

1922

Charles Blair Macdonald: architect

Seth Raynor: construction

CHAPTER SIXTEEN

PRACTICE COURSES

Eddie Moore Practice Course

Eddie Moore was treasurer of the USGA during the 1920s and a very good friend of Macdonald. No doubt influenced by the courses Macdonald had built for Thomas Suffern Tailer, Otto Kahn, William Stauffer, and Harry Payne Whitney, Moore asked Charlie to design a course for his estate in Roslyn, Long Island. Macdonald was against full-sized courses on private estates so he convinced Moore that he would be better off with a 3-green practice facility similar to the one built on the range at the National. Moore eventually consented.

> *This [idea] suggested to me the building of a practice ground on six acres by grouping three well-known classic greens, namely, a "Short" hole, an "Eden" hole, and a "Redan." By making a tee forty-two yards long by fifteen yards in width one would go to the front tee and play a ball to each green, then go to the middle tee and play a ball to each green, and then go to the third tee and play a ball to each green—that is nine balls in all—then walk to the different greens and play them out. Having done this, take the balls back to the tee again and instead of teeing them drop them so you will get the fairway practice the same as [if] you were playing through the green.*
>
> —*Scotland's Gift—Golf*

Although Macdonald inferred that this was his idea, a number of such plans were suggested, designed, and/or built more than twenty years before in the British Isles.

The three-hole course at the National was in the current practice area, eliminated long ago. Drawings for it exist and there is some interest at the club in reconstructing it. No doubt it would further add to the special mystique of that "living museum."

Opposite: Copy of the original sketch of the layout of the 3-green Eddie Moore Practice Course. The course was laid out with a "Short," an "Eden," and "Redan." (George Bahto Graphics)

Harry Payne Whitney Private Estate Course

Manhasset, Long Island, New York
1922
Seth Raynor (with input from C.B. Macdonald): architect
9-hole course

One of Long Island's social elite was Harry Payne Whitney. In 1922, Whitney commissioned Macdonald and Raynor to design and build a course on his private estate in Manhassett.

Whitney had been one of the National's original founders and had been instrumental in organizing several clubs where Macdonald and Raynor had designed courses. Initially, Whitney conceived of constructing a full-size 18-hole course on his estate.

Instead, they routed a 9-hole "minicourse" through 25 acres behind the main house. The layout was quite unique; a striking example of what can be accomplished in a relatively confined area. Although there was adequate room available for 18 holes, the land did not lend itself to the creation of an ideal course without enormous expense.

Although yardages of each hole could not be determined from early photos, it's clear there were three par 3s, one long hole, and five par 4s. Segments of the original Macdonald/Raynor course remain on the property today.

> *When Payne Whitney proposed building an eighteen-hole golf course on his property in Manhasset there was plenty of room, but the land was not adapted to it, and I persuaded him to build a nine-hole course and to build it on some twenty or thirty acres immediately in the back of his home. I grouped three classic holes in the centre of the land which had to be played at different angles. In this way, it was perfectly simple to get nine good holes on a small acreage. It could easily take care of ten or twelve men playing, and I doubt very much if there were ever more than that number golfing over his course. It was beautifully kept up and one had as many fine golfing shots as he could have had on any golf course. This suggested to me the building of a practice ground on six acres by grouping three well-known classical greens, namely a Short hole, an Eden Hole, and a Redan.*
>
> —*Scotland's Gift—Golf*

Opposite: Reproduction of the 1922 Harry Payne Whitney Private Estate Course routing on Long Island. Seth Raynor designed it with input from Macdonald. (George Bahto Graphics)

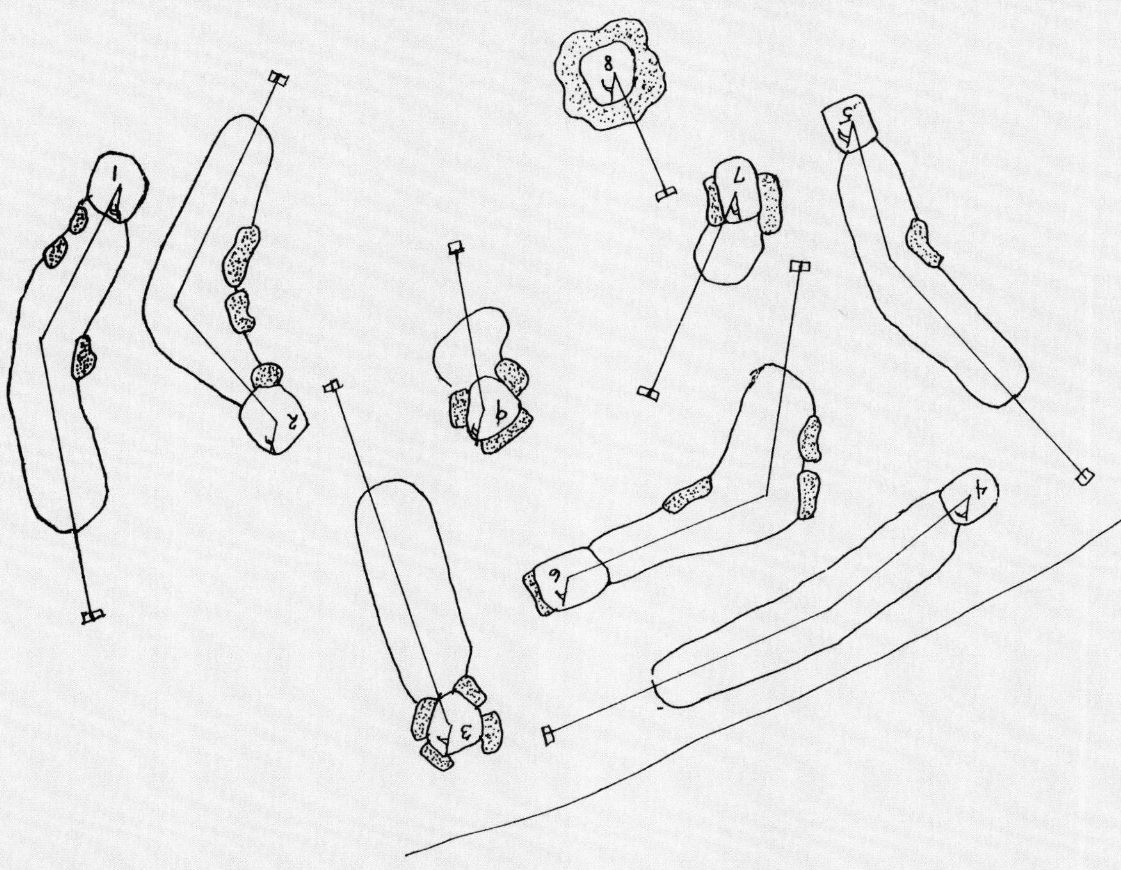

An 1894 graduate of Yale University, Harry Payne Whitney had been groomed from an early age to assume the enormous tobacco, oil, and mining empire of his father, W.C. Whitney. The family was also involved in high finance with Guaranty Trust, J. P. Morgan & Guggenheim. Harry's mother was a member of the Payne family, whose control of Standard Oil made her marriage to W.C. as much a business merger as a social event.

The Whitney family was descended from English Puritans that had arrived in the American colonies about 1635, eventually settling in Watertown, NY. An avid sportsman, Harry Payne was a noted polo player. He captained the American polo team that defeated England in the 1909 National Cup, and successfully defended it in 1911 and 1913.

Along with his passion for golf, he pursued horse racing and breeding. Among his philanthropic ventures was his financing of an expedition by the American Museum of Natural History to collect birds of Polynesia.

His Georgian brick manor was located on 1,000 rolling acres, and it included a racing stable with Tudor-style architecture. The stable once housed 72 prize horses and a collection of antique carriages and polo carts.

Harry Whitney eventually married Gertrude Vanderbilt, the famed sculptress and heiress.

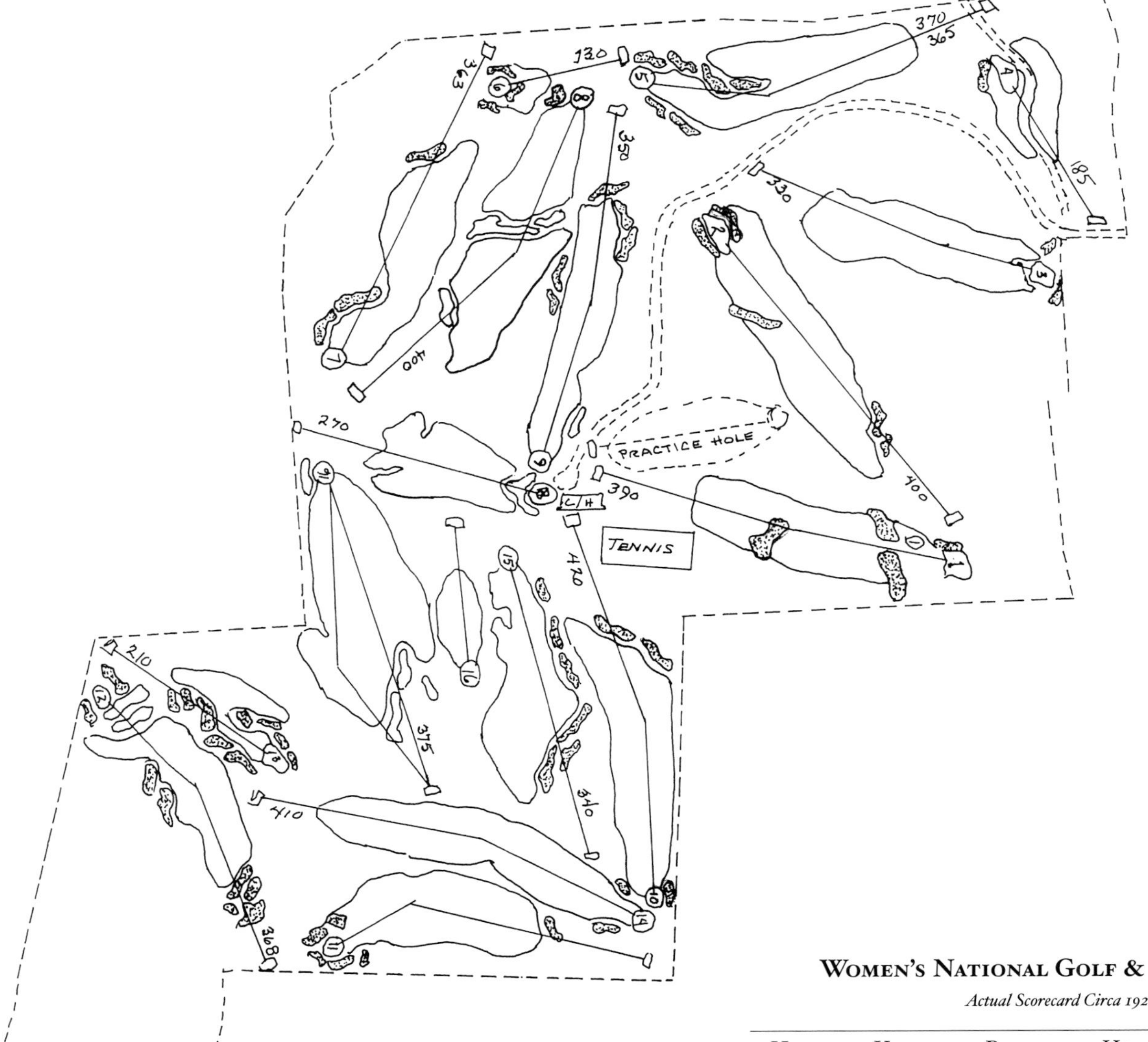

Women's National Golf & Tennis Club

Actual Scorecard Circa 1928

Hole	Yards	Par	Hole	Yards	Par
1	392	4	10	337	4
2	319	4	11	377	4
3	360	4	12	136	3
4	188	3	13	322	4
5	334	4	14	426	5
6	370	4	15	468	5
7	225	4	16	113	3
8	411	5	17	393	4
9	378	4	18	441	5
	2977	36		3013	37

5990 yards Par 73

1922–1923
Great Neck, Long Island, New York
Devereux Emmet: architect
C. B. Macdonald & Seth Raynor: consultation and drawings
Olmsted Bros.: landscape architect
Women's National sold to Glen Head C.C.—
1948: Women's National merged with Creek Club

CHAPTER SEVENTEEN

WOMEN'S NATIONAL GOLF & TENNIS CLUB

The first golf course designed specifically to present appropriate challenges for women—and the shorter distances they hit the ball—was the dream of the Marion Hollins, the 1921 U.S. Women's National Amateur Champion.

As one of the America's most influential sportswomen, and one of the outstanding women golfers of the 1920s, Miss Hollins saw the need to establish a club for women only that would help nurture a new generation of women champions in a less intimidating environment. In 1922, she founded the Women's National Golf & Tennis Club. Her thinking was:

> *I felt a course of this kind should not be of the usual standard type designed for men because it is impossible for women players, despite the great advance made by their sex during the past few seasons, to cope with a man's course on equal terms with par or even bogey.*

The simple introduction of forward tees, without regard to placement of hazards, or distance of approach shots, was nearly always inadequate. Hollins's approach was a revolutionary concept in the '20s, and even in the modern era is still a rarity. In her view, due consideration to the location and difficulty of hazards and proportional lengths of holes needed to be addressed. She championed the individuality of women.

Miss Hollins continued:

> *With this in mind the organization of the Women's National Golf & Tennis Club at Glen Head, Long Island was formed. Devereux Emmet was the retained architect, with Charles B. Macdonald and Seth Raynor assisting on the plans, and when it is completed the course will develop into what is expected to be the last word in golf.*

Emulating the original ideas of Charles Macdonald—the use of the best strategies of the great golf holes of the world—Hollins traveled to Europe the year before to acquire information on holes that she thought bestfitted women's play. She spoke with knowledgeable players of her plans, and was open for suggestions to improve her ideas.

> *During this trip I made sketches and jotted down data. Therefore one finds in the tentative plan which has been submitted for consideration several holes which are practically copies of famous holes on other courses while others have been*

Opposite: 1922 Map of the original Women's National course that was designed by Devereux Emmet with input from Macdonald and Raynor. The course no longer exists. (George Bahto Graphics)

laid out to embody superlative features of some of those which impressed me.

When she returned, Hollins found the organizational work by the committee at home had progressed, and that an ideal property of 160 acres had been secured at Glen Head, Long Island. It included twenty-five acres that had been set aside to develop an "exclusive bungalow colony as soon as the course has been finished." An old-fashioned farmhouse on site was moved to a high knoll, and remodeled to accommodate a locker room and dining facilities. As many of the members were tennis players, courts were also constructed.

The location was ideal, for the "vast majority of members, many of them socially elite, are residents of the Metropolitan area." Women's National also boasted members from other parts of the country who wished an intimate setting during their trips to New York.

"After careful scientific measurements," Hollins arrived at a benchmark length of 175 yards as the basic distance for a woman's drive when hit properly. Devereux Emmet was given these parameters along with the instructions that "generous leeway be made for the slightly shorter hitters or for shots which were just a little off."

Like at National Golf Links, it permitted the shorter hitter a safe play to the green, although usually costing an extra stroke. The fairways were generous and the greens were not bunkered as severely as a challenging man's golf course. The course featured four par 5s (any hole over 400 yards was a 5) and only three par 3s. The par 4s ranged from 210 yards to 375 yards. The total yardage was 5,990 yards, and par was 73.

A twist to the story involves an article written by Marion Hollins a year later that included the actual scorecard of the course. What was odd was that it did not resemble the Emmet blueprint of the year before. Uncovered in a blueprint shop in Southampton in the early 1990s was a card file indicating that Seth Raynor had drawn up the plans for Women's National. Whether it was fully implemented by Miss Hollins or not is not known, although there was certainly dramatic change by the time the course was built.

Emmet and Macdonald were close friends, and both Macdonald and Raynor concentrated much of their design efforts on courses in the area (Piping Rock, Creek Club, North Shore, etc.). Given the final product at Women's National, with the familiar configurations and brush strokes of their work, it is inconceivable that the course was not heavily influenced by Raynor (and therefore Macdonald, too).

Sadly, though Miss Hollins's concept of a women's only course was both revolutionary and valid, financial problems arising during World War II doomed the club to closure. The nearby Creek Club, where many of the member's husbands belonged, had its own mortgage called during the 1940s and it was decided that the interests of both clubs would be better served if Women's National sold its property and merged with Creek; a solution in 1941 that solved the financial problems of both clubs but shattered the lofty dreams of Marion Hollins.

In 1948 the original site was purchased by the newly formed Glen Head Country Club, which operates the course today.

Marion Hollins eventually relocated to California's Monterey Peninsula and helped found the Cypress Point Club. She initially chose Seth Raynor to lay out the course. After his untimely death in 1926, Dr. Alister MacKenzie took over and completed the work.

Above: Marion Hollins, the founder of Women's National, sought advice from many architects prior to building her course. Her admiration for Seth Raynor eventually led to her commissioning him to design and build the Cypress Point Club in California in 1925. But he died before the course could be routed and completed. (*Golf Illustrated*))

The 3rd hole at Women's National,
a 360-yard, par 4. (*Golf Illustrated*)

The treacherous green at the 113-yard, par-3 16th
presented many obstacles to the players. (*Golf Illustrated*)

Gibson Island, Maryland
1921–1922
Charles Blair Macdonald & Seth Raynor: architects
Seth Raynor: construction
Olmsted Bros.: landscape architects
Club founded: 1921
Renovations: unknown and/or in-house shortening of the course as a result of the stock market crash of 1929

CHAPTER EIGHTEEN

GIBSON ISLAND CLUB

Gibson Island is a 1,100-acre enclave of rolling woodlands near Annapolis, Maryland that juts out in a northern finger of the Chesapeake Bay. It is not really an island because it is connected to the mainland by a narrow sandbar, now an automobile causeway. The privacy of the island is protected by a guard who turns away inquisitive visitors unless expected by local residents. It's quaint, private, and has been a retreat for "bankers, corporate executives and military brass from the Washington and Baltimore [area] for nearly seventy-five years."

The "island" was once the summer campgrounds of various tribes of the Maryland Indians and was the subject of grants to settlers by King Charles II of England beginning in 1668. John Gibson Jr. replaced William Worthington as the largest landowner in 1771 (over 2,240 acres) and he attached his name to the land.

By 1910, a Captain Jefferson Cook owned much of the land but became a victim of mortgage problems. Financial assistance came from W. Stuart Symington Jr. When asked how much of the island he would like if he would pay off Cook's bank note of $165,000, Symington drew a line across a map that indicated over half the property. Symington, who later became a Baltimore judge, had a vision of Gibson Island being the site of "a fine family club where the best of residential facilities would be available and where golf could be played in a lovely setting." A financier as well as an inventor, Symington became the founding father of the island and owned a home that overlooked the 8th and 9th holes out on Goat Point.

Symington next called in the Olmsted Bros. architectural firm of Brookline, Massachusetts to look over the feasibility of developing a planned residential community in a country club setting. Charles Macdonald and Seth Raynor were then called in to render their opinion about building a golf course and where it might best be placed. C.B. stated that Gibson Island was one of the few courses he had an interest in designing.

The year was 1921 and a trip from Baltimore to Gibson Island took about 2½ hours, a distance of less than 20 miles as the crow flies. There was only one auto on the island at the time, a Model T Ford panel truck. The roads on the island were dirt, and there were only three houses. Water was obtained from hand-pumped wells, kerosene lamps were used for light, and wood stoves for heat and cooking. Telephones were all "party lines" shared by everyone in Anne Arundel County.

Although nine holes remain of the original Macdonald/Raynor layout, what's left is just 2,966 yards of original 1921

Opposite: The original 18 holes at Gibson Island as seen from this aerial photo. (National Golf Links)

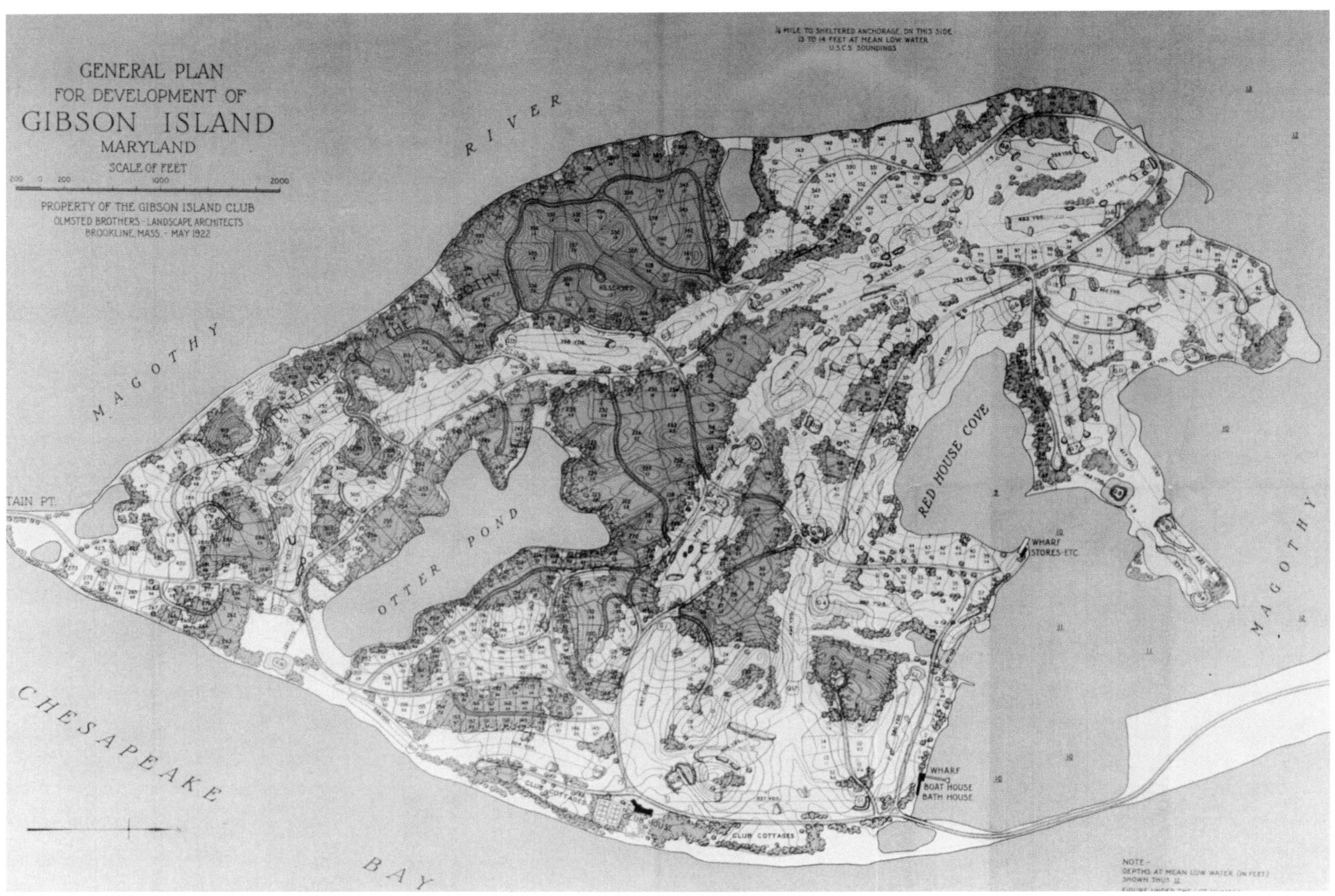

Above: Original Olmsted Bros. concept showing a 36-hole facility along the Chesapeake Bay in Maryland. Only one of the 18-hole layouts was constructed. (Olmsted Brothers)

Opposite top: Sketch of a part of the Gibson Island layout dubbed the "Peninsula Holes" that reflects the heroic nature of this layout by Seth Raynor. (George Bahto Graphics)

Opposite right: Copy of a rare letter sent by Seth Raynor to Mr. W.S. Symington in reference to building the course at Gibson Island. (George Bahto Collection)

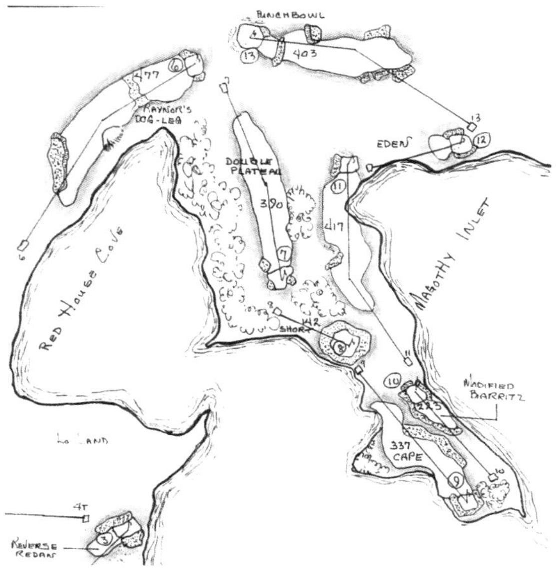

layout. The outer holes were abandoned during difficult times, and a combination of the holes nearest the clubhouse were combined to make up the existing short course.

For all but the current membership, Gibson Island has been thought of as being originally built as a nine-hole course with short yardage. Examination of the original Gibson Island development plan of the Olmsted Bros., however, shows an 18-hole plan, housing and a second 18-hole layout to be constructed as needed.

The original plans show a stout Macdonald design with a number of impressive holes not often seen on Raynor plans. Most notable was the 3rd, a sweeping reverse-Redan jutting into the water of Magothy Narrows. In fact, a number of holes were played over tidewater areas with the trademark Macdonald echelon carries off the tee.

There was a fine stretch of holes between #6 and #13, out and back over a narrow strip of land to Goat Point, barely wide enough for two holes side by side (see drawing above).

Another victim of the Great Depression, the original Gibson Island course had a good version of the "Raynor's Dogleg," the "Double Plateau," "Short," "Cape" (at the end of Goat Point), a modified "Biarritz," "Levan," "Eden," and "Punchbowl" that were abandoned and later sold off for homesites. Many of these lost holes still exist on private property, still there today with trees growing out of their putting surfaces.

Southampton, N.Y.
May 4th, 1922
Mr. W.S. Symington
Maryland Club
Baltimore, Md.

Dear Sir:

Your cheering letter received, I can be in Baltimore Monday or Tuesday of next week (8th).

The first thing for us to do is to contract for the clearing and get the water system started, water is an absolute necessity if we seed this fall. In the meantime it might be well to start plowing where it is already cleared and seeding with cow peas or some other good crop, also to have a gang of men clear out the fairways where they are covered with light stuff, such as peach trees etc. as this could be done cheaply and the contractor would not have to figure on this.

It would facilitate matters to know where we could procure 1000 tons of manure immediately and how to get it delivered to the best advantage.

Grass is very expensive this year, we will have to decide the first of the week what kinds of seed and how much we will need, so the order can go in immediately, as the market is about bought up.

Very truly yours,
(signed) Seth J. Raynor

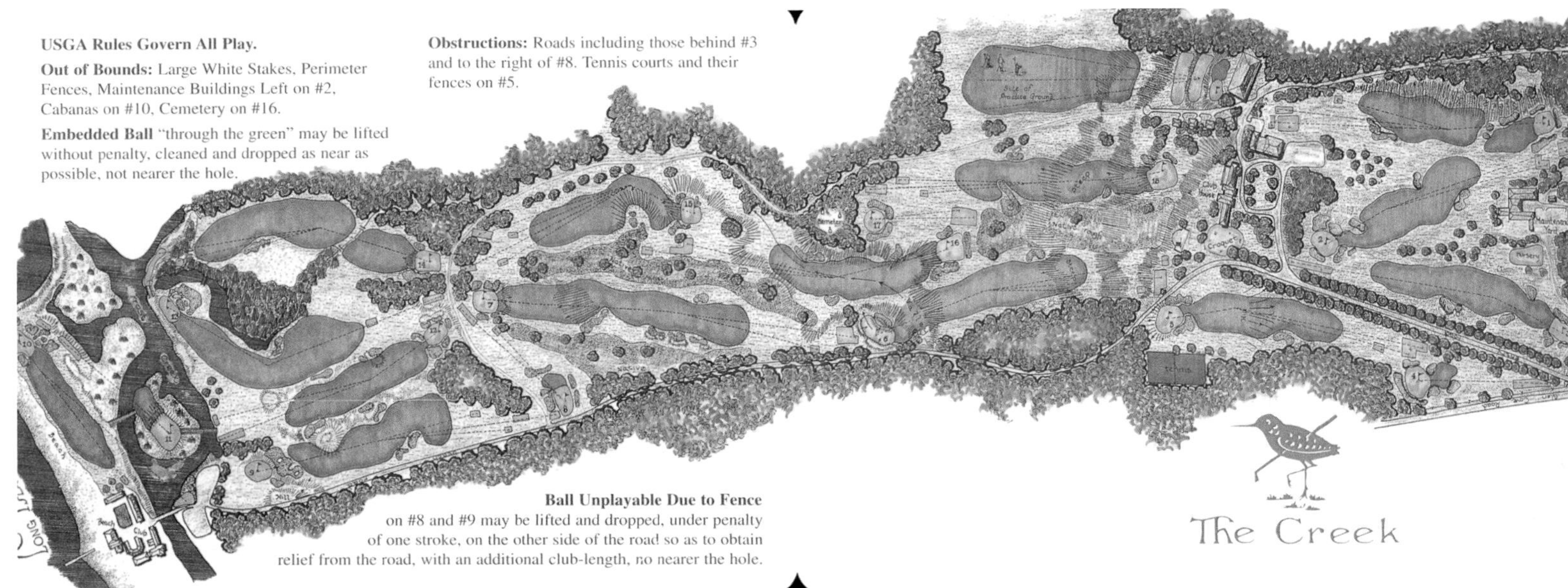

1922–1923

Locust Valley, New York

Charles Blair Macdonald & Seth Raynor: architects

Seth Raynor: construction

Alex Balfour: construction engineer (clubhouse)

Olmsted Bros.: landscape architects

Renovations:

William Flynn, 1940s (bunker alterations)

CHAPTER NINETEEN

CREEK CLUB

In response to a need for an intimate and more family-oriented club nearer Manhattan, a syndicate headed by Henry Davidson purchased the 600-acre estate of a prominent local attorney in Locust Valley on Long Island, Paul Karavath. Henry Gibson, the president of Manufacturer's Trust Bank (and a member at Piping Rock), was approached with the idea. He brought in Frank L. Crocker, who had been heavily involved with C.B. Macdonald in the financing and construction of the nearby Lido Golf Links on the southern shore of Long Island. Crocker suggested that "we consult and obtain the views of Charles B. Macdonald, the father of golf and the person who laid out many famous courses in the East."

Macdonald agreed to meet with the organizers and review the property, which extended from Harbor Hill Ridge down to a sandy beach on the North Shore of Long Island. After some careful planning and surveying with Seth Raynor, they concluded that the possibilities for a fine golf course existed, and together assembled a proposed routing plan for the founders.

This amount of participation was increasingly rare for Macdonald, who aside from the Creek Club and Gibson Island, had not been involved in design work since the beginnings of the Lido project, confining his architectural activities to the role of occassional advisor to Raynor.

Shortly after C.B. and Raynor got involved, Davidson was diagnosed with a terminal illness so he gave his blessing to Henry Gibson and Frank Crocker to continue on with the plans. They quickly assembled a committee of the most distinguished (and wealthiest) sportsmen on Long Island. This committee consisted of Vincent Astor, George F. Baker, Crocker, Marshall Field, Harvey D. Gibson, Macdonald, Clarence H. Mackay, John D. Ryan, Herbert L. Pratt, J. Pierpont Morgan, and Harry Payne Whitney.

Named after Frost Creek, an inlet of Long Island Sound, the Creek Club winds its way along the tree-lined terrain atop Harbor Hill Ridge for the first five holes. They are fine holes—particularly the first, with its boldly contoured green sliding from right to left. However, the soothing parkland setting that introduces the first section of the Creek Club gives no clue of what is to come.

The 5th rises uphill to the crest of the ridge, a panorama overlooking a stunning valley of gently rolling linksland and the Long Island Sound with Connecticut in the distance. From this exhilarating perch, the 6th (aptly named "Soundview") leaps off the ridge top and races down the steep hillside in a swooping left turn, opening up to a magnificent two-level, punchbowl green.

Opposite: Scorecard designed by architect Gil Hanse. (Gil Hanse)

The green, one of Raynor's finest, should be approached from the left, as near as possible to the tree line. The green is oriented at a severe angle from left to right and tilted away, presenting a strategic similarity to a reverse-Redan green. Approaches from the correct angle of the fairway can take advantage of the funnel effect of the green to work the ball in. Bailouts to the right side must directly confront the deep bunker standing guard on the short side of the green, obscuring the target and leering back down the fairway. The 6th is certainly one of the great par 4s on Long Island.

After a straight par 5 at No. 7 with a tee shot over a berm, the 8th hole presents one of Raynor's best adaptations of their classic par 3s—a 190-yard left-to-right Redan. A high shoulder on the left of the steeply banked green again feeds the correctly placed ball toward the pin, but will dismiss overly bold shots into the rear bunkers. Timid approaches are given little respect, as tee shots left short are punished with a nearly impossible downhill sliding pitch.

The front ends with a 400-yard par 4. The green is set on a high knoll and is steeply banked on all sides and surrounded by sandy waste. Finding this elevated green is only half the challenge—the humps, bumps, and knobs on the putting surface make par an excellent score.

The tee at the 10th ("Cape") is set at the entrance to the Beach Club, where members of another era often docked their yachts and teed off. The echelon tee shot on this short par 4 challenges players to find the narrow ribbon of fairway between the tidal marshlands to the right and the raised dune area on the south shore of the Sound to the left. Both the tee shot and the approach are made more difficult by the ever-present wind that sweeps across the water. The closer the tee shot skirts the right side tideland, the better the angle to the green. Conservative tee shots are discouraged by a pesky bunker on the left-front.

Fully exposed to the crossing breeze from an inlet of Frost

Above: The 6th hole green complex, one of the finest Raynor ever built. Also, a view of other parts of the front nine. (The Creek Club)

Opposite: One of the most unique Biarritz holes designed–the Creek's 11th. From the middle tees, it plays 167 yards. (The Creek Club)

Through the years leading up to the Depression, the Creek Club flourished. But during the 1930s and into the war years, there were financial problems at most courses and the Creek was no exception. The bank carrying the mortgage surprisingly exercised its option to demand payment in full from the club, resulting in a financial crisis.

The nearby Women's National Golf and Tennis Club, whose membership roster included wives and relatives of many Creek members, was also in financial straits and it was decided that the two clubs merge. The new club was renamed the Cedar Creek Club until 1948, when the club readopted its original name.

The course was tinkered with over the years, most notably by William Flynn in the 1940s, and then by Joseph Dey Jr. longtime executive director of the USGA and later commissioner of the PGA Tour. Sensing an obligation to restore the Creek to its original brilliance, the club brought in Tom Doak (Renaissance Golf Design) after witnessing the excellent results of his restoration of nearby Piping Rock while assisting Pete Dye.

Doak, a noted restoration specialist of golden age architecture, used aerial photos and archive information in an attempt to recapture the original flow and aesthetic balance of hazards at the Creek. Happily, with few exceptions, the course is once again a clear and relatively authentic articulation of the philosophy and concepts of C.B. Macdonald and Seth Raynor.

Long Island Solves a Golfing Problem

By R.E. Porter

The development of the Creek Club in the Locust Valley section of Long Island is particularly interesting for the colony in which it is situated and also because of its individual membership. Few clubs in this country, in fact, I might say no other club in this country, can boast of such a membership, including as it does men whose names are prominent in every walk of life and who are in many ways an important factor in the phases of life they are connected with. These men, having large estates in the fashion of country houses on or near the North Shore, organized this club and limited its membership to two hundred as a means of offsetting the ever-increasing congestion on the other courses on which they played. In other words, they will have golf as they desire to play it within easy access of their palatial homes.

Clarence Mackay, President
J. Pierpont Morgan, Vice-president
Marshall Field, Secretary
Harvey D. Gibson, Treasurer

Board of Governors

Harry Payne Whitney
Edward S. Harkness
Herbert L. Pratt
Vincent Astor
Charles B. Macdonald
Frank Crocker

The property secured for the course is that formerly owned by Paul D. Cravath, a one-hundred and eighty-three acre tract of rolling ground with magnificent views. Traversed by Frost Creek the course is fortunate in its water hazards, and Charles B. Macdonald, with his usual enthusiasm, has taken full advantage of this, while the board, recognizing that they had a good design, backed up the architect with every possible resource. The first tee is in the rear of what is known as the Dormie House, but members and their guests who arrive at the Creek by water do not have to lose any time in starting. The tenth hole is located on the shore of Long Island Sound and players are permitted to cut in there. Incidentally players may pause here on their way from the ninth green to take a dip before they tackle the second nine, for there is a bathing pavilion at hand. The course embodies upland, valley and seaside holes. Several of the fairways are literally in trees, while others lead out in the great open spaces and some run right down to the water's edge. There are no less than four water holes in the layout. All in all, the course affords good golf and enhances this with its natural surroundings and scenic beauty. The Creek should prove an attractive and eagerly sought Mecca for golfers who may be so fortunate as to play there.

—*Golf Illustrated*, August 1924

Creek is the enormous island double-green of the 11th. This rendition of a Biarritz measures 220 yards; the green measures well over 200 feet from front to back. The putting surface is also bisected by a swale (softened over the years due to tide-level difficulties) running across the middle of the green. Although the front portion of the green complex (in front of the traditional swale) was not originally putting surface, the Creek Club decided in the early 1990s to convert it to full putting surface. Historical records indicate that though several courses with the Raynor/Macdonald pedigree now feature a similar "double putting surface," the 9th at Yale was one of the few Biarritz holes originally designed that way.

After the shortish par-4 12th, the course turns back into the wind from a terraced tee on the long 439-yard 13th. It is a moderate rendition of a "Road" hole, a sweeping dogleg right with sandy waste and tideland at the inside corner of the dogleg. The left side of the green is fiercely guarded by marshland; the right by Frost Creek. The courageous drive that dares the inside of the dogleg gains the advantage of a shorter carry and more favorable angle to the green.

The 14th—called "Water Gate"—is a hole on the fringes of par. Originally a par 4 but converted to a par 5 with a tee set back in the marsh, the 439-yard uphill hole is complicated by a forced carry across the creek to an elevated green at the top of a rise. Even with the wind, to reach it in two shots requires a drive to the corner followed by a full shot far enough to bound up the closely cropped front fringe. Unsuccessful approaches roll back down the hill.

The drive-and-a-pitch 15th features a long tee shot over a fairway bunker set into the hill. The topography moves violently, and tee shots avoiding the carry are left with an awkward pitch from a hanging lie to a sharply contoured green featuring a rear plateau.

"Oak," the 16th, sweeps into a valley and banks up the hillside in a dogleg-left to another raised green with closely mowed fringe in the front. There is nothing particularly overwhelming about the hole, yet it is often pointed to by members as one of the most aesthetically pleasing on the course. Perhaps like the short 17th and par-5 18th, which climbs back up the ridge, it owes its appeal to the natural routing of the course, wandering the property much as one would on an afternoon stroll. First through the parkland, then down to the water and tidelands, and finally back up the hill to the elegant and understated clubhouse, which presides proudly over the tumbling expanse of classic golf at the Creek Club.

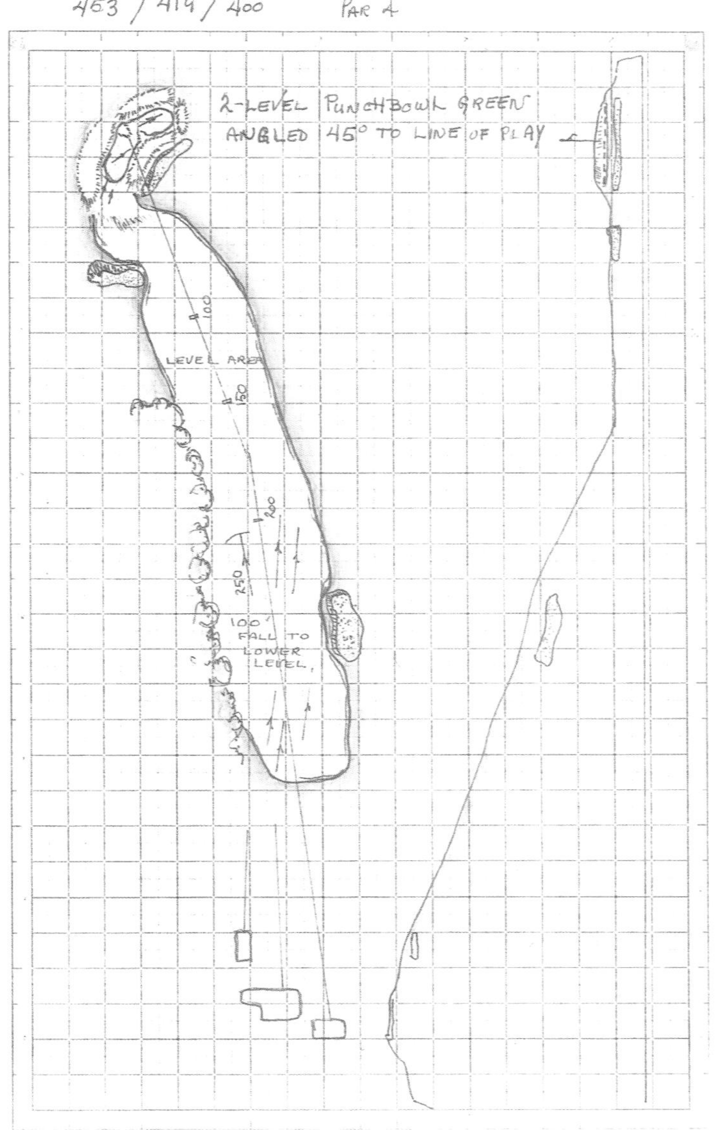

Above: Hole # 6 at the Creek Club, "Soundview." The strong par 4 drops 100 feet from the tee and plays to a two-level reverse Redan punchbowl green. (George Bahto Graphics)

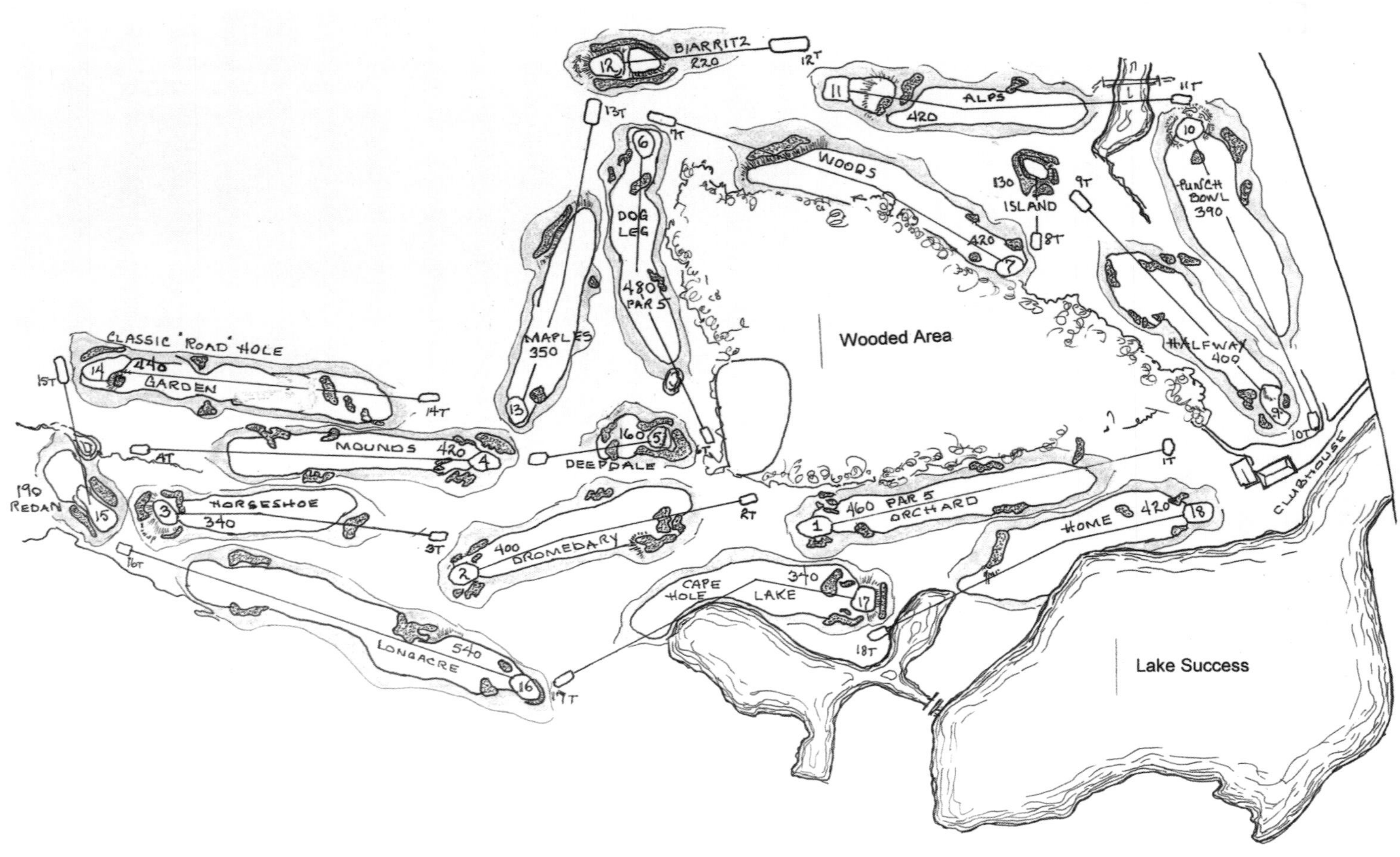

Great Neck, New York
1924–1925 (playable by 1926; completed by Charles Banks 1926–1927)
Charles Blair Macdonald (with input from Seth Raynor): architect
Seth Raynor & Charles Banks: construction
Warren & Wetmore: clubhouse architect
Portions of the course now part of the Lake Success C.C.
Not to be confused with the present Dick Wilson-built Deepdale C.C. in Manhasset, New York

Deepdale Golf & Country Club

Hole	Yards	Name	Par	Hole	Yards	Name	Par
1	460	Orchard	5	10	390	Punch Bowl	4
2	400	Dromedary	4	11	420	Alps	4
3	340	Horseshoe	4	12	220	Biarritz	3
4	420	Mounds	4	13	350	Maples	4
5	160	Deepdale	3	14	440	Garden	4
6	480	Dog's Leg	5	15	190	Redan	3
7	420	Woods	4	16	540	Longacre	5
8	130	Island	3	17	340	Lake	4
9	400	Halfway	4	18	420	Home	4
3470			36		3310		35
					6780		71

CHAPTER TWENTY

DEEPDALE GOLF & COUNTRY CLUB

The original Deepdale Golf Club and its course reflect the intense interest in sports of famous sportsman and philanthropist William Kissam Vanderbilt II. It was originally intended to be a private course on William K.'s 200-acre estate, his former summer home in Great Neck, Long Island. As the project began to evolve, some of his friends proposed to Mr. Vanderbilt a plan for organizing that included them as well. It would be a small club, with a small membership sharing all costs among themselves. Most of these friends were also members of the National but it was that old bugaboo, the arduous two-hour train trip to Southampton. Midweek golf was important to their membership. This seems to be an ongoing story of all the Macdonald/Seth Raynor courses in Nassau County, Long Island. Many of these same men held memberships at the Links, Piping Rock, Creek Club, and the Lido, plus many non-Macdonald/Raynor ventures such as Garden City and Nassau Country Club. Granted, the Roaring Twenties was financially explosive and money seemed to multiply at will, but one wonders how many courses one needed to belong to.

The proposed plan was to have a limited membership of about 200 who would pay only sustaining dues sufficient to maintain Willie K.'s course. The idea was accepted and the Deepdale Golf Club was incorporated in 1926. But the title of the property remained with Mr. Vanderbilt.

The Vanderbilt family is one of the most intriguing and interesting families in America. William Kissam Vanderbilt II (1878-1944), one of many Vanderbilts, was the third generation of the Vanderbilt clan after "Commodore" Vanderbilt. As the Vanderbilt wealth grew over the generations, given the large number in the various branches, some members opted for less involvement in the many family ventures. William K. II was content to leave the bulk of the operation to his younger brother Harold while he continued much in the manner of his father—a "sportsman," yachtsman, world traveler, adventurer. He did, however, serve on various boards or held offices in many companies; Western Union, C & N W Railroad, Metropolitan Opera Company, Long Island Motor Parkway, to name a few.

Reflecting the times, William K. was yet another of the wealthy men during the incredible 1920s who wished to have a private golf course built on his property. He was a member of all the great country clubs and an active investor in many of C. B. Macdonald's projects.

In 1925 he turned to his close friend Charlie to build a full eighteen-hole layout on the estate of his summer home at

Opposite: This hand-drawn map shows the layout of Deepdale Golf Club. (George Bahto Graphics)

Lake Success, Long Island. William knew of Macdonald's objections to estate courses (too hard for an individual to maintain; after the novelty wears off and the individual's ego comes down to earth, boredom is sure to settle in). It fell on deaf ears—William Kissam II was determined to continue. These were times of extravagances and of self-indulgence. Rich men were building mansions all over the country and in competition among themselves. Long Island's North Shore was attempting to emulate what Newport, Rhode Island did in the 1890s. The construction of new mansions on the North Shore reached a point of ostentatiousness that boggled the mind. These were men of wealth and men who were used to getting nothing short of what they wanted.

William Vanderbilt had a marvelous property overlooking Lake Success in Great Neck on Long Island and "at the behest of William Kissam Vanderbilt, the Deepdale course was designed...under the direction of Charley Macdonald using portions of the lake as a water hazard." The actual construction of the course was overseen by Seth Raynor and his new partner Charles Banks. Macdonald had long since ceased to be involved with course design but because of their close relationship he agreed to be involved with this venture —to what extent, no one knows.

Raynor and Banks were entering their most prolific period, a workload that nearly pushed them to the breaking point. New construction stretched from South Carolina to Wisconsin to California.

Deepdale was only partially complete at the time of Seth Raynor's death in January of 1926, but limited play was allowed by the end of the year. The official opening of the course was in 1927.

The Vanderbilt family was an active sporting family, largely devoted to sailboat racing, car racing and polo. The senior William Kissam Vanderbilt drew worldwide attention to the Long Island "Gold Coast" area by initiating the Vanderbilt Cup races in 1904.

Cornelius Vanderbilt Sr. (1794-1877) amassed an enormous fortune of more than $100 million, initially by securing a monopoly in New York steamship lines. He later parlayed the sale of the steamship lines into railroads, primarily the New York Central. It was said that at the turn of the century, Commodore Vanderbilt had more money than the United States Treasury.

William Kissam Vanderbilt II was one of two sons of the senior William Kissam. William II and his brother continued the operation of the then huge New York Central Railroad lines. His younger brother, Harold Sterling Vanderbilt, was the operating officer and between them they continued its successful operation, as well as the many other business ventures and philanthropic activities.

The original Deepdale course that Seth Raynor built on the Vanderbilt estate was of near championship quality but with a bit of "tooth" taken out of a few of the more difficult holes. The 6,520-yard course was a beauty and was complemented by a beautiful Spanish style clubhouse, its broad verandas overlooking Lake Success. The clubhouse "was appointed in the manner requisite of its wealthy membership" and was designed to serve the membership's needs in the style with which they were accustomed.

Although the holes Raynor built were not as sensational as those at Macdonald's National, the beautiful rolling terrain at Lake Success afforded him the opportunity to construct "a grouping of fine golf holes."

Perfect natural inclines were found for Raynor to build a "Redan" hole. A very nice "Cape" hole was named "Lake." And the course's penultimate hole was designed around a risky, angled, heroic carry over the corner of Lake Success. The favorite among the golfers, though, was "Biarritz," the

Above: Portrait of William Kissam Vanderbilt Jr., a close friend of C.B. Macdonald. (*Golf Illustrated*)

Opposite top: The original members of Deepdale Golf Club, Lake Success, N.Y. (Deepdale Golf Club)

Opposite bottom: The original dining room at William Vanderbilt's Deepdale. Note the wall mural of the golf course on the left. (*Golf Illustrated*)

220-plus-yards 12th. The 12th was described as requiring "a good poke with a spoon which will cover the distance and also avoid the traps—to the right and left is a disaster."

Deepdale was a par 71 (36-35), and it featured "named" holes in the fashion of the day. No. 2 was named "Dromedary." No. 5 was named "Deepdale." The 6th was a moderate version of Raynor's Prize dogleg at 480 yards. The "Short" was hole #8 and was named "Island." On the back nine there was a most difficult start, with a 390-yard "Punchbowl," a 420-yard (sans mountain) "Alps" that featured a full view of the green, then the 220-yard "Biarritz." The back nine continued with a drive and pitch (350 yards), a very long 440-yard 14th, a 190-yard Redan, a "Long" styled after the 14th at St. Andrews, followed by the aforementioned "Cape," and finishing with a long 420-yard "Home" hole. Interestingly, the incoming nine was 100 yards longer than the outgoing but the par was one less.

"The clubhouse at Deepdale is a smallish, beautiful stucco building of Spanish design." It was built by the noted architectural firm of Warren and Wetmore and it opened in September of 1926, its Spanish motive "consistently and harmoniously carried out to the smallest detail." The lounge was described as "restful quality"—a room that led to a balcony overlooking Lake Success. The dining room was delightful, with scenes that were hand-painted. One wall contained a reproduction of the routing plan of the course. The beautiful locker room featured walnut walls and lockers with cushioned seating in front of the lockers. The chairs were wicker and the sofas were upholstered in "modernistic fabrics." The furniture in the grill room was English eighteenth century design and the walls were natural oak.

Disaster struck the club in 1954 when the Long Island Expressway was routed through the northern portion of the course. The membership sold the original facility to the Lake Success Country Club, purchased the 175-acre W.R. Grace estate, and hired course architect Dick Wilson to design and construct an entirely new course for the Deepdale membership. It opened in 1956.

Only a few of the original Raynor-built, Banks-constructed holes remain on the present Lake Success course. All of the lockers, however, are still in use.

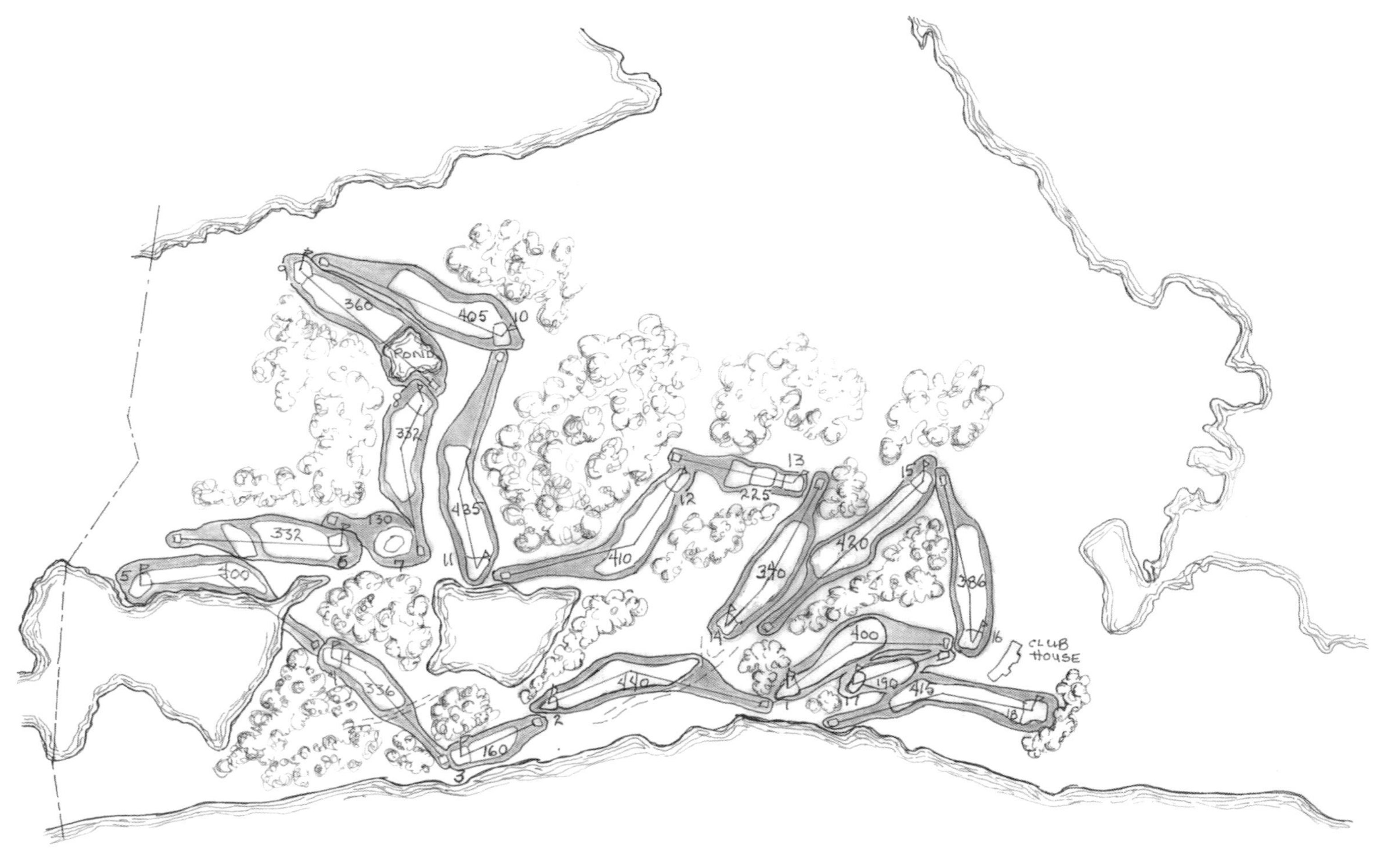

Tuckerstown, Bermuda

1922–1924

Charles Blair Macdonald with Seth Raynor: architect

Seth Raynor with Charles Banks & Ralph Barton: construction

Warren & Wetmore: clubhouse architects

Frederick Law Olmsted: landscape architect

Club opened: 1924

CHAPTER TWENTY-ONE

MID OCEAN CLUB

I first went to Bermuda in 1904, and every few years afterward visited the island again. There was no golf course in Bermuda worthy of the name in 1919. When the eighteenth amendment was passed and the nineteenth abolished, I discussed with a number of friends the propriety of having a golf course in Bermuda. Many friends thought it was better to go to Cuba, but I felt confident Bermuda was the place.

—Scotland's Gift—Golf

LOOKING OUT OVER THE CRYSTAL BLUE Gulf Stream that gives Bermuda its nearly perfect weather the year around, Mid Ocean Club, in Tuckerstown, is surely one of the world's most delightful spots. Routed along the cliff tops and fertile valleys between Harrington Sound and Castle Harbour, this intimate club became a home away from home for Macdonald and friends during the cold Long Island winters.

The idea for what became Mid Ocean originated when the Furness, Withy Steamship Company took an interest in developing this tiny British outpost some 570 miles off the coast of Cape Hatteras, North Carolina. Sir Frederick Lewis, one of the owners of the shipping line, decided to divert one of his steamships to the island and asked Macdonald and architect Charles Wetmore to accompany him and investigate.

They found what looked to be an ideal spot for a course just a few miles from the capital city of Hamilton, and attempted to purchase 500 acres for what they were led to believe would be between $150,000 and $200,00.

Word quickly spread amongst the locals that someone wanted to build a resort and it suddenly became far more difficult to secure the land they were looking at, most of which was devoted to growing onions, potatoes and Easter lilies.

Practically every one of the owners who had given an option on the property went back on his contract, and I think everybody in Bermuda connected with the situation lay awake nights wondering how they could get something out of it. Well, it's a long story, but finally it resulted in about 600 acres of property at a cost of about $600,000.

—Scotland's Gift—Golf

Planning and construction of the course was complicated. Only citizens of the Crown were permitted to own land on the island, so owing to their having an agent there, the property was purchased as part of a consortium made up of

Opposite: A rough routing plan of Mid Ocean Club. (*Scotland's Gift–Golf*)

Macdonald, Charles Wetmore, and H.C. Blackiston of the steamship company.

Soon after, a series of soil samples revealed that the only useable soil was in the valleys, and then less than a foot in depth. The majority of the hilly land was solid coral rock, further magnifying the difficulty—though there were several natural lakes to provide a water supply and hazards.

Macdonald and Raynor traveled to the island and drew up several possible routings from relief maps of the area, finally settling on one. Once the planning stages were complete, Macdonald left Raynor to tend to the actual construction, assisted by Charles Banks and Ralph Barton, a construction supervisor. It was Banks who later built the Castle Harbour course on the adjoining property.

When the course opened in 1924, Mid Ocean set a new standard as the finest island course in the world. Rather than succumb to the temptation of forcing scenic cliff-top holes at the expense of good golf, Macdonald and Raynor showed great restraint by skillfully routing Mid Ocean to take full advantage—first and foremost—of the natural contours of the site. This is not to suggest that Mid Ocean is not beautiful because it most certainly is. But much of its appeal, as it wanders through valleys and lakes, communicates a more subtle and refined elegance.

The first hole begins with a hard dogleg-left par 4, with fairway bunkers arranged to reward the bold, successful tee shot and punish the reckless or greedy one. The hole sits atop a ridge at the highest point on the course, with the well-guarded green snug against the edge of a cliff. Fully exposed to the ever-shifting winds, this hole can require a drive and a pitch one day, and a full brassie approach the next.

After a fairly forgiving short par-5 2nd hole, which still demands a truly struck drive, the Eden 3rd is a cliff-side par 3 often played in an awkward crosswind. Miss wide of the mark, and a devilish green full of subtle humps, bumps, and hollows awaits.

The 4th, with a tee shot across the road to town, is an uphill par 4 of only 350 yards with an entirely blind second shot. Distance control on the approach must be exact, as the two-tiered green is severely sloped with putts that can break 5 feet or more.

Then comes No. 5. The "Cape Hole," as it is known (and copied) throughout the world, is the best rendition of this

Left: Mid Ocean's famous Cape hole, the 5th, a dogleg left. It's the opposite of the Cape at National Golf Links. (Mid Ocean Club)

Opposite: An architectural sketch of the 5th at Mid Ocean. (George Bahto Graphics)

Macdonald detailed the activities in a letter sent to Sir Frederick's shipping partner when construction began. It stated in part:

"Regarding the Mid-Ocean Club in Bermuda the following is a description which I think will convey the beauty, charm and excellence of the Links. The contours of the property are unsurpassed, delightful valleys, one hundred to two hundred yards in width, winding through coral hills from twenty to seventy-five feet in length along the line of play; well wooded with vegetation. The contours are inviting to the golf architect to construct unique and scientific putting greens consistent with the length of the hole demanded. Mr. Seth Raynor, who for some fourteen years has been associated with me and who has my models and data, was employed to carry out the practical work in Bermuda. Mr. Raynor is most competent, having now to his credit some hundred and fifty courses."

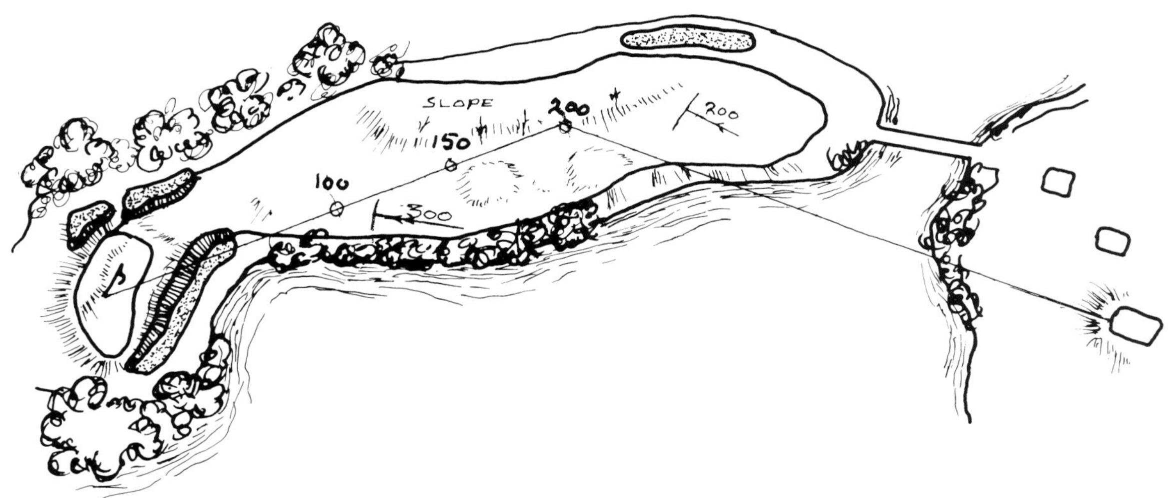

classic Macdonald original. The drive, from a high plateau above Mangrove Lake, demands to know how much water the golfer has the courage to carry to gain a shorter approach to this brilliantly contoured green.

As with many water holes, a safe landing is perhaps a bit farther than it looks. With disaster just a slight pull away, many golfers give the water a wide berth, taking the much longer route to the far right on this dogleg-left, 433-yard par-4.

Macdonald contoured the right side of the putting surface with a steep right-to-left tilt as a backstop. Players who successfully placed their drives near the water from the tee, thereby gained a more favorable angle into the green.

By contrast, this same feature punishes timidity from the tee by deflecting balls from the far right side of the fairway across the green and into the bunker or water. Macdonald so loved his creation that rather than build his home in Bermuda facing the ocean, he instead ordered it constructed to overlook the Cape hole. The home, which bears his name, still stands guard on the hillside over Mangrove Lake.

The 6th, with a tee shot along a rolling ridge, plummets abruptly into a valley, rewarding a long straight drive with a birdie opportunity. This is followed by a medium-length par 3, a "Short" that even though it is fronted by water, still has a generous green. The 8th is an uphill 339-yard par 4 that gently curves to the right, with some pesky fairway bunkers to the left and around the smallish green.

The front nine ends with a 406-yard uphill par 4. The tee shot here not only must clear a pond but land safely between two bunkers that squeeze in from both sides. The approach to this Alps hole rendition, with a punchbowl green, is mostly blind, and made more difficult by bunkering front and rear.

The journey home begins with a 404-yard downhill par 4 with a fairway sloping hard right in the landing area. A straight drive down the left side will send the ball scampering to the middle, but the landing area is contoured to shoulder away the slightest push, leaving a very difficult diagonal approach over a steep gathering bunker. This is followed by the short par-5 11th, a sharp dogleg left that—provided you keep the ball in play—can be reached in three shots fairly comfortably. However, those who succumb to temptation and try for the green in two will find the green site littered with guarding bunkers.

The 12th is a long par 4 of 437 yards, made more difficult by a tee shot skirting a shoulder of hillside from the left, and an uphill approach to a steeply contoured green guarded by deep bunkers. It is perhaps the most demanding hole at Mid Ocean.

The 233-yard 13th is a familiar Biarritz par 3, with clear sailing and an inviting ramp short of the green, but strips of bunkers snug against the green left and right. A short par 4 comes next at the 14th, with the left side guarded by fairway bunkers. The hole is notable for the classic bunkering that fronts and obscures the putting surface. The flat green is much larger than it looks from the fairway on this modified version of a Leven hole, where only a tee shot skirting the fairway bunker on the left leaves an open view of the green.

The 15th, a 500-yard par 5 littered with bunkers, rolls up a hillside. Two well-struck woods will leave only a pitch, but the putting surface is dangerously sloped and balls above the cup won't need much more than a tap. It is the last real chance for a birdie, as Mid Ocean stiffens the challenge considerably for the final threesome.

With a blind tee shot up the hillside that must be threaded between the trees on the left, and a deep grassy basin of fairway on the right, the 16th bears some resemblance to the 2nd hole at National. Even for players who have successfully found the ribbon of fairway and have the target in sight, the ever-present breeze on this hilltop green makes the approach—even with a short iron—a dicey proposition.

The Redan hole comes next. Measuring 225 yards (originally 190), it rests in the elbow between the first hole and the last. This particular version is downhill, and with the breeze swirling along the hillside, the choice of club is crucial. Like the original Redan at North Berwick, much of the difficulty of number 17 lies in the array of confusing strategic options a player must wade through in deciding how to attack the hole.

The finish at Mid Ocean returns to the ocean, with the tee set on the cliffs overlooking the pink sandy beach. The drive must skirt the right side and avoid a troublesome

Opposite top: Players teeing off the 7th hole at Mid Ocean Club in Bermuda. (*Golf Illustrated*)

Opposite bottom: The clubhouse at Mid Ocean Club, Tuckerstown, Bermuda. Warren & Wetmore were the clubhouse architect's and Frederick Law Olmsted was the landscape architect. The clubhouse formally opened on June 7, 1924. (*Golf Illustrated*)

Below: The 18th green at Mid Ocean, circa 1920s. (*Golf Illustrated*)

bunker in order to set up a shorter approach. Golfers taking too safe a route to the left on this 425-yard par 4 will play their next shot from a fairway bunker, and probably in front of an audience on the clubhouse veranda. With any luck it will be a final swing to the well-guarded and undulating green along the bright blue Atlantic.

Even today, in making comparisons with more modern island courses, there are perhaps a few that are more scenic than Mid Ocean, or whose routing offers more dramatic do-or-die shots. Yet there are few with the kind of classic shot values and design brilliance that separated the work of Macdonald and Raynor from their peers.

The great Babe Ruth, on a visit to Mid Ocean, once fell victim to Macdonald's Cape. Upon reaching the 5th hole, the "Bambino," a notoriously long hitter of the golf ball, boasted that he could reach the green from the tee. When told it was impossible, he insisted on a sizable wager—which his playing partners gladly accepted. The Babe reared back, took a mighty swing...and fell short. Still convinced it could be done—after all, he was Sultan of Swat!—he demanded another wager. And then another...and then another. After 11 tries, and out of balls, the Babe paid up, and stalked off the course.

Yale University Golf Course

Original Yardage—Three Courses—circa 1926 yardage from the middle of the tee to middle of the green

Hole	Long	Med	Short	Long Par	Hole	Long	Med	Short	Long Par
1	410	399	379	4	10	405	373	342	4
2	365	349	388	4	11	425	370	295	4
3	380	370	310	4	12	406	340	340	4
4	440	426	284	5	13	190	190	190	3
5	135	131	117	3	14	372	335	320	4
6	350	342	318	4	15	185	170	135	3
7	368	348	323	4	16	445	420	410	4
8	415	409	372	4	17	425	415	415	4
9	225	210	190	3	18	608	510	470	5
	3088	2984	2681	35		3461	3123	2917	35
						6549	**6107**	**5598**	**70**

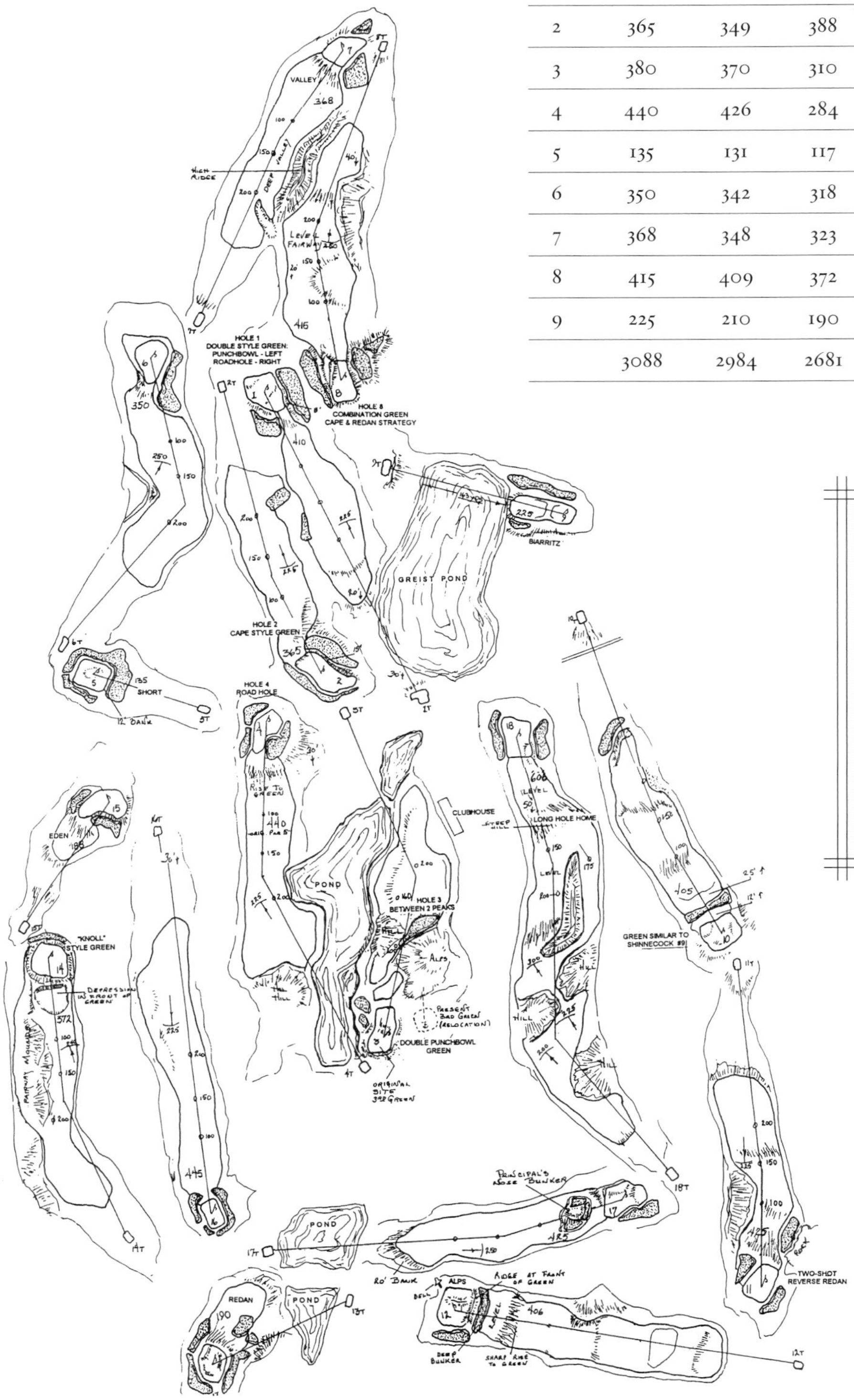

New Haven, Connecticut

1923–1926 (work began January 1924)

Seth J. Raynor: design and construction

C. B. Macdonald: advisory board

Charles Banks &

Ralph Barton: construction

Club opened: 1926

Project completed by: Charles Banks 1926

CHAPTER TWENTY-TWO

YALE UNIVERSITY GOLF COURSE

Much has been said about the Yale University Golf Course, but little has been said about the man who was mainly responsible for the creation and construction of the course. It was the late Seth J. Raynor who wormed his way through woods and thick underbrush, over land strewn with boulders and covered with ledge rock, and who picked his way through swamp areas, finally to emerge with a picture in his imagination of what is today considered by many to be the outstanding inland golf course of America... Mr. Macdonald, who served on the advisory committee, was familiar with the plans from the outset, but Mr. Raynor was the real genius of this masterpiece, who made the layout, designed the greens, and gave the work of construction his supervision from start to finish.

But if Mr. Raynor was responsible for the creation of the Yale course, Mr. Macdonald's genius was also seen in the work for it was he who started Mr. Raynor on his career as a golf architect, and it was he who, through a number of years thereafter, acted as Mr. Raynor's tutor and advisor. Mr. Raynor once remarked to me: 'I used to think my ears would grow to be like asses' ears, for I was always stretching them to take in every word that Mr. Macdonald uttered on the subject of golf.'

—Charles Banks, 1929

Opposite: Replica of the original map of Yale University Golf Course designed by Seth Raynor with C.B. Macdonald serving as an advisor. (George Bahto Graphics)

DURING 1923, C. B. MACDONALD was contacted by the administration of Yale University to study a newly acquired 700-acre tract to determine where, or if, a championship golf course could be built on the rugged property. Though Macdonald was 67 years old when first contacted by Yale and had long since retired from building courses, he understood the importance of the project to both Yale and to Seth Raynor's growing architecture firm.

Once again lured from his home in Southampton, Macdonald's name was added to an impressive panel of advisors. The 700-acre property was the largest forest and wildlife preserve in Connecticut, abounding with elk, deer, and other animals living undisturbed in their natural habitat.

The land was donated by Mrs. Ray Tompkins of Elmira, New York. It was offered "to stand as a memorial for her husband [and used for] encouraging the outdoor sports among the [Yale] undergraduates." RayTompkins was one of Yale University's finest athletes and the legendary captain of the 1883 football team.

Although the master plan for the property encompassed a variety of sports and activities, the board of the Yale Athletic Association decided that the first priority should be the construction of a golf course. The entire 700 acres were placed at the disposal of the members of the advisory panel, as well as a remarkably large (for the time) allocation of $400,000 earmarked for the project.

Originally, the plan called for the eventual construction of two eighteen-hole courses. The second course was routed on paper by Raynor, a service he frequently provided for clients, and put aside for future use if need be (it still exists). Playing privileges were to be extended only to students, faculty, and graduates of Yale University and their guests. Student fees were $20 per semester or $35 annually.

Following the approval of the routing and construction plans, a blue-ribbon panel—again led by Macdonald—was appointed to oversee the construction. Also appointed were two previous United States Amateur Champions, Bob Gardner (Yale, 1912) and Jesse Sweetser (Yale, 1924).

Right: Construction of the 2nd hole at Yale University Golf Course, circa 1925. (Yale University)

Below: The 5th (Short) at Yale University Golf Course during construction in the early 1920s. Note the soil deposit on the surface, and the beginnings of the famous "horseshoe" feature so often used on this genre. (Yale University)

The donation of the property was much appreciated by the institution, but it was going to be difficult turning a portion of it into a golf course. Unfortunately, much of the tract was stone outcropping, heavy forest, and swamp. It was also nearly devoid of useable soil. Successful construction would require enormous labor, tons of dynamite, and the talent of Seth Raynor.

The plan called for par 71-layout that from either of three different measurements: 6,549 yards (Championship), 6,107 yards (Middle), and 5,598 yards (Short). The jagged topography, described by Macdonald as "a veritable wilderness," needed to be literally dynamited out of rock. Raynor, Charles Banks, Ralph Barton, and a company of Italian laborers forged ahead with mules, ploughs, and sleds and cleared 102 acres of the rugged terrain. Of those acres, 28 were swamp and 43 were stone outcropping. That left only about 30 acres of land for them to cultivate.

Transforming this crude and gnarled terrain into a golf course would clearly test Raynor's engineering expertise. It's doubtful that many architects of the era would have summoned the courage to take on such a daunting challenge.

Though much of the Tompkins memorial site was thought to be a nearly unuseable, the funds that were available and the free hand that was given to Raynor provided him with enough latitude to build something truly special—especially since he was allowed to select any portion of the property to use. The major difficulty of finding useable topsoil was solved when Macdonald and Raynor were searching the property on foot. "Within the property a large deposit of sea-sand was found, indicating that the sea had swept the land during the glacial period; there was also a bog a quarter mile long filled with deep black muck."

The availability of these deposits to fill in the rocky terrain with soil so that a seed base could be prepared was instrumental in the successful completion of the course. Without it, most of the terrain only had about an inch of leaf mold. Long before he became a course builder, Raynor knew that proper drainage was also vital if a good stand of grass was to be maintained.

The final result of their effort was a landmark achievement of the Macdonald/Raynor design school—the boldest of brush strokes on a broad canvass. So dramatic and challenging was the terrain, that embellishment of fairways with bunkers was mostly unnecessary.

Yale is an expansive course proportioned with enormous and complex greens to match the dramatic rolls and jagged topography of the property. The greens average over 10,000 square feet, and sometimes contain two and even three different classical elements synthesized into one. The first green, for example, courageously combines a "Road Hole"-style putting surface on the right...with a "Punchbowl"-type surface on the left. The course is unique in that every move of the flagstick dramatically changes the characteristics of the hole, and that makes it a very difficult layout to master.

Charles Banks, a Yale graduate, was thrilled with the outcome of the course. In an article, he raved about the "rugged and massive features that will stir the golfer's soul...Here the architect has fashioned an Alps Hole, here a Cape, here a hint of the well known Road Hole. Not a single hole on the course is even fairly suggestive of any other one on the entire eighteen. Each hole has its own peculiar appeal—its own individuality. As a result, there is no monotony. The appeal to the eye is continuous and the appeal to the golfing sense is unfailing.

Carved through the woods, with a great variety of topography, and with an abundance of natural features, the Yale course is outstanding. It was my good fortune as an associate of Mr. Raynor during the latter part of his life to have many talks with him. During these discussions as to what really constitutes a great golf course he said, 'Well, one thing is for certain: no course can be great without a beautiful setting.' The Yale course can without a doubt lay claim to this requirement."

Yale Hole *by* Hole

Hole 1—Par 4—410 | 399 | 379

"Road Hole green on the right—Punchbowl on the left"

With a carry of 135 yards across the corner of Greist Pond, the fairway rises from the water, sweeping up to the green on a gradual slope. The bold play hugs the woods to the right, leaving an approach to the hole from a more favorable angle. The huge green is a combination Road Hole type on the right, and a Punchbowl on the left set in a gentle hollow.

"The play of the long and the bold may hug the woods to the right with increased water carry but shorter total distance to the hole and an easier second. The greens at Yale are so huge there can easily be two different styles of greens on the same hole. The green is a huge double green of the Road Hole type on the right and a Punchbowl on the left set into a bit of a hollow bunkered left and right. The play to the left half of the green is over a deep bunker about the front and left side of the green, requiring a lofted ball. The play to the right of the green is a direct shot to the high shoulder of the approach with a kick in to the green. The right half of the green has a deep bunker all along the right side but a clear approach permitting a run up. It is evident that the play of the second shot is considerably dependent upon the placing of the first shot." (Charles Banks, circa 1931)

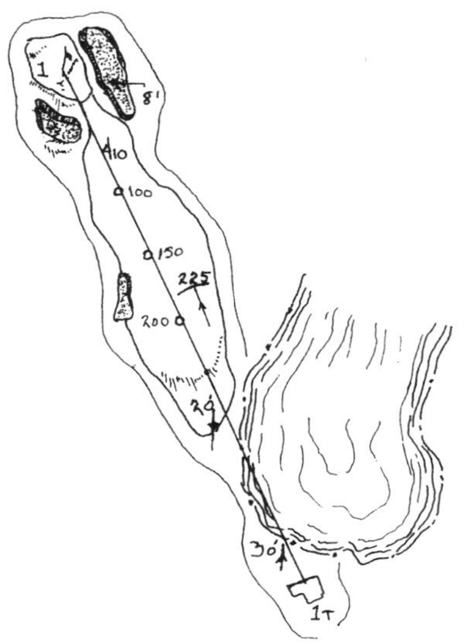

Though the individual holes now have an intimate feel about them, Yale, like many courses of the era, had far fewer trees. The first tee once provided a stunning vantage point of the rolling and broken nature of the property, though the integrity of the design is still intact. The only notable change to the hole has been the removal of a left fairway bunker.

Hole 2—Par 4—365 | 349 | 338

"Green: natural to the right—but similar to Cape overall."

Thoughtful placement of the tee ball is crucial on the 2nd hole for the best angle to the green. Although the hole is not very long, the approach is extremely hazardous. The ideal tee ball is up the right side of the fairway, which opens up the entrance to the green. The target is oriented on a severe right to left angle, and is perched precariously over a steep falloff to the left.

"This is a natural green heavily bunkered on the left with a rather narrow approach on the right. Much of the green is on natural ground though along the left it has been dramatically built up and features one of the most feared bunkers on the course; a sandpit with a depth in excess of 20 feet. Balls missing this green further left than this bunker will fall into deeper oblivion. In general the green can be considered a 'Cape setting,' jutting out, seemingly into mid-air, rather than out into a body of water." (Banks, circa 1931)

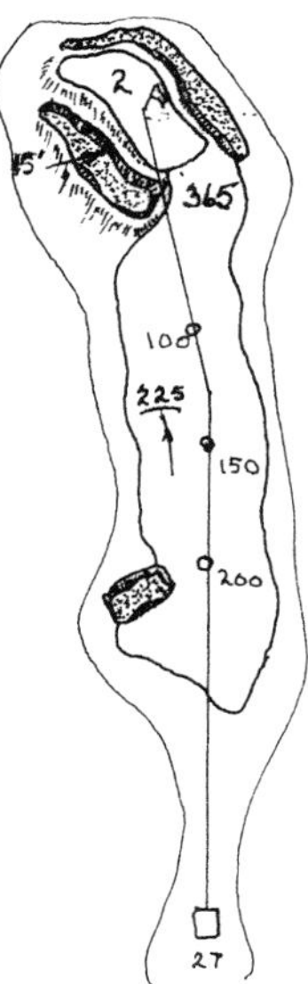

Once again, the green is very large, but contoured to accept an approach from the correct fairway angle. Good tee ball placement rewards a shot that will feed to the pin. A miss left from the tee leaves a hanging approach over a wall of grass and sand to the short side of the green.

Hole 3—Par 4—380 | 370 | 310

"Second played between two knolls to blind, double-punchbowl green."

Author's note: The original characteristics of the approach on this hole have been altered dramatically. (*See Yale map for location of Seth Raynor's original green.*) The hole has been misidentified as an Alps hole for many years because the present green (now 30 feet to the left of the original), sits hidden behind a high hill. The current small and flat green replaced the original—an expansive double punchbowl on the edge of the lake ploughed up years ago. It is thought this was done for speed of play issues. The following is the original description.

"The second water hole on the course has a [diagonal] water carry of 118 yards. The hole forces water play as there is no way around. Across the water, the fairway runs parallel to the water on the right and is flanked on the left by high ledges and knolls. The play of the second shot is directly over the saddle between two knolls into a groove between these knolls and a second line of knolls, or directly to the green over the right knoll. The groove leads directly to the green which is blind all the way. A long sand trap stretches in front of the first line of knolls. The green is a double punchbowl with water along the batter [Ed: backside of an upward slope] on the right and back of it. The fairway undulations of this hole are natural and the hole is most attractive to the eye and furnishes interesting play. There is a close and narrow pitch approach to the green on the right but is very dangerous." (Banks, circa 1931)

Hole 4—Par 5—440 | 426 | 284

"Often inaccurately referred to as a 'Cape.' In fact, it is a 'Road Hole'—similar in strategy to 17th St. Andrews."

At hole #4 we have another misunderstood hole at Yale Golf. Primarily because of the diagonal water carry off the tee, with a secondary finger of water encroaching into the right side landing area, the hole has been incorrectly referred to as a "Cape."

Though there is some validity to this, the 1931 text clearly states the hole was designed to be a "Road Hole," primarily because of the green complex.

Over the years, the front-left pot bunker, originally a representation of the Road Bunker, has expanded. Today it is even deeper, leering back down the fairway at golfers hoping to find the green. Strip bunkering behind the green simulates the road at St. Andrews.

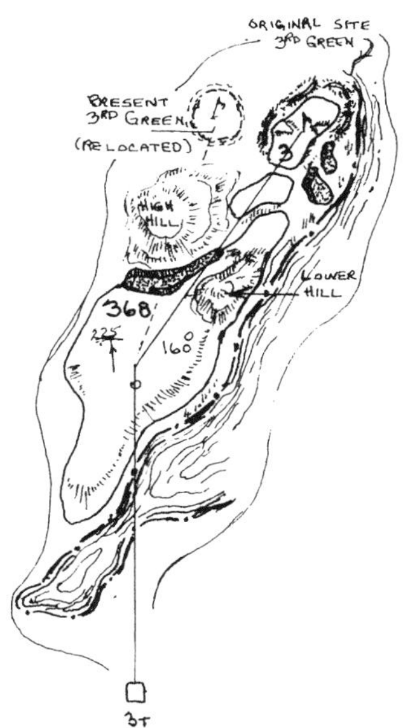

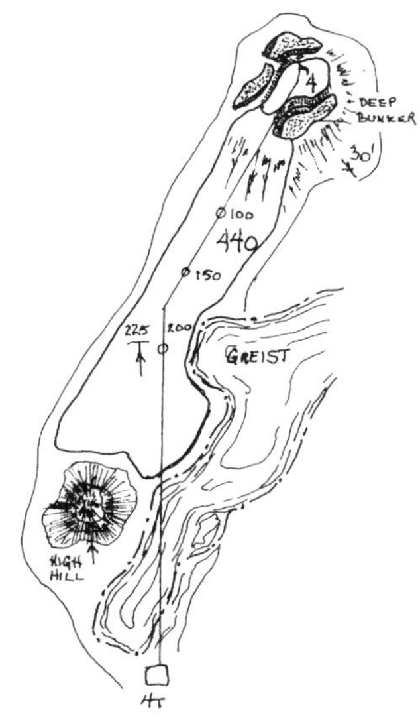

"The fourth hole has a water carry of 132 yards on the line of play. Play to the left of the line of play lengthens the hole and shortens water carry while a shot to the right of the line of play not only does the opposite to left play but also puts the ball in danger from a second arm of the lake, for play to the right of the line of play is upon a peninsula. The approach to the green requires a long, up-hill second shot compelling distance, height and hold due to the nature of the green which is of the Road Hole of the St. Andrews (Old Course) type, wherein a pot bunker is tangent to the line of play in front of the green and the left approach is lifted. The player may, by using different tees and varying the angle of the dog-leg, play the hole with the same distance as that of the original hole". (Banks, circa 1931)

One of the primary keys of this hole lies in the realization that there is little advantage to skirting the hazard to the right. The tee has been moved to the left of its original position, but it has little bearing on the strategy of the hole.

Ben Crenshaw has stated the 4th at Yale is "A perfect use of water as a driving hazard."

Hole 5—Par 3—135 | 131 | 117

"Short—modeled after the 6th hole at the National Golf Links."

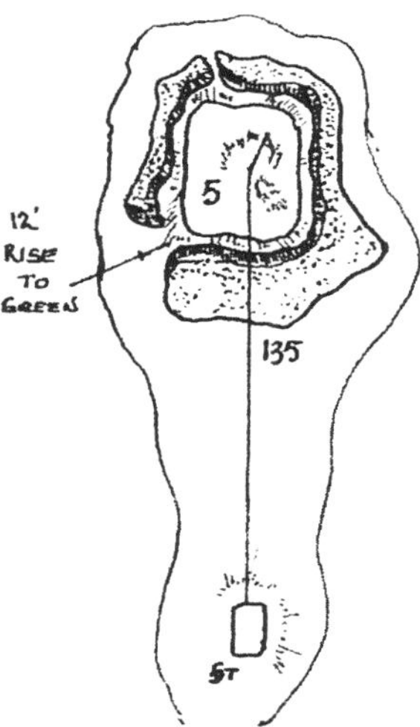

Below: A most revealing photo of the 3rd green taken from the 4th tee in its original location. The "double punchbowl" par 4 of 380 yards was unfortunately plowed under and replaced by a bland, flat putting surface behind the mound, losing the integrity of the Seth Raynor design. (Yale University Archives)

The "Short," suggested to Macdonald by the 5th hole at Brancaster (now Royal West Norfolk), is a beautifully natural version here at Yale. The plateau height is higher and the rise to the green is more abrupt than many of Raynor's Short hole versions.

"The hole is original with Messrs. Macdonald and Raynor and was first put up on the National Golf Links of America as hole number six. This is one of the four short holes of the course, i.e., each short hole is designed for a single shot to the green with a particular club. No. 5 is a mashie hole. The tees are slightly above the green level. The green is completely surrounded by sand, making it an island green elevated 12 feet above the level of the sand in the bunker. The contours of the green mark a horseshoe around the pin which is placed in the center of the green." (Banks, circa 1931)

Hole 6—Par 4—350 | 342 | 318

"The 7th hole has many attributes of a Leven."

The 6th hole at Yale pits the golfer against himself. The dogleg is classic risk/reward strategy where the long hitter can gain significant advantage, but there is a definite danger of driving through the fairway with a drive to the right of center. The corner of the dogleg is on low ground, affording little roll.

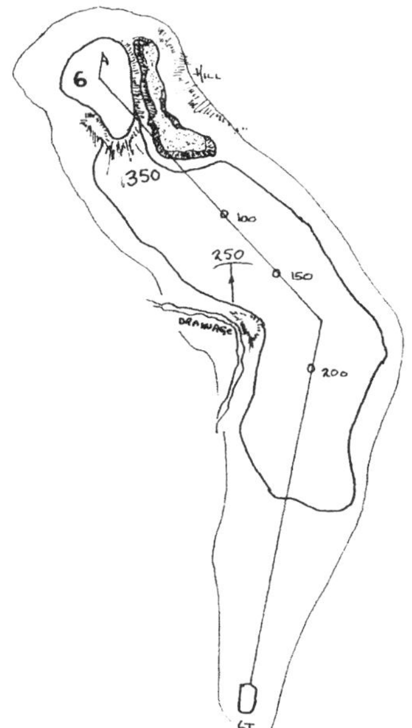

The fairway rises to a putting surface, hidden behind the right greenside bunker. Normally a short approach, the 6th has been lengthened by 66 yards from its original yardage.

"On April 1, 1924, this whole hole was a large swamp impassable except with high top boots. Filling and drainage have brought it to its present pleasant contours. The surface of the present green is six feet above the original land surface. A sharp angle of the swamp remaining on the left cuts in on the left a little more than half way up the fairway. This angle is guarded by a sand dune. The safest shot is close to this dune and yet clearing it. Safety and distance increase with play to the right. The second shot is a pitch to the green possibly over a broad bunker on the right or avoiding a sand dune on the left. An over-shot is dangerous." (Banks, circa 1931)

Hole 7—Par 4—368 | 348 | 323

"A typical Macdonald / Raynor / Banks 'Valley' hole."

From an elevated tee, the 7th swoops into a valley bordered to the left by the woods and a rough-hewn stony ridge along the right. The second shot is played to a green perched at the top of a sharply rising fairway.

"This hole reminds one of Indian Summer. It is pleasant,

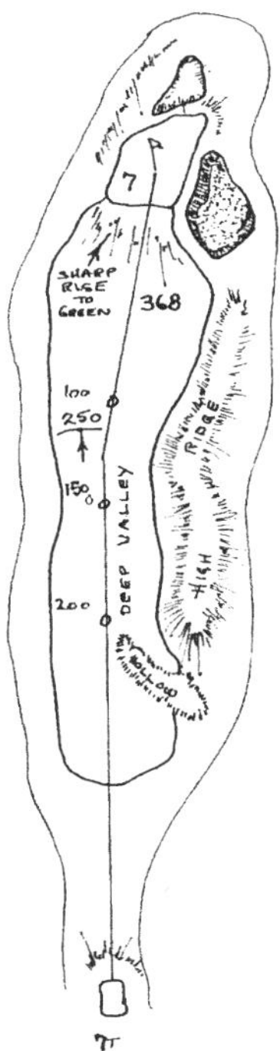

Above: View of the original greenside bunker on the 7th hole at Yale University. (Yale University Archives)

inviting and a trifle lazy. The fairway is a natural lane between two ledges on the right, cleared and bare, and tree covered ledges on the left. The approach to the green is a well rounded knoll and the green winds to the right on the top of the knoll. There is a wide bunker to the right of the green. Play on this hole is better if made to the left hugging the trees so as to get a better entry to the green. In the construction of this hole six feet of solid ledge was taken off the knoll approach and the balance of the fairway was an impassable swamp." (Banks, circa 1931)

Hole 8—Par 4—415 | 409 | 372

"Combination green—'Cape' and 'Redan' strategy."

One of the great holes at Yale, the 8th is played into a stunning combination of sloping land flowing in from the left, countered by a gentle bank on the right. The movement of the hills and vales along the route to the green makes the tee shot placement awkward—players caught in the valley on the left are often left with a blind shot to a unnerving combination Cape and Redan green.

"The first shot of this hole is 180 yards to a saddle crossing the fairway. A roll up or carry of the knoll gives a roll down the other side of the saddle into a broad level basin making 220 yards not difficult. The basin is the playing area for the

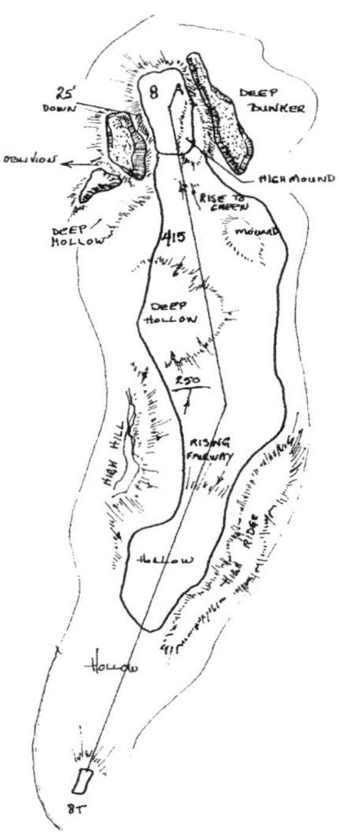

second shot. The second shot should be for a kick in from the front right corner of the green. The green combines characteristics of both the Cape and the Redan." (Banks, circa 1931)

The green complex, as dramatic as the 2nd, is one of Yale's best. A fearsome bunker guards the left front, countering the high shoulder of the Redan approach on the right side that seemingly blends into the green.

Hole 9—Par 3—225 | 210 | 190

"Biarritz—hole origin: Chasm hole #3, Biarritz, France – 1888."

The Yale version of the Biarritz hole is the most dramatic version ever built, and the most recognizable hole on the course. Exemplifying the original design in the best manner, the 9th begins with a water carry from a tee perched on a hillside overlooking an enormous green. The two plateaus of the putting surface are divided by a perpendicular trench taller than the average man through which bounding tee balls, often from over 225 yards away, cannot be controlled. The trench is a representation of the "Valley of Sin," which guards the left front of the 18th at St. Andrews.

Precise placement on the green is crucial, as trying to control the distance of a stroke from the wrong section of the

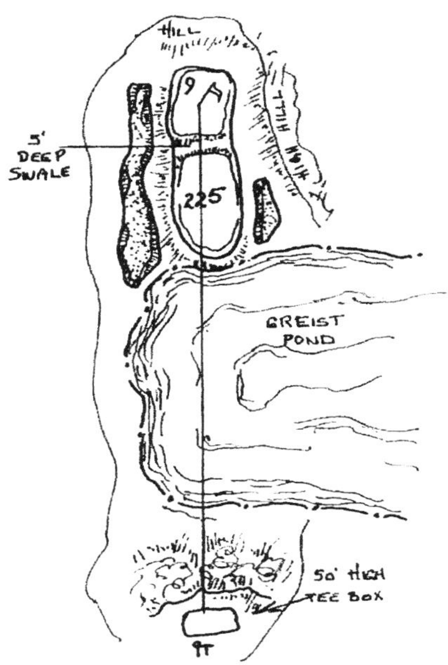

green introduces one of the world's most maddening lag putts.

The hole has long been a fixture on the list of best 100 holes in the world, and is one of the only versions of Biarritz that employs two full putting surfaces. Most correct representations of the hole feature only a rear section of the putting surface, with the trench and approach area simply presented as closely mowed grass.

"This is the second of the short holes and is planned for a single shot to the green with the driver. There is a 163 yard water carry from the back tee. The green proper is behind a deep trench in the approach. The approach is about the same size as the green itself and is bunkered heavily both right and left with water jutting in on the right front. The 'fairway' is the lake. The tees are elevated above the lake. The green is heavily battered at the back and the right and the whole psychology of the hole is to let out to the limit. The distance, however, is not as great as it seems, due to the water, and a moderate stroke with care is safer than a slam. Correct play for this green is to carry to the near edge of the groove or trench and come upon the green with a roll. The disappearance and reappearance of the ball in the groove adds to the interest of the play. The carry for this play is 180 yards from the back tee. This hole has its original on the Biarritz Course at the famous watering place in France of the same name." (Banks, circa 1931)

Bottom left: Modern view of the "Biarritz" (9th) at Yale University Golf Course. The hole can be stretched to a full 250 yards, but usually plays around 170-175 yards. (Bahto Golf Graphics)

Below: Yale's 9th hole is one of the most famous versions of the Biarritz design and at one time was one of only two versions that had the entire landing area planted and mowed as complete putting surface. This rare construction photo clearly shows the drama that lies ahead. The tee shot is played from a highly elevated location across Greist Pond to the green some 170+ yards beyond. (Yale University Archives)

Hole 10 — Par 4 — 405 | 373 | 342

"Green complex similar to the present 9th green at Shinnecock Hills."

Another fine hole is the 10th, a par 4 highlighted by the most severely undulating putting surface at Yale, a complex and slippery green set high on a hillside terrace that severely punishes careless placement from the fairway approach. Regardless of the pin's position on the rolling, swaying green, even the shortest putts have an alarming tendency to creep by the hole and wander far away. The hole bears a strong resemblance to the famous 9th at Shinnecock. The green is highly undulated so as to furnish a sure landing when a ball reaches it. The play for this hole is to get as much distance on the first plateau as possible in order to make the second shot reach the green...the second shot requires both height and distance." (Banks, circa 1931)

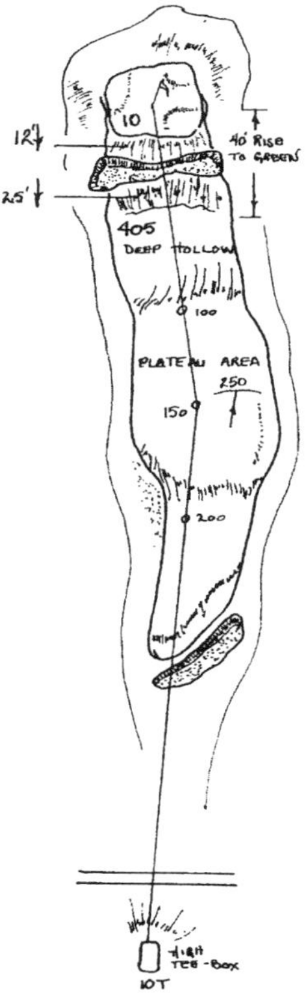

Hole 11 — Par 4 — 425 | 370 | 295

"Valley hole — two-shot reverse-Redan green."

Hole 11 leaps off the hillside, leaving a good drive with a short iron pitch to an elegantly bunkered green complex. Also perched on high ground, the green is a "reverse-Redan" that accepts an approach shot properly carved in from left to right.

"As contrasted with number ten which is practically all up hill, number 11 is practically all down hill. The tee is high above the green and the fairway immediately in front. In fact the tee is at the highest point of the course. From the tee Long Island and the Sound are readily visible when not covered by fog. The play of this hole is to reach the second knoll and catch a roll over the far shoulder when there is an easy pitch to the green. The green is a reversed Redan and the whole is a two shot Redan. Play to the right of the line of play direct to the green gives a little better facing to the green for the kick-in play to which the green is best adapted. The green is backed on the left by a long bunker and has a long bunker on the right. The hole is essentially a drive and pitch hole." (Banks, circa 1931)

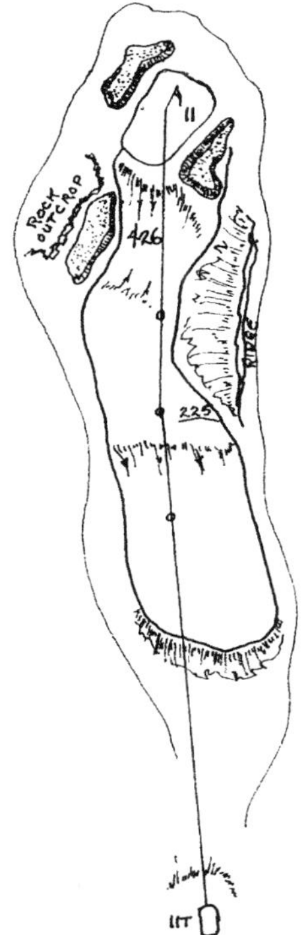

Hole 12 — Par 4 — 406 | 340 | 340

"This was the original Alps hole."

"This hole is intended in its original form to give the player the feeling of playing up on the side of a mountain to a hidden pocket. From the back tee of this hole the ledge at the back of the green is visible in outline above the elevation in front of the green. Men on the green are entirely out of view. From the position of the second shot only the mound in front of the green is visible.

The second shot is to play over the mound in front of the green. A roll up and over this mound is punished by a bunker on the left side and is highly undulated. For the first shot a carry of 176 yards from the back of the tee catches the near side of a knoll for a roll over to the level playing ground for the second shot." (Banks, circa 1931)

Years ago, the essential elements of this "Alps" hole was altered dramatically near the green site. Though the hole still maintains the general concept of a blind approach, the deep cross-bunker in front of the green was filled in, and the hilltop ridge was flattened to improve target visibility from the fairway. Still a fine hole, but sadly no longer the true Alps as conceived by Raynor.

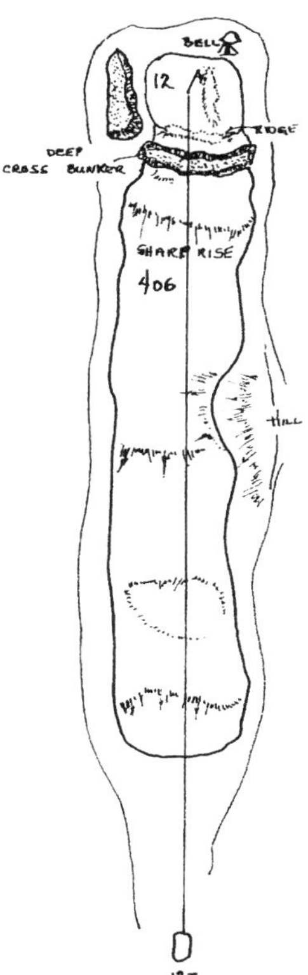

Hole 13 — Par 3 — 190 | 190 | 190

"Those who say all Redans are the same should visit Yale's Redan."

Yale's Redan is a departure from the customary strategic arrangement commonly presented by Macdonald and Raynor. The traditional Redan features a ground-level teebox positioned to obscure all but the front edge of the putting surface. At Yale, play at the 13th begins from a hillside terrace overlooking a pond with a clear view of the sprawling green. Though the front-to-back tilt is unconventionally gentle, Raynor presents an ingenuous challenge by introducing imaginative ripples and wrinkles throughout what is essentially a modified version of the classic Redan hole.

"The third water hole is the regular Redan or one shot hole for the cleek. The original hole is on the No. Berwick course in Scotland. In levels and undulations this green closely resembles the original but has a different setting. The line of play cuts the green diagonally from front to back right cor-

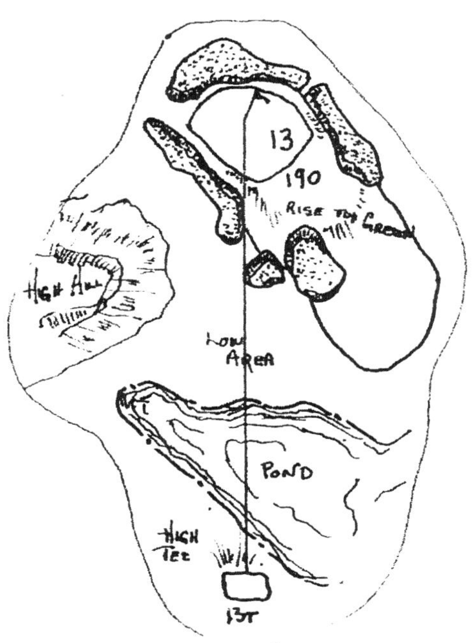

Above: Yale's Redan is marked in the top 100 holes in the United States. Played from a high teeing ground, rare for its genre, this hole leaves a lasting impression on those who play it. (George Bahto Collection)

ner. The green slopes down to the back. The pin is set at the back left corner for championship play. The approach to the green rises to the green proper whence the green slopes away to the back with the front right corner the highest point on the green. From the above it is evident that the play for the green is to catch the approach a little above and beyond its center for a kick in or carom off the right corner and a curving roll across the green to the pin at the back left corner. When properly executed the play of this green is one of the most pleasing and interesting plays in golf. The tee for this hole is 48 feet above the surface of the water, partially crossing the fairway.

Directly in front of the approach a broad bunker runs across the fairway necessitating a carry of 150 yards to safety. The fairway is flanked on either side by high knolls so that straight shooting and a 150-yard carry are the compelling influence of the hole. The green is bunkered along the right and left sides making short cuts dangerous." (Banks, circa 1931)

Hole 14—Par 4—372 | 335 | 320

"'Knoll'– hole origin: hole 4, Scotscraig, Scotland."

"Number 14 offers in its first shot three different attacks on the playing ground for the second shot. The first of these from the back tee plays for a kick in to the right from a knoll on the left side of the fairway at the angle of the dog leg with a consequent roll to low ground in front of the green. The shot from the regular tee offers the same shot with a distance to the target 37 yards less, or if desired, a straight shot to the playing ground over the trees. The shot from the short tee is straightaway down the fairway with the green in sight all the way, All: of these shots lead to the same playing ground for the second shot. The second shot is a lift and a hold [author: an interesting expression]. The green is elevated on all sides and slopes to the left. There is a large bunker at the back." (Banks revision, circa 1931)

The Knoll hole design, first introduced at Piping Rock and later at Lido, traces its origin to the 4th hole at Scotscraig Golf Club in Scotland. It is at once a startling target, and one that seems to shrink smaller and smaller the longer one looks at the edge of the knoll, which shoulders away poor shots that then tumble down the hillside.

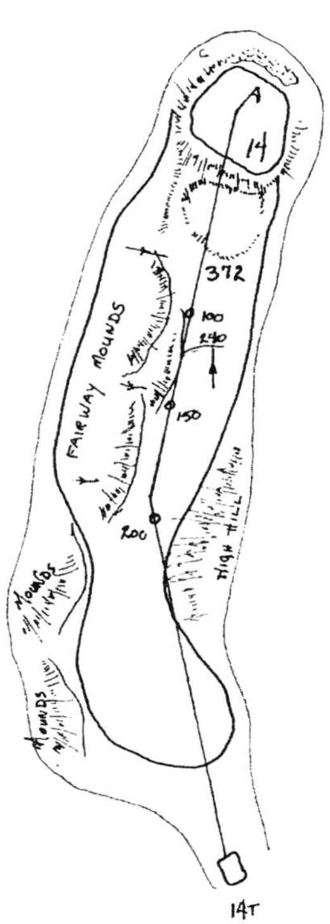

Hole 15—Par 3—185 | 170 | 135

"Eden—from the 11th at St. Andrews."

"This is the Eden hole which has its original on the St. Andrews course in Scotland. This is the fourth and last of the short holes and is a one shot hole with the iron. The regular tee gives the customary distance for the iron (175 yards).

In its original setting this green has the river Eden flowing along the back. From the tee it appears that the river touches the back of the green but in reality the river is beyond the bunker which crossed the back of the green. The bunkers on the right and left of this green are named Strath Bunker on the right and the Shelley Bunker on the left [Ed: "Shelley" later it became known as "Hill"].

This green has a different setting. In the case of the short holes the fairway of the fairgreen is missing and the intervening space is rough. From all holes the rough extends some 129 yards from the tee before the smooth fairgreen begins." (Banks, circa 1931)

A slightly more forgiving interpretation of the design mentioned most often as the outstanding short hole in the British Isles, Yale's "Eden" hole is an essential ingredient of the classic Macdonald/Raynor course.

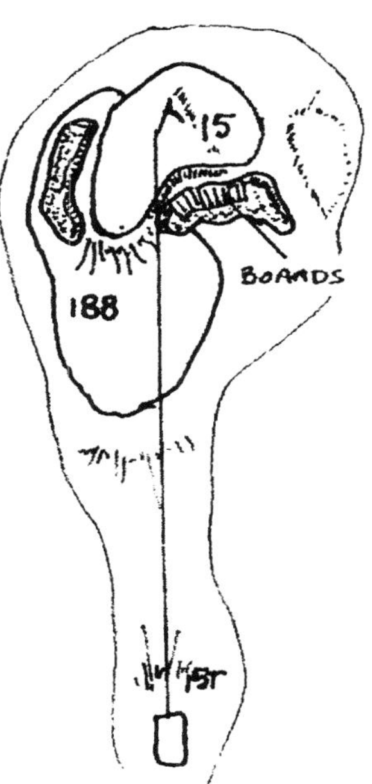

Hole 16—Par 4—445 | 420 | 410

"Originally a short par 5 – 50 yards have been added."

Appropriate yardage has been added to this relatively short par 5, compensating for modern equipment, and restoring the integrity of Raynor's original conception. Here players have a chance to gather their breath before the challenging finish.

"Number sixteen is a rather long rolling fairway leading to a broad level green. The hole should be found somewhat of a let-down from the preceding and following holes of the second nine. The second shot of this hole is the critical one and should bring the ball up from an easy pitch to the green. The green is hidden from the tees and a shot for a narrow transverse saddle in the fairway should open up the hole for the second and third." (Banks, circa 1931)

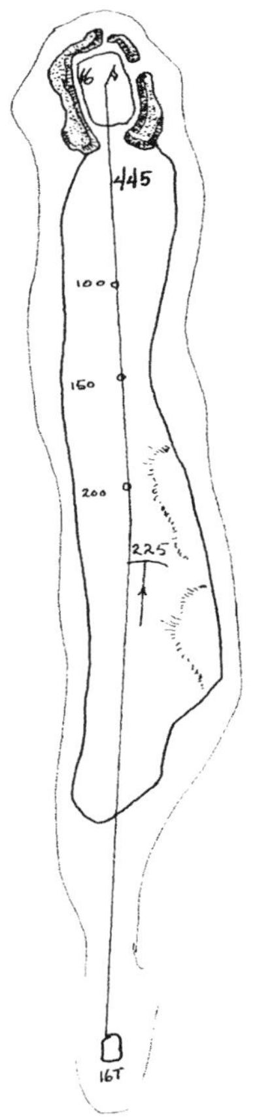

Hole 17—Par 4—425 | 415 | 415

"Double-Plateau."

Yale's 17th hole combines two important features of classic design. The "Principal's Nose" fairway hazard, positioned a short distance from the front of the green, is intended to partially obscure the target—in this case a rolling double-plateau green. Again, every move of the flagstick to a different section of the green suggests a different approach strategy. The Principal's Nose, once a hillock bunker, has been left unmaintained and is now a mound of unkempt love grass.

"The play from the tee is over the last of the six water fairways at the far side of which is a lift of 20 feet from the water's surface. The carry to the top of the lift opens up the hole. The ground from the edge of the lift slopes down to the green at a good angle so that a good roll may be expected. The green is composed of three plateaus. With an opening at the back between two of them and upon the low one. The approach to the green on the left is guarded by a mound

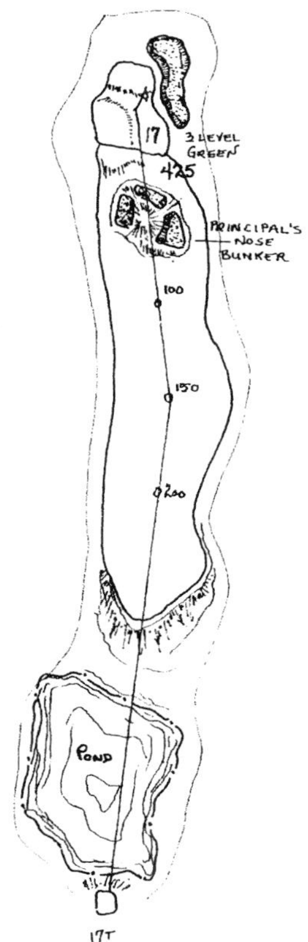

flanked with bunkers, one at the left, one at the right, both visible from the playing ground for the second shot and a third behind the knoll next to the green which is hidden from the player making his second shot. This hazard is known as the Principal's Nose and originates on the St. Andrews Course. The approach on the right is smooth but not broad and travel that way may present a putting hazard unless the pin is on the low plateau." (Banks, circa 1931)

Hole 18 — Par 5 — 608 | 510 | 470

"Home."

The climatic path back to the clubhouse begins with a steep climb to the top of a ridge, and an exhilarating leap off a hillside that is Yale's most dramatic — and severe — topography. A labyrinthine maze of options, Yale's finishing hole is a sophisticated puzzle that will suggest as many alternative routes to the green as there are golfers who play it. If the truest measure of a hole's worthiness lies in the furious debates it ignites, then Yale's theatrical finish might be the most captivating of all.

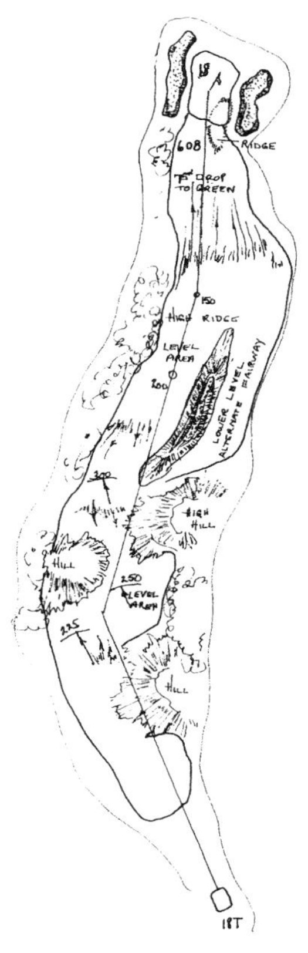

"This is the long fellow. To relieve the tedium of the drag through a long hole where distance is the only commendation, this hole has been broken up into three distinct parts with an option of still another line of play after the first shot.

The first shot should carry over a shoulder at the right and at the angle of the dog leg. By carrying the brow of this shoulder and making a roll over, the ball is brought to a smooth area of playing ground for the second. The second plays to the top of a hill which has been leveled off and cut down so as to make the green visible from this second play area. The shot is to the green on the third. Should the player desire to avoid the hill he may play around to the right with a penalty of increased distance. The two playing grounds for the second and third shots are practically two greens to shoot at but of twice or three times the area of the ordinary putting greens." (Banks, circa 1931)

Below: The 18th green at Yale. The top photo was taken in 1925 and the bottom photo was taken in 2001. The design of both the green and bunkering have been altered considerably. (Top: *Golf Illustrated*, Bottom: George Bahto Collection)

TIME LINE *of* EVENTS

THE FOLLOWING PAGES represent a comprehensive chronology of the biographical and architectural activities of Charles Blair Macdonald, Seth Raynor and Charles Banks.

Of particular interest is the explosion of activity as Raynor, nearing his untimely death in early 1926, established himself as one of America's premier golf course designers. One could only speculate about what might have been had he lived longer.

Please note their respective ages at various points throughout the Time Line, something we seldom think of.

The Time Line also serves as an illustration of the astonishing geographic dispersion of Raynor's work in an era of train and ship travel. His partnership with Charles Banks was brief before his death in 1926, leaving the nearly impossible task of completing unfinished projects littered throughout the nation.

Banks, a victim of unfortunate timing, established his own successful design business before the crash of 1929 put an end to most golf course construction.

Opposite: Twilight on the Punchbowl 16th at National golf Links. (L.C. Lambrecht)

Macdonald age 16 1872	Macdonald age 17 1873	Macdonald age 18 1874	1875—through	1891
Charles B. Macdonald to Scotland for formal education 1872 / 1873 / 1874.		Macdonald returns to Chicago, fall 1874.	Macdonald's "Dark Ages," nearly 20 years of virtually no golf.	

Charles B. Macdonald
November 14, 1855–April 21, 1939

Seth J. Raynor
May 7, 1874–January 23, 1926

Charles H. Banks
June 3, 1883–March 20, 1931

> Indicates golf course under construction; < Indicates golf course is completed.

Macdonald age 36 1892	Macdonald age 37 1893	1894	1895	1896
Spring Senator Farwell Estate, 7 holes **Summer** Chicago Golf Club > 9 holes—Belmont, IL (A. Haddow Smith farm)	< Chicago Golf Club adds 2nd 9 holes in Spring. First 18-hole course in America. Chicago Golf Club, Belmont, IL, chartered on July 18, 1893.	Chicago Golf Club > in Wheaton, IL purchases 200 acre Patrick Farm. Originally 2967-2910–5877 yds, later opened at par 73 3305-3078–6383 yds. Belmont course abandoned. Macdonald loses 1st attempt at U.S. Amateur on "Rocky Farm" course of Newport CC in September but results canceled. 1st U.S. Amateur replayed, Macdonald loses again at St. Andrews, NY "Grey Oaks" course. Results again canceled. Macdonald marries Frances Porter. American Golf Association of the United States is formed New York City at the Calumet Club. It is later renamed the United States Golf Association.	New Chicago Golf Club built in Wheaton. Macdonald wins 1st official U.S. Amateur October 1-3, Newport RI.	H.J. Whigham* wins 2nd official U.S. Amateur at Shinnecock Hills, Southampton, NY Macdonald loses 1st round match.

*Henry James Whigham: 1869-1954—died age 85

MACDONALD AGE 41 1897	MACDONALD AGE 42 1898	1899	1900	1901
Macdonald writes article about the "Ideal Golf Course" in Britian's *Golf Illustrated*.	Macdonald leaves USGA Executive Committee.		Macdonald moves to New York City.	"Best Hole Discussion" article published (British) *Country Life*.
H.J. Whigham wins 3rd official U.S. Amateut at Chicago Golf Club.	Findlay Douglas wins U.S. Amateur at Morris County GC.	H.M. Harriman wins at U.S. Amateur at Onwentsia Club.		Macdonald proclaims himself Father of American Golf Architecture, coins phrase "Golf Architecture."
Macdonald loses in semifinals at Amateur.	Macdonald loses in semifinals at U.S. Amateur.	Macdonald loses in semifinals at U.S. Amateur.	Macdonald does not compete in U.S. Amateur.	Macdonald loses in quarterfinals of U.S. Amateur at CC of Atlantic City.

Macdonald age 46 1902	1903	**Macdonald age 48** 1904	1905	**Macdonald age 50** 1906
Macdonald decides to build an "Ideal Golf Course."	Macdonald plans his "Ideal Golf Links" and locates land. ········➤			Southampton, LI, NY. Macdonald & friends acquire 205 acres in Sebonac Neck.
Macdonald goes abroad to consider feasibility of plan.		Macdonald Goes abroad again for more detailed information		Macdonald goes abroad to complete research.
Macdonald abroad during Amateur.	Macdonald abroad during Amateur.	Macdonald does not qualify for U.S. Amateur at Baltusrol, Springfield, NJ	Macdonald loses in 1st round at U.S. Amateur	Macdonald does not compete in U.S. Amateur; loses in 1st round of British Amateur
				Macdonald retires from competitive golf

Macdonald age 51 1907	Macdonald age 52 1908	Macdonald age 53 1909	Raynor age 37 1910	1911
Construction of > National Golf Links of America begins, Whigham & Emmet consultants.	National Golf Links > incorporated on March 11, 1908.	National—(6100 yds) > is barely playable.	National Golf Links > un-official Opening Tournament held, July 24, 1910.	< National Golf Links formal opening on Sept 11, 1911. 3090-3234 / 6324 yds, par 73.
Seth J. Raynor, local surveyor, hired.			New clubhouse location planned by architect Jarvis Hunt. 9s are reversed.	New National clubhouse opens
Mortimer S. Payne, local contractor, hired to construct National course.	National greens rebuilt.	National greens restored.		
		Original contact made by Piping Rock Club >		Piping Rock >
Raynor retained by Macdonald to assist in construction at the National at first seeding. National greens all lost—totally rebuilt.	Macdonald becomes member of powerful R&A Rules Committee, 1908–1926.	H.J. Whigham marries Macdonald's daughter Frances. Shinnecock Inn burns. Original clubhouse lost.	Seth Raynor retained by Macdonald to help build Piping Rock & Sleepy Hollow.	Sleepy Hollow >
Macdonald does not qualify for U.S. Amateur.	Macdonald does not qualify for U.S. Amateur.	Macdonald does not qualify for U.S. Amateur.	Macdonald does not qualify for U.S. Amateur.	Macdonald does not qualify for U.S. Amateur.

Macdonald age 56 1912	Raynor age 39 1913	Macdonald age 58 1914	Raynor age 41 1915	1916
Seth Raynor retained by Macdonald to help build courses for St. Louis CC & White Sulphur Springs, VA. >	Macdonald contacted about Lido	Lido Club project begins >	Lido >	Lido >
	St. Louis CC > White Sulphur Springs	St. Louis CC > White Sulphur Springs	< St. Louis CC	Shoreacres >
	#1 "Old White" >	< #1 "Old White"	Shinnecock redesign >	Shinnecock redesign >
		CC Fairfield contact / landfill begins.	CC Fairfield > Bellport >	CC Fairfield > < Bellport
< Piping Rock		Westhampton > Greenwich > Mountain Lake 1st 9 >	< Westhampton Greenwich > Mountain Lake 1st 9 >	< Greenwich Mountain Lake 1st 9 >
Sleepy Hollow >	Sleepy Hollow >	< Sleepy Hollow		
			Blind Brook >	Blind Brook >
			J.P. Whitney Private Estate Gardiner's Bay >	< Gardiner's Bay
				Hollywood GC (NJ) asks Raynor for advice on course.
In his final appearance, Macdonald does not qualify for U.S. Amateur.			Maidstone hires Raynor to assist C. Wheaton Vaughan in expanding course.	

US enters WWI Apr 1917	WWI Armistice Nov 1918	Macdonald age 63 1919	Raynor age 46 1920	Macdonald age 65 1921
Lido >	< Lido	Ocean Links >	< Ocean Links	
				Chicago redesign >
Shoreacres >	Shoreacres >	Shoreacres >	Shoreacres >	< Shoreacres
< Shinnecock redesign	Links Club >	< Links Club		Greenbrier #3 >
				Brookville >
CC Fairfield >	CC Fairfield >	CC Fairfield >	CC Fairfield >	< CC Fairfield
		Somerset CC >	Somerset CC >	< Somerset CC
		Midland Hills >	Midland Hills >	Midland Hills >
Mountain Lake 1st 9 >	Mountain Lake 1st 9 >	Mountain Lake 2nd 9 >	Mountain Lake 2nd 9 >	< Mountain Lake 2nd 9
Blind Brook >	< Blind Brook			Metairie GC >
				Minnesota Valley >
				Gibson Valley >
Seth Raynor, age 43. During World War I served on many home front committees and activities assisting veteran's & families. Also worked with Liberty Loan Drives, Legal Legal committee for veterans, War Committee, New York Bar Association		Ralph Barton works 2 summers with Seth Raynor.		Ralph Barton leaves University of Minnesota
	Everglades Club 1st 9 >	< Everglades Club 1st 9		
Oakland GC (NY) >	< Oakland GC (NY)			
			Babson Park G & YC >	< Babson Park G & YC
			Grand Hotel	
Morris County GC >	Morris County GC >	Morris County GC >	< Morris County GC	Fleischmanns—1920s
Olympic Club: Raynor in California during 1917-1918: submitted plans for Lake Course design that was not accepted until 1924—Raynor, probably too busy to return.				Wanumetonomy >
				White Sulphur Springs "Old White" redesign>
Spring A "Santa Barbara" course (probably La Cumbre) design not accepted				
Sequoyah Hills plans drawn: inconclusive if built by Raynor				

Macdonald age 66 1922	Raynor age 49 1923	Macdonald age 68 1924	Banks age 41 1925	Raynor age 51 1926
Creek > Chicago GC redesign >	< Creek < Chicago GC redesign	(Banks works part-time this summer)	**Charles Banks** joins **Seth Raynor**	Seth Raynor age 51 dies January 23
Maidstone redesign work Greenbrier #3 > < Brookville	Camargo > Greenbrier #3 > North Shore (NY) > Yale University >	Camargo > < Greenbrier #3 < North Shore (NY) Yale University>	Camargo > Southampton > Barton leaves Raynor Yale University >	< Camargo Southampton > Statesville (NC) > < Yale University
Otto Kahn (OHEKA) > < Midland Hills	< Otto Kahn (OHEKA) Mid Ocean >	Riddles Bay Mid Ocean >	< Mid Ocean	Banks loses Monterey contract plus others
Thousand Island Club > < Metairie GC < Minnesota Valley Gibson Island > Dedham C & YC >	< Thousand Island Club Hotchkiss School > Fox Chapel > < Gibson Island < Dedham C & YC	Blue Mound> < Hotchkiss School Fox Chapel > Eddie Moore 3-hole practice course	Blue Mound > Lookout Mountain > < Fox Chapel Fishers Island >	< Blue Mound Lookout Mountain > Fishers Island >
National Golf Links hosts Walker Cup.	Elkridge CC > Berwind CC (PR) > Crawford CC (NY) >	< Elkridge CC < Berwind CC (PR) < Crawford CC (NY)	Deepdale G&CC > Essex County CC East NJ > Yeamans Hall > Rock Spring CC >	< Deepdale G&CC Essex County CC East NJ > < Yeamans Hall Rock Spring CC >
Women's National seeks advice on design from Macdonald & Raynor —plans by Raynor submitted but course by Devereux Emmet.	Rumson—(date unclear) > early 1920s	< Rumson (NJ)	Dunes—Monterey CC > Green Park—Norwood >	< Dunes—Monterey CC < Green Park—Norwood
	Plans submitted for course in Westchester (Westchester Hills or Westchester Biltmore) exact information unclear	Mid Pacific >	Knollwood CC > Roselle GC (NJ) Mid Pacific > Hackensack CC > Waialae CC Hawaii >	Knollwood CC > Mid Pacific > Hackensack CC > Waialae CC Hawaii >
Wanumetonomy >	Wanumetonomy >	< Wanumetonomy	Cypress Point routed by Seth Raynor: contract lost in 1926 along with 2 others.	
< "Old White" redesign	Essex Fells (NJ) plans delivered for course built by William Braid in 1928 to Raynor's drawings	CC Charleston >	< CC Charleston	Essex County Park> Commission
Raynor hired to build 9-hole course at White Sulphur Springs.		Everglades Club 2nd 9 >	Everglades Club 2nd 9 >	< Everglades Club 2nd 9 Raynor dies during opening.
J.P. Knapp 3-green course on Southampton estate. (date unclear)				
William E. Stauffer estate course. New Orleans (date unclear)	Nassau CC—1 green	Breton Woods plans (NH)	Augusta CC—Lake >	< Augusta CC—Lake

Banks age 43 1927	Macdonald age 72 1928	Banks age 45 1929	1930	Banks dies age 47 1931
Charles Banks on his own	Macdonald does no work with Charles Banks	**Stock Market Crash** November 1929—The Great Depression continues		Charles Banks dies April 21, 1939, age 47
< Southampton < Statesville (NC)	Whippoorwill Club > The Knoll > Tamarack CC >	Whippoorwill Club > < The Knoll < Tamarack CC Forsgate CC >	< Whippoorwill Club Hotchkiss redesign 2 holes Castle Harbour > Forsgate CC >	< Castle Harbour < Forsgate CC
Cavalier Y & CC > Forest Hill FC (NJ) > < Lookout Mountain	< Cavalier Y & CC < Forest Hill FC (NJ) Wyantenuck 3 holes	< Cavalier Y & CC Mountain Lake major renovation.	Silver Spring (CT) > designed by Banks.	Silver Spring (CT) > built by Robert White after Banks's death to Banks's plans
Montclair GC—4th 9 >	Montclair GC—4th 9 >	< Montclair GC—4th 9	North Hempstead 2nd green only.	
< Fishers Island	Annapolis Roads >	< Annapolis Roads		
< Essex County CC—East Essex County CC—West >	< Essex County CC—West			
< Rock Spring CC < Knollwood CC	**Four Courses built by Banks in South America between 1928 and 1931:** Caracas CC—Venezuela (exact dates unclear). Junko CC—Venezuela (exact dates unclear). CC Bogota—Colombia (exact dates unclear). Prince of Wales—Chile (exact dates unclear).			
Mid Pacific > < Hackensack CC < Waialae CC Hawaii North Palm Beach CC > Westhampton adjustment > Westhampton Oneck >	< Mid Pacific Essex Fells built by William Braid < North Palm Beach CC < Westhampton adjustment Westhampton Oneck >	Crossing CC (NJ) designed—never built (Great Depression) < Westhampton Oneck		
Essex County Park > Commission aka: Branch Brook or Hendrick's Field	< Essex County Park Commission			

Macdonald continues tinkering & fine-tuning National Golf Links; moving bunkers, tees, and even greens through 1929. Course probably completed by Banks (data unclear).

Macdonald age 76 1932	**Macdonald age 78** 1933–1938	**Macdonald age 83** 1934	1939
			Charles B. Macdonald dies at age 83 on April 23 1939 in Southampton, NY. Interred in the Southampton Cemetery. ***The End of an Era***

< Silver Spring (CT), built by Robert White.

COMPOSITE LISTING *of* COURSES

Course	Year	Architect(s)	Notes
Annapolis Roads—Maryland	1928-1929	B	(drawings-1926)—18 (36 planned)—only 9 built.
Augusta CC—Georgia	1925-1926	R & B	Advertised by Bon Air-Vanderbilt Hotel for guests.
Babson Park Golf & Yacht Club I NLE—Florida	1920-1921	R	Barton construction (probably).
Bellport GC—New York	1915-1916	R	
Berwind: Porto (Puerto) Rico I NLE	1923-1925	R	Originally Condado-Vanderbilt Hotel, San Juan.
Blind Brook Club—New York	1915-1918	R	Assisted by William Rusack: George Low bunkering.
Blue Mound G&CC—Wisconsin	1924-1926	R & B	Completed by Banks.
Brookville CC—New York	1921-1922	R	
Camargo Club—Ohio	1923-1926	R & B	2 holes completed in-house.
Caracas CC—Venezuela	1928-1930	B	
Castle Harbour GC—Bermuda	1930-1931	B	
Cavalier Yacht & CC—Virginia	1927-1929	B	
Chicago GC (Wheaton)—Illinois	1895	M	
Chicago GC (Wheaton)—redesign	1921-1923	R (with M)	Probably all Raynor, but politically Macdonald.
Chicago GC (Belmont)—Illinois I NLE	1892-1893	M	Haddow Smith farm—9 holes; 9 added 1893.
Country Club of Bogota—Colombia I NLE	1930-1931	B	
Country Club of Charleston—South Carolina	1924-1925	R	
Country Club of Fairfield—Connecticut	1914-1921	R	Long time landfill.
*Cow Neck CC-see Southampton CC—New York		R	Original Southampton plan—never built.
Crawford Country Club—New York	1923-1924	R	Redesign.
Creek Club—New York	1922-1923	M & R	
*Crossing CC—designed-never built—New Jersey	1930	B	Due to the Great Depression.
Cypress Point Club—Seth Raynor routing	1925	R	Raynor routed it, then died. Completed by Alister MacKenzie.
Dedham Country & Polo Club—Massachusetts	1923	R	Recently confirmed.
Deepdale G& CC—New York I NLE	1925-1926	R & B	William K. Vanderbilt Jr.
Downers Grove GC (9)—Illinois I NLE	1893	M	Club traces its roots to Macdonald.
Dunes Club of Monterey Peninsula CC—California	1925-1926	R & B	Drew plans for Shore course—contract lost.
Elkridge CC—Maryland	1923-1924	R	

*Indicates design plans were drawn but not implemented.

Course	Year	Architect(s)	Notes
Essex County CC (East)—New Jersey	1925-1927	R & B design	Banks built course.
Essex County CC (West)—New Jersey	1927-1928	B	Solo contract.
Essex County Park Commission Course—New Jersey	1926-1928	B	
Essex Fells CC—New Jersey	1923-1928	R plans 1923	William Braid-built to Raynor plans 1928.
Everglades Club—Florida	1919-1926	R	1st 9—1919; 2nd 9-1924–1926
Farwell: Senator John B.'s estate—Illinois | NLE	1892	M	7 holes.
Fishers Island Club—New York	1925-1927	R	Completed by Banks.
Forest Hill Field Club—New Jersey	1927-1928	B	
Forsgate CC (East)—New Jersey	1930-1931	B	
Fox Chapel GC—Pennsylvania	1923-1925	R	Completed by Banks.
Gardiner's Bay CC—New York	1915-1916	R	
Gibson Island GC—Maryland	1921-1923	R	Original 9 holes—some Macdonald involvement.
Grand Hotel GC—New York	1920s	R	9-hole resort hotel course.
Green Park—Norwood GC—North Carolina	1925-1926	R & B	Now Blowing Rock CC.
Greenwich CC—Connecticut	1915-1916	R	
Hackensack CC—New Jersey	1925-1927	R & B	
Hotchkiss School GC—Connecticut	1923-1924	R	9 holes.
Hotchkiss School GC—redesign	1930	B	Redesigned 2 holes.
Junko CC—Venezuela | NLE	1930-1931	B	
Kahn, Otto—Estate Course—New York	1922-1923	R	Some bunkering by Kahn—now Cold Spring Harbor CC
Knapp, J.P. (3-green course)—New York | NLE	1920s	R	Southampton estate.
Knoll CC—New Jersey	1928-1929	B	
Knollwood CC—New York	1925-1927	R & B	
Lido Club—New York | NLE	1914-1918	M & R	
Links Club—New York | NLE	1918-1919	M & R	
Lookout Mountain GC—Georgia	1925-1927	R & B	Built by Banks.
Maidstone GC—New York	1916	R	Raynor with C. Wheaton Vaughan—expansion.
Maidstone GC—renovation	1922	R	Some modifications.
Metairie Golf Club—Louisiana	1921-1922	R	Joe Bartholomew construction.

Course	Year	Architect(s)	Notes
Midland Hills CC—Minnesota	1919-1922	R	
Mid Ocean Club—Bermuda	1923-1925	M & R w/B & Bar	
Mid Pacific CC (original 9 holes)—Hawaii	1924-1928	R & B	9 holes built by Banks.
Minnesota Valley CC—Minnesota	1921-1922	R	
*Montauk Downs GC—New York | NLE	1923-1924	M	Advisory capacity to H.C.C. Tippett.
Montclair GC—4th nine—New Jersey	1927-1929	B	
Moore, Edward S.—(3-green course)—New York | NLE	1924	R	Private estate on Long Island.
Morris County GC—New Jersey	1916-1920	R	Mapping, 1915.
Mountain Lake Club—Florida	1915-1921	R	1st 9-1915–1919;-2nd 9-1920–1921.
Mountain Lake Club—major redesign	1929	B	Hole 5—Eden.
Nassau CC (1 green)—New York	1923	R	5th green only.
National Golf Links of America—New York	1907-1910	M	
North Hempstead CC—New York	1930	B	2nd green.
North Palm Beach CC—Florida	1927-1928	R	Built by Banks—Raynor's final design (1926).
North Shore CC—New York	1923-1924	R	
Oakland GC—New York | NLE	1920-1921	R	
Ocean Links (9)—New York | NLE	1919-1920	M & R	
*Olympic Club (Lake Course)—California	1917	R	Hired, drew plans, never built.
Piping Rock Club—New York	1911-1912	M & R	
Prince of Wales CC—Chile	1927-1928	B	
Riddles Bay G&CC—Bermuda	1924-1925	R	Raynor design—may have been built by Emmet.
Rock Spring CC—New Jersey	1925-1927	R & B	Completed by Banks.
Roselle GC (9 hole course)—New Jersey	1925-1927	R	
Rumson Country Club—New Jersey	1920s	R	
*Santa Barbara GC—California	1917	R	Plans submitted.
*Sequoyah CC of Oakland	1917	R	Plans submitted.
Shinnecock Hills GC—New York | NLE	1915-1917	M & R	5+ holes remain.
Shoreacres—Illinois	1916-1921	R	
Silver Spring CC—Connecticut	1939+	B—plans	Built by Robert White to Banks plans after Banks died in 1931.

COURSE	YEAR	ARCHITECT(S)	NOTES
Sleepy Hollow CC—New York	1911-1914	M & R	
Somerset CC—Minnesota	1919-1921	R	
Southampton GC—New York	1925-1927	R & B	Completed by Banks.
St. Louis CC—Missouri	1913-1915	M & R	
Statesville CC (9-holes)—North Carolina I NLE	1926-1927	R & B	Designed by Raynor, built by Banks.
Stauffer, William E.—Estate Course—Louisiana	1921-1922	R	New Orleans.
Tamarack CC—New York	1928-1929	B	
Thousand Island Club—New York	1922-1923	R	
Waialae CC—Hawaii	1925-1927	R & B	Completed by Banks
Wanumetonomy G&CC—Rhode Island	1921-1924	R	1st 9: 1921–1922; 2nd 9: 1923 -1925.
Westchester Hills GC—New York	1923	R	Raynor drew plans; unknown if he built course or if his plans were used
Westhampton CC—New York	1914-1915	R	1st solo course.
Westhampton CC—redesign	1928-1929	B	
Westhampton CC (Oneck Course)—New York I NLE	1927-1930	B	
Whippoorwill Club—New York	1928-1929	B	
White Sulphur Springs (Old White)—West Virginia	1913-1914	M & R	
White Sulphur Springs (The Greenbrier)—West Virginia I NLE	1921-1922	R	Replaced by Jack Nicklaus design.
White Sulphur Springs (2nd Lakeside 9 hole course)—West Virginia	1921-1923	R	Course redesigned when he built Greenbrier.
White Sulphur Springs (Old White)—West Virginia	1922	R	Redesign.
Whitney, H.P.—Estate Course—New York I NLE	1915	R	9 holes.
*Women's National G&CC—New York I NLE	1922-1923	R	M & R as advisors to Marion Hollins—built by Devereux Emmet.
Wyantenuck CC—Massachusetts	1928	B	Banks design—mostly built in house.
Yale University GC—Connecticut	1923-1926	M & R	Barton assisted Raynor.
Yeamans Hall CC—South Carolina	1925-1926	R & B	

THE EVANGELIST *of* GOLF

by H.J. Whigham, *Country Life* Magazine, September 1939

It is hard to realize that the whole history of American golf is comprised within half the lifetime of one man.

Charlie Macdonald had lived thirty-six years before he could persuade any friends in this country to take up the game he had played as an undergraduate of the University of St. Andrews in Scotland. To him, young Tom Morris and Davie Strath were the heroes of a great game in which all his friends could take part if they would only follow his lead; and he lived to see that his own unceasing efforts had made the supremacy of American golf possible.

Now that Charlie Macdonald is gone, and the present generation takes all that he did for granted—believing, I suppose that there never was a time when beautifully kept golf courses did not lie within easy reach of any American city it may be worth while for history's sake to point out who and what made the greatness of American golf.

It all began, of course, with the building of links at Belmont, west of Chicago, and the St. Andrews Golf Club (originally an apple orchard) up Yonkers way, in 1892. Macdonald was the prime mover at Chicago, and John Reid, another grand old Scotchman, at St. Andrews. It is quite unimportant whether New York or Chicago can make good its claim to the discovery of golf. Nor would it be safe to say that if John Reid and Charlie Macdonald had never existed golf would not have taken root in the United States. Because, for some curious reason which has never been explained, the Scotch game suddenly spread out through the world in the early '90s and took a grip of the imagination of the Anglo-Saxon world.

Golf was almost unknown in England in 1890 outside of a few places like Hoylake, near Liverpool, where many Scotchman live, and Black Heath, a public common on the southern outskirts of London where Scotchmen pursued their favorite sport and drank their famous brew. At Oxford in 1890 no one but a few old dons and one or two Scotch undergraduates ever attempted to play. Those who could stand the ridicule were permitted to use the well-named Cowley Marshes, but only in winter; the marshes dried out in summer and became cricket fields. When the few golfers asked for a "blue," or at least a half blue, for representing Oxford against Cambridge, they were laughed to scorn.

Yet England overnight became golf conscious. By 1892 Oxford had a real golf course on the Hinkley Meadows where cricketers, football blues, and great oarsmen were out playing the despised game. So I am quite sure that even without the efforts of the great pioneers, golf would have come to America in about 1892.

Nor is it in the least important that Charlie Macdonald won the first Amateur Championship of America under the auspices of the U. S. G. A. in 1895. It was no great feat in those days for anyone who had played fairly well in Scotland to defeat a field of middle-aged Americans who had suddenly taken up a new game. Golf was still practically unknown in the colleges. Larry Waterbury, afterwards a famous polo player, won the long-driving competition at Shinnecock in 1896, when he was very young, and the late Rossiter Betts got into the finals at Chicago in 1897 while still an undergraduate. But the fields in those early years were mainly composed of grown-up amateurs who had had very little experience, and Charlie Macdonald, though he was as keen as mustard to win, never thought a great deal about his victory in 1895. (Yet most of the notices written after his death recorded merely that he had started golf in Chicago in 1892 and had won the Amateur Championship in 1895.)

More important than his victory that year was the fact that it took place at Newport. Through no fault of John Reid or Charlie Macdonald, golf in its early days over here fell into the hands of a few smart country clubs. It required a fabulous sum of money to buy two hundred acres of real estate within easy reach of a big city just for a game, so golf, like yacht racing and polo, tended to become a sport of the rich, and you had to smile when you called a man a golf player.

Consult Mr. Dooley, in 1898. He reads an account of a game to his friend Hennessy and winds up with the names of the Misses This and the Mesdames, who were among those present,

> *"'It sounds more like a society affair than a game of goluf,' said Hennessy.*
>
> *"'It's the same thing,' says Mr. Dooley."*

Peter Dunne, the creator of Dooley, later became an enthusiastic though execrable player, but his satire was valid at the time it was written. In the eyes of every good journalist it was a dude game.

To make matters worse, it was actually a game of skill. The elderly gentlemen who took to golf in the early '90s because it was fashionable soon discovered that they could not compete with the experts at all. A missed shot with the old "gutty" ball went nowhere, but it did knock up the face of the wooden club and tear the skin off the fingers. So golf gradually began to lose its devotees, and some of the smart clubs, like Meadow Brook, closed down their courses.

The invention of the rubber-cored ball by Haskell in 1898 came just in time to save the game. Inferior players found that the new ball was much easier to hit and was certainly less destructive of clubs and hands than the old gutty. From that time on golf began to flourish as the ideal sport for the incompetent. And there I believe it would have remained if it had not been for Charlie Macdonald.

The links in those days were laid out rather like race courses. Each hole was a fairly wide, straight strip of turf with narrow trenches dug across it at right angles to trap a poor shot. The fairway between trenches was as smooth and level as possible so as to make every shot an easy one. The greens were flat and slow. It was difficult to make a bad approach and almost impossible to take three putts on any green.

The golfers who played on these courses had only one object in mind and that was to lower their scores, by fair means or foul, and for them the best course was the one that presented the least difficulty. It is no wonder then that the game had little appeal for the young, imaginative, or athletic. Nor that Walter Travis, the greatest American golfer of the period, was a man who had little physique, had never played as a youth, and could drive only a mediocre distance. Granted that he was a marvelous example of the triumph of mind over matter, the fact remains that he was uninspiring to watch and that the courses he laid out owed as little as possible to imagination.

During the rather dreary years of this period Macdonald was planning the rebirth of American golf. Though a champion, he took little interest in tournaments or cups. He detested a man who counted his score except when obliged to do so in competition. For him golf was a battle in which individual character and courage and ingenuity were the things that counted, and in which all sorts of problems could be solved in all manner of ways. Rightly, I think, he saw that the score-counting habit, prevalent here and in England, but never countenanced in Scotland, was the cause of bad courses just as bad, dull courses encouraged the bad habit. What fun does the score counter get out of playing on a great links if he always has to take the safe line lest he should register an eight?

Pondering the grievous depths to which American golf had sunk, Macdonald conceived the idea of building a truly great links which would so change the minds of golfers that they would never again put up with the miserable game to which they were accustomed. With this in view he traveled England and Scotland to pick out eighteen holes on Britain's great seaside courses. He had these holes blueprinted so as to reproduce them in America.

Charlie was a perfectionist if nothing else. He was not content to build a course as good as Prestwick or St. Andrews or St. George's at Sandwich. He observed that all these classic courses were created mainly by nature and that the founders had taken what nature gave in her lavish moments but generally had had also to include one or two indifferent holes because nature had so ordained it. It never occurred to any Scotchman to change the eighteenth hole at Prestwick by putting in steam shovels and dynamite and entirely remaking the topography. The idea of creating out of whole cloth eighteen perfect holes, each presenting different and difficult problems for the player, was something entirely new, and to the average mind a trifle fantastic.

What was perhaps more fantastic was the fact that Macdonald expected to do it at a cost of $70,000. He had inspired seventy men with sufficient faith in his project to make them put up $1,000 apiece. I think even a fourth-rate golf course made to order today under favorable conditions of soil and climate would cost three times as much.

He did not, it is true, reproduce eighteen classic holes. The holes he copied in detail were the Redan at North Berwick, the Alps at Prestwick, and the Eden and the Road holes at St. Andrews. Several other holes at the National have features borrowed from Littlestone and Muirfield and elsewhere. But it very soon became apparent to Macdonald, once he had picked his ground on Peconic Bay, that nature, here too, had her own suggestions and it was far better, and certainly much more amusing to utilize existing features of the land than to copy slavishly from the great masterpieces. Indeed, what Macdonald actually accomplished was finer than what he had originally planned. He did produce a course with eighteen great holes, and in doing so created masterpieces of his own which have been reproduced in many parts of America.

In the meantime the idea of creating holes became fashionable. A competition, organized by *Country Life* in England, for which Macdonald gave the prize, produced some marvelous types, several of which were used in laying out the Lido at Long Beach.

It is hard to exaggerate the zest which was given to the whole conception of golf by the building of the National. The concrete effects were almost miraculous. Here is one example out of thousands.

I went out with Macdonald to ride over the land which is now the National, and on coming back to the Shinnecock Club for lunch we found four elderly members awaiting us with dire prophecies of what would happen if we selected a site so near their own club, one of the first three golf clubs in America and the most fashionable. Yet on that first Saturday of September in 1907 there were only four old members in their sixties or seventies in the clubhouse, and they confessed that they had to contribute a pretty penny each year to keep things going.

The very next year on the first Saturday of September I counted over fifty players at Shinnecock, many young people among them. The fame of the National had spread so far beyond Long Island that golfers from everywhere came to look over the project, and Shinnecock, instead of being hurt by the proximity of the National, had taken on a new lease of life.

Clubs all over the country asked Macdonald to remodel their courses. Since he was every inch an amateur, golf architecture for him was entirely a labor of love, and it was quite impossible for him to do all that was asked of him. So he used to send Seth Raynor to do the groundwork, and he himself corrected the plans.

Raynor had an extraordinary career as a golf architect. He was a surveyor in Southampton whom Macdonald had called in to read the contour maps he had brought from abroad. Raynor knew nothing about golf and had never hit a ball on any links, but he had a marvelous eye for a country. Having helped lay out the eighteen great holes on the National, he was able to adapt them to almost any topography. The Macdonald-Raynor courses became famous all over America. Among the most famous are Piping Rock, the Merion Cricket Club at Philadelphia, the Country Club of St. Louis, two beautiful courses at White Sulphur, the Lido (literally poured out of the lagoon), and that equally amazing Yale course at New Haven, which was hewn out of rock and forest at an expense of some seven hundred thousand dollars. From coast to coast and from Canadian border to Florida you will find Macdonald courses. And in hundreds of places he never heard of you will discover reproductions of the Redan and the Eden and the Alps.

Not only did the great links spring into existence by the magic of the Macdonald touch, but others were started independently with the idea of emulating the National. Pine Valley is almost a contemporary. The late George Crump discovered a curious outcrop of sand dunes in New Jersey only forty minutes out of Philadelphia and immediately set out to build a super-links out of his own inner consciousness. He did ask Macdonald to look it over in its early stages, and followed a few of his suggestions, but to all intents and purposes Pine Valley was a George Crump creation and a noble work of golf architecture.

Twenty years ago Pine Valley was the chief rival of the two outstanding Macdonald creations, the National and the Lido. And nothing would annoy Charlie Macdonald more than mentioning these three in the same breath. He always maintained that Pine Valley was too difficult and had too many trees. He was probably right, for one of the cardinal points of his faith was that a good golfing hole should be equally interesting and playable for the duffer and the champion. He was indeed so jealous of the National's reputation that he even disliked listening to praise of his own Lido.

Here again he was right. For the National has been much more than just a good golf course: it has been the inspiration of every great course in this country, though plenty of them will not show a trace of the Macdonald style. Take MacKenzie's Cypress Point, for example. Here is a finished product which fits perfectly into magnificent scenery; every hole is a masterpiece and pure MacKenzie. But Cypress Point would never have been conceived at all if the National had not shown the way.

As it happened Macdonald ran right into the panic of 1907 the very year that his great work was to take shape. That never bothered him at all: nearly all his seventy founders came across with their subscriptions and he gaily went into his own pocket for the rest. Being a born leader and evangelist he managed to collect about him an extraordinarily able group of men.

Among his founders and associate members are historic names like Robert Lincoln, Robert Bacon, Andrew Mellon, and Alfred E. Smith. Naturally, since Charlie Macdonald was one of the most picturesque figures in Wall Street, the world of business and finance was well represented. Henry Frick, Judge Gary, Eugene Grace, Walter Chrysler, Edward Harkness, and Herbert L. Pratt are a few of the names that leap out of the list. Charlie Sabin was a tower of strength through many years. Dan Pomeroy is still there, and Charles Steele, Harry Davison, Harold Stanley, and Charlie Mitchell. Two of the most gallant figures in the world of sport in 1908 were Harry Payne Whitney and William K. Vanderbilt Jr. Both were original founders. Vincent Astor was an early associate member. Bernard Baruch is perhaps the most typical representative of the Stock Exchange, and Nicholas Murray Butler stands for learning. The National had its fair share of wits when Patrick Francis Murphy was alive, and Peter Dunne, and De Lancey Nicoll. I am afraid it will be hard to fill their places.

And where, someone might ask, are the golfers in all this array? Remember that Macdonald was far more intent on the spirit of the golfer than on the skill with which he played, and you will realize that the most famous names on the list were chosen for their character rather than their golfing record. Among the champions the National had Findlay Douglas, E. G. Byers, and Herbert Harriman; among presidents of the U. S. G. A. Washington B. Thomas, founder, Fritz Byers, George H. Walker (who gave the Walker Cup), "Jack" Ramsey, John Jackson, and Archie Reid, present holder of the title.

It would be easy to go on enumerating the men preeminent in other walks of life who have been members of the National, lawyers like Morgan O'Brien, architects like John Cross, publishers like Condé Nast, journalists like Grantland Rice, and great figures in sports like Bob Wrenn and Dev Milburn. All whom I have mentioned here joined the National as followers of Charlie Macdonald. They believed in his sporting spirit and admired his perfectionism, whether it was manifested in the marvelous beauty of the National's landscape or the surpassing quality of the National's food.

They even followed him in the beginning when he thought a clubhouse was an unnecessary luxury, though they were glad that the Shinnecock Hills Hotel burned down and a clubhouse had to be built. But even then the entire house and furnishings cost, I think, less than $50,000 because Macdonald believed that the play was more important than creature comforts. They enthusiastically endorsed his dislike of tournaments and cups. Only one professional tournament has been held at the National, and one Walker Cup match—the first.

And what a match that was! Bobby Jones, Cyril Tolley, Jesse Guilford, Roger Wethered, and Francis Ouimet played. Wethered had to make a four for a 76 going to the eighteenth hole in the club tournament but didn't even qualify in the first sixteen because he took a ten—and quite easily, too. How that pleased Macdonald! He didn't like to see 80 broken too often and was sure that 70 could never be beaten. There never will be a Walker Cup match like that one again. There were no gate receipts and not even a big crowd. But the spirit was there.

Charlie Macdonald was a born leader who would inevitably have achieved success in any pursuit that he chose. He happened to put his tireless energy and enthusiasm and vision to the service of the game he liked to play. And in so doing he probably did more for health and happiness of the American people than most statesmen, inventors, or philanthropists.

(Mike Tureski Family)

Charles Blair Macdonald
November 14, 1855–April 21, 1939
Age 83 Years

ACKNOWLEDGMENTS

My heartfelt gratitude to the National Golf Links of America and especially Karl Olson and David Mullen. Without their cooperation, guidance and friendship, this book could not have been written.

In addition, I would like to thank the club for their generosity and trust in granting me full access to their library. The historical items housed there, in many respects, represent the original seeds from which golf grew in America.

So many people and clubs have lent their support through the years as I have tried to put this complex puzzle together. If I inadvertently omit anyone, please forgive me:

At the United States Golf Association: Library Curator Rand Jerris, Patty Moran, Nancy Stulack, and Andy Mutch. Architects Tom Doak and Gil Hanse. The many dedicated course superintendents—gentlemen all: Karl Olson, Rich Spear, Bill Jones, Mike Rewinski, Jim Yonce, Pat Sisk, Tim Davis, Chuck Martineau, Rich Tacconelli, Carl Grassl, Mark Merrick, Sean Klotzbach, Benny Zukosky (then age 92), and Greenbrier historian Bob Conte, whose assistance was indispensable.

Writers Dr. Bill Quirin, Geoff Shackelford, Brad Klein, Daniel Wexler, David Goddard.

Artist/historian Charles Ferguson; photographer Jerry Rizzo; collector John Keough; the aerial photography of Air Views and Sky Shots. As strange as it may sound, I would like to thank architect Seth Raynor for NOT documenting his work. That so little information on his activities and thoughts were ever recorded, this circumstance spurred me into the substantial research project needed to write this chronology. In some measure, my hope is this tome validates Seth Raynor's oft forgotten lofty position in golf's architectural history. It was virtually an archeological dig. A special thanks to the administration archivists, golf committees and personnel at Yale University. Their meticulous records were invaluable in shedding light on Raynor's work on that landmark golf course.

I would also like to express my gratitude to Brian Tureski, grandson of the former long-time superintendent at National Golf Links. He provided a mother lode of archival information about the National, much of it original documents written in the hand of Macdonald himself. To the many clubs who allowed me access to their archives and their courses, I thank you and hope the information provided in this book helps to clarify the proud pedigree your club carries in American golf history.

I'd like to thank Shirley, my wife of more than 50 years, who understood what it took for a rookie writer to complete this book.

And finally, I'd to thank my editor, Gib Papazian, who undertook the difficult task of making sense of my ramblings. I selected Gib from a group of volunteers who offered to edit my book because of his love for the National Golf Links and the architecture of Macdonald and Raynor. His was a labor of love with me realizing the plaudits, so here I offer my heartfelt gratitude for his magnificent effort. I do not think it was easy making me sound like a "better me." He refers to himself as "your faithful editor, Gib" but it has become much more than that. I treasure his enduring friendship even more than his work on "our book."

— *George Bahto*

EDITOR'S NOTE

Golf courses—and indeed golfers themselves—can be roughly divided between the objective and the subjective. Which side of the line you fall speaks volumes on how you view the game of golf, and perhaps ultimately the game of life.

The objective sort prefers a straightforward test, abhorring injustice and condemning the odd bounce or blind hole as defects in the architecture.

However, for those who look at golf and life as a whimsical adventure full of puzzles and choices—where skill and luck remain inextricably bound together—the legacy of golf courses left behind by Charles Blair Macdonald and Seth Raynor are the benchmark.

So, how did a guy from the San Francisco Peninsula, several thousand miles from the bulk of their courses, end up editing this book? The answer begins in 1988.

On a whirlwind tour of historic courses along the East Coast, my friend Rick Short suggested I include the National Golf Links of America on our itinerary. Off we went to Pinehurst, Merion, Oakmont, Winged Foot, Shinnecock Hills, the list goes on; each different, but supreme in its own way. If truth were told, we nearly skipped National—described by a humorless scratch player as "quirky, tricked up and old fashioned."

Some people are not capable of appreciating genius.

There is an ethereal atmosphere about National Golf Links that altered far more than my understanding of golf architecture. In truth, it forever changed how I view the game itself. For that epiphany I remain eternally grateful—though a bit cursed as well.

Jabbering ceaselessly for ten years that I had discovered American golf's Holy Grail bought me some strange looks, since almost nobody on the West Coast had ever heard of National Golf Links. A few vaguely recalled seeing a windmill in the distance from the Shinnecock Hills clubhouse.

My introduction to the book's author, George Bahto, came by happy accident. I am indebted to Geoff Shackelford—an outstanding researcher and writer in his own right—for suggesting we may have a thing or two to talk about.

Though separated by 30 years and three thousand miles, George has become my teacher and golf mentor. His supernatural ability to locate pieces of the puzzle in the most unlikely of places never ceases to astonish me—almost as if providence has guided him from the beginning.

I have been extremely fortunate to visit and closely study many of the world's revered golf courses. Still, nothing inspires in me more excitement than the prospect of playing a Macdonald or Raynor course—at once endearingly familiar, but intricate enough to never become tiresome.

Yet from this corner, the National Golf Links of America remains a separate entity—there is nothing even remotely like it in the world.

Charles Blair Macdonald's gothic masterpiece stands as the ultimate expression of one man's love for the game of golf—a beacon from the distant past, left behind as a guidepost for the future.

—Gib Papazian

Publisher's Note: Gilbert "Gib" Papazian II is a freelance writer and weekly essayist for the San Mateo Times. He is also an architectural design consultant with Neal Meagher Golf and a national panelist for *GolfWeek* Magazine. Mr. Papazian lives in Burlingame, California with his wife Amy and two children.

INDEX

A

Allison, Charles, 176
Alps (hole), 31, 33, 37, 43, 65, **88**, 144
  Deepdale Golf & Country Club, 222
  Fishers Island, 43
  Lido, 175
  Links Club, **199**, **200**
  Mid Ocean Park, 227
  National Golf Links, 43, **43**, **64**, 87-89
  Piping Rock, 152
  Prestwick Golf Club, 31, 36, 37, 43, 87, 88
  St. Louis Country Club, 43, 160
  Yale University Golf Course, 233, 241
Alps-Punchbowl, 56, 160
Amateur Golf Association, 24-26
American Golf Association, 26
Amory, F.J., 28
Anderson, Willie, 159
Apawamis, 76
"Apple Tree Gang," 18
Armour, Tommy, 79, 112
Arnold, Arthur T., 192
Ashford General Hospital, 167
Astor, John Jacob, 155
Astor, Vincent, 215, 218
Atkinson, Henry M., 61
Atlanta Athletic Club, 28
Atlantic City Country Club, 27
Aylmer, C.C., 78, 79

B

Baird, David, 93
Baker, George L., 215
Balfour, Alex, 214
Ballyshear, **63**, 66
Baltusrol Golf Club, 27, 76
Banks, Charles, 65, 141, 142, 175
  Bottle Hole, 49
  Hog's Back, 96
  Long, 108, 110
  Punchbowl, 56
  Redan, 94
  Road Hole, 102, 103
  Short, 51, 99
  Women's National Golf & Tennis Club, 142
  See also Deepdale Golf & Country Club, Mid Ocean Club, National Golf Links of America, Yale University Golf Course
Banks, Josh. *See* Banks, Charles
Barber, T.H., 24
Barton, Ralph, 141, 224, 226, 230, 233
Bauer, Aleck, 109
Behr, Max, 69, 76
Bellport, 140, 172
Belmont Golf Club, 17
Beman, Deane, 161
Bement, Gerald, 28
Betts, Rossiter, 27, **149**
Biarritz (hole), 42, 142, **148**, 164
  Biarritz Golf Club, 37, 42, 150
  Chicago Golf Club, 42
  Creek Club, **217**, 219
  Cypress Point, 42
  Deepdale Golf & Country Club, 222-223
  Fishers Island, 42
  Gibson Island Club, 213
  Lido, 174
  Links Club, 199
  Mid Ocean Club, 227
  National Golf Links, 42
  Piping Rock, 42, 149, 150
  Yale University Golf Course, 42, **42**, 219, 238-239, **239**
Biarritz Golf Club, 37, 42, **150**
Bixby, Harold, 160
Blackiston, H.C., 226
Blind Brook, 140, 172
Bobby Jones Award for Distinguished Service to Golf, 80
Boldt, George, 140
Bonnet, Theodore, 143
Boston Sprinkler Company, 126
Bostwick, G. Jr., 194
Bottle Hole, 49
  Essex County Country Club, 49, **49**, 139
  National Golf Links, 104-106, **104**, **105**
  Sunningdale, 49, 104
Bourne, George, 192
Bowers, John M. 61
Bradley, Alva, 167
Braid, James, 30, 32
Brancaster, 31, 35, 36, 51, 98-99, 101-102, 237
British Amateur Championship, 27, 30, 31
British Open, 79, 80
Brookline, 66
Broughton, Urban, 16, 17, 61
Budke, Mary, 161
Bull, Henry, 170

Bull Head's Bay, 62
Bunn, Oscar, 187
Burke, Jack, 79
Burns, George, 194
Byers, Fritz, 79

C

Cambridge Golfing Society, 27
C&O Railroad Company, 165, 167
Cape (hole), 54
  Creek Club, 216
  Deepdale Golf & Country Club, 222
  Gibson Island Club, 213
  Lido, 175
  Mid Ocean Club, 54, **54**, 121, 226-227, **226**, 229
  National Golf Links, 54, **64**, **74**, 121-124, **122**, **123**
  St. Louis Country Club, 160
  Yale University Golf Course, 54, 121, 234
Cape/Redan, 238
Carter, Phillip, 76
Caven, J., 78
Cedar Creek Club, 216
Channel Hole, 36, 53
  Harbour Town Links, 53
  Lido, 36, 53, **53**, 176, **183**
Charles Blair Macdonald Cup Match, 161
Chasm Hole. *See* Biarritz Golf Club
Chatfield-Taylor, Horace, 15, 16, **16**
Chauncey, Daniel, 61
Cherry Hills, 189
Chicago Golf Club, **14**, 24, 27, 28, 75, 77
  Biarritz, 42
  Double Plateau, 48
  early history of, 17, 18-20
  Eden, 44
  Short, 51
Choate, A.O., 155
Claxton, C., 28
Cleveland, John, 80
Colgate, James, 155
Collett, Glenna, 161, 162, 165
Colt, Harry, 19, 176
Columbian Exposition, 15-16
Congressional Country Club, 81
Cook, Jefferson, 211
Cooper, Harry, 79
Corrkran, D. Clarke, 195
Country Club, The (Brookline), 18, 21, 24, 28
Country Club of Charleston, 141
Country Club of Fairfield, 140, 172
Crater, 160
Cravath, Paul, 218
Creek Club, 206, 208, **214**, 215-219, **219**
  Charles Blair Macdonald Cup Match, 161
  Redan, 41, 216
Crenshaw, Ben, 100, 236
Crocker, Frank L., 192, 201, 215, 218
Cromwell, James, 187
Cross, Elliot, 201
Cross, John W., 201
Cruickshank, Bob, 79
Crump, George, 93
Curtis, Laurence, 18, 24, 28
Cuyler, Thomas, 170
Cypress Point Club, 42, **141**, 142, 208

D

Darwin, Bernard, 18, 72-73, 77, 84, 88, 99, 117, 119, 176, 177
Davidson, Henry, 215
Davis, Willie, 23, 184, 185
Deepdale Golf & Country Club, 220, **220**, 221-223, **223**
Dey, Joseph Jr., 216
Dixon, George A., 189
Doak, Tom, 146, 152, 216
Double Plateau (hole), 48
  Chicago Golf Club, 48
  Fishers Island, 48
  Gibson Island Club, 213
  National Golf Links, 48, **48**, 112-114, **113**
  North Shore, 48
Douglas, Findlay S., 27, 80
Dunn, Jamie, 11, 195
Dunn, Willie, 11, 18, 28, 42, 148, 184, 185, 187, 188, 195
Dye, Pete, 53, 88, 146, 152, 216

E

East Lake Country Club, 28
Eddie Moore Practice Course, 202-203
Eden, 44, 65, 157, 164
  Chicago Golf Club, 44
  Gibson Island Club, 213
  Lido, 44, 174
  Links Club, 201
  Mid Ocean Club, 226
  National Golf Links, 44, **44**, 65, 149, 117-120, **117**
  practice course, 202, 204
  St. Andrews, 31, 44, 117-120, **118**, **119**, 243
  St. Louis Country Club, 44
  Yale University Golf Course, 243
Edgewater Golf Club, 76
Edward, William, 192
Egan, Chandler, 27
Ekwonok Golf Club, 76
Emmet, Devereux, 33, 58, 61, 62, 69, 81, 142, 206, 207, 208
Essex County Country Club, 24, 28, **106**
  Bottle Hole, 49, **49**, 139
Evans, Chick, 18, 19, 76, 78, 79, 161
Everglades Club, 142

F

Fairlawn, 15
Farquhar, W.R., 17
Farrell, Johnny 79, 177, 178
Farwell, Charles B., 15, 16, 17
Field, Marshall, 140, 215, 218
Field, Stanley, 140
Findlay, Alex, 164, 166
Fishers Island, 141
  Alps, 43
  Biarritz, 42
  Double Plateau, 48
  Punchbowl, 56
Flagler, Henry, 141
Flynn, William, 93, 94, 184, 185, 186, 188, 189, 214, 216
Forgan, James B., 17, 18, 19
Foulis, James, 28, 75
Foulis, Robert, 75
Fowler, Herbert, 31
Fownes, William C., 76, 79
Francis Byrne Golf Club, 106
Frick, Henry Clay, 187

G

Garden City (hole), 58
Garden City Golf Club, 27, 58, 76, 77, 81, 93, 126, 147
Gardener, Robert, 19, 78, 79
Gardiner's Bay, 140, 172
Gardner, Bob, 161, 232
Gibson Island Club, 141, **210**, 211-214, **212**
Gibson, Harvey D., 215, 218
Gibson, Henry, 215
Gibson, John Jr., 211
Girard, Alick, 79
Glen Head Country Club, 206, 208
Goddard, David, 185-186
Goelet, Robert, 170
Gold Mashie Tournament, 193-195
Goodner, Ross, 189
Gowell, Guy, 146
Grace, J. Peter, 61, 83, 121
Grace, W.R., 223
Greenbrier Resort, 163-167
  Greenbrier Course, 165
  Lakeside, 166
  Old White, 164, 165, **166**, 167
Greenwich, 140
Grey Oaks Course, 23-24
Grier, John, 61
Guilford, Jesse P., 78, 79, 161, 195

H

Hagen, Walter, 79, 112
Hallock, Mary Araminta, 138, **138**, **139**
Harbour Town Links, 53
Harding, Horace, 61
Harkness, Edward S., 218
Harmon, Tommy, 177
Harriman, H.M., 27, 61
Harriman, Oliver, 155
Harris, Robert, 77, 78, 79
Harry Payne Whitney Private Estate Course, 204-205
Havemeyer, Theodore, 18, 21, 24-25, 187
Havemeyer Trophy, **25**, 28. *See also* Havemeyer, Theodore
Herd, Alexander, 30
Herreshoff, Fred, 69, 76
Hewitt, Cooper, 156
Hill, Cynthia, 161
Hilton, H.H., 30, 31-32, 35
Hilton, Harold, 76-77, 144
Hog's Back (hole), 50
  Lido, 175
  National Golf Links, 50, **50**, 94-96, **94**
Holderness, Ernest, 78
Hollins, Marion, 142, 207-208, **208**
Hooman, C.V.L., 78, 79
Howe, Richard F., 192
Hoylake, 30, 31, 77
Hunt, Jarvis, 61, 73, 141
Huntingdon Valley, 189
Huntington, C.P., 164
Hutchinson, Horace, 19, 30, 31, 36, 67, 96, 102, 171, 176
Hutchinson, Jock, 79

I

Ingleby, Halcome, 102
Island Golf Links, 81

J

Johnson, Elizabeth, 137, **139**
Johnson, Ford, 192
Johnson, William, 13
Jones, Rees, 154
Jones, Robert Trent, 146, 154, 158, 182
Jones, Robert Tyre Jr. (Bobby), 28, 74, 78, **78**, 79, 80, 117, 161
Jones, W. Alton, 80

K

Kahn, Otto, 140, 170, 203
Karavath, Paul, 215
Kirkwood, Joe, 79
Knapp, Joseph P., 62, 69, 76
Knight, Harry, 160
Knoll Hole, 52, 142, 243
  Lido, 175
  Piping Rock, 52, **52**, **150**, 152
Knoll Golf Club, 50
Kravath, Paul, 170

L

Lake Forest Club, 17
Lake Success Country Club, 223
Lakeside Country Club, 143-45
Lawrence, W.G. (Willie), 21-23, 23, 24
Leatherstocking, 81
Leeds, Herbert, 66
Lees, Peter, 168, 171-172, **171**, 173, 174, 177
Leven (hole), 40
  Gibson Island Club, 213
  Links Club, 199
  Mid Ocean Club, 228
  National Golf Links, 40, 130-133, **130**, **131**, **132**
  Yale University Golf Course, 237
Leven Links, 36, 37, 40
Lewis, Frederick, 225, 226
Lido Golf Club, 63, 140, 142, 168-183
  Alps, 175
  Biarritz, 174
  Cape, 175
  Channel, 36, 53, **53**, 176, **183**
  clubhouse, 178, **181**
  construction, 171-174, 172
  Eden, 44, 174
  Hog's Back, 175
  Knoll, 175
  Long, 55, **107-108**, 108, 176, **180**, **181**
  Ocean, 174
  Punchbowl, 174, **175**
  Raynor's Prize Dogleg, 45, **176**
  Redan, 174
  routing plan, **168**
  Short, 174
  Strategy, 59, 174-175
  tournaments, 177-178
Lincoln, Robert, 61
Lindbergh, Charles, 160
Links Club, 76, 196-201, **198**
  Alps, **199**, **200**
  Leven, 199
  map, **196**
  Reverse Redan, 201
Littlestone, 35, 36, 53, **182**, 183
Livingston, Louis, 69
Long (hole), 31, 55
  Deepdale Golf & Country Club, 222
  Lido, 55, **107-108**, 108, 176, **180**, **181**
  Links Club, 201
  National Golf Links, 55, **55**, 107-110
  St. Andrews, 31, 55, 107, **108**, **109**, 176, **180**
Long Island Railroad, 186
Lookout Mountain, 142
Low, John L., 30, 36
Lyle, Sandy, 127
Lyon, George S., **25**

M

Macdonald, Charles Blair, **17**, **20**, **26**, **60**, **62**, **65**, **69**, 77
  Amateur Golf Association, 24
  Ballyshear, **63**, 66
  as competitor, 21-28, 29
  Creek Club, 214-219
  Deepdale Golf & Country Club, 220-223
  early golf course design, 32-38
  early life in St. Andrews, Scotland, 9-11
  family, 13, 16, 17, 61, 75, 83, 138. *See also* Whigham, Henry J.
  Gibson Island Club, 210-214
  medals, **76**
  memorabilia, **74**
  Mid Ocean Club, 225-229
  practice courses, 202-205
  statue of, **67**, 74
  Women's National Golf & Tennis Club, 142, 206-208
  See also Chicago Golf Club, Greenbrier Resort, Lido Club, Links Club, National Golf Links of America, Ocean Links, Piping Rock, Shinnecock Hills Golf Club, Sleepy Hollow Country Club, St. Louis Country Club, Yale University Golf Course, *specific holes*
Macdonald, Frances (daughter), 16, 17
Macdonald, Frances Porter, 17
Macdonald, Godfrey, 13
Macdonald, Janet, 17
Macdonald, Mary Blackwell, 13
Macdonald, William, 10
Macdonald Invitational Tournament, 68
"Macdonald's Folly," 149
MacFarlane, Willie, 80
Mackay, Clarence, 61, 147, 215, 218
MacKenzie, Alister, 42, **141**, 142, 176-177, 208
Mackenzie, Willis, 78, 79
Macy, V. Everit, 155
Maidstone Club, 138, 140, 187
Marston, Max, 79
Martin, Gould, 193-194
Maxwell, Perry, 196
Meadow Brook, 24, 28
Mehlhorn, Bill, 79
Melville, Leslie Balfour, 31
Merion Cricket Club, 93
Metropolitan Open (1992), 177
Mid Ocean Club, 138, **224**, 225-229, **227**, **228**
  Cape, 54, **54**, 121, 226-227, **226**, 229
  Charles Blair Macdonald Cup Match, 161
Mid Pacific, 142
Millen, Woody, 146
Mitchell, William, 184
Mizner, Addison, 141
Montague, Russell, 164
Montclair Country Club, 56
Monterey Peninsula Country Club, 142
Moore, Eddie, 203
Moorman, John, 163
Morgan, J. Pierpont, 215, 218

Morgan, W. Forbes, 170
Morris, Tom (Old), 10, **11**, **13**, 21, 43, 52, 195
Morris, Tom (Young), 11, **11**, 93
Morris County Country Club, 27, 75, 76
Moschowicz, Paul, 193
Mountain Lake, 141
Muirfield, 36, 46, 127, 129
Mullen, David, 83
Musselburgh, 195
Myopia Hunt Club, 34, 66

N

Narrows (hole), 46, **46**, 124-127, **125**
Nassau County Club, 51, 76
Naste, Conde, 192
National Amateur (1912), 19
National Golf Course. *See* National Golf Links of America
National Golf Links of America, 12, 27, 61-136, **64**, **246**
  Alps, 43, **43**, **64**, 87-89
  Biarritz, 42
  blueprint, **63**
  Bottle, 104-106, **104**, **105**
  Cape, 54, **64**, **74**, 121-124, **122**, **123**
  Charles Blair Macdonald Cup Match, 161
  clubhouse, 73, **74**
  construction, 64-68
  Double Plateau, 48, **48**, 112-114, **113**
  early plans, 61-63,
  Eden, 44, **44**, 65, 149, 117-120, **117**
  Gold Mashie Tournament, 194
  Hog's Back, 50, **50**, 94-96, **94**
  hole description, 82-135
  irrigation system, 67, 126
  Leven, 40, 130-133, **130**, **131**, **132**
  library, 74-76
  logo, 76
  Long, 55, **55**, 107-110
  lunch, 74
  Narrows, 46, **46**, 124-127, **125**
  neighbor to Shinnecock, 110, 185-187
  Punchbowl, 56, **56**, **64**, 127-129, **128**
  Raynor, Seth, 137-138
  Redan, 41, **40**, **41**, 65, **90**, 90-94, 149
  Road Hole, 47, 69, 99-103, **100**, **101**, **102**, **103**
  Sahara, 57, **57**, 65, 69, 84-86, **84**
  Sebonac, 114-116
  Shippen, John, 187
  Short, 51, **51**, **64**, **65**, 96-99, 149
  St. Andrews hole. *See* Road Hole
  tiles, 74-76
  tournaments, 67-70, 76-77, 79-80
  turf, 66-67
  Valley, 58, **58**, 69, **82**, 82-84
  Walker Cup, 77-79
  windmill, 129, **246**
New York Metropolitan Golf Association, 80
Newport Country Club, 18, 21-23, 24, 26-28, 140, 191, 192, 193
Nicklaus, Jack, 165, 166
Nocco, Rocco, 192
North Berwick Golf Club, 35, 41
  Redan, 29, 31, 36, 90, 92, 93
North Berwick Links, 72
North Hempstead, Short, 51
North Shore Country Club, 47, 48, 58

O

Oakhurst Club, 164
Oakmount Country Club, 76
O'Brien, Morgan, 61, 74, 75, **75**, 189
Ocean Links, 140, 190-196, **190**
  Gold Mashie Tournament, 193-196
  paintings of, **192**
  Raynor's Prize Dogleg, 45
  Short, **193**
  Valley, 58
O'Laughlin, Marty 178
"Old White," **162**
Olmstead, Frederick Law, 126, 224, 229
Olmstead Bros., 141, 206, 210, 211, 213, 214
Olson, Karl, 83, 98, 113
Olympic Club, 143
Onwentsia Club, 17, 27, 75
Ouimet, Francis, 18, 78, 79, 161, 193, 195

P

Palmer, Arnold, 134
Park Willie, 30, 49, 195
Parrish, Samuel, 24, 189
Payne, Mortimer S., 67, 137–138
Peconic Bay Realty Company, 61
Pennick, Frank, 84
Pervis, W. Laidlaw, 53
Peters, Richard, 26-28
PGA Tour, 162
Philadelphia Country Club, 28
Phillips, Joe, 197
Philp, Hugh, 195
Pine Valley, 63, 78, 93, 111, 140
Pinehurst, 94
Piper, C.V., 62
Piping Rock Club, 75, 141, **146**, **149**, 147-153, 170
  Alps, 152
  Biarritz, 42, 149, 150
  Charles Blair Macdonald Cup Match, 161
  Knoll Hole, 52, **52**, **150**, 152
  Redan, 41, 93, 152
  Road Hole, 47, **47**, 152, **153**
  routing plan, 146
Pomeroy, Dan, 129
Pope, John Russell, 193-194
Porter, Frances, 17
Porter, R.E., 218
Pratt, Herbert L., 215, 218

Prestwick Golf Club, 35
Alps, 31, 36, 37, 43, 87, 88
Punchbowl (hole), 56, **64**, 142
Deepdale Golf & Country Club, 222
Fishers Island, 56
Gibson Island Club, 213
Lido, 174, **175**
National Golf Links, 56, **56**, **64**, 127-129, **128**
St. Louis Country Club, 56
Westhampton Country Club, 56
Yale University Golf Course, 233, 234
Punchbowl/Alps, 160
Punchbowl/Eden, 56
Purves, W. Laidlaw, 76

R

Rainsford, William, 26
Rawlins, Horace, 28
Ray, Ted, 18, 117
Raynor, Seth J., 20, **136**, 137-146, **138**, **142**
Alps, 86, 88-89, 139
Biarritz, 42
Cape, 139
Creek Club, 214-219
Deepdale Golf & Country Club, 220-223
Garden City, 58
Gibson Island Club, 210-214
Lakeside, 143-145
Mid Ocean Club, 225-229
National Golf Links, 62
practice courses, 202-205
Raynor's Prize Dogleg, 45, **176**, 213, 223
Redan, 91, 139
Road Hole, 102, 103
Shoreacres, **97**
Short, 51, 99
Strategy, 59
Valley, 58
Women's National Golf & Tennis Club, 142, 206-208
See also Greenbrier Resort, Lido Club, Links Club, National Golf Links of America, Ocean Links, Piping Rock, Shinnecock Hills Golf Club, Sleepy Hollow Country Club, St. Louis Country Club, Yale University Golf Course
Raynor's Prize Dogleg, 45, **45**
Gibson Island Club, 213
Lido, 45, **176**
Ocean Links, 45
Deepdale Golf & Country Club, 223
Redan (hole), 33, 41, 44, 65, 90-94, 142, 157, 164
Creek Club, 41, 216
Deepdale Golf & Country Club, 222
Lido, 174
Mid Ocean Club, 228
National Golf Links, 41, **40**, **41**, 65, 90-94, **90**, 149
North Berwick, 29, 31, 36, 90, 92, 93
Piping Rock, 41, 93, 152
practice course, 202, 204
reverse, 156, 201, 213, 240
Shinnecock Hills, **188**, 189
St. Louis Country Club, 160
Yale University Golf Course, 240, 241-242, **242**
Reid, John, 18, 23, 24
Reid, Wilfrid, 143
Reverse Redan (hole), 156, 201, 213, 240
Rice, Grantland, 70-72
Riviera Country Club, 93
Road Hole, 31-32, 47, 99-103, **99**, 152, **153**
Creek Club, 219
Links Club, 199
National Golf Links, 47, 69, 99-103, **100**, **101**, **102**, **103**
North Shore, 47
Piping Rock, 47, **47**, 152, **153**
St. Andrews, 12, 31-32, 47, 90, **100**, **101**
Yale University Golf Course, 233, 234, 235-236
Robertson, Allan, **12**, 47, 101, 195
Rockefeller, John D., 141, 143
Rockefeller, William, 155, 156
Rocker, Frank, 147
Rocky Farm Golf Course, 21, **22**, 27
Rogers, Archibald, 24
Roosevelt, Theodore, 159
Ross, Arthur, 178
Ross, Donald, 62, 94
Royal and Ancient Golf Club, 10-11, 77, 101
Royal Liverpool Golf Club, 23, 27, 76
Royal Mid-Surrey Golf Club, 171
Royal St. George Golf Club (Sandwich), 31, 57, 75, 84
Royal West Norfolk, 51, 101-102, 237
Ruth, Babe, 229
Ruth, Frederick, 141
Rutherford, William, 24, 28
Ryan, John D., 215
Ryder Cup, 162, 166
Ryerson, Arthur, 24

S

Sabin, Charles, 61, 62, 170, 201
Sahara (hole), 36, 57, 65
National Golf Links, 57, **57**, 65, 69, 84-86, **84**
Royal St. George, 31, 57, 84
Sands, Charles, 27, 28
Sandwich, 31, 35, 36, 37, 86
Sarazen, Gene, 79, 112, 117, 177, 178
Sayers, Ben, 41, 72, 92
Scotscraig Golf Club, 52, **151**, 152, 243
Scott, George A.H., 17
Sears, Samuel, 24
Sebonac Creek, 65
Senior PGA Tour, 162
Shepard, Elliot, 155

Shinnecock Hills Golf Club, 61, 76, 94, 138, 140, 184-189
Macdonald and Raynor design, 187-189
national championships, 21, 27, 91
neighbor to National Golf Links, 185-187
Redan, **188**, 189
routing, **184**
Shinnecock Indian Reservation, 187
Shippen, John, 187
Shoreacres, 97, 138, 140
Short (hole), 51, 142, 157
Chicago Golf Club, 51
Deepdale Golf & Country Club, 222
Gibson Island Club, 213
Lido, 174
Links Club, 199, **200**
Mid Ocean Club, 227
National Golf Links, 51, **51**, **64**, **65**, 96-99, 149
North Hempstead, 51
Ocean Links, **193**
practice course, 202, 204
Royal West Norfolk, 51
St. Andrews, 98
St. Louis Country Club, 160
Yale University Golf Course, **232**, 236-237
Simons, W.R., 76
Simpson, Tom, 31, 176
Singer, Paris, 141, 142
Sleepy Hollow Country Club, 75, 93, 141, **154**, 155-157, 161, 170
Sloane, William D., 61
Smith, A. Haddow, 17
Smith, Walter B., 27
Snead, Sam, 161, 162, 166-167
Society of St. Andrews Golfers, 101
Solheim Cup, 162
Somerset Country Club, 140, 172
Spear, Richard, 146, 152
St. Andrews, 11, 35-38
Clubhouse, **10**
Eden, 31, 44, 117-120, **118**, **119**, 243
Long, 31, 55, 107, **108**, **109**, 176, **180**
Road Hole, 12, 31-32, 47, 90, **100**, **101**
Robertson, Allan, 12, 44
Short, 98
Walker Cup, 77
St. Andrews (town), 9–11
St. Andrews Golf Club (Yonkers), 18, 21, 23-24, 27
St. Louis Country Club, 139, **158**, 159-161
Alps, 43
Charles Blair Macdonald Cup Match, 161
Eden, 44
Punchbowl, 56
Stauffer, William, 203
Sterling, J. Carlos, 17
Stewart, Charles, 80
Stillman, James A., 61, 62, 155, 170, 201
Stoddart, Lawrence, 23-24
Strategy (hole), 59
Lido, 59, 174-175
Westhampton Country Club, 59
Strath, David, 11, 90, 92, 93, 117
Sunningdale Golf Club, 19, 36, 49, 104
Swasey, W. Albert, 168, 178
Sweetser, Jesse, 78-79, 193, 195, 232
Symington, W. Stuart Jr., 211, 213

T

Tailer, T. Suffern, 45, 140, 190, 191-192, 193, **194**, 195, 203
Tailer, Tommy, 194, **194**, 195
Tallmadge, Henry, 24, 26
Taylor, J.H., 30, 117, 171
Thomas, George C. Jr., 93, 106
Thomas, Washington B., 61
Thorpe, J.G., 27
Tillinghast, A.W., 154, 156, 192
Tolley, C.J.H., 78, 79
Tolley, Cyril, 161
Tompkins, Ray, 231, 233
Toomey, H., 184
Toronto Golf Club, **25**
Torrence, W.B., 78, 79
Trammel, Niles, 80
Travis, Walter J., 18, 27, 62, 69, 81, 93
Troubetzkoy, Prince, **67**
Tucker, Sam, 28
Tull, Alfred, 81
Turnesa, Joe, 79
Tuxedo, 24
Tweedie, H.J., 17, 75
Tweedie, Herbert, 17
Tweedie, Lawrence, 17
Tyng, Lucien, 187

U

United States Golf Association, 18, 19, 26, 77, 80, 185, 195
U.S. Amateur Championship, 21-24, **22**, **25**, 26, 75, 80, 161
U.S. Open, 18, 28, 30, 79, 80, 91, 159, 161, 185, 187
U.S. Women's National Amateur, 161, 162, 165, 207

V

Valley (hole), 58, 82-84
Links Club, 201
National Golf Links, Valley, 58, **58**, 69, **82**, 82-84
North Shore Country Club, 58
Ocean Links, 58
Yale University Golf Course, 237-238
Vanderbilt, Cornelius, 155, 170, 221, 222
Vanderbilt, Gertrude, 205
Vanderbilt, Harold, 221, 222
Vanderbilt, Percy, 155
Vanderbilt, William K. I, 18, 155, 187, **222**

Vanderbilt, William K. II, 61, 221-222, **222**
Vanderlip, Franklin, 155, 156
Vardon, Harry, 18, 30, 32

W

Waialae, 142
Walker, Bert, 192
Walker, Cyril, 80
Walker, George H., 77
Walker Cup, 25, 74, 77-79
Ward, John, M., 69, 70
Warren (architect), 220, 223, 224, 229
Watson, William, 76
Wee Burn, 81
Wendeback, Cliff, 141
Westhampton Country Club, 56, 59, 140
Wethered, R.H., 78, 79
Wetmore, Charles, 141, 220, 223, 224, 225, 226, 229
Wheeler, Fred, 76
Whigham, Henry J., 74, 85, 92-93, 97-98, 121, 135
  course layout by, 17, 18, 19, 62, 75, 81
  as player, 16, 27, 36
Whigham, Jim, 156
Whippoorwill, 141
White, Robert, 66-67
White, Stanford, 18, 23, 33, 141, 155, 184
White Sulphur Springs, 162-167
Whitney, Harry Payne, 61, 170, 203, 204-205, 215, 218
Whitney, W.C., 205
Wilmerding, Harry, 17
Wilson, Dick, 166, 189, 220, 223
Wilson, Hugh, 93
Windeler, Herbert, 66
Winthrop, Roger, 147, 169, 170, 171
Winton, Tom, 154
Women's National Golf & Tennis Club, 142, **206**, 207-208, **209**, 216
Wood, Craig, 79, 112
Wood, Henry, 15, 16
Worsham, Lou, 161
World's Fair (1893), 15-16
Worthington, Edward, 17
Worthington, James S., 171
Write, Henry, 158

Y

Yale University Golf Course, 149, **230**, 231-245
  Alps, 233, 241
  Biarritz, 42, **42**, 219, 238-239, **239**
  Cape, 54, 121, 234
  Cape/Redan, 238
  Double Plateau, 244-245
  Eden, 243
  hole description, 234-245
  Knoll, 243
  Leven, 237
  Punchbowl, 233, 234
  Redan, 240, 241-242, **242**
  reverse Redan, 240
  Road, 233, 234, 235-236
  Short, **232**, 236-237
  Valley, 237-238
Yates, Danny, 194
Yeamans Hall, 141
Young, Robert R., 167

Z

Zukosky, Benny, 197

ORIG.
8 TEE
ORIGINAL
12th T
HIGH
HILL
POND
POND
ORIGINAL
GREEN